THE FLASH®

ARCHIVES ▾ VOLUME 1

JOHN BROOME ROBERT KANIGHER CARMINE INFANTINO
FRANK GIACOIA JOE GIELLA JOE KUBERT

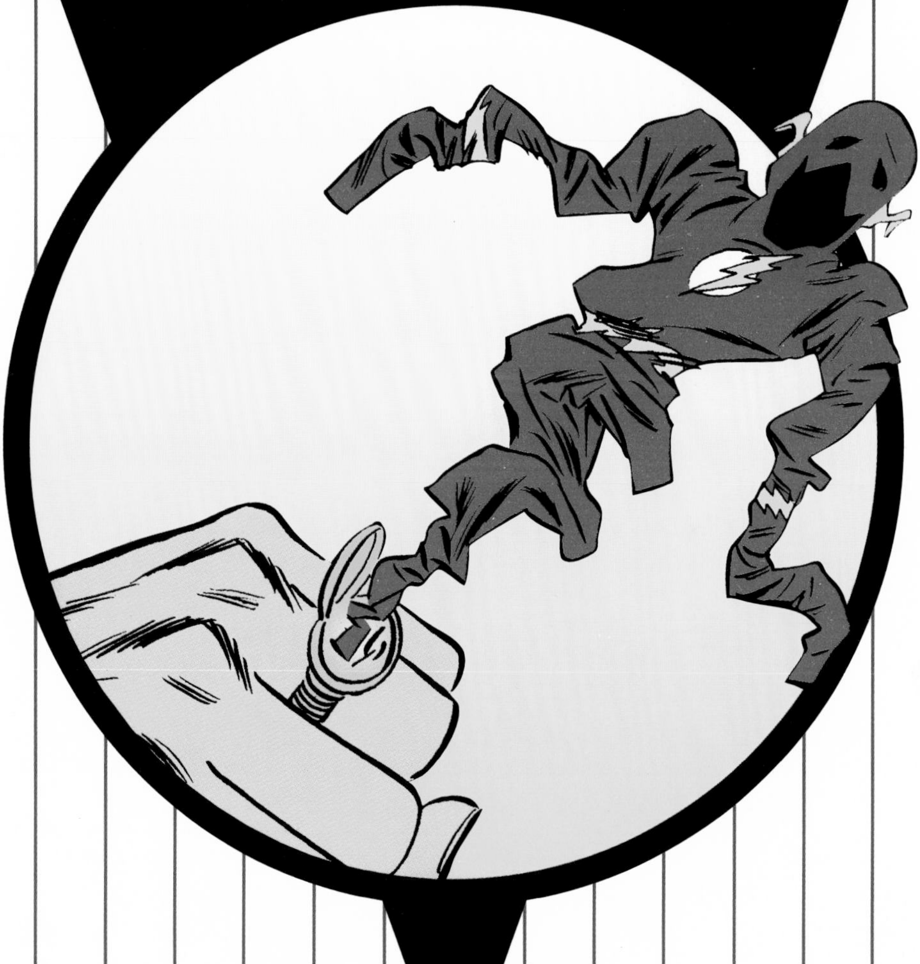

ARCHIVE DC EDITIONS

DC COMICS

JENETTE KAHN
PRESIDENT & EDITOR-IN-CHIEF

PAUL LEVITZ
EXECUTIVE VICE PRESIDENT &
PUBLISHER

MIKE CARLIN
EXECUTIVE EDITOR

JULIUS SCHWARTZ
EDITOR-ORIGINAL STORIES

BOB KAHAN
EDITOR-ARCHIVE EDITION

GEORG BREWER
DESIGN DIRECTOR

ROBBIN BROSTERMAN
ART DIRECTOR

RICHARD BRUNING
VP-CREATIVE DIRECTOR

PATRICK CALDON
SENIOR VP-FINANCE &
OPERATIONS

DOROTHY CROUCH
VP-LICENSED PUBLISHING

TERRI CUNNINGHAM
VP-MANAGING EDITOR

JOEL EHRLICH
SENIOR VP-ADVERTISING &
PROMOTIONS

ALISON GILL
EXECUTIVE DIRECTOR-
MANUFACTURING

LILLIAN LASERSON
VP & GENERAL COUNSEL

JIM LEE
EDITORIAL DIRECTOR-
WILDSTORM

JOHN NEE
VP & GENERAL MANAGER-
WILDSTORM

CHERYL RUBIN
VP-LICENSING &
MERCHANDISING

BOB WAYNE
VP-SALES & MARKETING

THE FLASH
VOLUME ONE

ISBN 1-56389-139-5

PUBLISHED BY DC COMICS.
COVER, COMPILATION AND FOREWORD
COPYRIGHT ©1996 DC COMICS.

ORIGINALLY PUBLISHED IN SINGLE
MAGAZINE FORM IN FLASH COMICS 104,
SHOWCASE, 4, 8, 13, 14, THE FLASH 105-108.
COPYRIGHT 1949, ©1956-59 DC COMICS.
ALL RIGHTS RESERVED.

THE FLASH AND ALL RELATED CHARACTERS,
THE DISTINCTIVE LIKENESSES THEREOF, AND
ALL RELATED INDICIA ARE TRADEMARKS OF
DC COMICS. THE STORIES, CHARACTERS, AND
INCIDENTS FEATURED IN THIS PUBLICATION
ARE ENTIRELY FICTIONAL.

DC COMICS
1700 BROADWAY
NEW YORK, NY 10019

A DIVISION OF WARNER BROS. -
AN AOL TIME WARNER COMPANY
PRINTED IN HONG KONG.
THIRD PRINTING.

THE DC ARCHIVE EDITIONS

COVER ILLUSTRATION BY CARMINE
INFANTINO AND JOE KUBERT

SERIES DESIGN BY ALEX JAY/STUDIO J

PUBLICATION DESIGN BY EDDIE ORTIZ

BLACK-AND-WHITE RECONSTRUCTION OF
SOME INTERNAL MATERIAL BY RICK KEENE

COLOR RECONSTRUCTION BY RICK TAYLOR
AND TOM McCRAW

TABLE OF CONTENTS

TABLE OF CONTENTS

FOREWORD

Considering they were about to change the course of the entire comic-book industry, the men sitting around the conference table that afternoon in 1955 were rather blasé about the situation. It was, in fact, as routine a meeting as one can imagine; the editorial director of DC Comics sitting with his editorial staff, trying to determine what feature would fill the pages of an upcoming issue of the new title, SHOWCASE.

SHOWCASE was, itself, something of an experiment, a bimonthly comic created to introduce new characters and titles without DC having to take the financial risk of launching numerous new series. Such caution was well founded in 1955, an era when the 1940s flood of super-hero comics had receded, leaving the newsstands full of genre comics. Westerns. Crime. Horror. Romance. Funny animals. Television and movie star licenses. Aside from Superman, Batman, and Wonder Woman, no other costumed super-hero appeared in namesake titles, and only a handful of secondary characters like Aquaman and Green Arrow still held regular backup spots in other titles.

The first three issues of SHOWCASE featured the exploits of *Firefighters*, tales of *The Kings of the Wild*, and the aquatic adventures of *Frogmen*.

"So there we were, sitting around at our monthly meeting," Schwartz said of that fateful editorial conference. "Irwin Donenfeld was in charge. We sat around, shooting out ideas of what was going to appear in SHOWCASE #4. Someone suggested, and I really don't remember who it was, that maybe we should bring back the Flash. Someone else objected, saying that the Flash had failed once. Why bring back a character that had failed?"

That had been in 1949 when, after nine years and 104 issues, the last issue of FLASH COMICS had been published. Hardly, it can be argued, a failure. Rather, it was the drastic change in the comic-book market of the 1940s, the years that would come to be known as comics' Golden Age, that was responsible for the cancellation of hordes of super-hero titles.

"Then someone pointed out that roughly five years had elapsed since the last issue, FLASH COMICS #104, had come out," Julie recalled in 1996, better than forty years since the events of that meeting. "It was an entirely new audience out there, because it was generally accepted back then that kids only read comics for maybe, tops, five years. So a whole new generation of readers had come around since we last published Flash. Unless anybody had any better ideas for the book, Donenfeld thought we should go with Flash."

Of course, that decision prompted the obvious question. Who was to spearhead and edit this revival?

Julie laughed. "I had been the last editor of the original Flash, so everybody looked at me."

Schwartz was the natural choice for the job, a conscientious and meticulous editor who came to the comic-book industry in 1944 from his first career as literary agent to some of the greatest names in the science-fiction field, including Ray Bradbury, Henry Kuttner, Edmond Hamilton, and Alfred Bester. At DC, he edited Flash, Green Lantern, All Star's Justice Society, Hawkman, and Atom during the Golden Age and, later, such genre titles as BIG TOWN, CHARLIE CHAN, and ALL-STAR WESTERN, as well as combining his love of science fiction with his chosen field of comics with such titles as MYSTERY IN SPACE and STRANGE ADVENTURES. "I asked how much time I had to prepare this new feature. The answer was, 'No time!' so I immediately went back to my office, which I shared with fellow editor Robert Kanigher, and said let's get to work!"

Kanigher's proximity to Schwartz wasn't the reason he got the assignment. Like Julie, he had been associated with the Golden Age incarnation of the fastest man alive as one of its regular writers, along with John Broome. (Of course, none of them had been in on the creation of the original Flash. That honor fell to writer Gardner Fox and artist Harry Lampert, who crafted the 1940 lead story from FLASH COMICS #1 about student Jay Garrick who, exposed to the fumes from "hard water" acquired the gift of superspeed.) By 1955, Kanigher was a veteran editor and writer, a talented creator known for his fertile imagination, innovative storytelling devices, and speed at the keyboard.

"I knew I would get the script out of Bob within a couple of days, which I did. My guess is, he probably sat right down at the typewriter during his lunch hour and started it right then and there," Julie said. "I insisted that the new Flash would have no relation to the original except for the name. Everything else would be different. *Everything...* including and above all, his origin.

"Lightning is the fastest thing that we know of, 186,000 miles a second, so we decided to tie the super-speed origin in with lightning, and have it flash into some chemicals as this Flash-to-be, whose civilian identity we hadn't yet decided, would be working with in a police laboratory — and have them splash all over him, endowing him with super-speed.

"By the way, the name of the new Flash's secret identity, Barry Allen, came from two show-business personalities I was very fond of in those days. One was radio announcer and talk-show host Barry Gray. The other was comedian Steve Allen, who had his TV program in those days.

"To motivate his becoming a super-hero, we had him remembering that his favorite comic book as a kid was FLASH COMICS, so that inspired him to adopt that name.

"Several years later, I was plotting a story with Gardner Fox when I recalled the idea that Barry Allen had been inspired by a comic-book hero he had read as a kid. We took it several steps farther, having the Flash visit the Flash of the comic books of his youth, and make him 'real,' actually alive on a different Earth! Gardner and I licked the plot right off — in a flash — conceiving the concept of parallel Earths, with the Golden Age Flash alive on what we now called Earth-Two, the parallel Earth where all the Golden Age characters existed. Actually, it should have been the other way around, since the Golden Age Flash came first, but in our haste, because we were so excited by the idea, we left it the way it was."

With Kanigher in place, Julie recognized the wisdom of bringing back another member of the Golden Age Flash creative team, penciller Carmine Infantino. Carmine was an experienced comic-book hand, proficient in drawing everything from super-heroes to Westerns. His quirky, unique style was recognized by his fellow professionals for its freshness of design and mastery of storytelling. "I called in Carmine. I needed a cover even before the interior art. Carmine came up with the idea, that now famous cover of Flash speeding through frames of film. This was strictly Carmine's idea, as was the design of Flash's new costume.

"Without question, Carmine really was the artist best suited to pencil the revival. His skill at drawing speedlines gave the impression that Flash was really moving!"

With Schwartz editing, Kanigher writing the origin, and John Broome at work on subsequent scripts for SHOWCASE #4 (as well as the issues to follow, #8, #13, and #14) while Infantino began pencilling, it seemed as though the Flash revival would be a total case of old home week. Only Golden Age inker Frank Giacoia was missing from the mix, due, according to Julie's recollection, to extenuating deadline pressures.

But an artist whose work had appeared regularly in comics since the mid-1940s, and who was a contributor to the Kanigher-edited war books of the day, was tapped to ink the first issue. "Since Joe Kubert wasn't one of my usual stable of artists, I asked him years later, 'How come, of all people, I asked you to ink the story?' Joe conjectures it may have been as simple as his being on hand when this hurry-up assignment hit my desk. It sure turned out to be a wonderful combination!"

The stories after SHOWCASE #4 were mainly written by John Broome. Says Julie, "John Broome was my best friend as well as one of my favorite writers to work with. We wanted to bring back the Golden Age team, so we brought back Kanigher and Infantino... and, of course, Broome." A wise move, considering all that Broome would bring to the Flash over the years to come, including the fastest man alive's infamous Rogues' Gallery, the collection of terrific villains who were created to bedevil Flash.

"John Broome and I agreed, once he came on as the regular Flash writer, that it was helpful to have a villain be the main focus of the story. So we had to build up a Rogues' Gallery, with John Broome creating every one of those villains, and Infantino designing the costumes. We'd come up with gags, like when all the villains were in jail at the same time, and having contests to see who would escape first and commit the most crimes. They all even went to the same tailor for their super-villain costumes, a character called Paul Gambi, named after Paul Gambicini, a major fan writer of the day. There was the Flash Museum. And Kid Flash. Bob Kanigher had created and named *Iris* West in the Flash origin as Barry Allen's girlfriend and the name West rang a bell with me, because there was a popular science-fiction writer named Wallace West. And that's who I named Kid Flash, Wally West, after." In the first eight issues of the new Flash's run, Schwartz and Broome introduced several major villains, including Mirror Master, Mister Element, Captain Cold, and Gorilla Grodd, who made three appearances in that span. The Top, Weather Wizard, Abra Kadabra, the Trickster and others followed.

Flash was a hit, making a total of four appearances in SHOWCASE before gaining his own title. "After I had the first issue of his own title ready, I asked Irwin Donenfeld what *number* to put on it: #1... or #105? [Of course, the Golden age title was FLASH COMICS and this was THE FLASH, so for all intents and purposes, this was an entirely new title.] But Irwin said, no doubt about it — it has to be #105. In those days, with a couple of hundred titles on the stand, if the potential buyer saw two side by side, one of them #105 and the other #1, which one would he buy? Number 105, of course, because it had a track record. Number one? He wasn't going to risk his ten cents on an unknown magazine!"

Wasn't it deliberate? Wasn't SHOWCASE #4 part of some brilliant scheme to revive the comic-book marketplace's interest in super-heroes? "Absolutely not! We had no idea we'd ever bring back super-heroes. We had moved on to other concepts — the Westerns, funny animals, romance, along with celebrated movie and television characters. We did Jackie Gleason, Bob Hope, Martin & Lewis, Pat Boone, Dobie Gillis."

But deliberate or not, Flash's debut — although Julie's Captain Comet feature in STRANGE ADVENTURES and Martian Manhunter in DETECTIVE COMICS beat him to the punch — was the defining event of the superheroic resurgence. Fast on the heels of Flash's success came still more Schwartz-spearheaded revivals from DC's 1940s heroes, including Green Lantern, Justice League of America, Atom, and Hawkman. All these SHOWCASE or BRAVE & BOLD features went on to receive their own titles... thereby sparking renewed interest in super-hero comics.

But nobody at that 1955 meeting knew that the off-handed suggestion to bring back the Flash in SHOWCASE #4 would act as a "Big Bang" to the kickstarting of the entire comic-book industry!

— **PAUL KUPPERBERG**

Paul Kupperberg has both written and edited THE FLASH (among many other comics) and hopes to one day grow up to be Julie Schwartz.

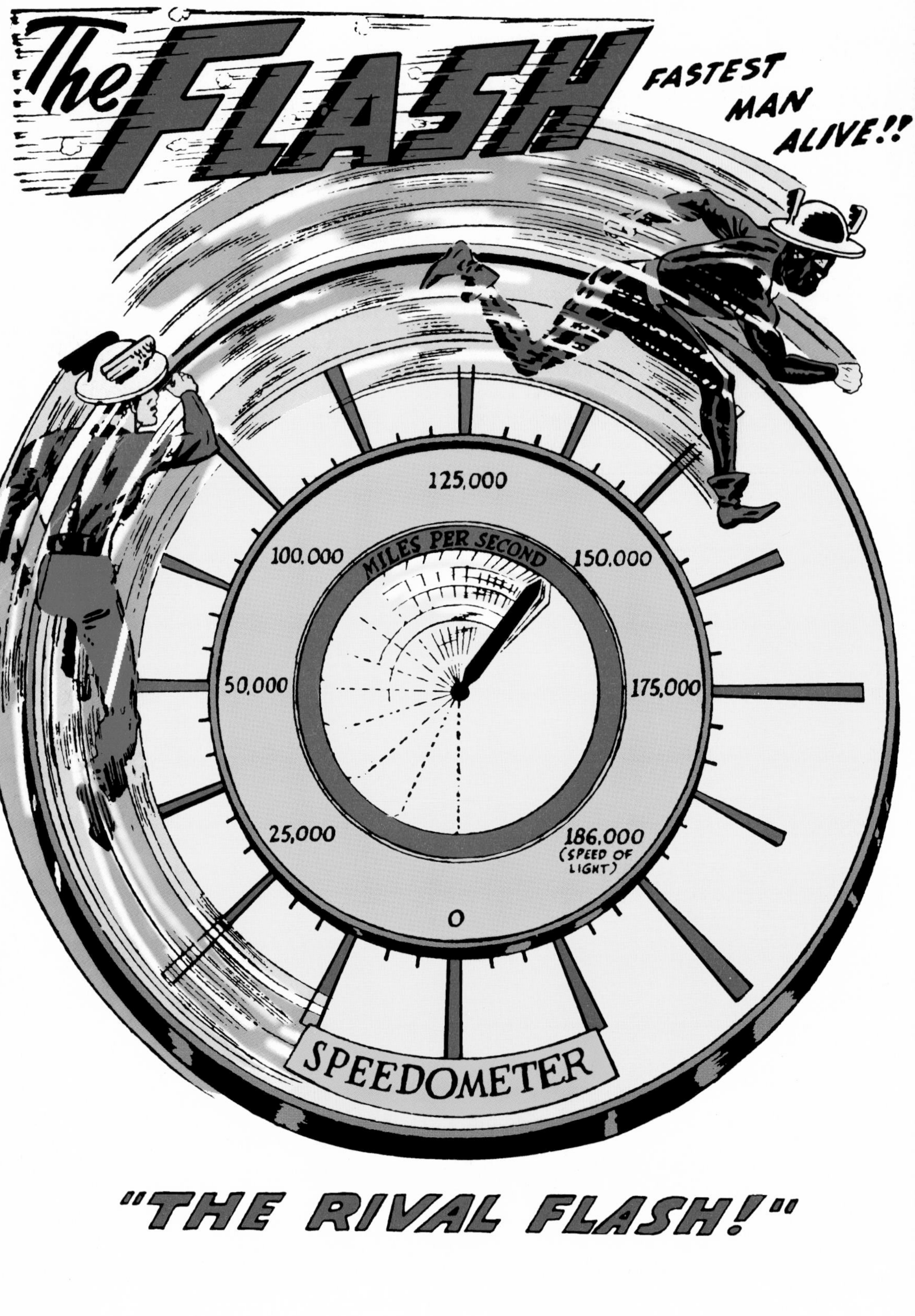
The FLASH
FASTEST MAN ALIVE!!
125,000
100,000
150,000
MILES PER SECOND
50,000
175,000
25,000
186,000 (SPEED OF LIGHT)
0
SPEEDOMETER
"THE RIVAL FLASH!"

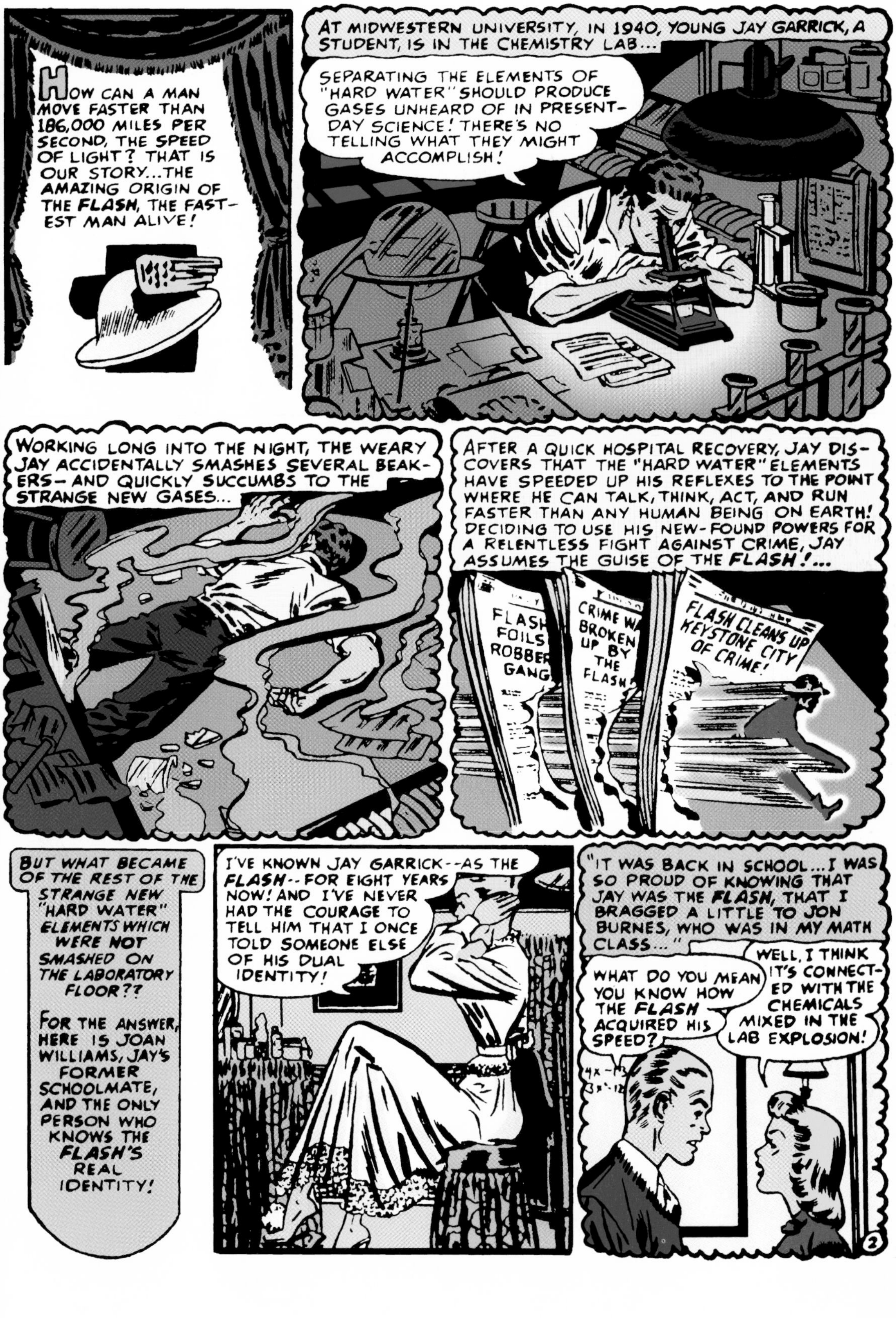
HOW CAN A MAN MOVE FASTER THAN 186,000 MILES PER SECOND, THE SPEED OF LIGHT? THAT IS OUR STORY...THE AMAZING ORIGIN OF THE FLASH, THE FASTEST MAN ALIVE!
AT MIDWESTERN UNIVERSITY, IN 1940, YOUNG JAY GARRICK, A STUDENT, IS IN THE CHEMISTRY LAB...
SEPARATING THE ELEMENTS OF "HARD WATER" SHOULD PRODUCE GASES UNHEARD OF IN PRESENT-DAY SCIENCE! THERE'S NO TELLING WHAT THEY MIGHT ACCOMPLISH!
WORKING LONG INTO THE NIGHT, THE WEARY JAY ACCIDENTALLY SMASHES SEVERAL BEAKERS-- AND QUICKLY SUCCUMBS TO THE STRANGE NEW GASES...
AFTER A QUICK HOSPITAL RECOVERY, JAY DISCOVERS THAT THE "HARD WATER" ELEMENTS HAVE SPEEDED UP HIS REFLEXES TO THE POINT WHERE HE CAN TALK, THINK, ACT, AND RUN FASTER THAN ANY HUMAN BEING ON EARTH! DECIDING TO USE HIS NEW-FOUND POWERS FOR A RELENTLESS FIGHT AGAINST CRIME, JAY ASSUMES THE GUISE OF THE FLASH!...
FLASH FOILS ROBBER GANG
CRIME WA BROKEN UP BY THE FLASH
FLASH CLEANS UP KEYSTONE CITY OF CRIME!
BUT WHAT BECAME OF THE REST OF THE STRANGE NEW "HARD WATER" ELEMENTS WHICH WERE NOT SMASHED ON THE LABORATORY FLOOR??
FOR THE ANSWER, HERE IS JOAN WILLIAMS, JAY'S FORMER SCHOOLMATE, AND THE ONLY PERSON WHO KNOWS THE FLASH'S REAL IDENTITY!
I'VE KNOWN JAY GARRICK--AS THE FLASH--FOR EIGHT YEARS NOW! AND I'VE NEVER HAD THE COURAGE TO TELL HIM THAT I ONCE TOLD SOMEONE ELSE OF HIS DUAL IDENTITY!
"IT WAS BACK IN SCHOOL...I WAS SO PROUD OF KNOWING THAT JAY WAS THE FLASH, THAT I BRAGGED A LITTLE TO JON BURNES, WHO WAS IN MY MATH CLASS..."
WHAT DO YOU MEAN YOU KNOW HOW THE FLASH ACQUIRED HIS SPEED?
WELL, I THINK IT'S CONNECTED WITH THE CHEMICALS MIXED IN THE LAB EXPLOSION!
2

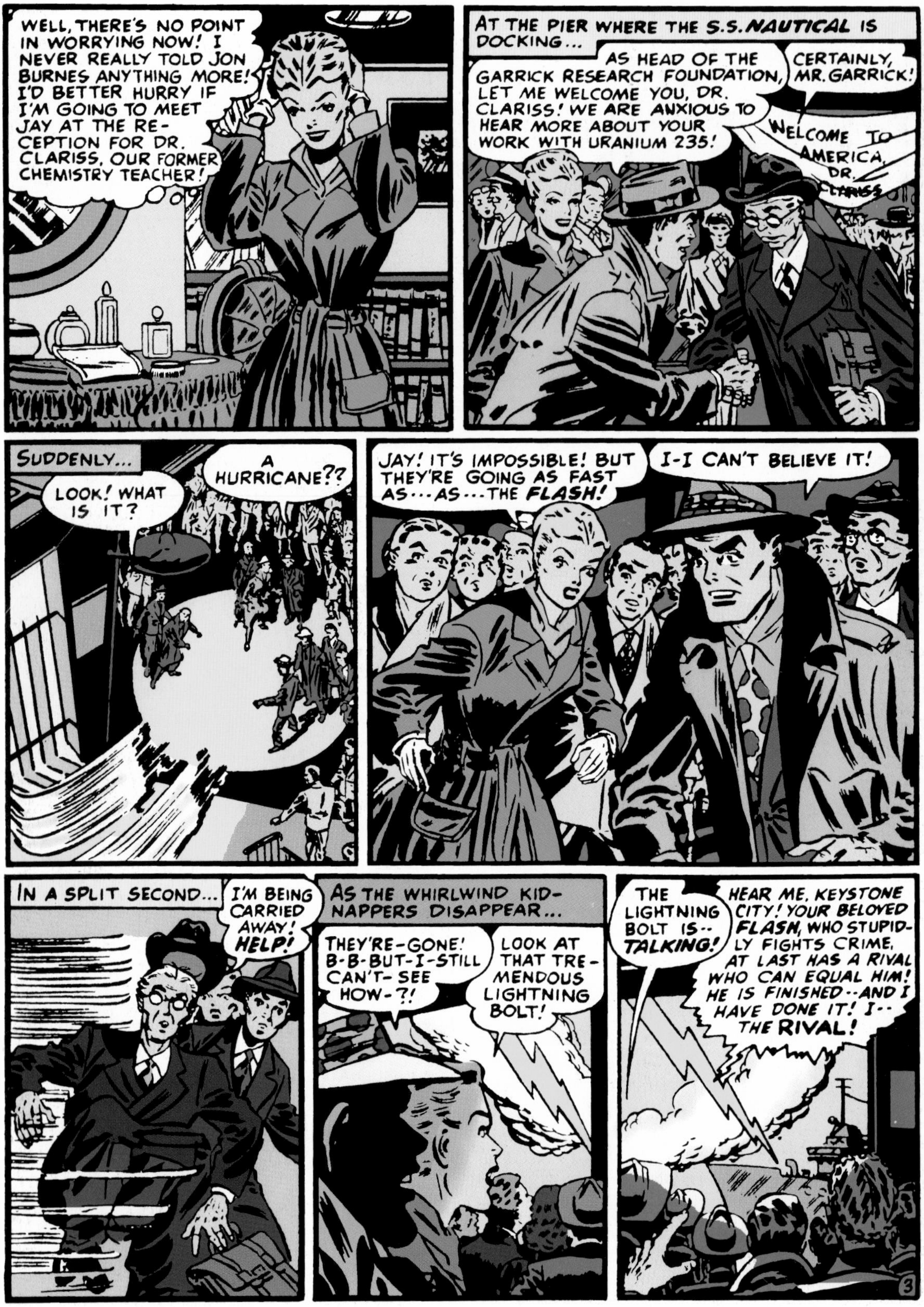
WELL, THERE'S NO POINT IN WORRYING NOW! I NEVER REALLY TOLD JON BURNES ANYTHING MORE! I'D BETTER HURRY IF I'M GOING TO MEET JAY AT THE RECEPTION FOR DR. CLARISS, OUR FORMER CHEMISTRY TEACHER!
AT THE PIER WHERE THE S.S. NAUTICAL IS DOCKING...
AS HEAD OF THE GARRICK RESEARCH FOUNDATION, LET ME WELCOME YOU, DR. CLARISS! WE ARE ANXIOUS TO HEAR MORE ABOUT YOUR WORK WITH URANIUM 235!
CERTAINLY, MR. GARRICK!
WELCOME TO AMERICA, DR. CLARISS
SUDDENLY...
LOOK! WHAT IS IT?
A HURRICANE??
JAY! IT'S IMPOSSIBLE! BUT THEY'RE GOING AS FAST AS...AS...THE FLASH!
I-I CAN'T BELIEVE IT!
IN A SPLIT SECOND...
I'M BEING CARRIED AWAY! HELP!
AS THE WHIRLWIND KIDNAPPERS DISAPPEAR...
THEY'RE-GONE! B-B-BUT-I-STILL CAN'T-SEE HOW-?!
LOOK AT THAT TREMENDOUS LIGHTNING BOLT!
THE LIGHTNING BOLT IS--TALKING!
HEAR ME, KEYSTONE CITY! YOUR BELOVED FLASH, WHO STUPIDLY FIGHTS CRIME, AT LAST HAS A RIVAL WHO CAN EQUAL HIM! HE IS FINISHED--AND I HAVE DONE IT! I--THE RIVAL!
3

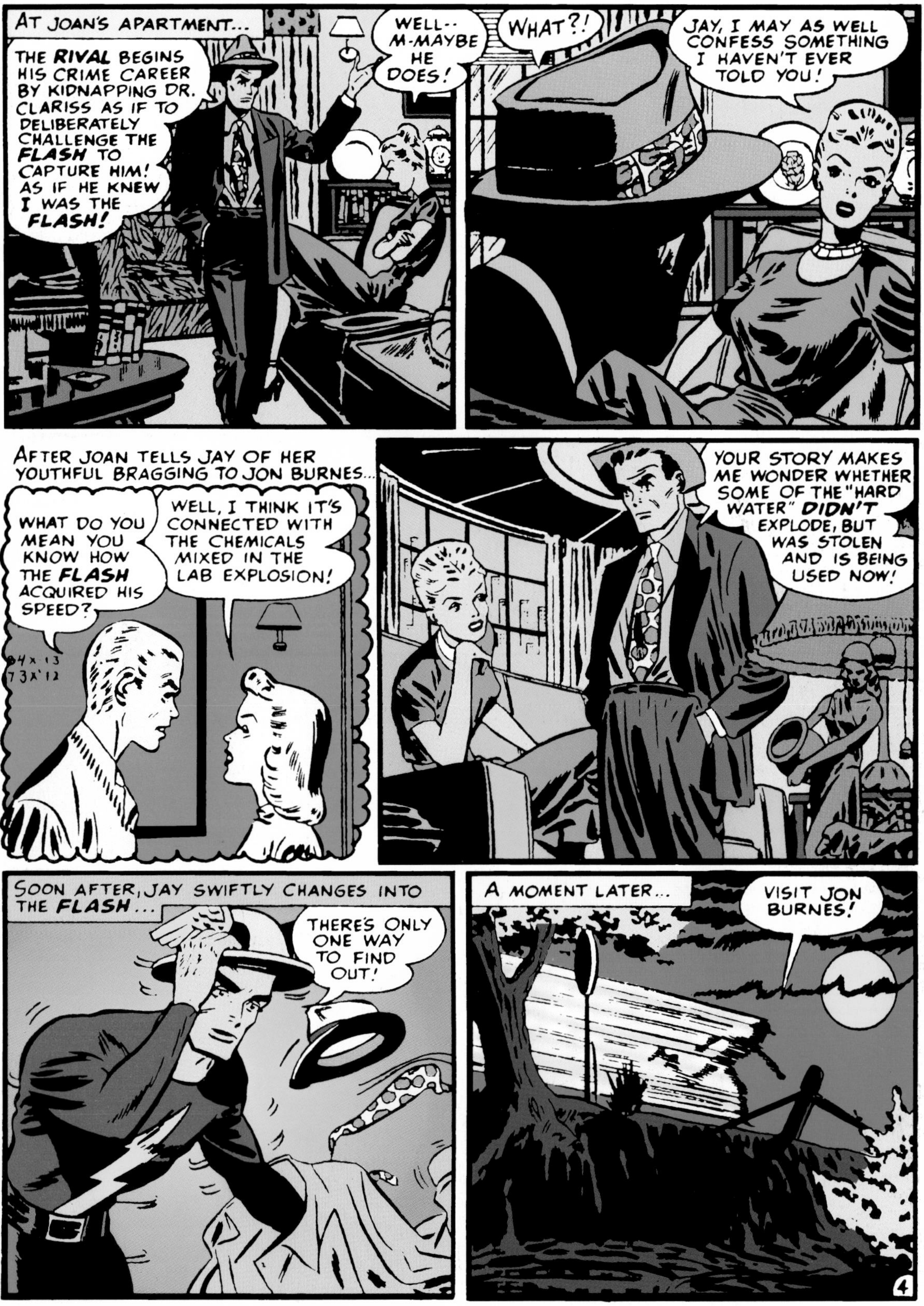
AT JOAN'S APARTMENT...
THE RIVAL BEGINS HIS CRIME CAREER BY KIDNAPPING DR. CLARISS AS IF TO DELIBERATELY CHALLENGE THE FLASH TO CAPTURE HIM! AS IF HE KNEW I WAS THE FLASH!
WELL-- M-MAYBE HE DOES!
WHAT?!
JAY, I MAY AS WELL CONFESS SOMETHING I HAVEN'T EVER TOLD YOU!
AFTER JOAN TELLS JAY OF HER YOUTHFUL BRAGGING TO JON BURNES...
WHAT DO YOU MEAN YOU KNOW HOW THE FLASH ACQUIRED HIS SPEED?
WELL, I THINK IT'S CONNECTED WITH THE CHEMICALS MIXED IN THE LAB EXPLOSION!
YOUR STORY MAKES ME WONDER WHETHER SOME OF THE "HARD WATER" DIDN'T EXPLODE, BUT WAS STOLEN AND IS BEING USED NOW!
SOON AFTER, JAY SWIFTLY CHANGES INTO THE FLASH...
THERE'S ONLY ONE WAY TO FIND OUT!
A MOMENT LATER...
VISIT JON BURNES!
4

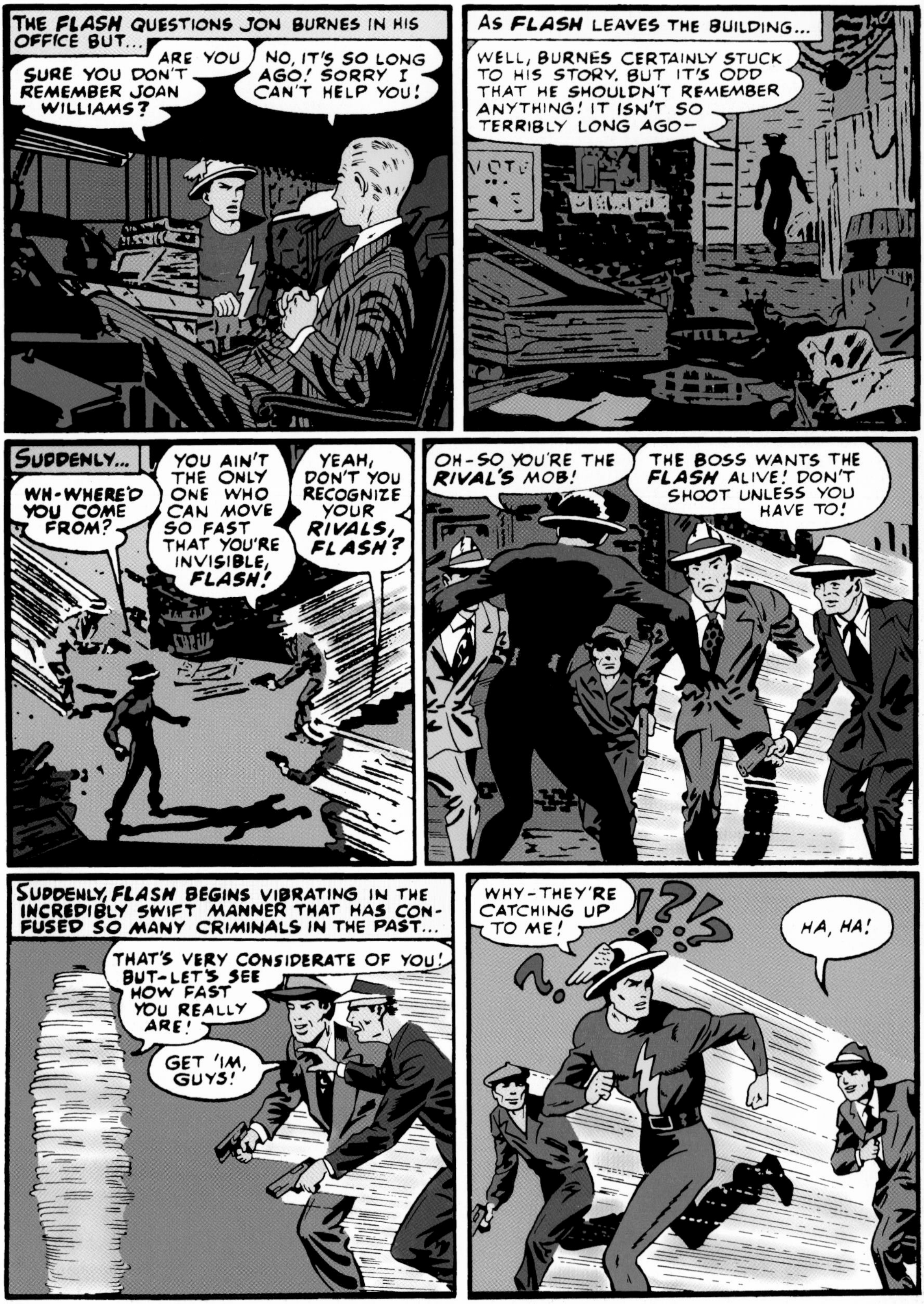
THE FLASH QUESTIONS JON BURNES IN HIS OFFICE BUT...
ARE YOU SURE YOU DON'T REMEMBER JOAN WILLIAMS?
NO, IT'S SO LONG AGO! SORRY I CAN'T HELP YOU!
AS FLASH LEAVES THE BUILDING...
WELL, BURNES CERTAINLY STUCK TO HIS STORY. BUT IT'S ODD THAT HE SHOULDN'T REMEMBER ANYTHING! IT ISN'T SO TERRIBLY LONG AGO—
SUDDENLY...
WH-WHERE'D YOU COME FROM?
YOU AIN'T THE ONLY ONE WHO CAN MOVE SO FAST THAT YOU'RE INVISIBLE, FLASH!
YEAH, DON'T YOU RECOGNIZE YOUR RIVALS, FLASH?
OH-SO YOU'RE THE RIVAL'S MOB!
THE BOSS WANTS THE FLASH ALIVE! DON'T SHOOT UNLESS YOU HAVE TO!
SUDDENLY, FLASH BEGINS VIBRATING IN THE INCREDIBLY SWIFT MANNER THAT HAS CONFUSED SO MANY CRIMINALS IN THE PAST...
THAT'S VERY CONSIDERATE OF YOU! BUT-LET'S SEE HOW FAST YOU REALLY ARE!
GET 'IM, GUYS!
WHY-THEY'RE CATCHING UP TO ME!
HA, HA!

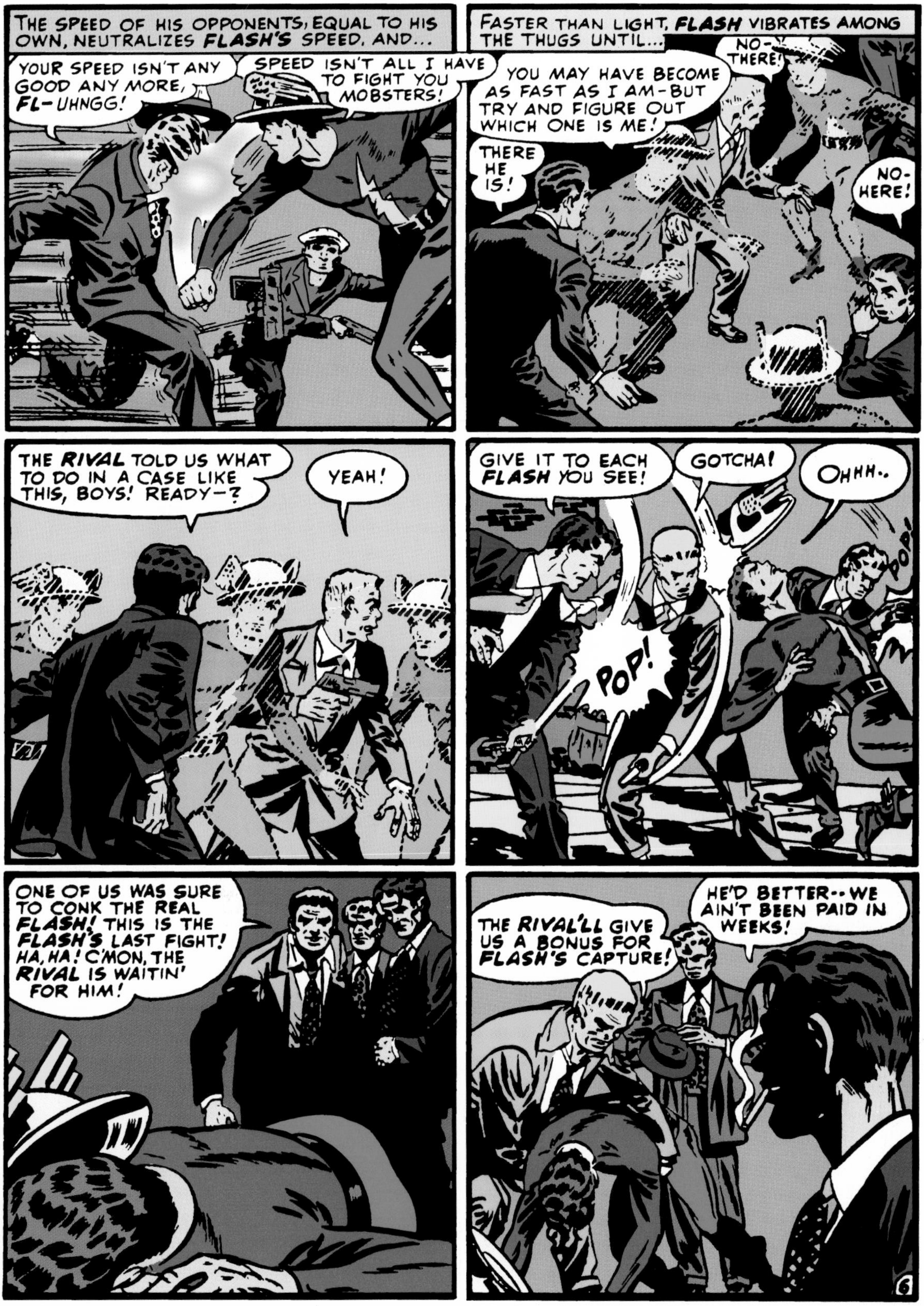
THE SPEED OF HIS OPPONENTS, EQUAL TO HIS OWN, NEUTRALIZES FLASH'S SPEED, AND...
YOUR SPEED ISN'T ANY GOOD ANY MORE, FL- UHNGG!
SPEED ISN'T ALL I HAVE TO FIGHT YOU MOBSTERS!
FASTER THAN LIGHT, FLASH VIBRATES AMONG THE THUGS UNTIL...
NO- THERE!
YOU MAY HAVE BECOME AS FAST AS I AM- BUT TRY AND FIGURE OUT WHICH ONE IS ME!
THERE HE IS!
NO- HERE!
THE RIVAL TOLD US WHAT TO DO IN A CASE LIKE THIS, BOYS! READY-?
YEAH!
GIVE IT TO EACH FLASH YOU SEE!
GOTCHA!
OHHH..
POP!
POP!
ONE OF US WAS SURE TO CONK THE REAL FLASH! THIS IS THE FLASH'S LAST FIGHT! HA, HA! C'MON, THE RIVAL IS WAITIN' FOR HIM!
THE RIVAL'LL GIVE US A BONUS FOR FLASH'S CAPTURE!
HE'D BETTER-- WE AIN'T BEEN PAID IN WEEKS!
6

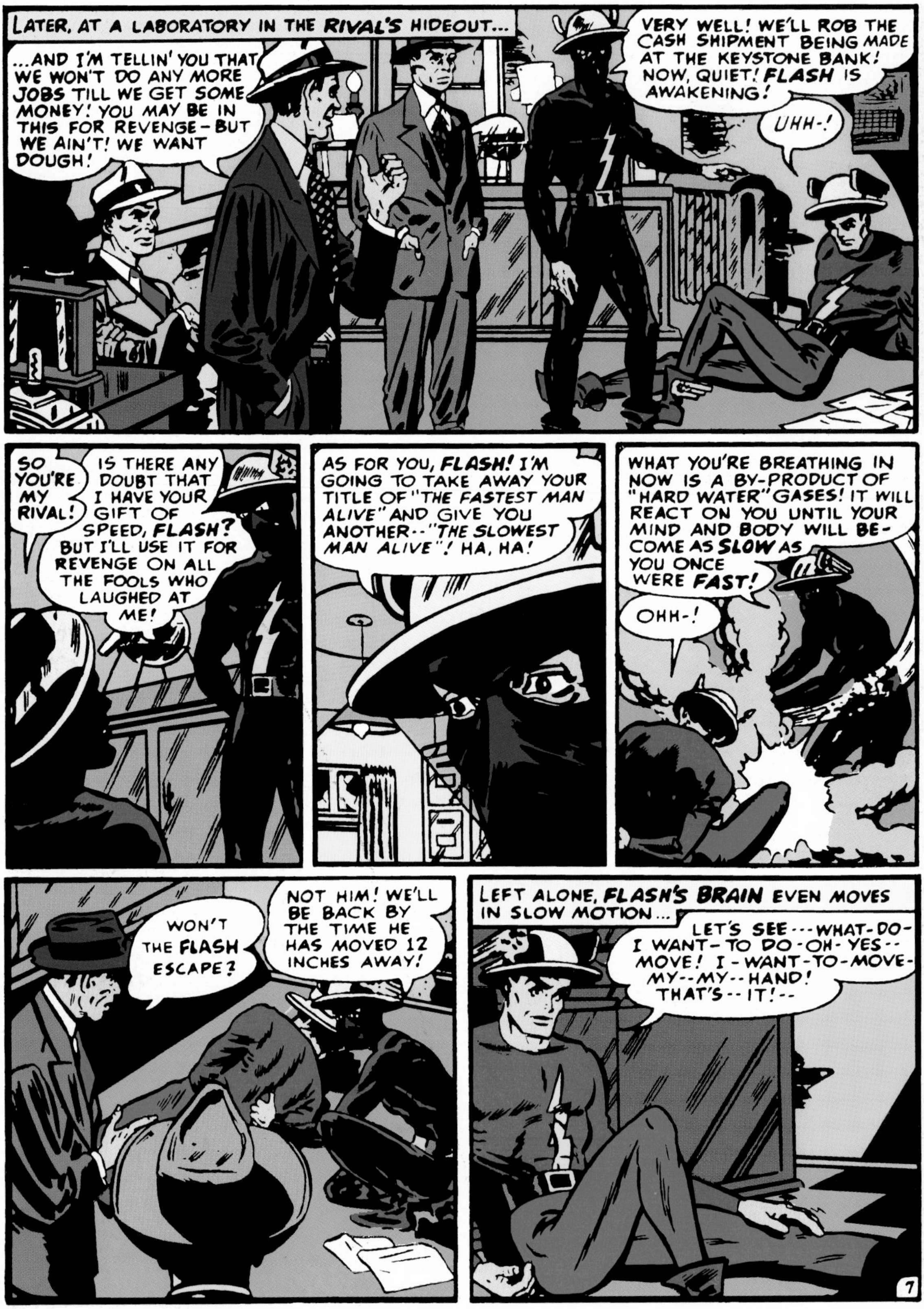
LATER, AT A LABORATORY IN THE RIVAL'S HIDEOUT...
...AND I'M TELLIN' YOU THAT WE WON'T DO ANY MORE JOBS TILL WE GET SOME MONEY! YOU MAY BE IN THIS FOR REVENGE - BUT WE AIN'T! WE WANT DOUGH!
VERY WELL! WE'LL ROB THE CASH SHIPMENT BEING MADE AT THE KEYSTONE BANK! NOW, QUIET! FLASH IS AWAKENING!
UHH-!
SO YOU'RE MY RIVAL!
IS THERE ANY DOUBT THAT I HAVE YOUR GIFT OF SPEED, FLASH? BUT I'LL USE IT FOR REVENGE ON ALL THE FOOLS WHO LAUGHED AT ME!
AS FOR YOU, FLASH! I'M GOING TO TAKE AWAY YOUR TITLE OF "THE FASTEST MAN ALIVE" AND GIVE YOU ANOTHER--"THE SLOWEST MAN ALIVE"! HA, HA!
WHAT YOU'RE BREATHING IN NOW IS A BY-PRODUCT OF "HARD WATER" GASES! IT WILL REACT ON YOU UNTIL YOUR MIND AND BODY WILL BECOME AS SLOW AS YOU ONCE WERE FAST!
OHH-!
WON'T THE FLASH ESCAPE?
NOT HIM! WE'LL BE BACK BY THE TIME HE HAS MOVED 12 INCHES AWAY!
LEFT ALONE, FLASH'S BRAIN EVEN MOVES IN SLOW MOTION...
LET'S SEE---WHAT-DO-I WANT-TO DO-OH-YES--MOVE! I-WANT-TO-MOVE-MY--MY--HAND! THAT'S--IT!--
7

LATER...AFTER MUCH EFFORT, *FLASH* MANAGES TO CRAWL FORWARD...

NOW—WHAT—DO—I—WANT—TO DO? OH—I KNOW—ESCAPE! HOW? —OH, YES—A—A— DOOR—I—MUST—GET—TO A—DOOR—

THE FLEET-FOOTED *FLASH*, FORMERLY THE FASTEST MAN ALIVE, INCHES IN THE SLOWEST OF SLOW MOTION ACROSS THE FLOOR!...

I—SMELL— SOMETHING— FAMILIAR! I—I—CAN'T— REMEMBER WHAT—IT— IS—IT'S—SO LONG—AGO! IF—I—COULD— ONLY—THINK!

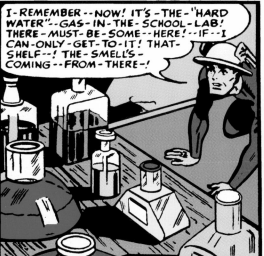

I—REMEMBER—NOW! IT'S—THE—"HARD WATER"—GAS—IN—THE—SCHOOL—LAB! THERE—MUST—BE—SOME—HERE!—IF—I CAN—ONLY—GET—TO—IT! THAT— SHELF—! THE—SMELL'S— COMING—FROM—THERE—!

SUMMONING ALL HIS STRENGTH AND WILL POWER, THE *FLASH* MANAGES TO TOPPLE THE CABINET OVER...

GOOD—THING—IT'S—ONLY MY—SPEED—AND— NOT—MY—STRENGTH THAT'S—BEEN AFFECTED! OH— NONE OF THESE ARE THE "HARD WATER" GASES!

A—HIDING—PLACE! I—WONDER— IF—THAT'S—THE—STUFF—?

AFTER WHAT SEEMS AN INTERMINABLE LENGTH OF TIME, *FLASH* RAISES HIMSELF TO THE HIDDEN SHELF AND...

IT—IS! HAVE— TO—BREATHE— DEEPLY—!

SMASH!

8

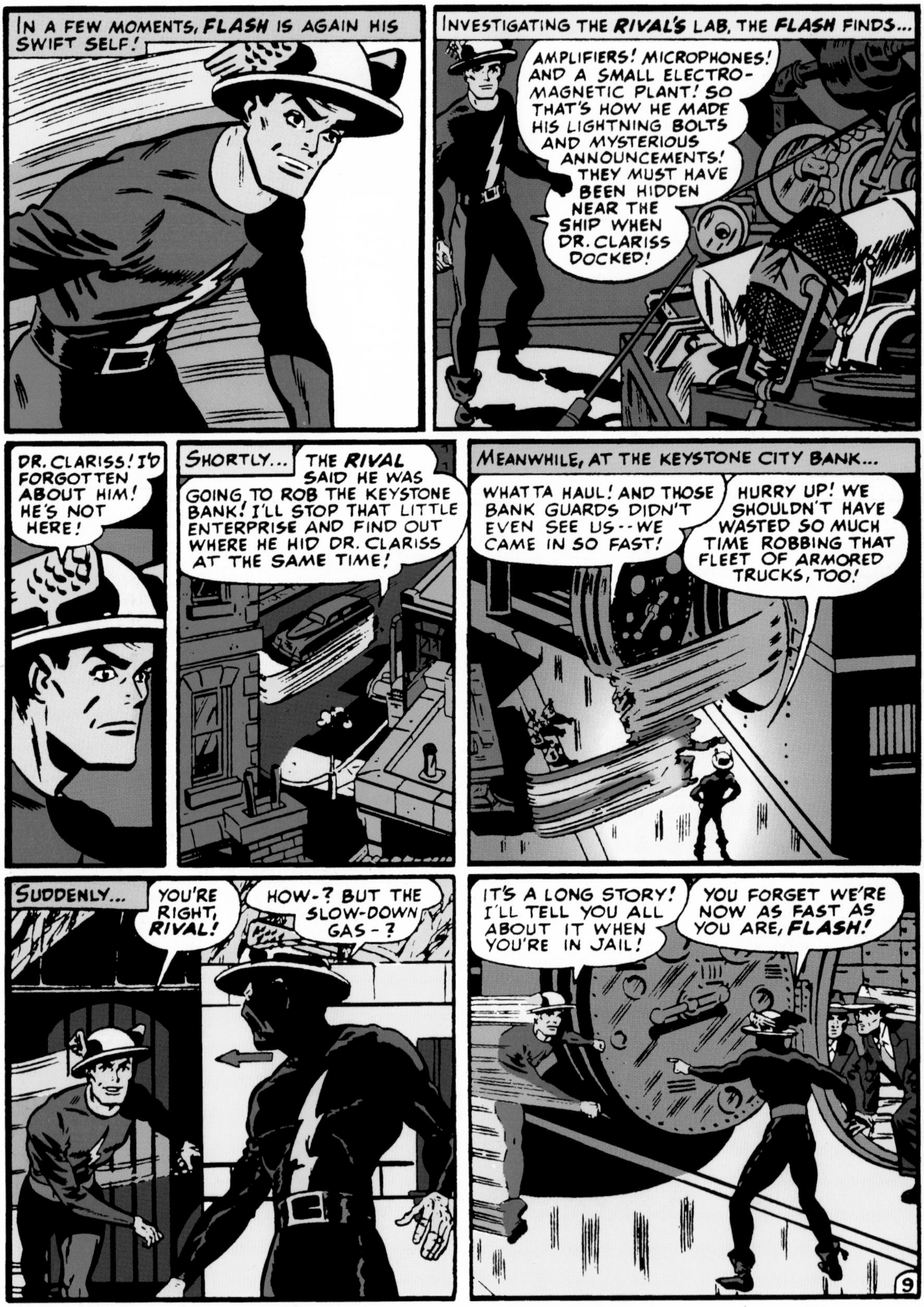
IN A FEW MOMENTS, FLASH IS AGAIN HIS SWIFT SELF!
INVESTIGATING THE RIVAL'S LAB, THE FLASH FINDS...
AMPLIFIERS! MICROPHONES! AND A SMALL ELECTRO-MAGNETIC PLANT! SO THAT'S HOW HE MADE HIS LIGHTNING BOLTS AND MYSTERIOUS ANNOUNCEMENTS! THEY MUST HAVE BEEN HIDDEN NEAR THE SHIP WHEN DR. CLARISS DOCKED!
DR. CLARISS! I'D FORGOTTEN ABOUT HIM! HE'S NOT HERE!
SHORTLY...
THE RIVAL SAID HE WAS GOING TO ROB THE KEYSTONE BANK! I'LL STOP THAT LITTLE ENTERPRISE AND FIND OUT WHERE HE HID DR. CLARISS AT THE SAME TIME!
MEANWHILE, AT THE KEYSTONE CITY BANK...
WHATTA HAUL! AND THOSE BANK GUARDS DIDN'T EVEN SEE US--WE CAME IN SO FAST!
HURRY UP! WE SHOULDN'T HAVE WASTED SO MUCH TIME ROBBING THAT FLEET OF ARMORED TRUCKS, TOO!
SUDDENLY...
YOU'RE RIGHT, RIVAL!
HOW-? BUT THE SLOW-DOWN GAS-?
IT'S A LONG STORY! I'LL TELL YOU ALL ABOUT IT WHEN YOU'RE IN JAIL!
YOU FORGET WE'RE NOW AS FAST AS YOU ARE, FLASH!
9

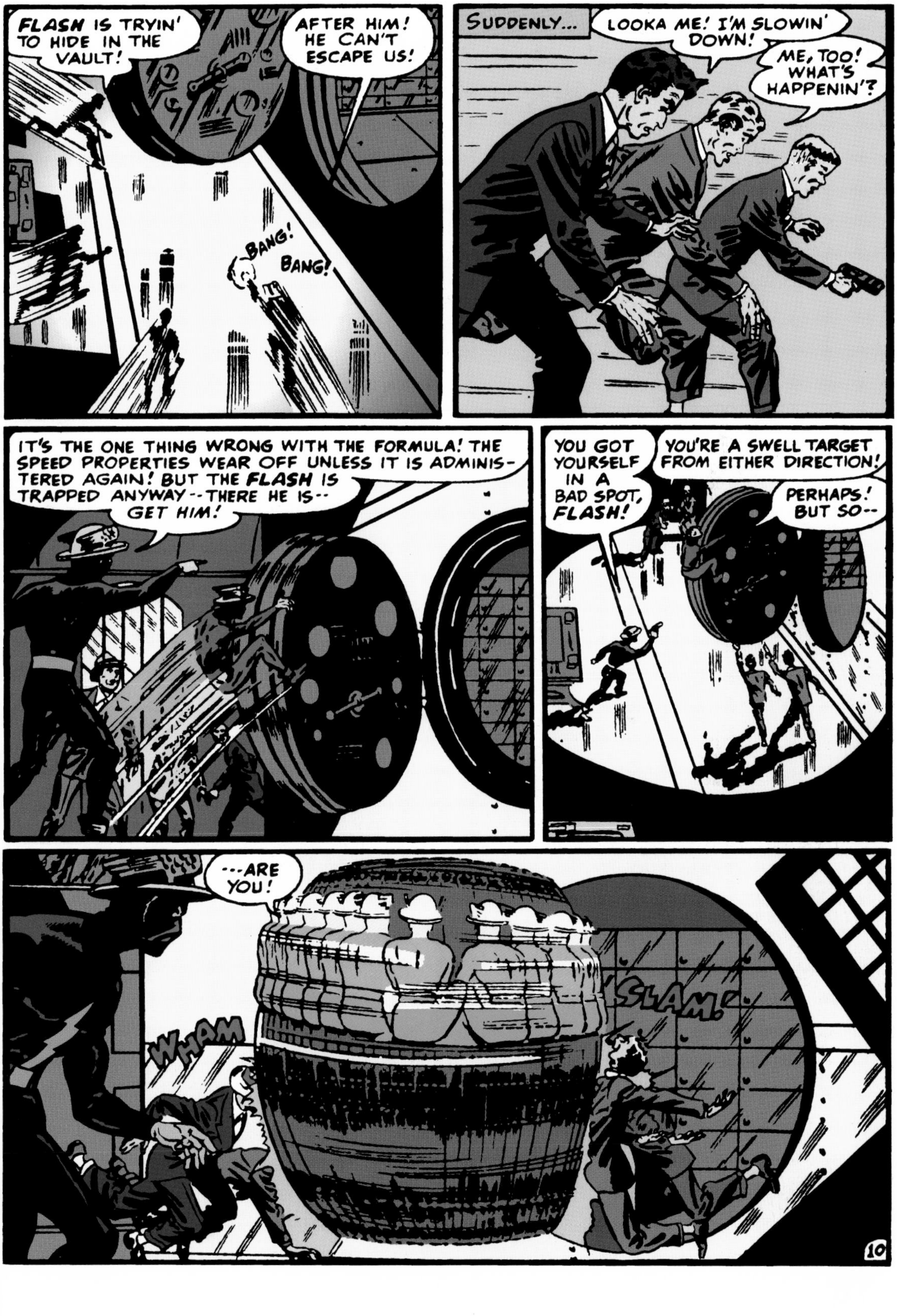
FLASH IS TRYIN' TO HIDE IN THE VAULT!
AFTER HIM! HE CAN'T ESCAPE US!
BANG!
BANG!
SUDDENLY...
LOOKA ME! I'M SLOWIN' DOWN!
ME, TOO! WHAT'S HAPPENIN'?
IT'S THE ONE THING WRONG WITH THE FORMULA! THE SPEED PROPERTIES WEAR OFF UNLESS IT IS ADMINISTERED AGAIN! BUT THE FLASH IS TRAPPED ANYWAY--THERE HE IS--GET HIM!
YOU GOT YOURSELF IN A BAD SPOT, FLASH!
YOU'RE A SWELL TARGET FROM EITHER DIRECTION!
PERHAPS! BUT SO--
---ARE YOU!
WHAM
SLAM!
10

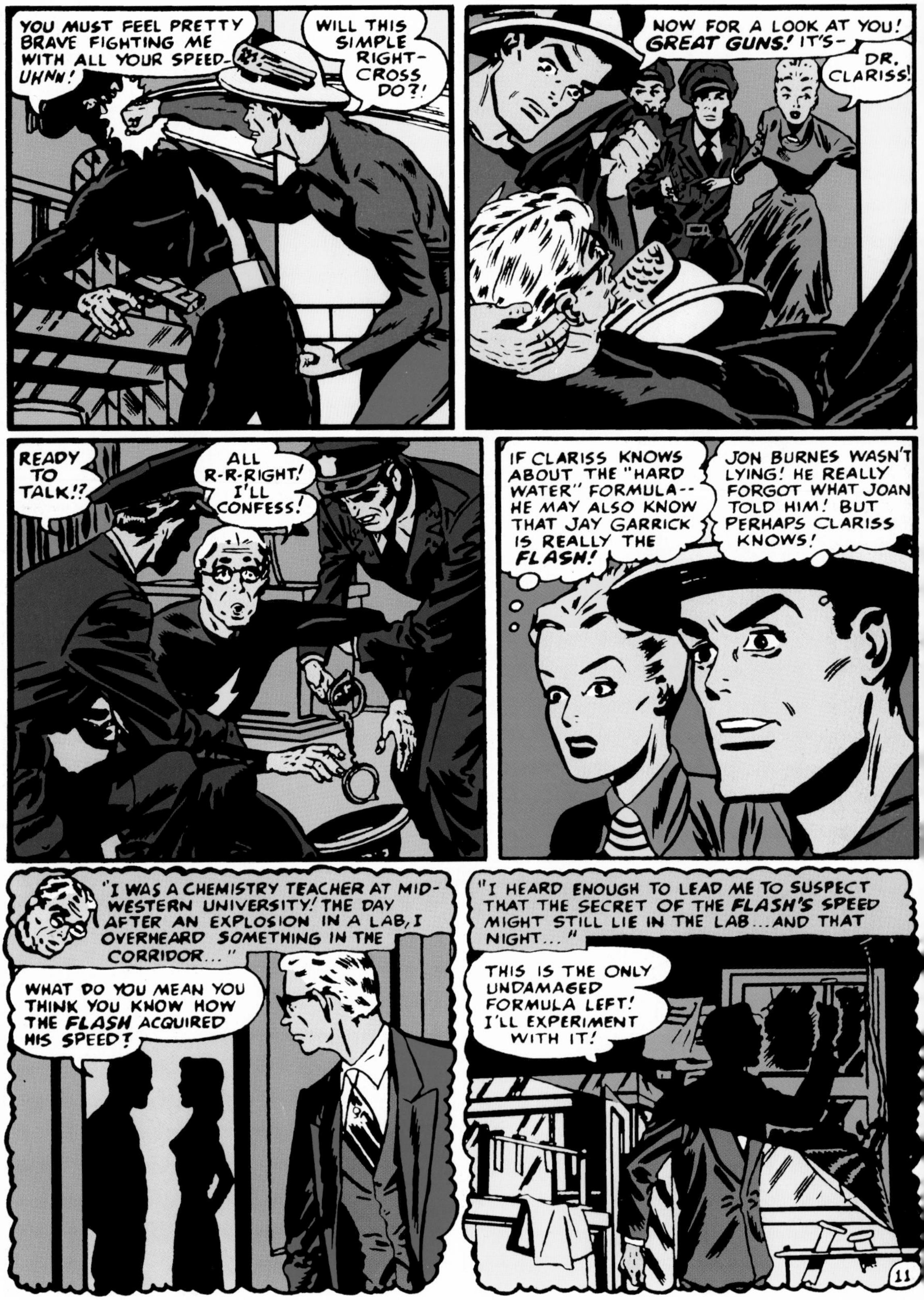
YOU MUST FEEL PRETTY BRAVE FIGHTING ME WITH ALL YOUR SPEED-UHNN!
WILL THIS SIMPLE RIGHT-CROSS DO?!
NOW FOR A LOOK AT YOU! GREAT GUNS! IT'S-
DR. CLARISS!
READY TO TALK!?
ALL R-R-RIGHT! I'LL CONFESS!
IF CLARISS KNOWS ABOUT THE "HARD WATER" FORMULA-- HE MAY ALSO KNOW THAT JAY GARRICK IS REALLY THE FLASH!
JON BURNES WASN'T LYING! HE REALLY FORGOT WHAT JOAN TOLD HIM! BUT PERHAPS CLARISS KNOWS!
"I WAS A CHEMISTRY TEACHER AT MID-WESTERN UNIVERSITY! THE DAY AFTER AN EXPLOSION IN A LAB, I OVERHEARD SOMETHING IN THE CORRIDOR..."
WHAT DO YOU MEAN YOU THINK YOU KNOW HOW THE FLASH ACQUIRED HIS SPEED?
"I HEARD ENOUGH TO LEAD ME TO SUSPECT THAT THE SECRET OF THE FLASH'S SPEED MIGHT STILL LIE IN THE LAB... AND THAT NIGHT..."
THIS IS THE ONLY UNDAMAGED FORMULA LEFT! I'LL EXPERIMENT WITH IT!
11

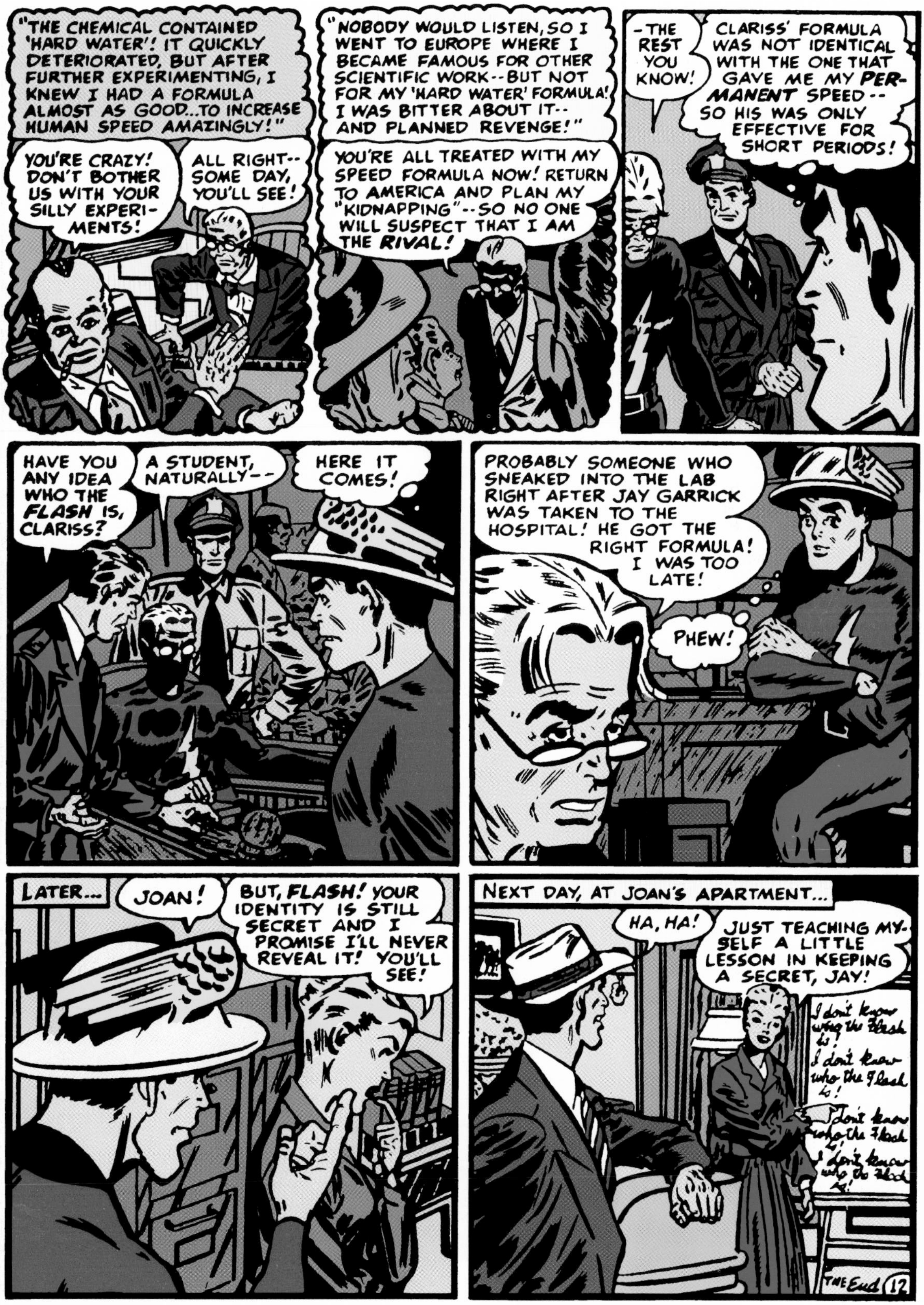
"THE CHEMICAL CONTAINED 'HARD WATER'! IT QUICKLY DETERIORATED, BUT AFTER FURTHER EXPERIMENTING, I KNEW I HAD A FORMULA ALMOST AS GOOD...TO INCREASE HUMAN SPEED AMAZINGLY!"
YOU'RE CRAZY! DON'T BOTHER US WITH YOUR SILLY EXPERIMENTS!
ALL RIGHT-- SOME DAY, YOU'LL SEE!
"NOBODY WOULD LISTEN, SO I WENT TO EUROPE WHERE I BECAME FAMOUS FOR OTHER SCIENTIFIC WORK--BUT NOT FOR MY 'HARD WATER' FORMULA! I WAS BITTER ABOUT IT-- AND PLANNED REVENGE!"
YOU'RE ALL TREATED WITH MY SPEED FORMULA NOW! RETURN TO AMERICA AND PLAN MY "KIDNAPPING"--SO NO ONE WILL SUSPECT THAT I AM THE RIVAL!
-THE REST YOU KNOW!
CLARISS' FORMULA WAS NOT IDENTICAL WITH THE ONE THAT GAVE ME MY PERMANENT SPEED-- SO HIS WAS ONLY EFFECTIVE FOR SHORT PERIODS!
HAVE YOU ANY IDEA WHO THE FLASH IS, CLARISS?
A STUDENT, NATURALLY--
HERE IT COMES!
PROBABLY SOMEONE WHO SNEAKED INTO THE LAB RIGHT AFTER JAY GARRICK WAS TAKEN TO THE HOSPITAL! HE GOT THE RIGHT FORMULA! I WAS TOO LATE!
PHEW!
LATER...
JOAN!
BUT, FLASH! YOUR IDENTITY IS STILL SECRET AND I PROMISE I'LL NEVER REVEAL IT! YOU'LL SEE!
NEXT DAY, AT JOAN'S APARTMENT...
HA, HA!
JUST TEACHING MYSELF A LITTLE LESSON IN KEEPING A SECRET, JAY!
I don't know who the Flash is!
I don't know who the Flash is!
I don't know who the Flash is!
I don't know who the Flash is!
THE End
12

SUPERMAN
DC
NATIONAL COMICS
OCT.
10¢
NO. 4
In this issue:
DETAILS and ENTRY BLANK for
Giant 5000 PRIZE CONTEST!
APPROVED BY THE COMICS CODE AUTHORITY
SHOWCASE
Presenting THE FLASH!
WHIRLWIND ADVENTURES OF THE FASTEST MAN ALIVE!

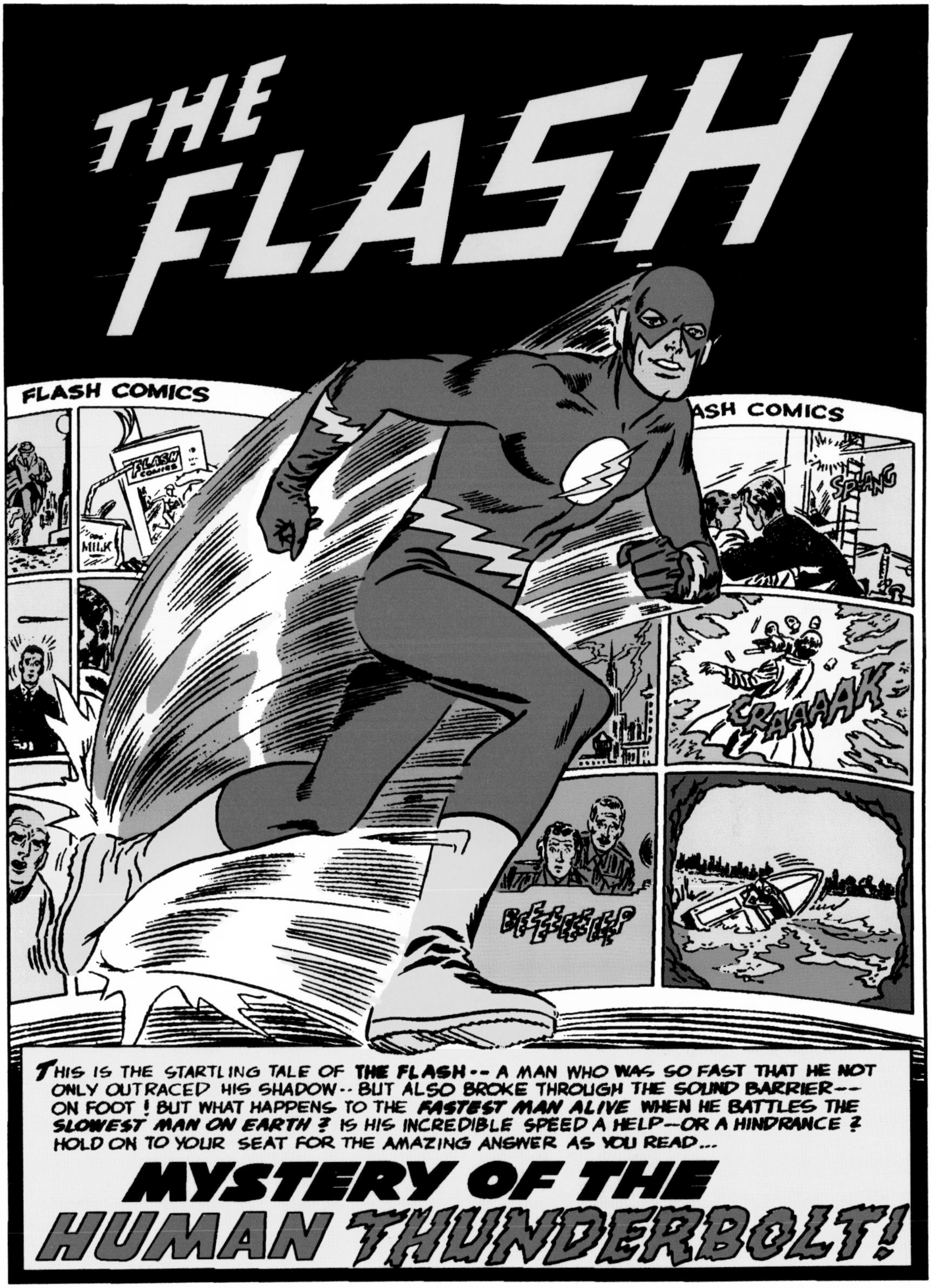
THE FLASH
FLASH COMICS
FLASH COMICS
MILK
ASH COMICS
SPANG
CRAAAAK
BEEEEEEP
THIS IS THE STARTLING TALE OF THE FLASH -- A MAN WHO WAS SO FAST THAT HE NOT ONLY OUTRACED HIS SHADOW -- BUT ALSO BROKE THROUGH THE SOUND BARRIER -- ON FOOT ! BUT WHAT HAPPENS TO THE FASTEST MAN ALIVE WHEN HE BATTLES THE SLOWEST MAN ON EARTH ? IS HIS INCREDIBLE SPEED A HELP--OR A HINDRANCE ? HOLD ON TO YOUR SEAT FOR THE AMAZING ANSWER AS YOU READ...
MYSTERY OF THE HUMAN THUNDERBOLT!

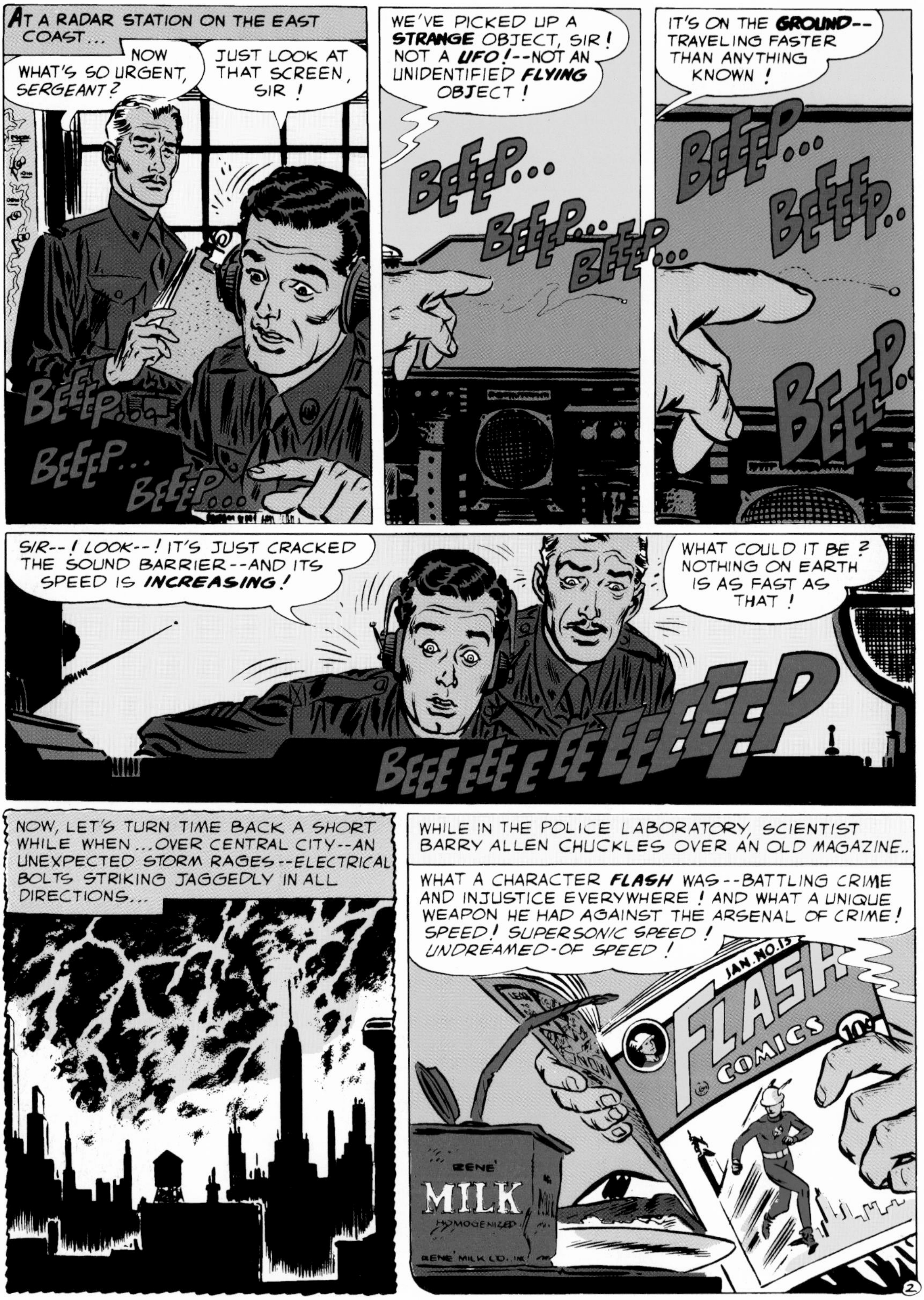
AT A RADAR STATION ON THE EAST COAST...
NOW WHAT'S SO URGENT, SERGEANT?
JUST LOOK AT THAT SCREEN, SIR!
BEEEP...
BEEEP...
BEEEP...
WE'VE PICKED UP A STRANGE OBJECT, SIR! NOT A UFO!--NOT AN UNIDENTIFIED FLYING OBJECT!
BEEEP...
BEEEP...
BEEEP...
IT'S ON THE GROUND--TRAVELING FASTER THAN ANYTHING KNOWN!
BEEEP...
BEEEP...
BEEEP...
SIR--! LOOK--! IT'S JUST CRACKED THE SOUND BARRIER--AND ITS SPEED IS INCREASING!
WHAT COULD IT BE? NOTHING ON EARTH IS AS FAST AS THAT!
BEEE EEE E EE EEEEEEP
NOW, LET'S TURN TIME BACK A SHORT WHILE WHEN ...OVER CENTRAL CITY--AN UNEXPECTED STORM RAGES--ELECTRICAL BOLTS STRIKING JAGGEDLY IN ALL DIRECTIONS...
WHILE IN THE POLICE LABORATORY, SCIENTIST BARRY ALLEN CHUCKLES OVER AN OLD MAGAZINE..
WHAT A CHARACTER FLASH WAS--BATTLING CRIME AND INJUSTICE EVERYWHERE! AND WHAT A UNIQUE WEAPON HE HAD AGAINST THE ARSENAL OF CRIME! SPEED! SUPERSONIC SPEED! UNDREAMED-OF SPEED!
JAN. NO. 13
FLASH COMICS
10¢
GENE' MILK HOMOGENIZED
GENE' MILK CO. INC.
2

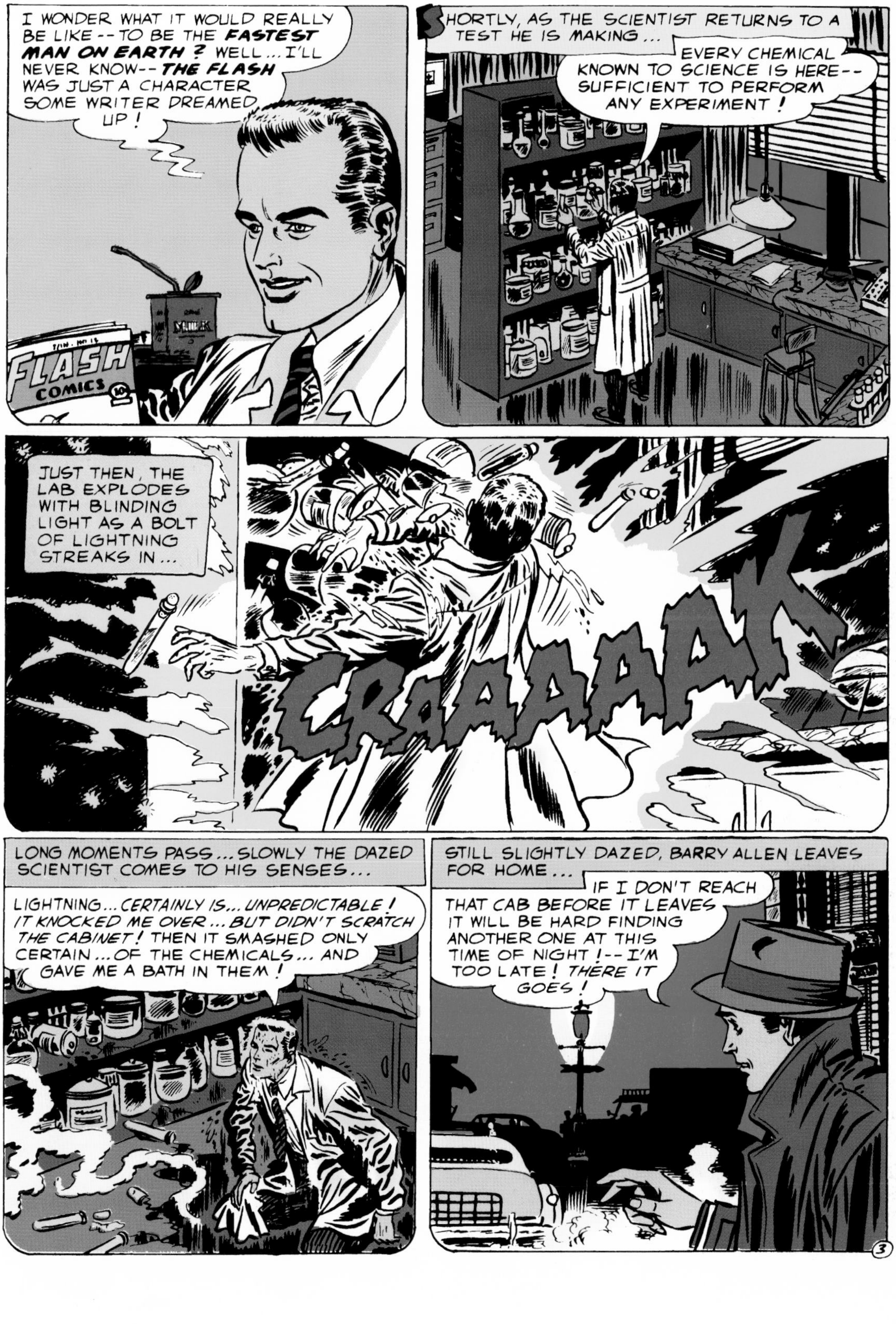

I WONDER WHAT IT WOULD REALLY BE LIKE -- TO BE THE **FASTEST MAN ON EARTH?** WELL... I'LL NEVER KNOW-- **THE FLASH** WAS JUST A CHARACTER SOME WRITER DREAMED UP!
FLASH COMICS
SHORTLY, AS THE SCIENTIST RETURNS TO A TEST HE IS MAKING...
EVERY CHEMICAL KNOWN TO SCIENCE IS HERE-- SUFFICIENT TO PERFORM ANY EXPERIMENT!
JUST THEN, THE LAB EXPLODES WITH BLINDING LIGHT AS A BOLT OF LIGHTNING STREAKS IN...
CRAAAAAK
LONG MOMENTS PASS... SLOWLY THE DAZED SCIENTIST COMES TO HIS SENSES...
LIGHTNING... *CERTAINLY IS... UNPREDICTABLE! IT KNOCKED ME OVER... BUT DIDN'T SCRATCH THE CABINET!* THEN IT SMASHED ONLY CERTAIN... OF THE CHEMICALS... AND GAVE ME A BATH IN THEM!
STILL SLIGHTLY DAZED, BARRY ALLEN LEAVES FOR HOME...
IF I DON'T REACH THAT CAB BEFORE IT LEAVES IT WILL BE HARD FINDING ANOTHER ONE AT THIS TIME OF NIGHT!-- I'M TOO LATE! *THERE IT GOES!*
3

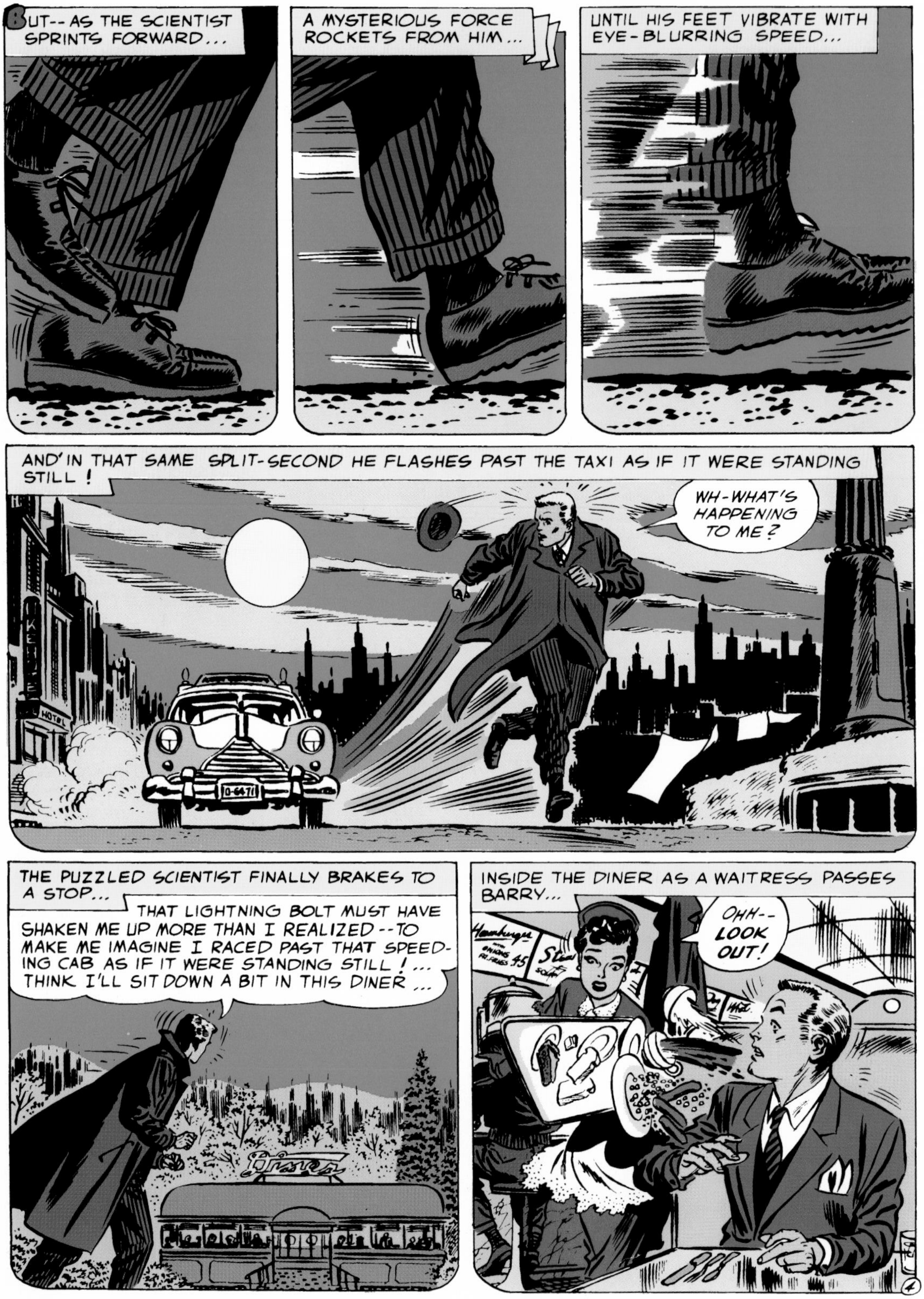
BUT-- AS THE SCIENTIST SPRINTS FORWARD...
A MYSTERIOUS FORCE ROCKETS FROM HIM...
UNTIL HIS FEET VIBRATE WITH EYE-BLURRING SPEED...
AND IN THAT SAME SPLIT-SECOND HE FLASHES PAST THE TAXI AS IF IT WERE STANDING STILL!
WH-WHAT'S HAPPENING TO ME?
HOTEL
THE PUZZLED SCIENTIST FINALLY BRAKES TO A STOP...
THAT LIGHTNING BOLT MUST HAVE SHAKEN ME UP MORE THAN I REALIZED --TO MAKE ME IMAGINE I RACED PAST THAT SPEEDING CAB AS IF IT WERE STANDING STILL!... THINK I'LL SIT DOWN A BIT IN THIS DINER...
INSIDE THE DINER AS A WAITRESS PASSES BARRY...
OHH-- LOOK OUT!
4

INSTINCTIVELY SHRINKING FROM THE FALLING OBJECTS, BARRY IS STARTLED TO SEE...

WHY--IT LOOKS AS IF THEY'VE **STOPPED** FALLING ! IT CAN'T BE HARD TO CATCH THINGS THAT ARE JUST **HANGING** IN THE AIR--AS IF THEIR **MOTION** IS STOPPED !

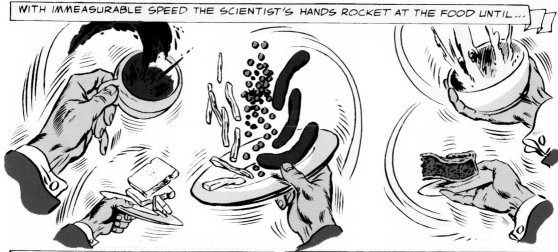

WITH IMMEASURABLE SPEED THE SCIENTIST'S HANDS ROCKET AT THE FOOD UNTIL...

AS THE FLEET SCIENTIST RETURNS THE RE-TRIEVED FOODS TO THE FLABBERGASTED WAITRESS...

I--I MUSN'T BE GETTING ENOUGH SLEEP !... I'M BEGINNING TO SEE TH-THINGS !... I COULD HAVE SWORN I DROPPED EVERY-THING AND Y-Y-YOU--NO ! IT'S IMPOSSIBLE !... EXCUSE ME, SIR !

SHE ISN'T THE ONLY ONE WHO'S SEEING THINGS ! THAT LIGHTNING BOLT TOSSED ME AROUND LIKE A SALAD IN A DRESSING OF CHEMICALS ! I'D BETTER GO HOME AND GET A GOOD NIGHT'S SLEEP !

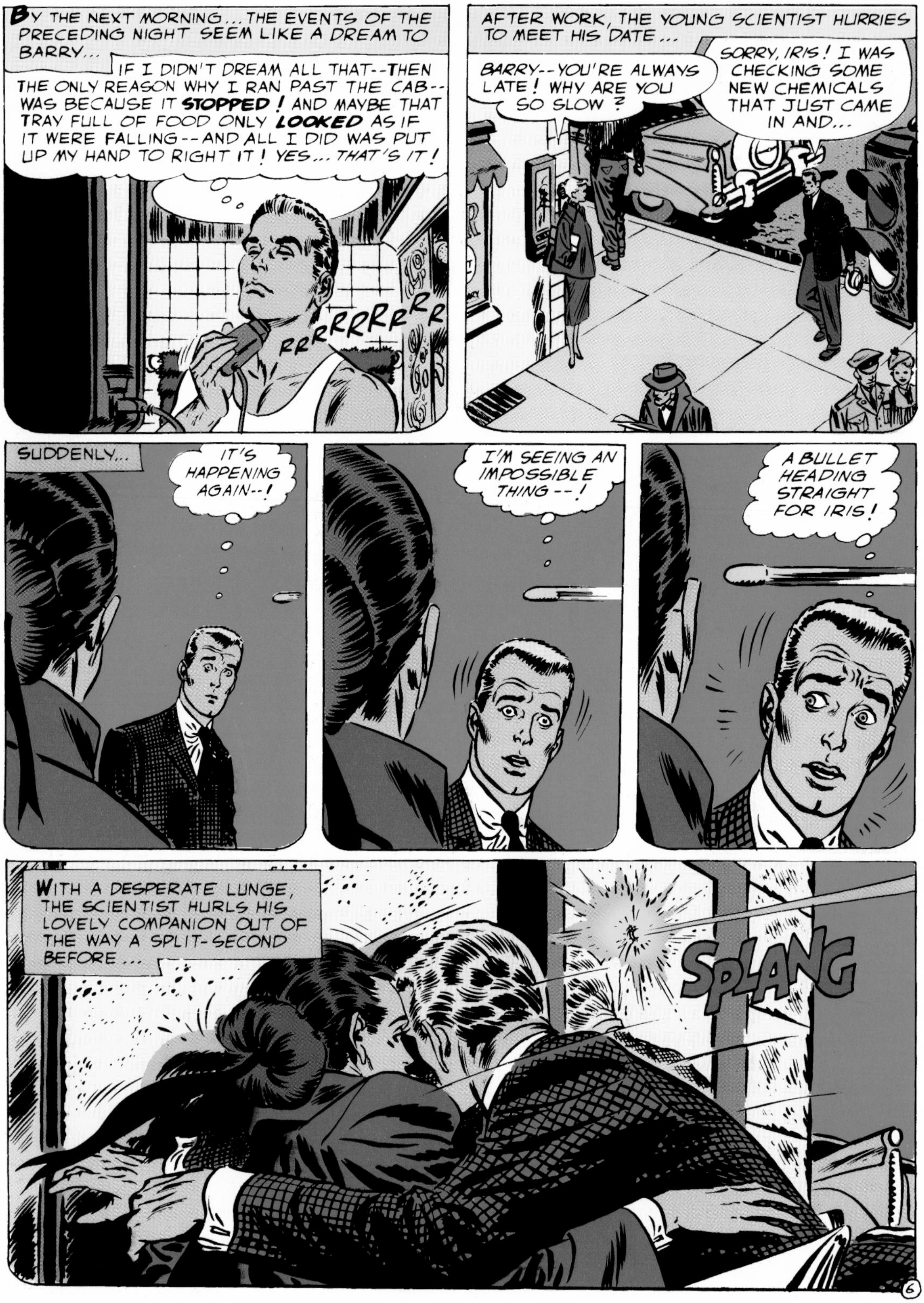
BY THE NEXT MORNING... THE EVENTS OF THE PRECEDING NIGHT SEEM LIKE A DREAM TO BARRY...
IF I DIDN'T DREAM ALL THAT--THEN THE ONLY REASON WHY I RAN PAST THE CAB--WAS BECAUSE IT **STOPPED**! AND MAYBE THAT TRAY FULL OF FOOD ONLY **LOOKED** AS IF IT WERE FALLING--AND ALL I DID WAS PUT UP MY HAND TO RIGHT IT! YES... THAT'S IT!
RRRRRRRRR
AFTER WORK, THE YOUNG SCIENTIST HURRIES TO MEET HIS DATE...
BARRY--YOU'RE ALWAYS LATE! WHY ARE YOU SO SLOW?
SORRY, IRIS! I WAS CHECKING SOME NEW CHEMICALS THAT JUST CAME IN AND...
SUDDENLY...
IT'S HAPPENING AGAIN--!
I'M SEEING AN IMPOSSIBLE THING--!
A BULLET HEADING STRAIGHT FOR IRIS!
WITH A DESPERATE LUNGE, THE SCIENTIST HURLS HIS LOVELY COMPANION OUT OF THE WAY A SPLIT-SECOND BEFORE...
SPLANG
6

BARRY--IF Y-YOU H-HADN'T ACCIDENTALLY STUMBLED AGAINST ME J-JUST BEFORE THAT STRAY BULLET STRUCK--I WOULD HAVE BEEN H-HIT!

GLAD YOU FOLKS WEREN'T HURT! THAT STRAY WAS FIRED BY THE *TURTLE MAN* -- MAKING A GETAWAY!

THE *TURTLE MAN?* THAT'S THE CRIMINAL CALLED "*THE SLOWEST MAN ON EARTH*"!

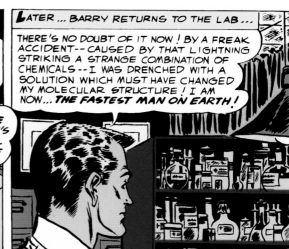

LATER ... BARRY RETURNS TO THE LAB ...

THERE'S NO DOUBT OF IT NOW! BY A FREAK ACCIDENT--CAUSED BY THAT LIGHTNING STRIKING A STRANGE COMBINATION OF CHEMICALS--I WAS DRENCHED WITH A SOLUTION WHICH MUST HAVE CHANGED MY MOLECULAR STRUCTURE! I AM NOW... *THE FASTEST MAN ON EARTH!*

THERE MUST BE *SOME* WAY I CAN USE THIS UNIQUE SPEED TO HELP HUMANITY!... HMMM--THIS GIVES ME AN IDEA!

FLASH COMICS
JAN. NO. 13
10¢

SOMETIME LATER... AT THE LAB...

THE REMOTE CONTROL HOOKUP I'VE FIXED UP WITH THE ALARM SYSTEM AT HEAD-QUARTERS IS PAYING OFF! IT'S SIGNALLING THAT THE BURGLAR ALARM AT THE CENTRAL BANK HAS BEEN TRIPPED!

BZZ Z ZZZ BZZZZZ

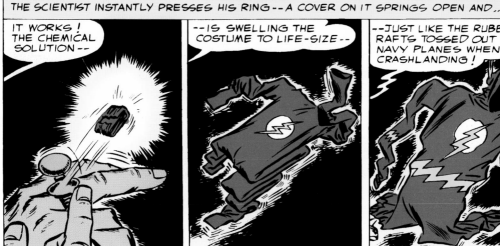

THE SCIENTIST INSTANTLY PRESSES HIS RING--A COVER ON IT SPRINGS OPEN AND...

IT WORKS! THE CHEMICAL SOLUTION--

--IS SWELLING THE COSTUME TO LIFE-SIZE--

--JUST LIKE THE RUBBER RAFTS TOSSED OUT BY NAVY PLANES WHEN CRASHLANDING!

7

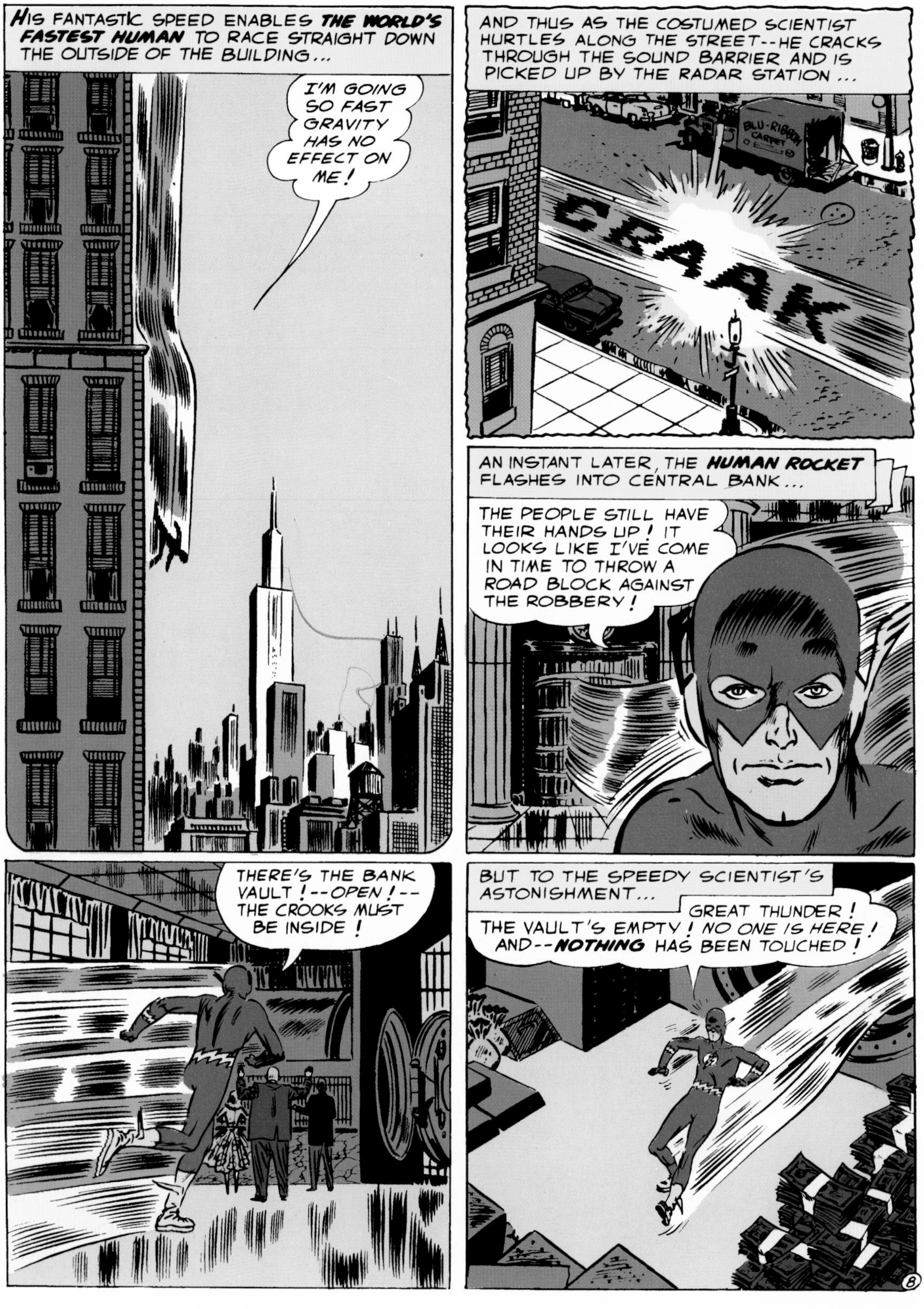
HIS FANTASTIC SPEED ENABLES THE WORLD'S FASTEST HUMAN TO RACE STRAIGHT DOWN THE OUTSIDE OF THE BUILDING...
I'M GOING SO FAST GRAVITY HAS NO EFFECT ON ME!
AND THUS AS THE COSTUMED SCIENTIST HURTLES ALONG THE STREET--HE CRACKS THROUGH THE SOUND BARRIER AND IS PICKED UP BY THE RADAR STATION...
BLU-RIBBON CARPET
CRAAK
AN INSTANT LATER, THE HUMAN ROCKET FLASHES INTO CENTRAL BANK...
THE PEOPLE STILL HAVE THEIR HANDS UP! IT LOOKS LIKE I'VE COME IN TIME TO THROW A ROAD BLOCK AGAINST THE ROBBERY!
THERE'S THE BANK VAULT!--OPEN!--THE CROOKS MUST BE INSIDE!
BUT TO THE SPEEDY SCIENTIST'S ASTONISHMENT...
GREAT THUNDER! THE VAULT'S EMPTY! NO ONE IS HERE! AND--NOTHING HAS BEEN TOUCHED!
8

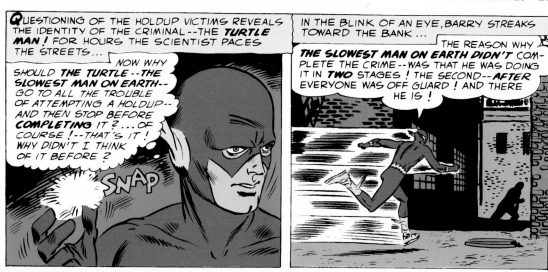

QUESTIONING OF THE HOLDUP VICTIMS REVEALS THE IDENTITY OF THE CRIMINAL --THE *TURTLE MAN!* FOR HOURS THE SCIENTIST PACES THE STREETS...

NOW WHY SHOULD *THE TURTLE* --THE *SLOWEST MAN ON EARTH* --GO TO ALL THE TROUBLE OF ATTEMPTING A HOLDUP-- AND THEN STOP BEFORE *COMPLETING* IT ? ...OF COURSE !--THAT'S IT ! WHY DIDN'T I THINK OF IT BEFORE ?

SNAP

IN THE BLINK OF AN EYE, BARRY STREAKS TOWARD THE BANK ...

THE REASON WHY *THE SLOWEST MAN ON EARTH DIDN'T* COMPLETE THE CRIME --WAS THAT HE WAS DOING IT IN *TWO* STAGES ! THE SECOND--*AFTER* EVERYONE WAS OFF GUARD ! AND THERE HE IS !

AT EYE-BLURRING SPEED...

THE SCIENTIST REACHES OUT FOR THE STATIONARY VILLAIN...

ONLY TO DISCOVER ...

HE TRICKED ME--THIS IS JUST A PAINTED SILHOUETTE --NOT A REAL SHADOW !

SO GREAT IS THE *HUMAN WHIRLWIND'S* SPEED --HE BORES THROUGH THE SOLID BRICK WALL LIKE A GIGANTIC DRILL ... AS THE *TURTLE MAN* TAUNTS...

HE...DOESN'T...KNOW...I...ANTICIPATED...HIS... RETURN...AFTER...I...SAW...HIM...ENTER... THE ..VAULT...WHERE ...I ...WAS...HIDING ... HA...HA...HA...

KRUNNNG

BY THE TIME BARRY REGAINS HIS SENSES...

I'VE GOT TO -- WATCH MYSELF! THE *TURTLE MAN* -- IS USING MY SPEED -- AS A WEAPON -- AGAINST ME! -- LOOKS LIKE HE WENT... UNDERGROUND!

INTO THE UNDERGROUND OPENING THE PURSUING SCIENTIST DROPS...

ALL THESE SEWERS EMPTY OUT ON THE RIVER! I'LL CATCH UP TO HIM THERE!

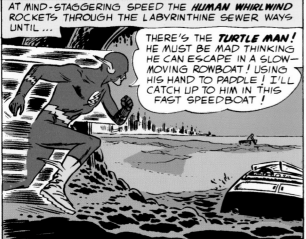

AT MIND-STAGGERING SPEED THE *HUMAN WHIRLWIND* ROCKETS THROUGH THE LABYRINTHINE SEWER WAYS UNTIL ...

THERE'S THE *TURTLE MAN!* HE MUST BE MAD THINKING HE CAN ESCAPE IN A SLOW-MOVING ROWBOAT! USING HIS HAND TO PADDLE! I'LL CATCH UP TO HIM IN THIS FAST SPEEDBOAT!

I MUST REMEMBER TO THANK THE OWNER OF THIS SPEEDBOAT FOR HELPING ME CAPTURE THE *TURTLE MAN!*

BRRRRRRRRRR

BUT AS THE SPEEDBOAT LUNGES FORWARD...

THIS BOAT'S SINKING RIGHT UNDER ME -- THE *TURTLE MAN* MUST HAVE BOOBY-TRAPPED IT!

HA... HA... HA...

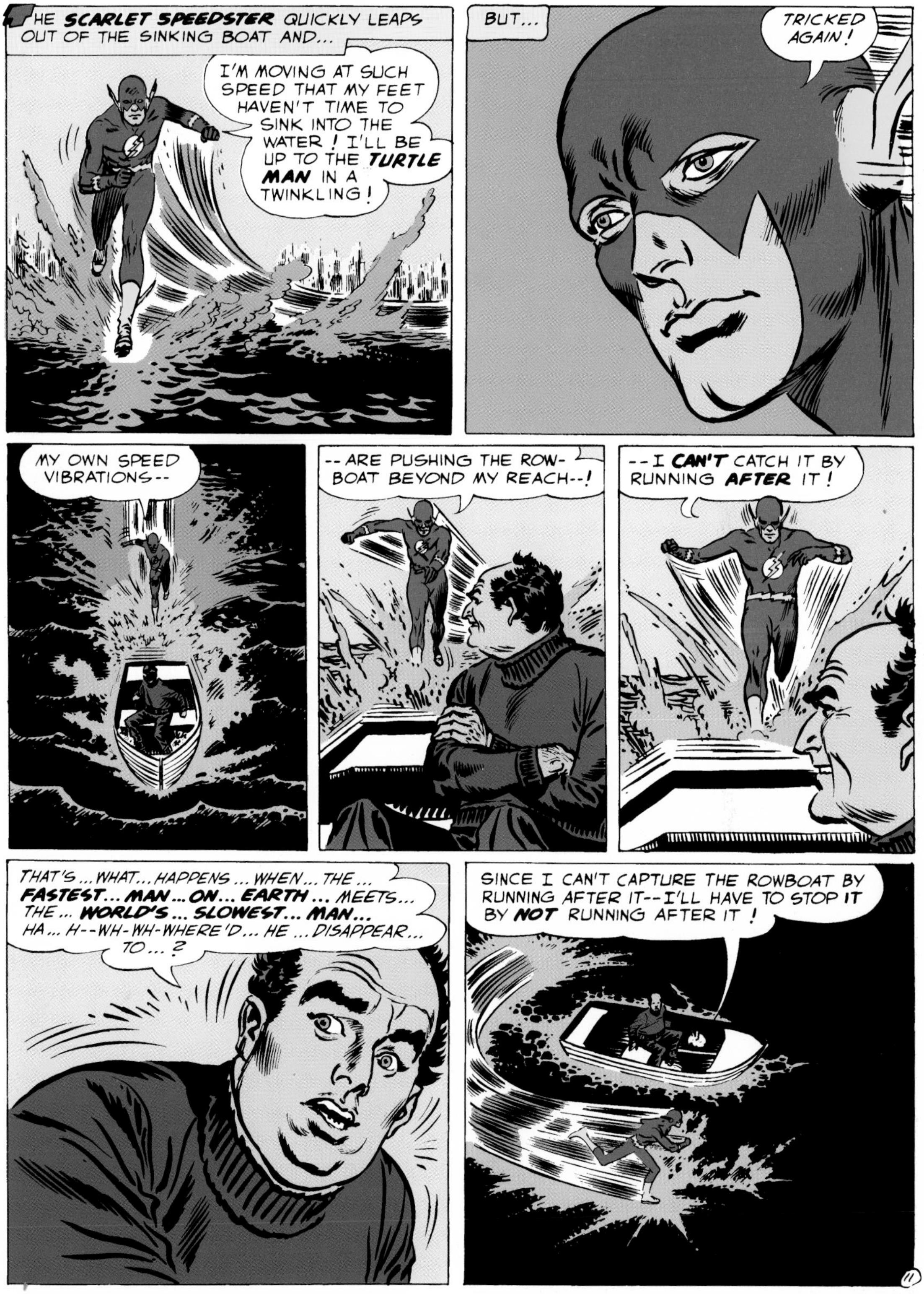
THE SCARLET SPEEDSTER QUICKLY LEAPS OUT OF THE SINKING BOAT AND...
I'M MOVING AT SUCH SPEED THAT MY FEET HAVEN'T TIME TO SINK INTO THE WATER! I'LL BE UP TO THE TURTLE MAN IN A TWINKLING!
BUT...
TRICKED AGAIN!
MY OWN SPEED VIBRATIONS--
--ARE PUSHING THE ROW-BOAT BEYOND MY REACH--!
--I CAN'T CATCH IT BY RUNNING AFTER IT!
THAT'S...WHAT...HAPPENS...WHEN...THE... FASTEST...MAN...ON...EARTH...MEETS... THE...WORLD'S...SLOWEST...MAN... HA... H--WH-WH-WHERE'D... HE...DISAPPEAR... TO...?
SINCE I CAN'T CAPTURE THE ROWBOAT BY RUNNING AFTER IT--I'LL HAVE TO STOP IT BY NOT RUNNING AFTER IT!
11

Circling the rowboat at supersonic speed, the human hurricane creates a vortex which...

HELP...!

I'LL BE GLAD TO!

Catching the dazed criminal, the speedy scientist rockets back to the river bank with him...

YOU... TRICKED ME...!

THAT'S WHAT HAPPENS WHEN THE *WORLD'S SLOWEST MAN* MEETS THE *FASTEST MAN ON EARTH!*

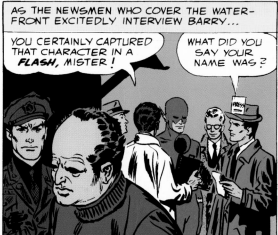

As the newsmen who cover the waterfront excitedly interview Barry...

YOU CERTAINLY CAPTURED THAT CHARACTER IN A *FLASH*, MISTER!

WHAT DID YOU SAY YOUR NAME WAS?

YOU JUST SAID IT-- *THE FLASH!*

Later, as the startling speedster returns to his secret identity...

READ ALL ABOUT THE FLASH-- THE FASTEST MAN IN THE WORLD!

HOW EXCITING IT WOULD BE TO MEET A MAN LIKE THAT! BUT I GUESS IT'S JUST AN IDLE DREAM!

SOMETIMES DREAMS COME TRUE, IRIS!

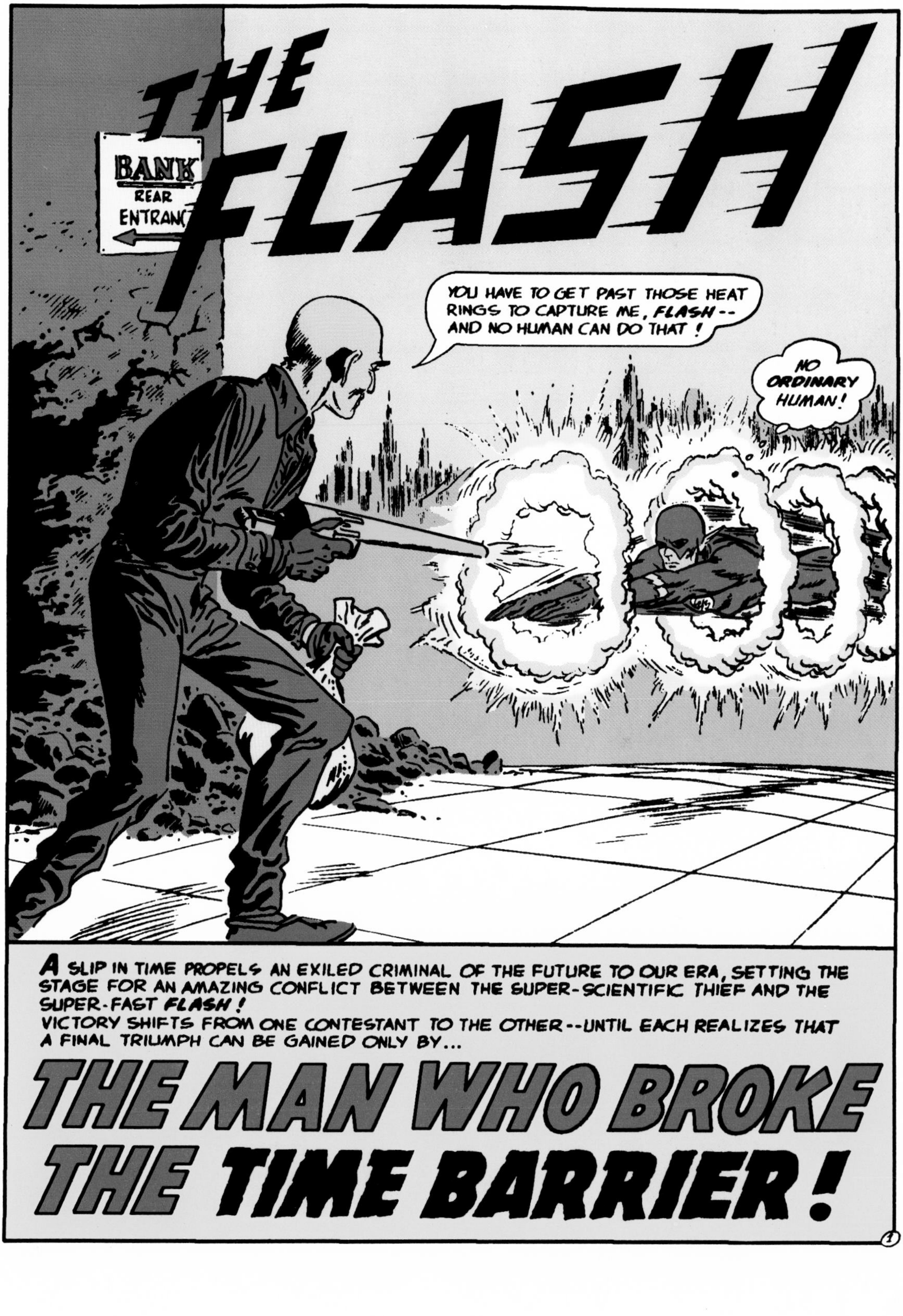
THE FLASH
BANK
REAR
ENTRANC
YOU HAVE TO GET PAST THOSE HEAT RINGS TO CAPTURE ME, FLASH -- AND NO HUMAN CAN DO THAT !
NO ORDINARY HUMAN!
A SLIP IN TIME PROPELS AN EXILED CRIMINAL OF THE FUTURE TO OUR ERA, SETTING THE STAGE FOR AN AMAZING CONFLICT BETWEEN THE SUPER-SCIENTIFIC THIEF AND THE SUPER-FAST FLASH !
VICTORY SHIFTS FROM ONE CONTESTANT TO THE OTHER--UNTIL EACH REALIZES THAT A FINAL TRIUMPH CAN BE GAINED ONLY BY...
THE MAN WHO BROKE THE TIME BARRIER!
1

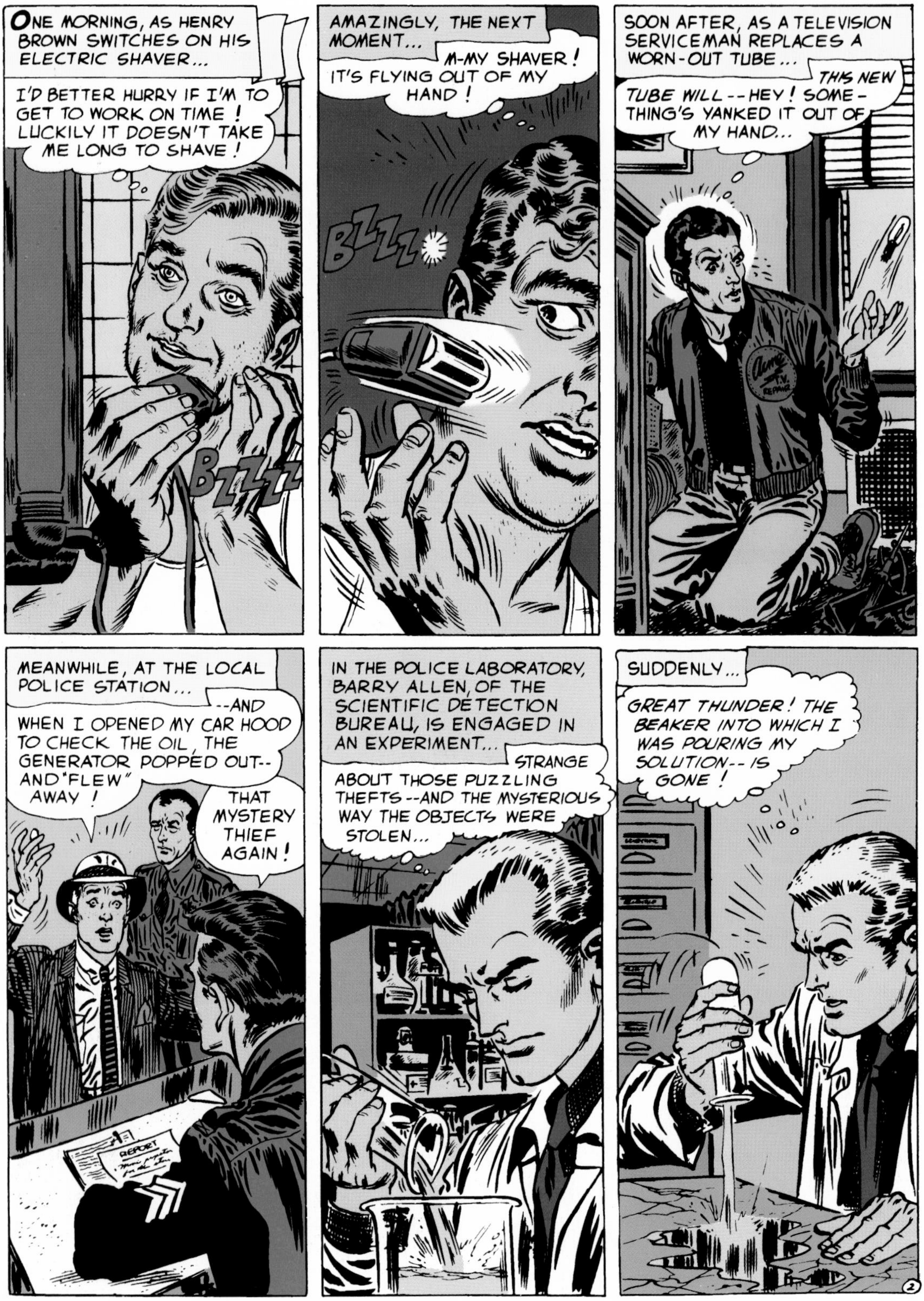
ONE MORNING, AS HENRY BROWN SWITCHES ON HIS ELECTRIC SHAVER...
I'D BETTER HURRY IF I'M TO GET TO WORK ON TIME! LUCKILY IT DOESN'T TAKE ME LONG TO SHAVE!
BZZZZ
AMAZINGLY, THE NEXT MOMENT...
M-MY SHAVER! IT'S FLYING OUT OF MY HAND!
BZZZ
SOON AFTER, AS A TELEVISION SERVICEMAN REPLACES A WORN-OUT TUBE...
THIS NEW TUBE WILL--HEY! SOMETHING'S YANKED IT OUT OF MY HAND...
MEANWHILE, AT THE LOCAL POLICE STATION...
--AND WHEN I OPENED MY CAR HOOD TO CHECK THE OIL, THE GENERATOR POPPED OUT--AND "FLEW" AWAY!
THAT MYSTERY THIEF AGAIN!
REPORT
IN THE POLICE LABORATORY, BARRY ALLEN, OF THE SCIENTIFIC DETECTION BUREAU, IS ENGAGED IN AN EXPERIMENT...
STRANGE ABOUT THOSE PUZZLING THEFTS--AND THE MYSTERIOUS WAY THE OBJECTS WERE STOLEN...
SUDDENLY...
GREAT THUNDER! THE BEAKER INTO WHICH I WAS POURING MY SOLUTION--IS GONE!
2

WITH STARTLING SPEED, THE YOUNG SCIENTIST WHIRLS...

WHO'S *THAT*--? SOMEONE GOING OUT! I'D BETTER SEE WHO THAT IS -- AT *SUPER-SPEED!*

AS BARRY ALLEN TOUCHES THE RING ON HIS FINGER, ITS COVER SNAPS OPEN -- AND A COLORFUL UNIFORM IS EJECTED... EXPANDING INSTANTLY...

...AND IN LESS TIME THAN IT TAKES TO NAME HIM, *FLASH* APPEARS...

FIRST THE CHEMICAL SOLUTION I WAS POURING VANISHES-- BEAKER AND ALL-- AND THEN AN UNKNOWN FIGURE SLIPS OUT OF THE LAB! I'VE GOT TO GET AFTER HIM!

A SPLIT-SECOND LATER, IN A SIDE STREET NEARBY...

THERE HE IS!

SOMEONE COMING AFTER ME!

AS THE *FASTEST MAN ALIVE* DARTS AT HIS TARGET...

SHOOTING RINGS AT ME -- RINGS OF INTENSE *HEAT!*

THE RINGS ARE GETTING HOTTER AND HOTTER! JUST LIKE FLAME, THE RED RINGS ARE THE LEAST HOT -- THE YELLOW ONES ARE HOTTER -- AND THE BLUE-WHITE ARE THE HOTTEST OF ALL!

SPINNING AROUND WITH INCREDIBLE SPEED, *FLASH* CREATES A WIND THAT COOLS OFF THE RINGS -- AND LIFTS THEM SKYWARD...

WHILE I WAS AVOID-ING THE BARRAGE OF HEAT RINGS, THE AMAZING THIEF WHO SHOT THEM AT ME ESCAPED!

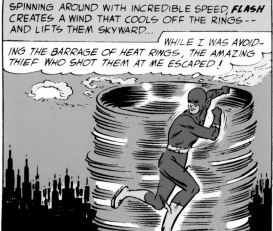

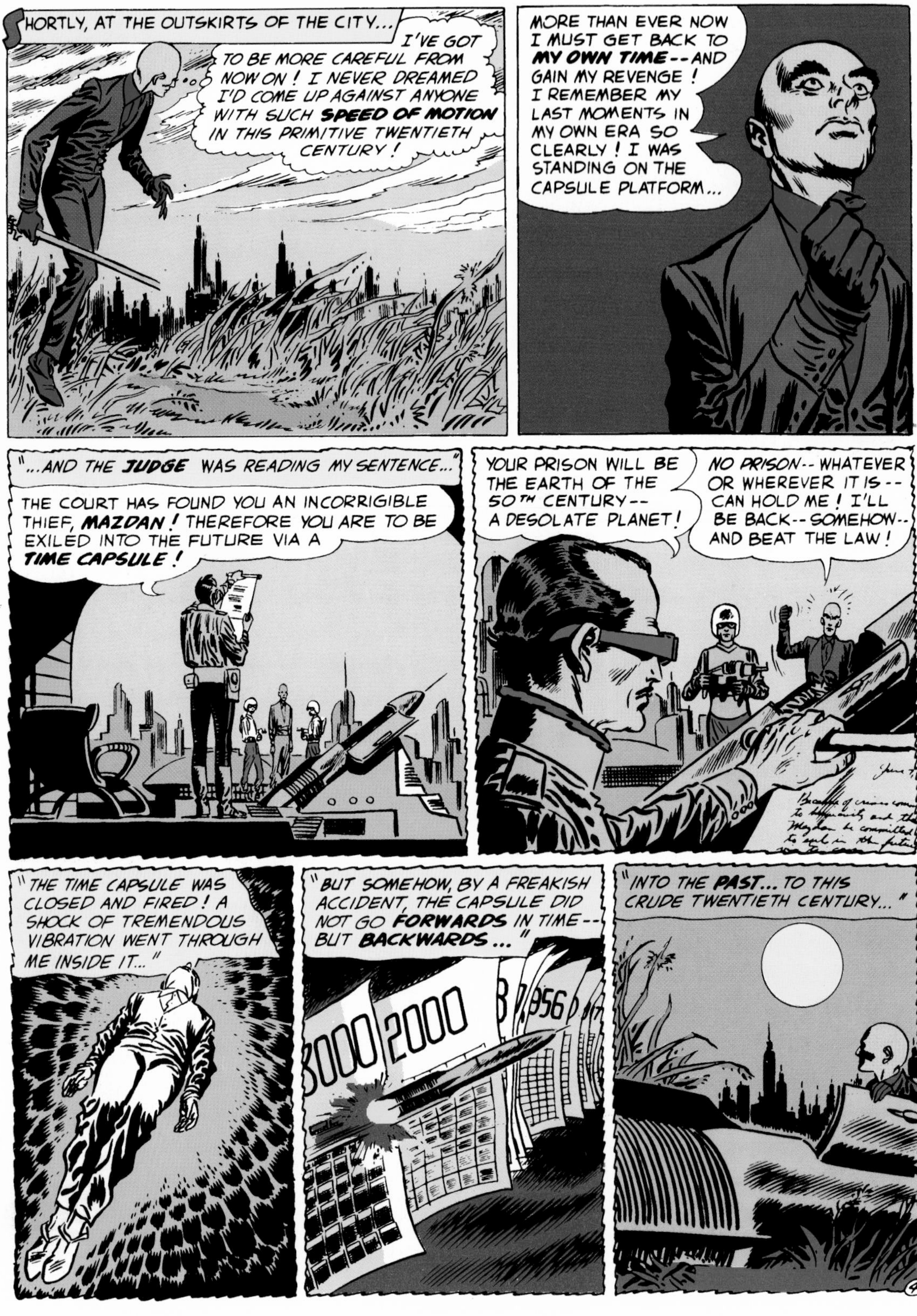
SHORTLY, AT THE OUTSKIRTS OF THE CITY...
I'VE GOT TO BE MORE CAREFUL FROM NOW ON! I NEVER DREAMED I'D COME UP AGAINST ANYONE WITH SUCH SPEED OF MOTION IN THIS PRIMITIVE TWENTIETH CENTURY!
MORE THAN EVER NOW I MUST GET BACK TO MY OWN TIME--AND GAIN MY REVENGE! I REMEMBER MY LAST MOMENTS IN MY OWN ERA SO CLEARLY! I WAS STANDING ON THE CAPSULE PLATFORM...
"...AND THE JUDGE WAS READING MY SENTENCE..."
THE COURT HAS FOUND YOU AN INCORRIGIBLE THIEF, MAZDAN! THEREFORE YOU ARE TO BE EXILED INTO THE FUTURE VIA A TIME CAPSULE!
YOUR PRISON WILL BE THE EARTH OF THE 50TH CENTURY-- A DESOLATE PLANET!
NO PRISON--WHATEVER OR WHEREVER IT IS--CAN HOLD ME! I'LL BE BACK--SOMEHOW--AND BEAT THE LAW!
"THE TIME CAPSULE WAS CLOSED AND FIRED! A SHOCK OF TREMENDOUS VIBRATION WENT THROUGH ME INSIDE IT..."
"BUT SOMEHOW, BY A FREAKISH ACCIDENT, THE CAPSULE DID NOT GO FORWARDS IN TIME--BUT BACKWARDS..."
3000
2000
1956
"INTO THE PAST... TO THIS CRUDE TWENTIETH CENTURY..."
4

WITH THE HELP OF MY MAGNETIC ROD, I'VE STOLEN THE OBJECTS I NEED TO PROPEL THE TIME CAPSULE BACK INTO THE FUTURE! NOW I HAVE TO STRENGTHEN THE CAPSULE'S SHIELDING METAL -- WITH GOLD!

SOON AFTER, THE TIME EXILE APPROACHES A BANK...

I REMEMBER FROM ANCIENT HISTORY BOOKS THAT THE PEOPLE IN THIS AGE SOMETIMES KEPT THEIR GOLD IN BANKS -- LIKE THIS ONE! IT'S CLOSED, BUT THAT WON'T STOP ME...

MOMENTS LATER, AS A FRANTIC POLICEMAN TELEPHONES HEADQUARTERS...

SEND HELP! THERE'S A GUY BLASTING HIS WAY INTO THE BANK ON CLOVER STREET! I TRIED TO STOP HIM-- BUT COULDN'T GET NEAR HIM!

AT POLICE HEADQUARTERS, AS THE SERGEANT REPORTS WHAT HAS HAPPENED...

...AND THE WEAPON HE'S CARRYING SHOOTS OFF RINGS OF HEAT! RUSH RIGHT OVER TO THE CLOVER STREET BANK!

RINGS OF HEAT?

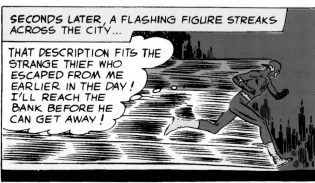

SECONDS LATER, A FLASHING FIGURE STREAKS ACROSS THE CITY...

THAT DESCRIPTION FITS THE STRANGE THIEF WHO ESCAPED FROM ME EARLIER IN THE DAY! I'LL REACH THE BANK BEFORE HE CAN GET AWAY!

THERE HE IS-- AND THIS TIME HIS HEAT-RINGS WON'T STOP ME FROM CAPTURING HIM!

THE SCARLET SPEEDSTER!

5

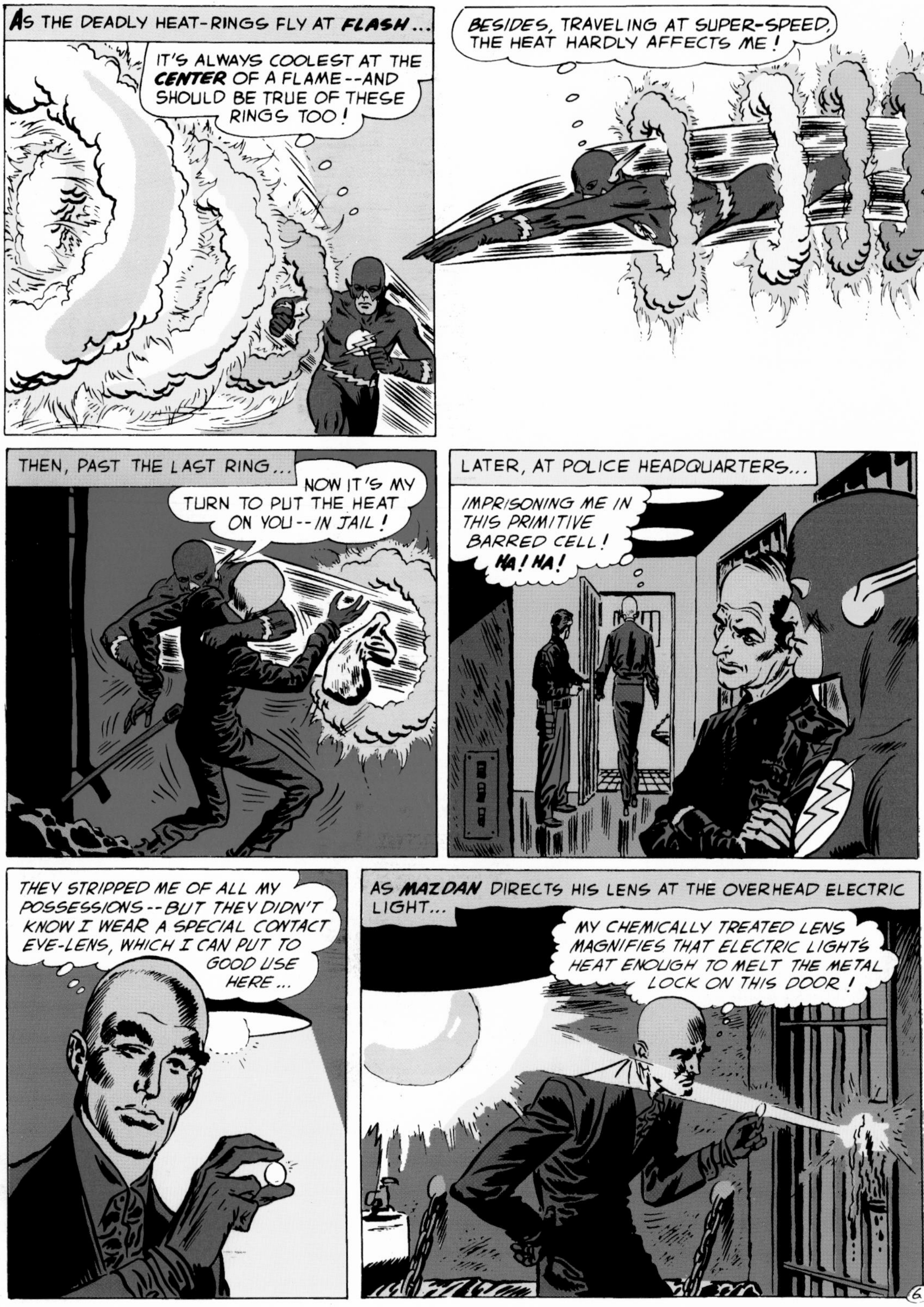

AS THE DEADLY HEAT-RINGS FLY AT FLASH...
IT'S ALWAYS COOLEST AT THE CENTER OF A FLAME--AND SHOULD BE TRUE OF THESE RINGS TOO!
BESIDES, TRAVELING AT SUPER-SPEED, THE HEAT HARDLY AFFECTS ME!
THEN, PAST THE LAST RING...
NOW IT'S MY TURN TO PUT THE HEAT ON YOU--IN JAIL!
LATER, AT POLICE HEADQUARTERS...
IMPRISONING ME IN THIS PRIMITIVE BARRED CELL! HA! HA!
THEY STRIPPED ME OF ALL MY POSSESSIONS--BUT THEY DIDN'T KNOW I WEAR A SPECIAL CONTACT EYE-LENS, WHICH I CAN PUT TO GOOD USE HERE...
AS MAZDAN DIRECTS HIS LENS AT THE OVERHEAD ELECTRIC LIGHT...
MY CHEMICALLY TREATED LENS MAGNIFIES THAT ELECTRIC LIGHT'S HEAT ENOUGH TO MELT THE METAL LOCK ON THIS DOOR!
6

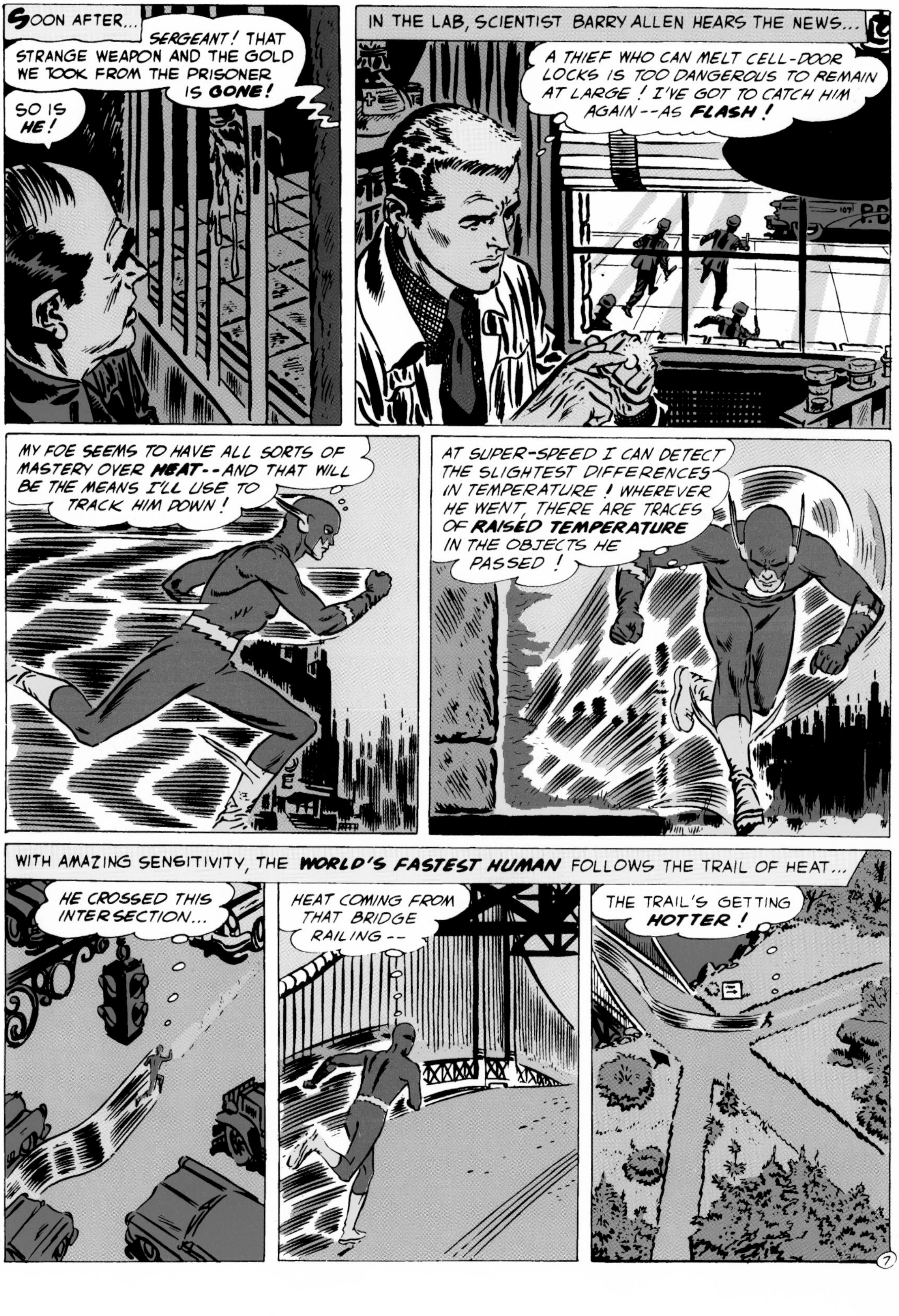
SOON AFTER...
SERGEANT! THAT STRANGE WEAPON AND THE GOLD WE TOOK FROM THE PRISONER IS GONE!
SO IS HE!
IN THE LAB, SCIENTIST BARRY ALLEN HEARS THE NEWS...
A THIEF WHO CAN MELT CELL-DOOR LOCKS IS TOO DANGEROUS TO REMAIN AT LARGE! I'VE GOT TO CATCH HIM AGAIN--AS FLASH!
MY FOE SEEMS TO HAVE ALL SORTS OF MASTERY OVER HEAT--AND THAT WILL BE THE MEANS I'LL USE TO TRACK HIM DOWN!
AT SUPER-SPEED I CAN DETECT THE SLIGHTEST DIFFERENCES IN TEMPERATURE! WHEREVER HE WENT, THERE ARE TRACES OF RAISED TEMPERATURE IN THE OBJECTS HE PASSED!
WITH AMAZING SENSITIVITY, THE WORLD'S FASTEST HUMAN FOLLOWS THE TRAIL OF HEAT...
HE CROSSED THIS INTERSECTION...
HEAT COMING FROM THAT BRIDGE RAILING--
THE TRAIL'S GETTING HOTTER!
7

SHORTLY, AT THE CITY'S OUTSKIRTS...

THERE HE IS--IN THAT STRANGE, GOLD-COATED PROJECTILE! I'VE GOT TO GET TO HIM BEFORE HE CAN CLOSE THAT DOOR!

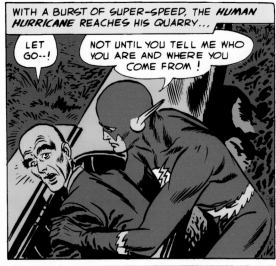

WITH A BURST OF SUPER-SPEED, THE *HUMAN HURRICANE* REACHES HIS QUARRY...

LET GO--!

NOT UNTIL YOU TELL ME WHO YOU ARE AND WHERE YOU COME FROM!

SHORTLY, AS THE TRAPPED THIEF FROM THE FUTURE TELLS HIS STORY...

...SO YOU SEE, IT'S TO YOUR INTEREST TO LET ME RETURN TO MY OWN AGE! I'LL NEVER COME BACK TO BOTHER YOU OR YOUR CIVILIZATION AGAIN!

SWIFTLY, *FLASH'S* KEEN, SCIENTIFIC MIND PROBES THE SECRETS OF THE TIME - VEHICLE...

YOUR TIME CAPSULE WORKS BY HEAT...*TREMENDOUS HEAT!* WHEN YOU TAKE OFF, THE RESULTANT BLAST WILL BE GREAT!

YES--IT WILL BLAST OUT A CRATER--AT LEAST TEN MILES IN DIAMETER!

DIDN'T YOU GIVE ANY THOUGHT TO THE PEOPLE WHO LIVE IN THAT AREA? THEY'LL ALL BE KILLED--

ONLY A FEW THOUSAND-- HARDLY IMPORTANT--

I CONSIDER THEM IMPORTANT, *MAZDAN*--AND TO MAKE SURE NO ONE IS HARMED, *I'M* GOING TO TAKE YOU BACK TO YOUR FUTURE ERA!

WITHOUT A TIME CAPSULE? IMPOSSIBLE!

8

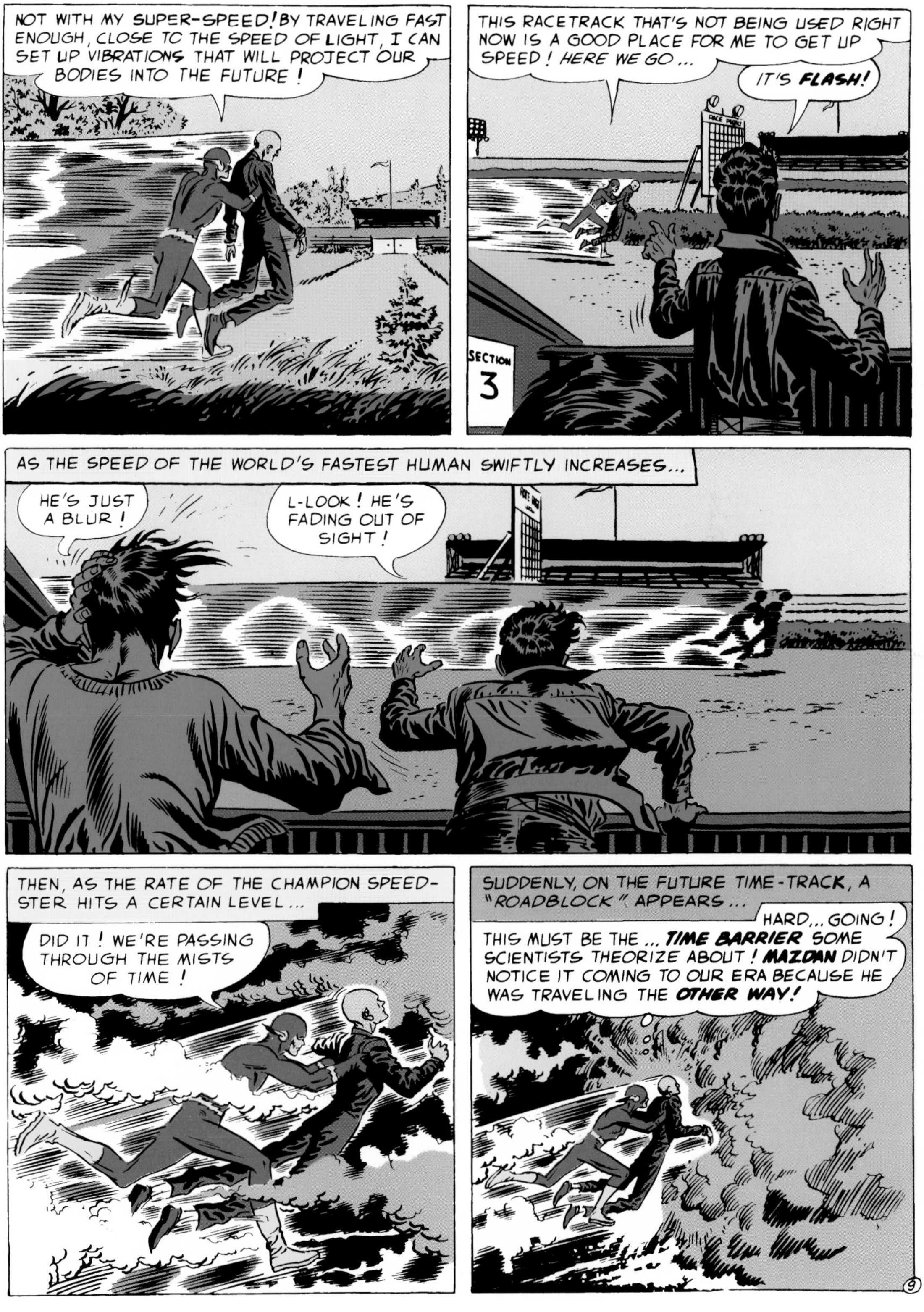
NOT WITH MY SUPER-SPEED! BY TRAVELING FAST ENOUGH, CLOSE TO THE SPEED OF LIGHT, I CAN SET UP VIBRATIONS THAT WILL PROJECT OUR BODIES INTO THE FUTURE!
THIS RACETRACK THAT'S NOT BEING USED RIGHT NOW IS A GOOD PLACE FOR ME TO GET UP SPEED! HERE WE GO...
IT'S FLASH!
SECTION 3
AS THE SPEED OF THE WORLD'S FASTEST HUMAN SWIFTLY INCREASES...
HE'S JUST A BLUR!
L-LOOK! HE'S FADING OUT OF SIGHT!
THEN, AS THE RATE OF THE CHAMPION SPEEDSTER HITS A CERTAIN LEVEL...
DID IT! WE'RE PASSING THROUGH THE MISTS OF TIME!
SUDDENLY, ON THE FUTURE TIME-TRACK, A "ROADBLOCK" APPEARS...
HARD... GOING!
THIS MUST BE THE ... TIME BARRIER SOME SCIENTISTS THEORIZE ABOUT! MAZDAN DIDN'T NOTICE IT COMING TO OUR ERA BECAUSE HE WAS TRAVELING THE OTHER WAY!
9

WITH EVERY ERG OF HIS SUPER-SPEED ENERGY, *FLASH* BATTLES THE TIME BARRICADE...

LIKE RUNNING ON A TREADMILL-- HARDLY MOVING FORWARD AT ALL!

FASTER, FASTER, GYRATE THE *FLASH'S* LEGS-- TILL FINALLY...

I BROKE THROUGH THE *TIME BARRIER!*

CRACK

SHORTLY, IN *MAZDAN'S* ERA...

...AND SO TO SEE JUSTICE DONE, I HAVE BROUGHT *MAZDAN* BACK TO THIS COURT, YOUR HONOR!

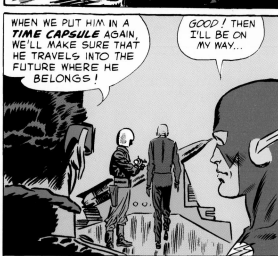

WHEN WE PUT HIM IN A *TIME CAPSULE* AGAIN, WE'LL MAKE SURE THAT HE TRAVELS INTO THE FUTURE WHERE HE BELONGS!

GOOD! THEN I'LL BE ON MY WAY...

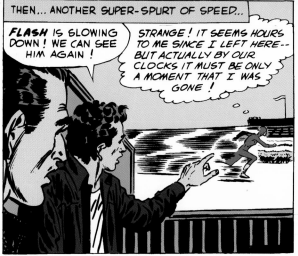

THEN... ANOTHER SUPER-SPURT OF SPEED...

FLASH IS SLOWING DOWN! WE CAN SEE HIM AGAIN!

STRANGE! IT SEEMS HOURS TO ME SINCE I LEFT HERE-- BUT ACTUALLY BY OUR CLOCKS IT MUST BE ONLY A MOMENT THAT I WAS GONE!

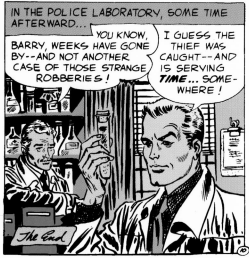

IN THE POLICE LABORATORY, SOME TIME AFTERWARD...

YOU KNOW, BARRY, WEEKS HAVE GONE BY--AND NOT ANOTHER CASE OF THOSE STRANGE ROBBERIES!

I GUESS THE THIEF WAS CAUGHT--AND IS SERVING *TIME*... SOME-WHERE!

The End

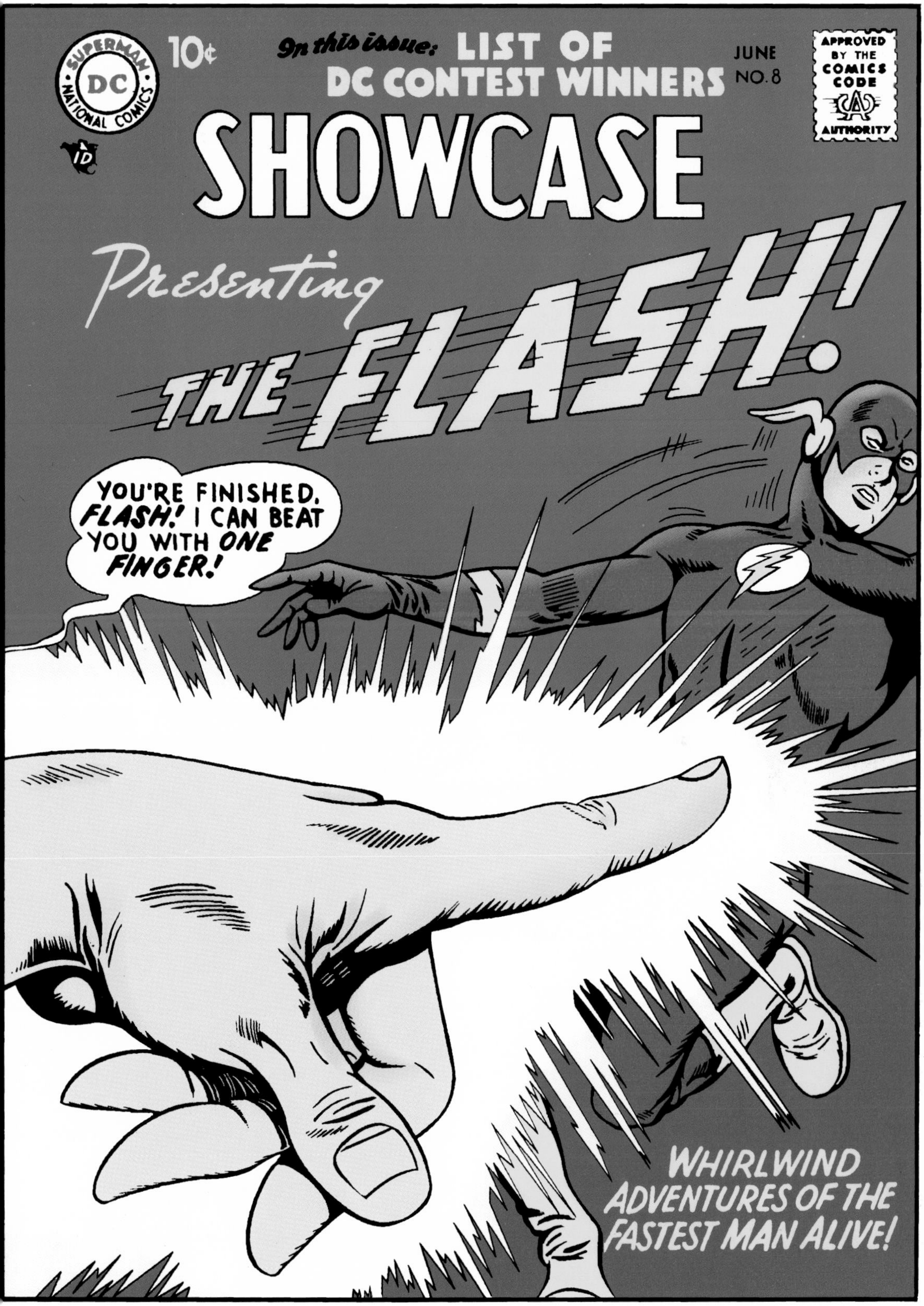

SUPERMAN DC NATIONAL COMICS
10¢
In this issue: LIST OF DC CONTEST WINNERS
JUNE NO. 8
APPROVED BY THE COMICS CODE AUTHORITY
SHOWCASE
Presenting THE FLASH!
YOU'RE FINISHED, FLASH! I CAN BEAT YOU WITH ONE FINGER!
WHIRLWIND ADVENTURES OF THE FASTEST MAN ALIVE!

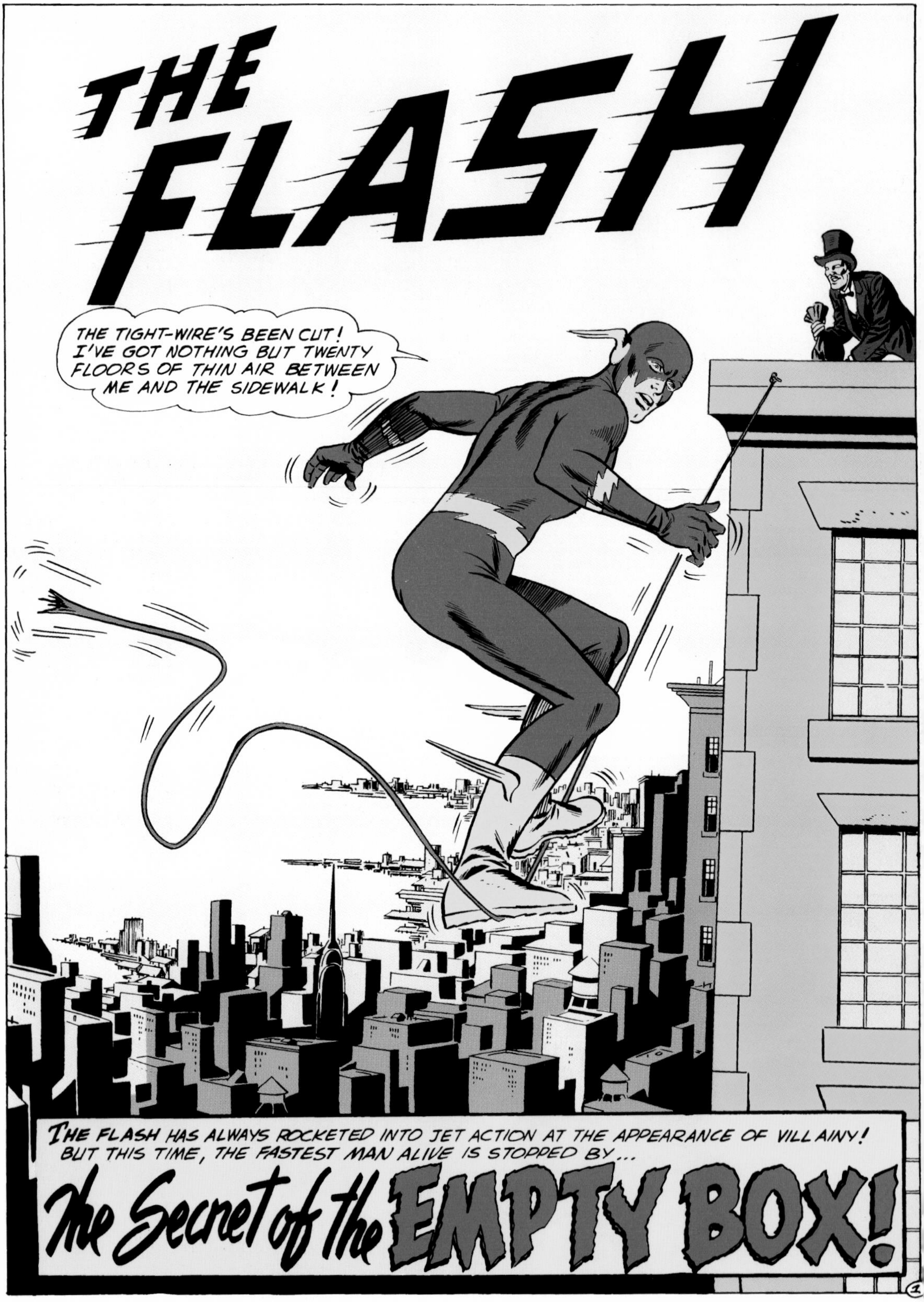
THE FLASH
THE TIGHT-WIRE'S BEEN CUT! I'VE GOT NOTHING BUT TWENTY FLOORS OF THIN AIR BETWEEN ME AND THE SIDEWALK!
THE FLASH HAS ALWAYS ROCKETED INTO JET ACTION AT THE APPEARANCE OF VILLAINY! BUT THIS TIME, THE FASTEST MAN ALIVE IS STOPPED BY...
The Secret of the EMPTY BOX!
1

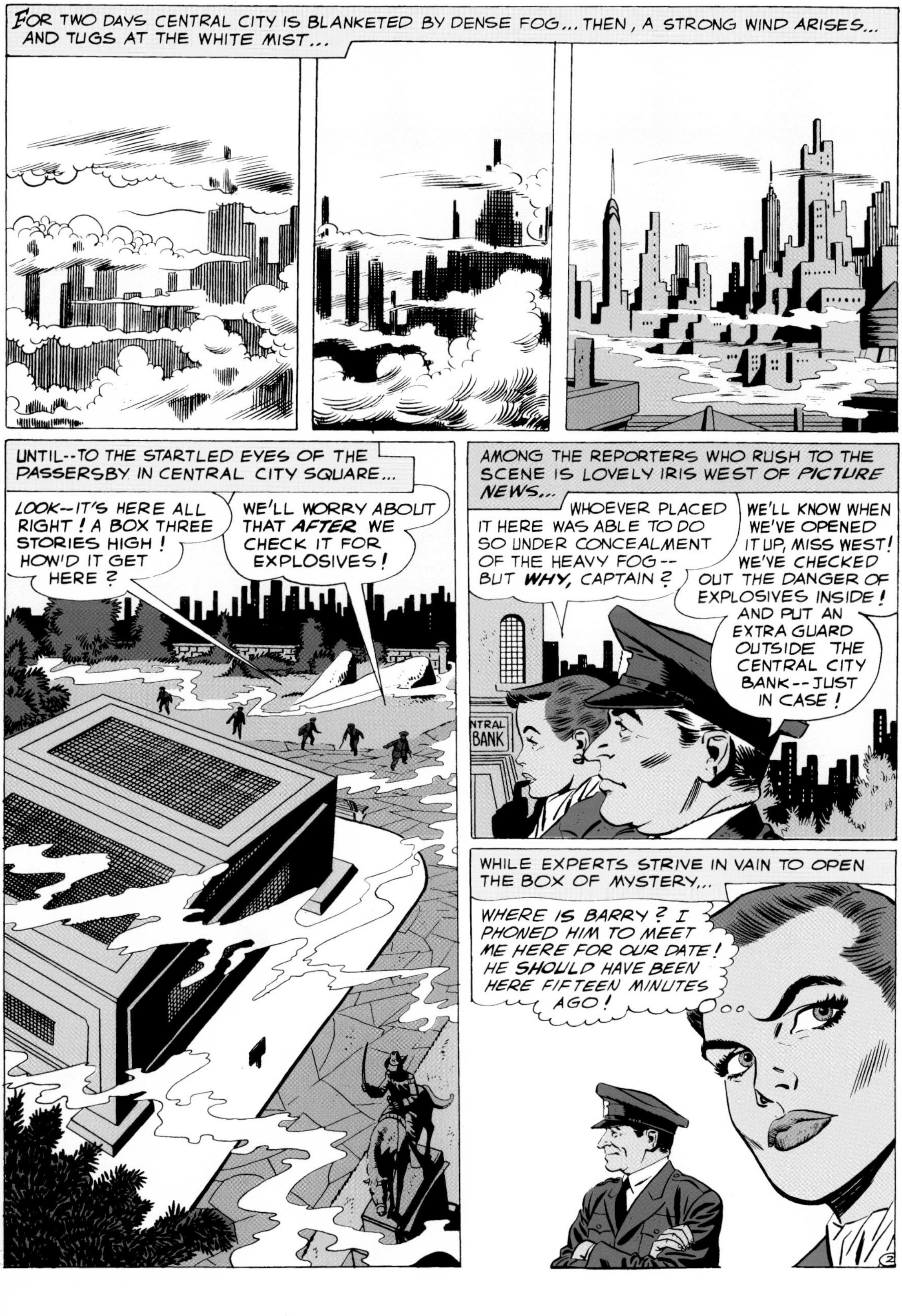
FOR TWO DAYS CENTRAL CITY IS BLANKETED BY DENSE FOG... THEN, A STRONG WIND ARISES... AND TUGS AT THE WHITE MIST...
UNTIL--TO THE STARTLED EYES OF THE PASSERSBY IN CENTRAL CITY SQUARE...
LOOK--IT'S HERE ALL RIGHT! A BOX THREE STORIES HIGH! HOW'D IT GET HERE?
WE'LL WORRY ABOUT THAT AFTER WE CHECK IT FOR EXPLOSIVES!
AMONG THE REPORTERS WHO RUSH TO THE SCENE IS LOVELY IRIS WEST OF PICTURE NEWS...
WHOEVER PLACED IT HERE WAS ABLE TO DO SO UNDER CONCEALMENT OF THE HEAVY FOG--BUT WHY, CAPTAIN?
WE'LL KNOW WHEN WE'VE OPENED IT UP, MISS WEST! WE'VE CHECKED OUT THE DANGER OF EXPLOSIVES INSIDE! AND PUT AN EXTRA GUARD OUTSIDE THE CENTRAL CITY BANK--JUST IN CASE!
NTRAL BANK
WHILE EXPERTS STRIVE IN VAIN TO OPEN THE BOX OF MYSTERY...
WHERE IS BARRY? I PHONED HIM TO MEET ME HERE FOR OUR DATE! HE SHOULD HAVE BEEN HERE FIFTEEN MINUTES AGO!
2

SCIENTIST BARRY ALLEN (*THE FLASH*), THE LOVELY REPORTER'S DATE, *DID* LEAVE THE POLICE LABORATORY IN PLENTY OF TIME...

I'M *NOT* GOING TO BE LATE THIS TIME!

POLICE LABORATORY

BUT, TWO BLOCKS FROM CENTRAL CITY SQUARE THE WORLD'S FASTEST HUMAN PAUSES WHEN...

I--I DROPPED MY--MY--RING--DOWN THERE! I--I CAN'T P-P-PICK IT UP!

DON'T CRY--I'LL GET IT FOR YOU!

I CAN'T GET THIS STRING TO CURL AROUND THE RING! I'LL HAVE TO TRY SOME OTHER WAY!

MY R-R-RING'S LOST!

YOU C-C-CAN'T GET Y-Y-YOUR HAND THROUGH--IT'S T-T-TOO NARROW! I ALREADY T-T-TRIED IT!

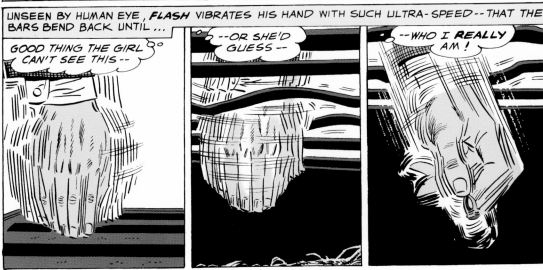

UNSEEN BY HUMAN EYE, *FLASH* VIBRATES HIS HAND WITH SUCH ULTRA-SPEED--THAT THE BARS BEND BACK UNTIL...

GOOD THING THE GIRL CAN'T SEE THIS--

--OR SHE'D GUESS--

--WHO I *REALLY* AM!

3

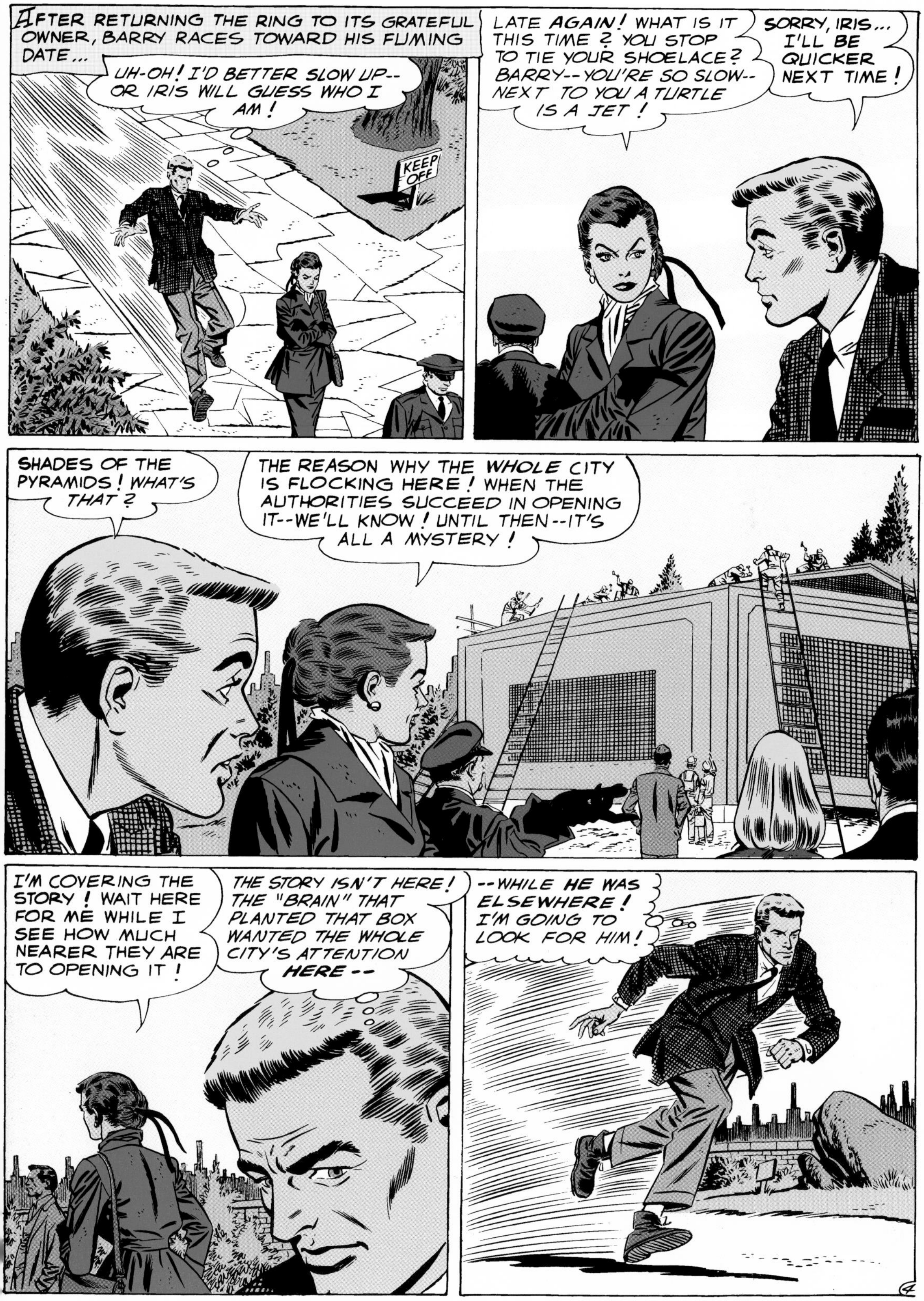
AFTER RETURNING THE RING TO ITS GRATEFUL OWNER, BARRY RACES TOWARD HIS FUMING DATE...
UH-OH! I'D BETTER SLOW UP-- OR IRIS WILL GUESS WHO I AM!
KEEP OFF
LATE AGAIN! WHAT IS IT THIS TIME? YOU STOP TO TIE YOUR SHOELACE? BARRY--YOU'RE SO SLOW--NEXT TO YOU A TURTLE IS A JET!
SORRY, IRIS... I'LL BE QUICKER NEXT TIME!
SHADES OF THE PYRAMIDS! WHAT'S THAT?
THE REASON WHY THE WHOLE CITY IS FLOCKING HERE! WHEN THE AUTHORITIES SUCCEED IN OPENING IT--WE'LL KNOW! UNTIL THEN--IT'S ALL A MYSTERY!
I'M COVERING THE STORY! WAIT HERE FOR ME WHILE I SEE HOW MUCH NEARER THEY ARE TO OPENING IT!
THE STORY ISN'T HERE! THE "BRAIN" THAT PLANTED THAT BOX WANTED THE WHOLE CITY'S ATTENTION HERE--
--WHILE HE WAS ELSEWHERE! I'M GOING TO LOOK FOR HIM!
4

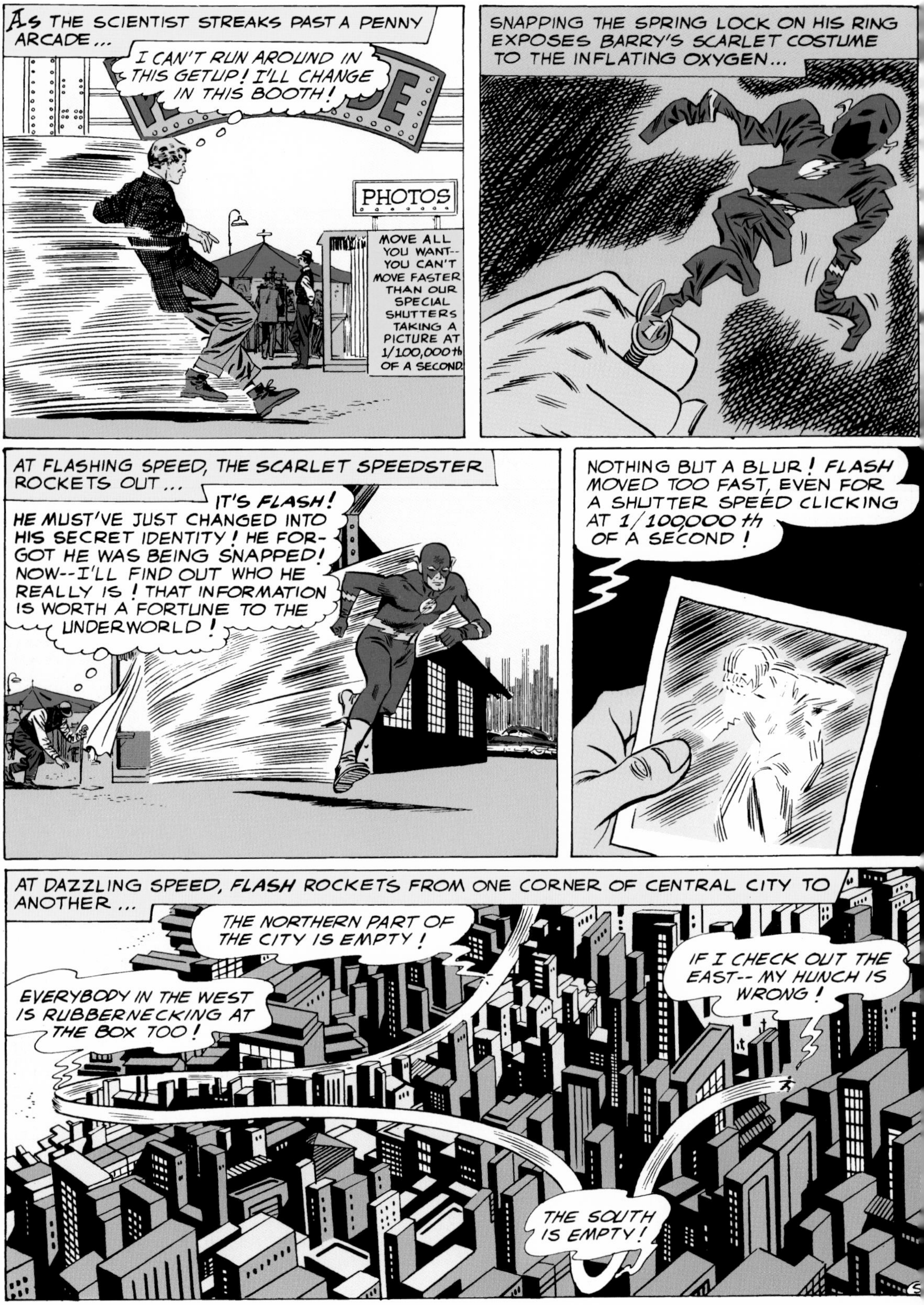
AS THE SCIENTIST STREAKS PAST A PENNY ARCADE...
I CAN'T RUN AROUND IN THIS GETUP! I'LL CHANGE IN THIS BOOTH!
PHOTOS
MOVE ALL YOU WANT-- YOU CAN'T MOVE FASTER THAN OUR SPECIAL SHUTTERS TAKING A PICTURE AT 1/100,000th OF A SECOND.
SNAPPING THE SPRING LOCK ON HIS RING EXPOSES BARRY'S SCARLET COSTUME TO THE INFLATING OXYGEN...
AT FLASHING SPEED, THE SCARLET SPEEDSTER ROCKETS OUT...
IT'S FLASH! HE MUST'VE JUST CHANGED INTO HIS SECRET IDENTITY! HE FORGOT HE WAS BEING SNAPPED! NOW--I'LL FIND OUT WHO HE REALLY IS! THAT INFORMATION IS WORTH A FORTUNE TO THE UNDERWORLD!
NOTHING BUT A BLUR! FLASH MOVED TOO FAST, EVEN FOR A SHUTTER SPEED CLICKING AT 1/100,000 th OF A SECOND!
AT DAZZLING SPEED, FLASH ROCKETS FROM ONE CORNER OF CENTRAL CITY TO ANOTHER...
THE NORTHERN PART OF THE CITY IS EMPTY!
EVERYBODY IN THE WEST IS RUBBERNECKING AT THE BOX TOO!
THE SOUTH IS EMPTY!
IF I CHECK OUT THE EAST-- MY HUNCH IS WRONG!

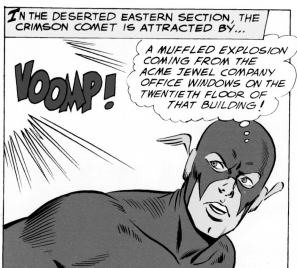

IN THE DESERTED EASTERN SECTION, THE CRIMSON COMET IS ATTRACTED BY...

A MUFFLED EXPLOSION COMING FROM THE ACME JEWEL COMPANY OFFICE WINDOWS ON THE TWENTIETH FLOOR OF THAT BUILDING!

VOOMP!

UP THE SIDE OF THE BUILDING RACES THE FLASH...

THIS WILL BE FASTER THAN THE ELEVATOR!

I WAS RIGHT! WHILE EVERYONE IS IN THE BLEACHERS AT THE SQUARE--WAITING TO SEE WHAT'S INSIDE THE BOX--THE "BRAIN" WHO PLACED IT *THERE*-- JUST WALKED THROUGH THAT EXIT WITH THE ACME JEWELS!

CLANG!

CAN'T--BUDGE--THIS--STEEL--DOOR! IF--I-- WAS--A--FLY--I--COULD--WALK--THROUGH-- THE--KEYHOLE! HMM--THAT--GIVES--ME-- AN IDEA!

IF YOU CAN'T FIT A KEYHOLE--

--MAKE THE KEYHOLE--

--FIT YOU!

6

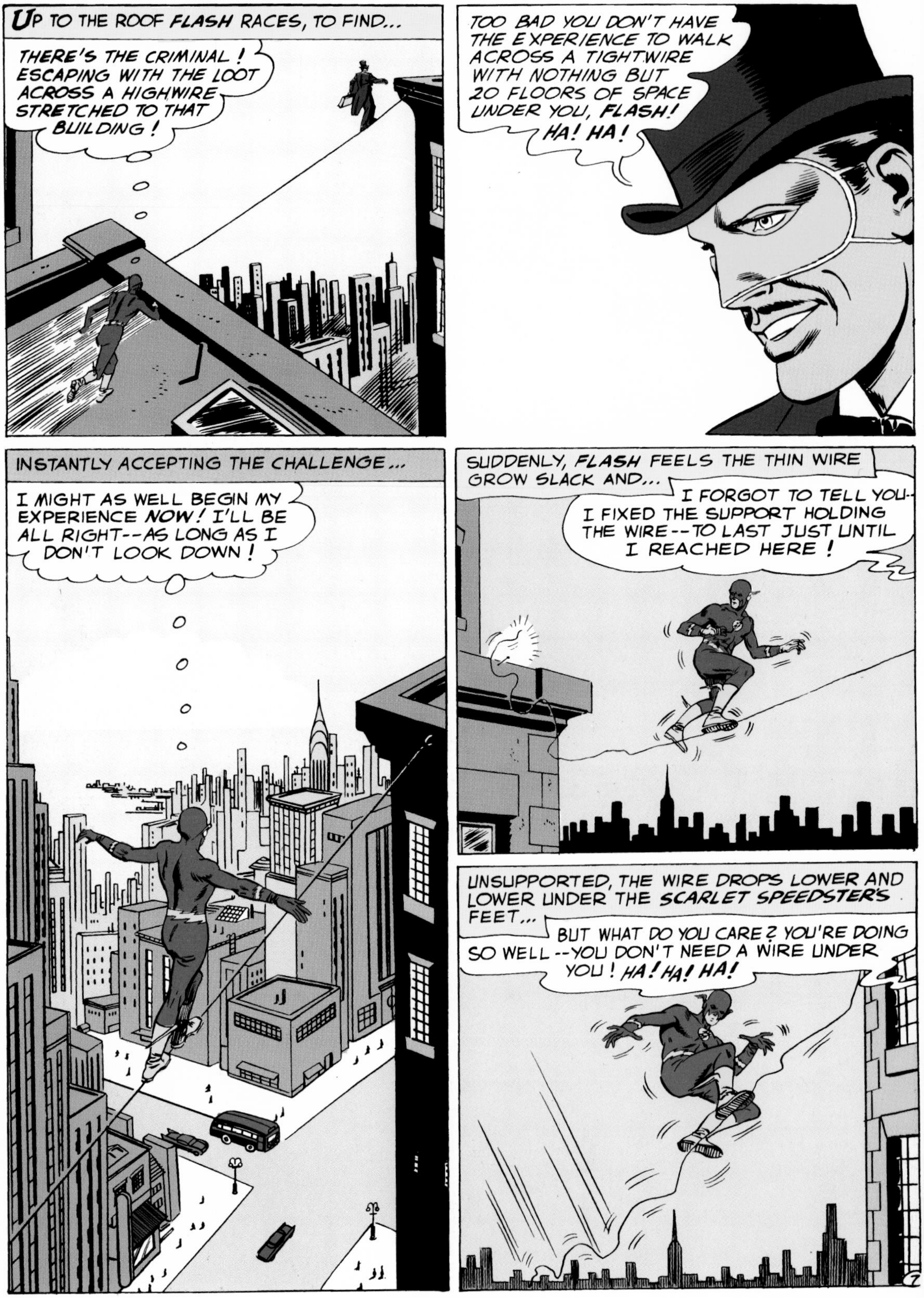
UP TO THE ROOF FLASH RACES, TO FIND...
THERE'S THE CRIMINAL! ESCAPING WITH THE LOOT ACROSS A HIGHWIRE STRETCHED TO THAT BUILDING!
TOO BAD YOU DON'T HAVE THE EXPERIENCE TO WALK ACROSS A TIGHTWIRE WITH NOTHING BUT 20 FLOORS OF SPACE UNDER YOU, FLASH! HA! HA!
INSTANTLY ACCEPTING THE CHALLENGE...
I MIGHT AS WELL BEGIN MY EXPERIENCE NOW! I'LL BE ALL RIGHT--AS LONG AS I DON'T LOOK DOWN!
SUDDENLY, FLASH FEELS THE THIN WIRE GROW SLACK AND...
I FORGOT TO TELL YOU-- I FIXED THE SUPPORT HOLDING THE WIRE--TO LAST JUST UNTIL I REACHED HERE!
UNSUPPORTED, THE WIRE DROPS LOWER AND LOWER UNDER THE SCARLET SPEEDSTER'S FEET...
BUT WHAT DO YOU CARE? YOU'RE DOING SO WELL--YOU DON'T NEED A WIRE UNDER YOU! HA! HA! HA!
7

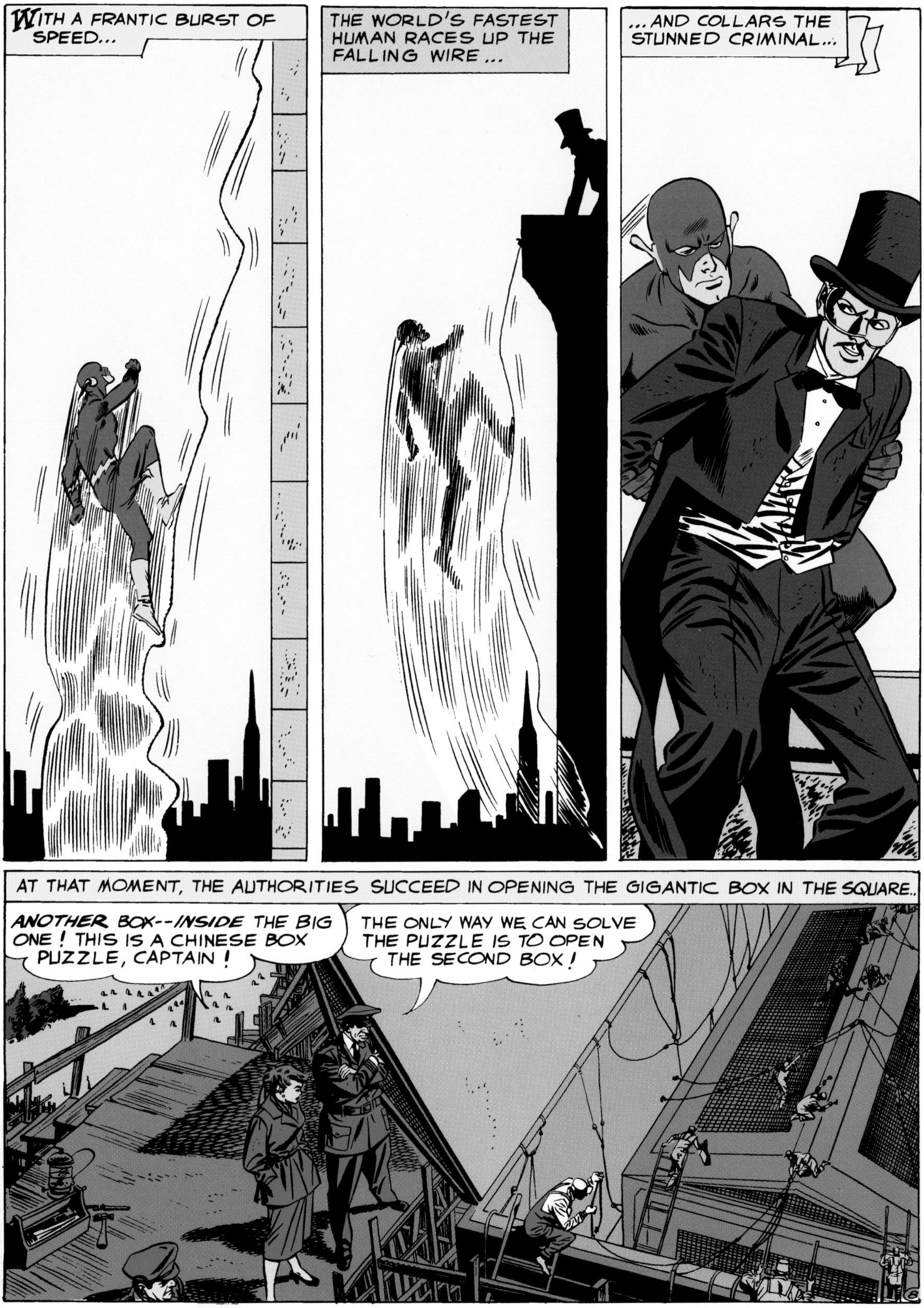
WITH A FRANTIC BURST OF SPEED...
THE WORLD'S FASTEST HUMAN RACES UP THE FALLING WIRE...
...AND COLLARS THE STUNNED CRIMINAL...
AT THAT MOMENT, THE AUTHORITIES SUCCEED IN OPENING THE GIGANTIC BOX IN THE SQUARE..
ANOTHER BOX--INSIDE THE BIG ONE! THIS IS A CHINESE BOX PUZZLE, CAPTAIN!
THE ONLY WAY WE CAN SOLVE THE PUZZLE IS TO OPEN THE SECOND BOX!
6

As FLASH LEAVES HIS PRISONER AT THE CENTRAL CITY JAIL...

THAT CROOK WAS LAUGHING AT ME AS IF I WAS WASTING MY TIME PUTTING HIM IN JAIL! THE SHOCK OF BEING CAPTURED MUST HAVE SHAKEN HIS WITS! I HOPE IRIS HASN'T DISCOVERED MY ABSENCE!

HA! HA! HA!

THE WORLD'S FASTEST HUMAN CHANGES BACK TO HIS IDENTITY OF BARRY ALLEN, SCIENTIST, JUST AS...

THERE'S ANOTHER BOX INSIDE THE BIG ONE! I'LL HAVE TO WAIT UNTIL IT'S OPENED! PLEASE GET ME A CONTAINER OF COFFEE, AND A SANDWICH-- AND BARRY, HONEY, TRY TO GET BACK THIS YEAR?

I'LL TRY TO HURRY, IRIS...

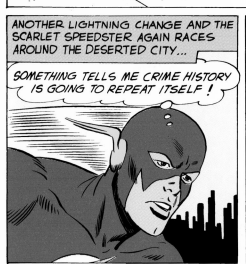

ANOTHER LIGHTNING CHANGE AND THE SCARLET SPEEDSTER AGAIN RACES AROUND THE DESERTED CITY...

SOMETHING TELLS ME CRIME HISTORY IS GOING TO REPEAT ITSELF!

CEASELESSLY CROSSING AND RECROSSING HIS TRACKS AT EYE-BLURRING SPEED, FLASH FINALLY COMES UPON...

AN ARMORED TRUCK--WITH A WHEEL BLOWN OFF! AND THERE'S THE "BRAIN" WHO DID IT! BY THE SANDS OF SAHARA! IS THAT A MIRAGE? OR THE SAME CHARACTER I JUST HAD LOCKED UP?

AS THE PERPLEXED CRIME-FIGHTER REACHES OUT FOR THE CRIMINAL...

HA! HA! HA!

HE TOOK OFF LIKE A ROCKET!

HA! HA! BY THE TIME FLASH FIGURES OUT THAT I'VE GOT A SPECIALLY-BUILT SPRING IN MY SHOES CATAPULTING ME HIGH INTO THE AIR-- I'LL HAVE OPENED MY CHUTE AND FLOATED OUT OF SIGHT!

BUT, **FLASH** ROTATES WITH SUCH ULTRA—SPEED THAT HE CREATES A DOWNDRAFT WHICH...

HE'S YANKING ME DOWN!

ARMORED

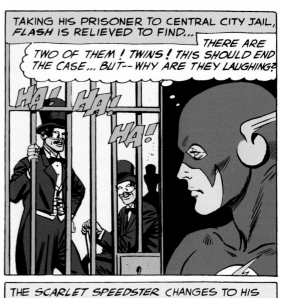

TAKING HIS PRISONER TO CENTRAL CITY JAIL, **FLASH** IS RELIEVED TO FIND...

THERE ARE TWO OF THEM! TWINS! THIS SHOULD END THE CASE... BUT—WHY ARE THEY LAUGHING?

HA! HA! HA!

THE **SCARLET SPEEDSTER** CHANGES TO HIS OTHER IDENTITY AND ROCKETS BACK TO THE SQUARE JUST AS...

I SEE YOU STILL HAVEN'T LEFT FOR MY COFFEE AND SANDWICH! OH, BARRY—YOU **ARE** THE SLOWEST HUMAN ON EARTH! BUT, IT DOESN'T MATTER! THEY'VE JUST OPENED THE SECOND BOX! YOU'VE PLENTY OF TIME!

WHAT DO YOU MEAN?

THERE'S A **THIRD** CLOSED BOX INSIDE IT!

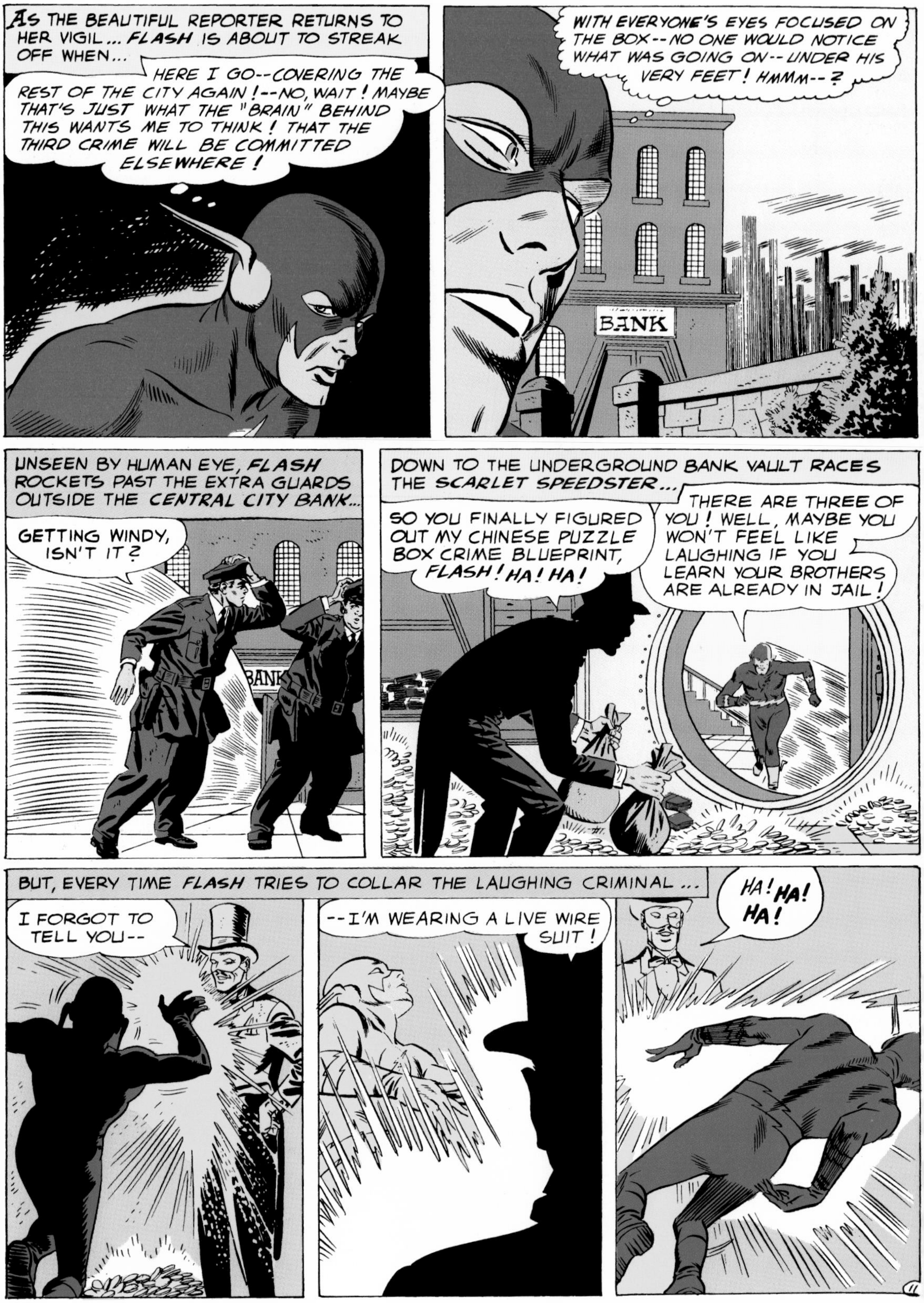
AS THE BEAUTIFUL REPORTER RETURNS TO HER VIGIL... FLASH IS ABOUT TO STREAK OFF WHEN...
HERE I GO--COVERING THE REST OF THE CITY AGAIN!--NO, WAIT! MAYBE THAT'S JUST WHAT THE "BRAIN" BEHIND THIS WANTS ME TO THINK! THAT THE THIRD CRIME WILL BE COMMITTED ELSEWHERE!
WITH EVERYONE'S EYES FOCUSED ON THE BOX--NO ONE WOULD NOTICE WHAT WAS GOING ON--UNDER HIS VERY FEET! HMMM--?
BANK
UNSEEN BY HUMAN EYE, FLASH ROCKETS PAST THE EXTRA GUARDS OUTSIDE THE CENTRAL CITY BANK...
GETTING WINDY, ISN'T IT?
DOWN TO THE UNDERGROUND BANK VAULT RACES THE SCARLET SPEEDSTER...
SO YOU FINALLY FIGURED OUT MY CHINESE PUZZLE BOX CRIME BLUEPRINT, FLASH! HA! HA!
THERE ARE THREE OF YOU! WELL, MAYBE YOU WON'T FEEL LIKE LAUGHING IF YOU LEARN YOUR BROTHERS ARE ALREADY IN JAIL!
BUT, EVERY TIME FLASH TRIES TO COLLAR THE LAUGHING CRIMINAL...
I FORGOT TO TELL YOU--
--I'M WEARING A LIVE WIRE SUIT!
HA! HA! HA!
11

AS THE PERPLEXED FLASH IS HURLED TO THE FLOOR AGAIN...
YOU CAN'T TOUCH ME, FLASH! EVEN IF YOU HAVE CAUGHT UP TO ME! AND MY LIVE-WIRE SUIT WILL HELP ME BLAST MY BROTHERS OUT OF JAIL! I PLANNED IT ALL-- EVERY STEP--AND YOU CAN'T STOP ME!
IF ONLY I HAD A NON-CONDUCTOR-- LIKE PAPER--I COULD GRAB HIM-- LIVE-WIRE SUIT AND ALL! HMM--! IF I HAVEN'T A NON-CONDUCTOR--I'LL USE THE BEST CONDUCTOR THERE IS--SILVER!
INSTANTLY, THE FASTEST MAN ON EARTH SHOWERS THE HUMAN LIVE WIRE WITH SILVER COINS..
DISCHARGE YOUR ELECTRICITY ON THIS--
TZING!
TZING!
TZING!
--UNTIL YOUR VOLTAGE IS DRAINED--
TZING!
TZING
TZING!
--AND I CAN GRAB YOU WITHOUT BEING SHOCKED!
LEAVING THE FLABBERGASTED CRIMINAL FOR THE GUARDS, THE FASTEST MAN ON EARTH RETURNS IN HIS OTHER IDENTITY TO THE SQUARE...
YOU STILL HAVEN'T LEFT FOR MY COFFEE AND SANDWICH! WELL, NEVER MIND! THE LAST BOX HAS BEEN OPENED! IT HAS AN OPENING IN IT WHICH LEADS TO THE BANK'S UNDERGROUND VAULT! INSIDE IS THE CROOK WHO PLANNED ALL THIS!
HOW ABOUT TAKING ME OUT TO DINNER, SLOW-POKE? THIS YEAR?
The End
12

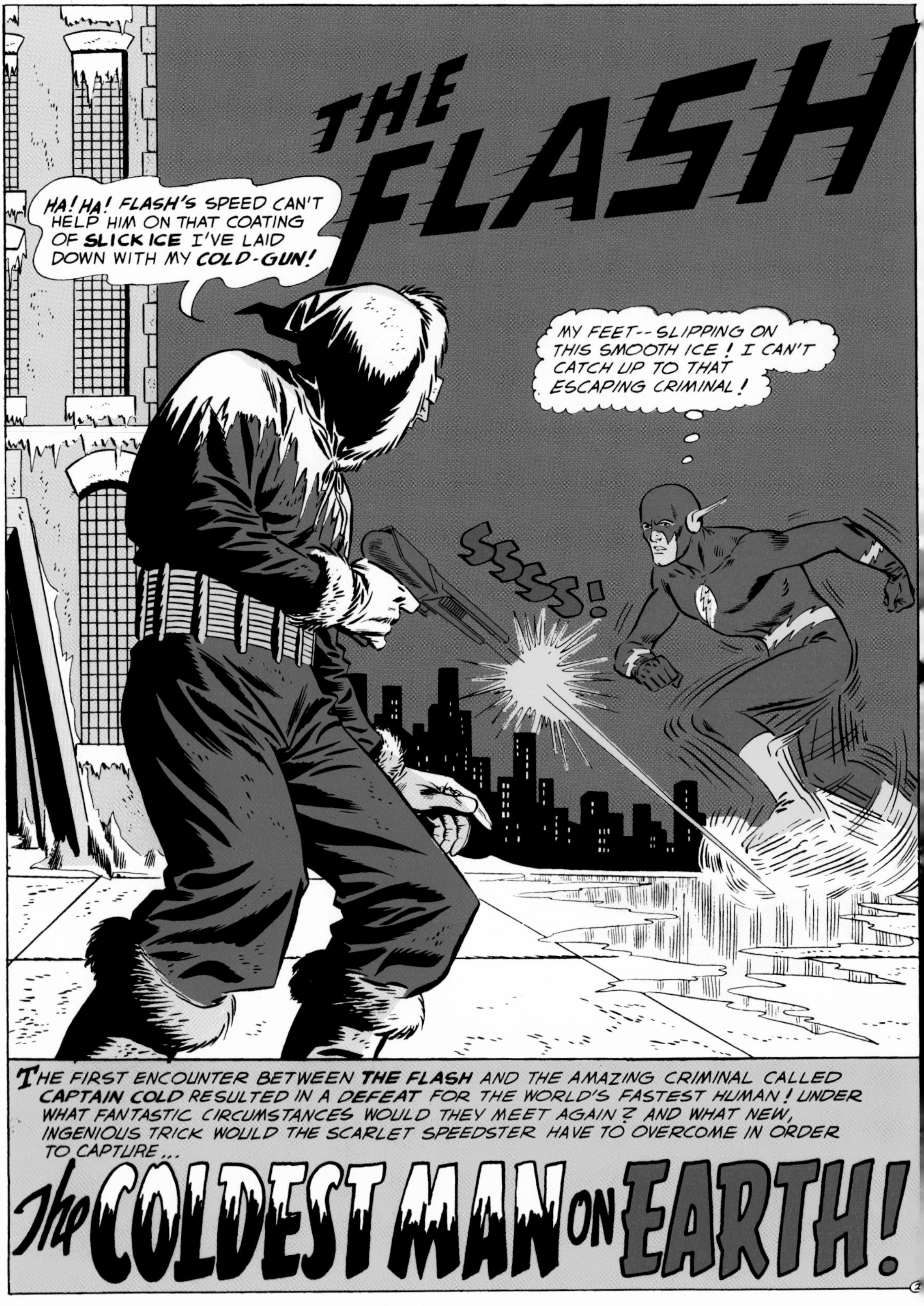
THE FLASH
HA! HA! FLASH'S SPEED CAN'T HELP HIM ON THAT COATING OF SLICK ICE I'VE LAID DOWN WITH MY COLD-GUN!
MY FEET--SLIPPING ON THIS SMOOTH ICE! I CAN'T CATCH UP TO THAT ESCAPING CRIMINAL!
SSSSS!
THE FIRST ENCOUNTER BETWEEN THE FLASH AND THE AMAZING CRIMINAL CALLED CAPTAIN COLD RESULTED IN A DEFEAT FOR THE WORLD'S FASTEST HUMAN! UNDER WHAT FANTASTIC CIRCUMSTANCES WOULD THEY MEET AGAIN? AND WHAT NEW, INGENIOUS TRICK WOULD THE SCARLET SPEEDSTER HAVE TO OVERCOME IN ORDER TO CAPTURE...
The COLDEST MAN ON EARTH!

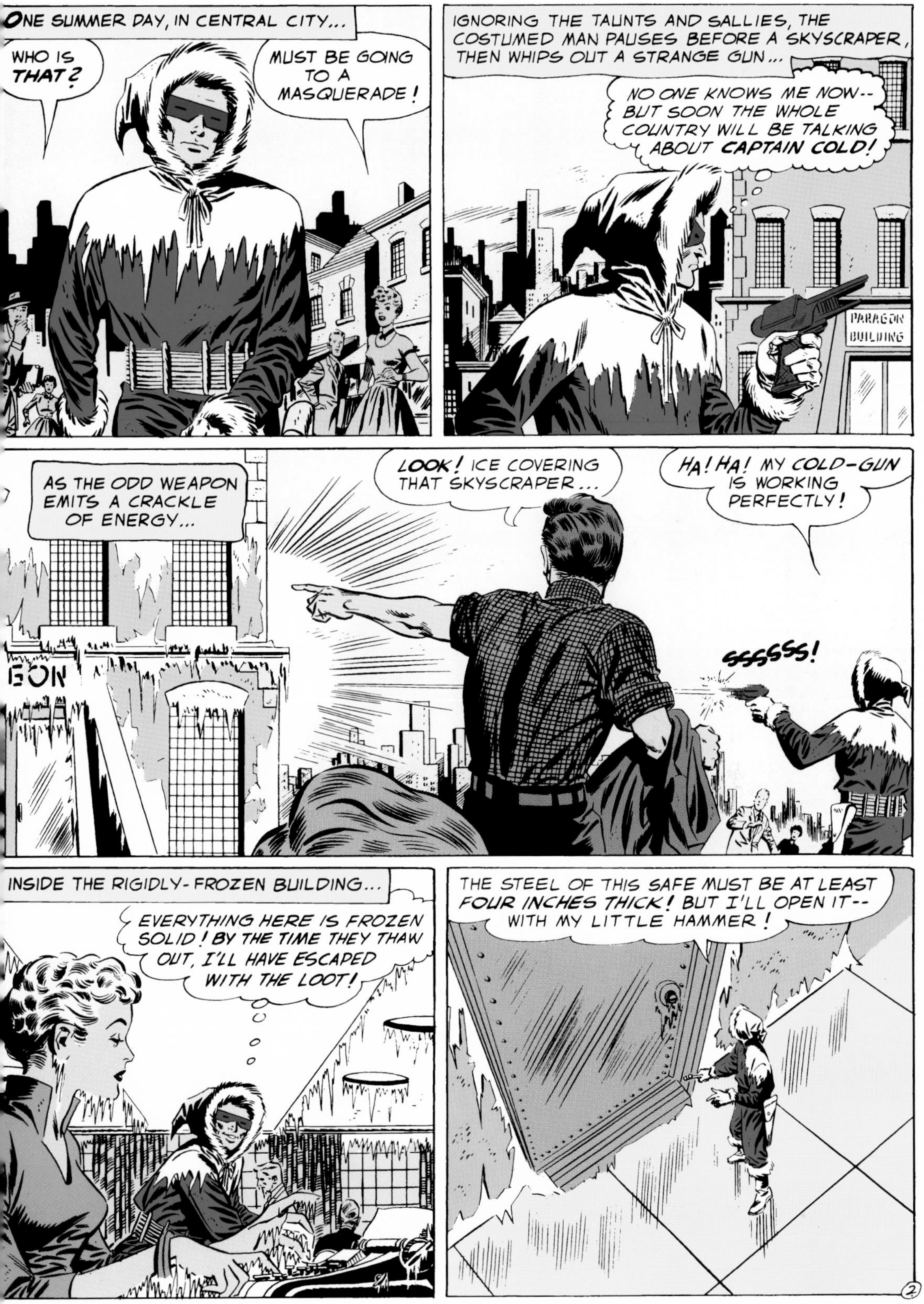
ONE SUMMER DAY, IN CENTRAL CITY...
WHO IS THAT?
MUST BE GOING TO A MASQUERADE!
IGNORING THE TAUNTS AND SALLIES, THE COSTUMED MAN PAUSES BEFORE A SKYSCRAPER, THEN WHIPS OUT A STRANGE GUN...
NO ONE KNOWS ME NOW-- BUT SOON THE WHOLE COUNTRY WILL BE TALKING ABOUT CAPTAIN COLD!
PARAGON BUILDING
AS THE ODD WEAPON EMITS A CRACKLE OF ENERGY...
LOOK! ICE COVERING THAT SKYSCRAPER...
HA! HA! MY COLD-GUN IS WORKING PERFECTLY!
SSSSSS!
GON
INSIDE THE RIGIDLY-FROZEN BUILDING...
EVERYTHING HERE IS FROZEN SOLID! BY THE TIME THEY THAW OUT, I'LL HAVE ESCAPED WITH THE LOOT!
THE STEEL OF THIS SAFE MUST BE AT LEAST FOUR INCHES THICK! BUT I'LL OPEN IT-- WITH MY LITTLE HAMMER!
2

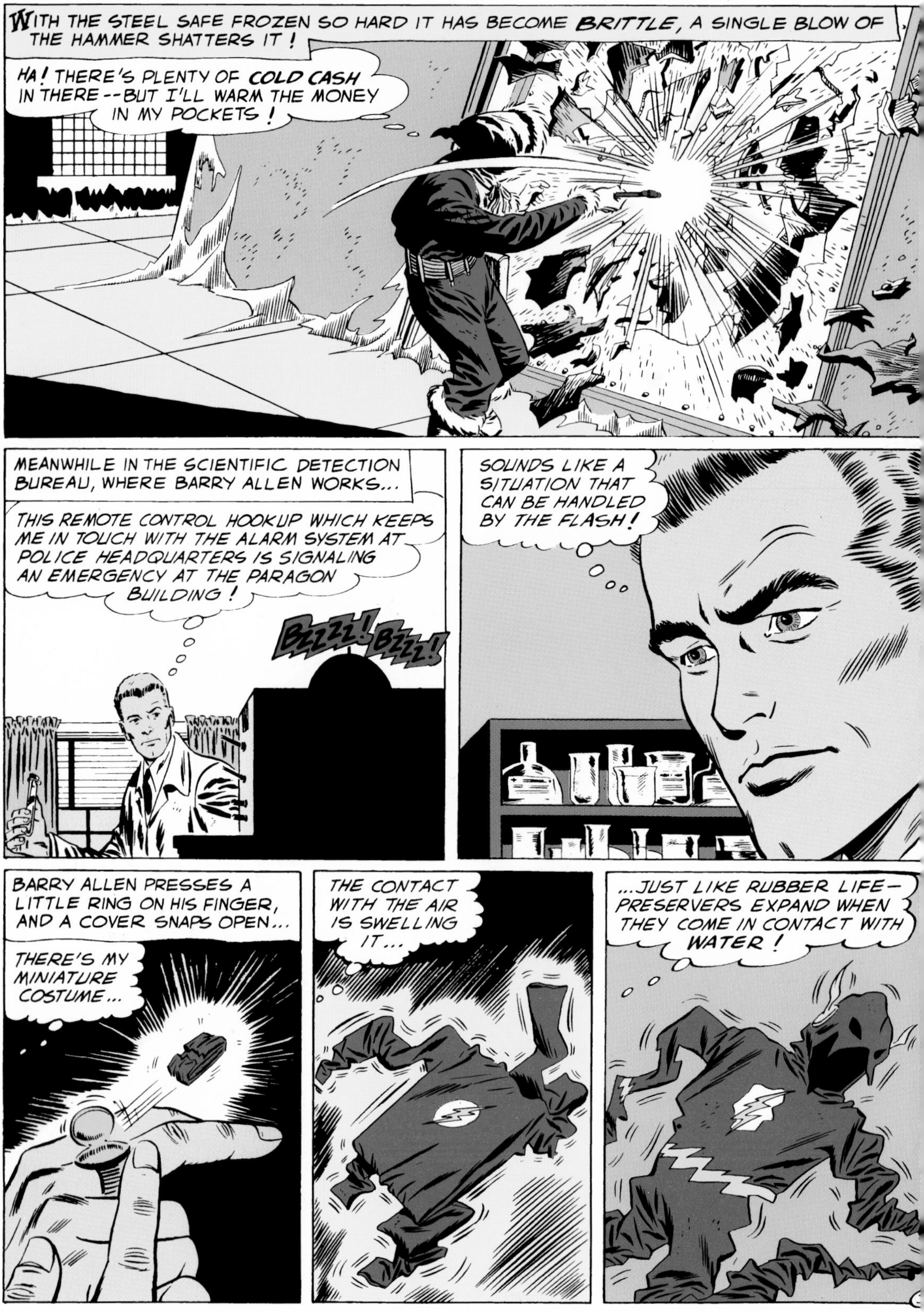
WITH THE STEEL SAFE FROZEN SO HARD IT HAS BECOME BRITTLE, A SINGLE BLOW OF THE HAMMER SHATTERS IT!
HA! THERE'S PLENTY OF COLD CASH IN THERE--BUT I'LL WARM THE MONEY IN MY POCKETS!
MEANWHILE IN THE SCIENTIFIC DETECTION BUREAU, WHERE BARRY ALLEN WORKS...
THIS REMOTE CONTROL HOOKUP WHICH KEEPS ME IN TOUCH WITH THE ALARM SYSTEM AT POLICE HEADQUARTERS IS SIGNALING AN EMERGENCY AT THE PARAGON BUILDING!
BZZZZ! BZZZ!
SOUNDS LIKE A SITUATION THAT CAN BE HANDLED BY THE FLASH!
BARRY ALLEN PRESSES A LITTLE RING ON HIS FINGER, AND A COVER SNAPS OPEN...
THERE'S MY MINIATURE COSTUME...
THE CONTACT WITH THE AIR IS SWELLING IT...
...JUST LIKE RUBBER LIFE-PRESERVERS EXPAND WHEN THEY COME IN CONTACT WITH WATER!

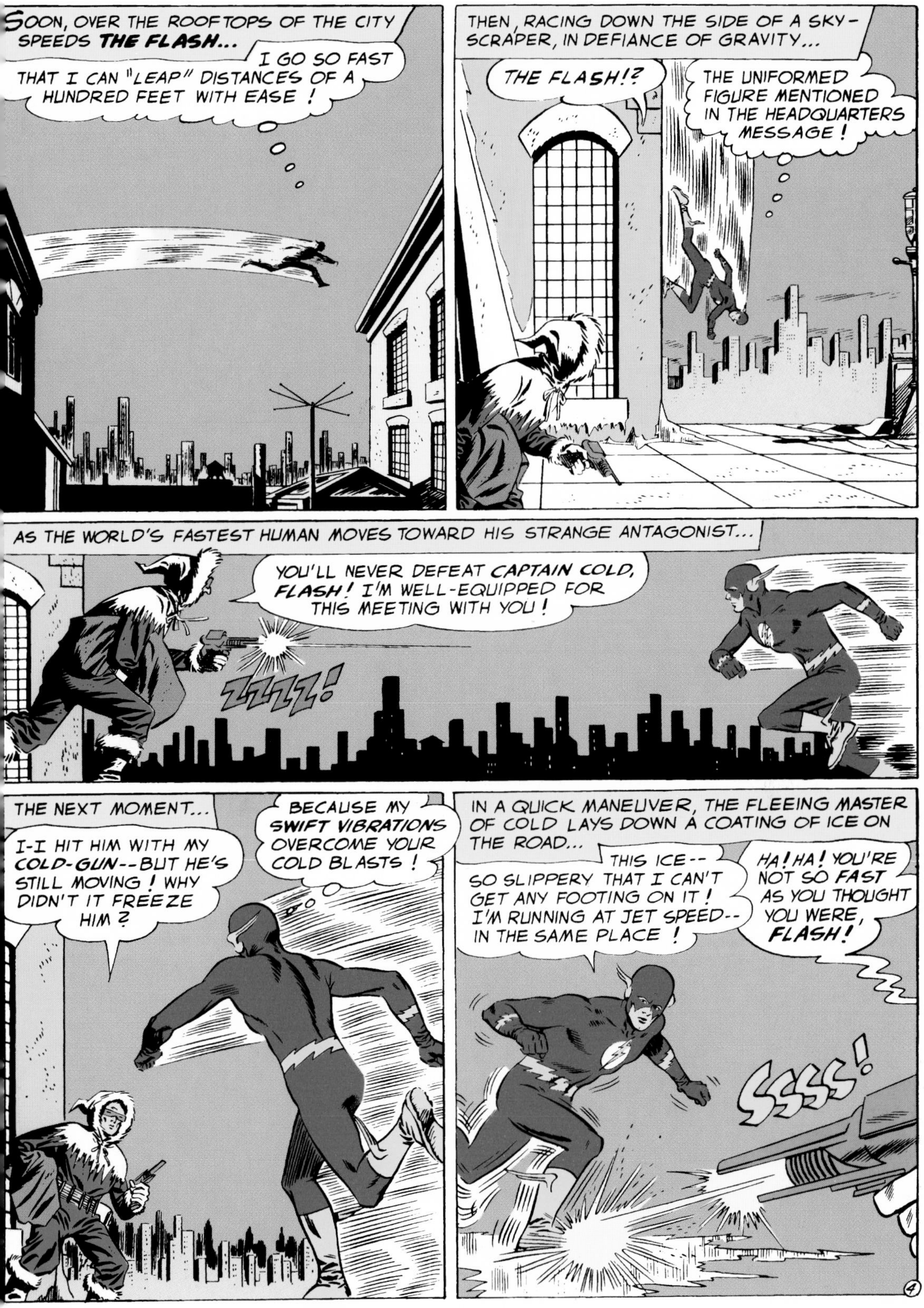
SOON, OVER THE ROOFTOPS OF THE CITY SPEEDS THE FLASH...
I GO SO FAST THAT I CAN "LEAP" DISTANCES OF A HUNDRED FEET WITH EASE!
THEN, RACING DOWN THE SIDE OF A SKY-SCRAPER, IN DEFIANCE OF GRAVITY...
THE FLASH!?
THE UNIFORMED FIGURE MENTIONED IN THE HEADQUARTERS MESSAGE!
AS THE WORLD'S FASTEST HUMAN MOVES TOWARD HIS STRANGE ANTAGONIST...
YOU'LL NEVER DEFEAT CAPTAIN COLD, FLASH! I'M WELL-EQUIPPED FOR THIS MEETING WITH YOU!
ZZZZ!
THE NEXT MOMENT...
I-I HIT HIM WITH MY COLD-GUN--BUT HE'S STILL MOVING! WHY DIDN'T IT FREEZE HIM?
BECAUSE MY SWIFT VIBRATIONS OVERCOME YOUR COLD BLASTS!
IN A QUICK MANEUVER, THE FLEEING MASTER OF COLD LAYS DOWN A COATING OF ICE ON THE ROAD...
THIS ICE--SO SLIPPERY THAT I CAN'T GET ANY FOOTING ON IT! I'M RUNNING AT JET SPEED--IN THE SAME PLACE!
HA! HA! YOU'RE NOT SO FAST AS YOU THOUGHT YOU WERE, FLASH!
SSSS!
4

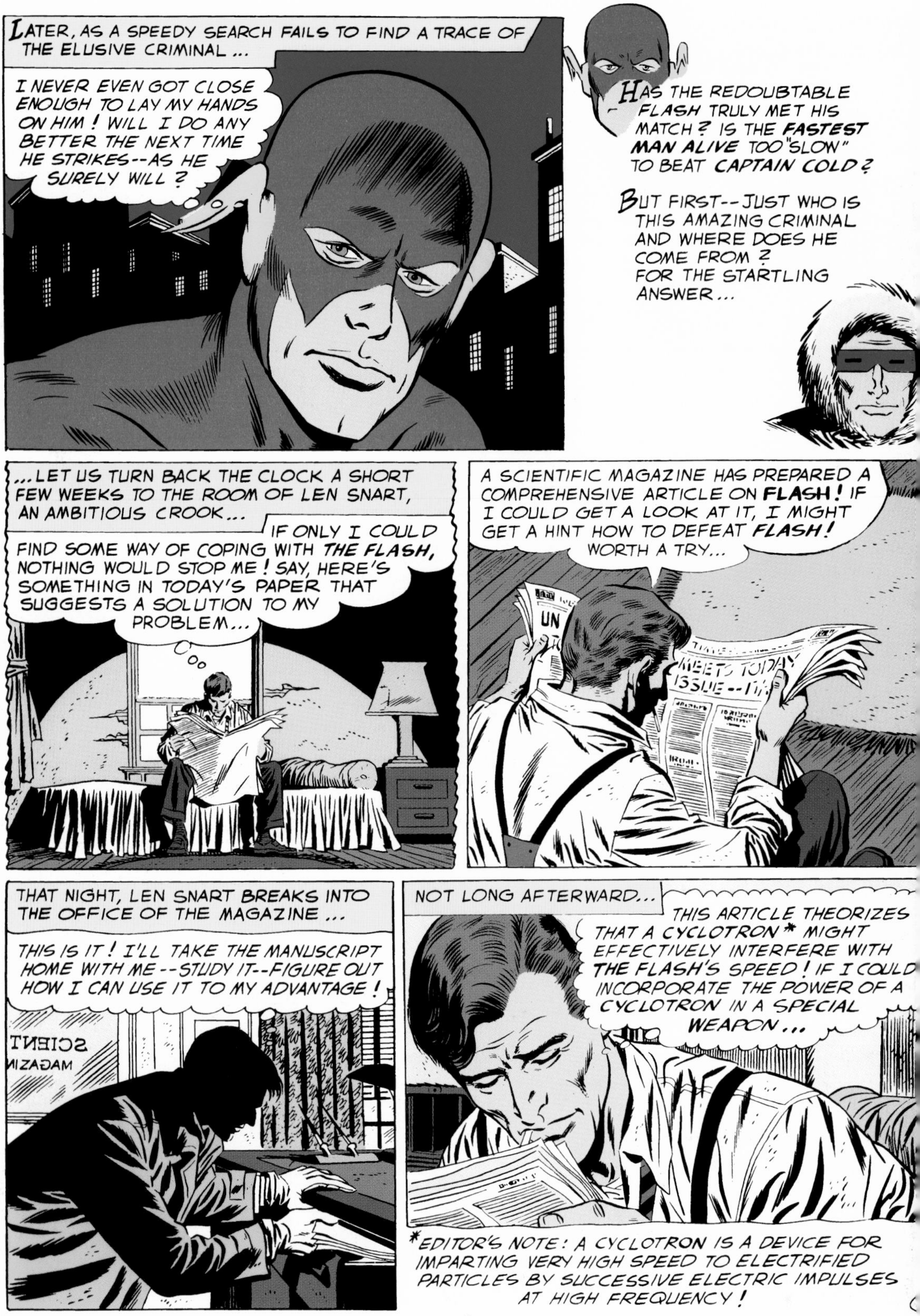
LATER, AS A SPEEDY SEARCH FAILS TO FIND A TRACE OF THE ELUSIVE CRIMINAL ...
I NEVER EVEN GOT CLOSE ENOUGH TO LAY MY HANDS ON HIM ! WILL I DO ANY BETTER THE NEXT TIME HE STRIKES--AS HE SURELY WILL ?
HAS THE REDOUBTABLE FLASH TRULY MET HIS MATCH ? IS THE FASTEST MAN ALIVE TOO "SLOW" TO BEAT CAPTAIN COLD ?
BUT FIRST--JUST WHO IS THIS AMAZING CRIMINAL AND WHERE DOES HE COME FROM ? FOR THE STARTLING ANSWER...
...LET US TURN BACK THE CLOCK A SHORT FEW WEEKS TO THE ROOM OF LEN SNART, AN AMBITIOUS CROOK...
IF ONLY I COULD FIND SOME WAY OF COPING WITH THE FLASH, NOTHING WOULD STOP ME ! SAY, HERE'S SOMETHING IN TODAY'S PAPER THAT SUGGESTS A SOLUTION TO MY PROBLEM...
A SCIENTIFIC MAGAZINE HAS PREPARED A COMPREHENSIVE ARTICLE ON FLASH ! IF I COULD GET A LOOK AT IT, I MIGHT GET A HINT HOW TO DEFEAT FLASH ! WORTH A TRY...
THAT NIGHT, LEN SNART BREAKS INTO THE OFFICE OF THE MAGAZINE ...
THIS IS IT ! I'LL TAKE THE MANUSCRIPT HOME WITH ME--STUDY IT--FIGURE OUT HOW I CAN USE IT TO MY ADVANTAGE !
NOT LONG AFTERWARD...
THIS ARTICLE THEORIZES THAT A CYCLOTRON* MIGHT EFFECTIVELY INTERFERE WITH THE FLASH'S SPEED ! IF I COULD INCORPORATE THE POWER OF A CYCLOTRON IN A SPECIAL WEAPON...
*EDITOR'S NOTE: A CYCLOTRON IS A DEVICE FOR IMPARTING VERY HIGH SPEED TO ELECTRIFIED PARTICLES BY SUCCESSIVE ELECTRIC IMPULSES AT HIGH FREQUENCY !

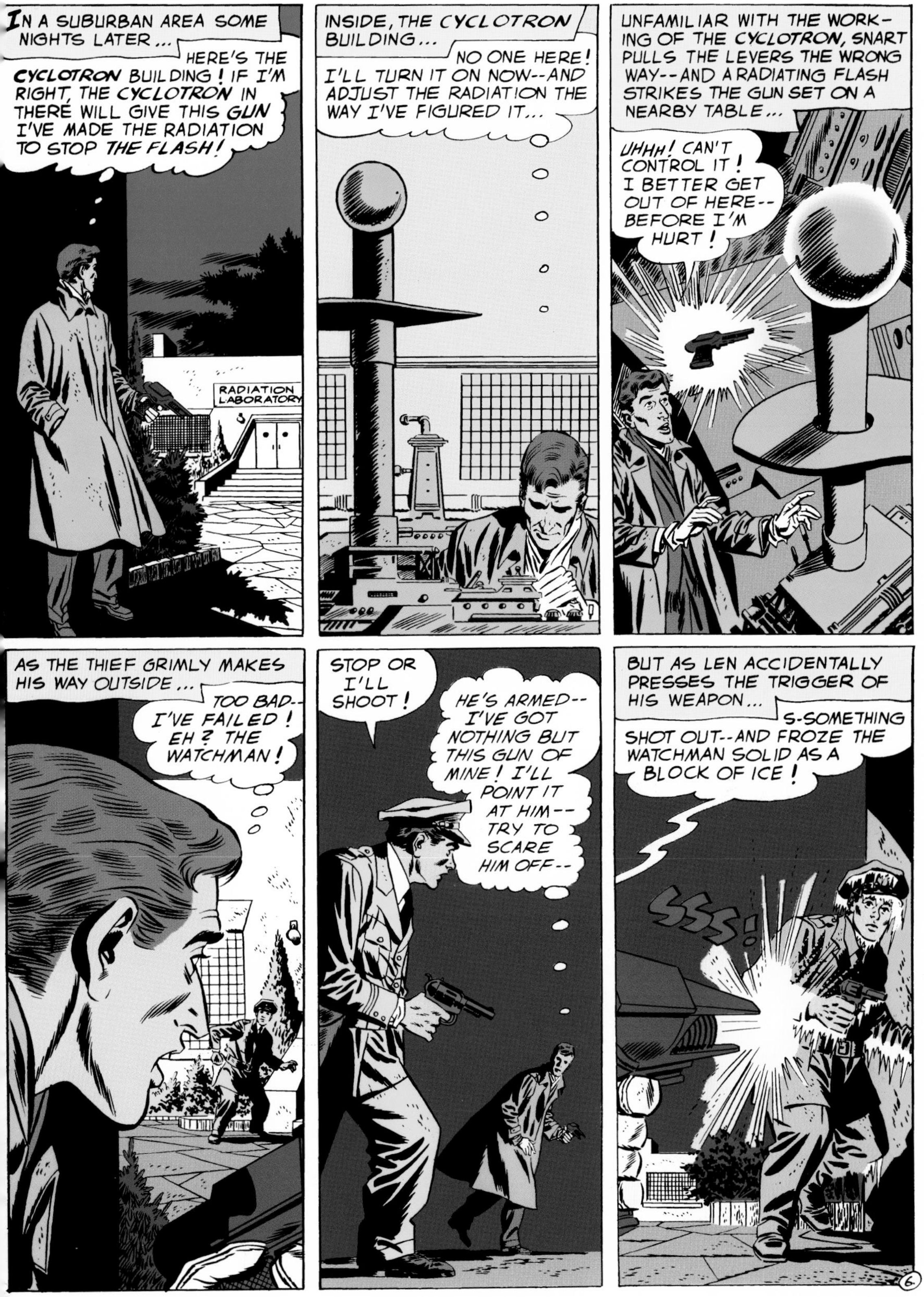
IN A SUBURBAN AREA SOME NIGHTS LATER...
HERE'S THE CYCLOTRON BUILDING! IF I'M RIGHT, THE CYCLOTRON IN THERE WILL GIVE THIS GUN I'VE MADE THE RADIATION TO STOP THE FLASH!
RADIATION LABORATORY
INSIDE, THE CYCLOTRON BUILDING...
NO ONE HERE! I'LL TURN IT ON NOW--AND ADJUST THE RADIATION THE WAY I'VE FIGURED IT...
UNFAMILIAR WITH THE WORKING OF THE CYCLOTRON, SNART PULLS THE LEVERS THE WRONG WAY--AND A RADIATING FLASH STRIKES THE GUN SET ON A NEARBY TABLE...
UHHH! CAN'T CONTROL IT! I BETTER GET OUT OF HERE--BEFORE I'M HURT!
AS THE THIEF GRIMLY MAKES HIS WAY OUTSIDE...
TOO BAD--I'VE FAILED! EH? THE WATCHMAN!
STOP OR I'LL SHOOT!
HE'S ARMED--I'VE GOT NOTHING BUT THIS GUN OF MINE! I'LL POINT IT AT HIM--TRY TO SCARE HIM OFF--
BUT AS LEN ACCIDENTALLY PRESSES THE TRIGGER OF HIS WEAPON...
S-SOMETHING SHOT OUT--AND FROZE THE WATCHMAN SOLID AS A BLOCK OF ICE!
SSS!
6

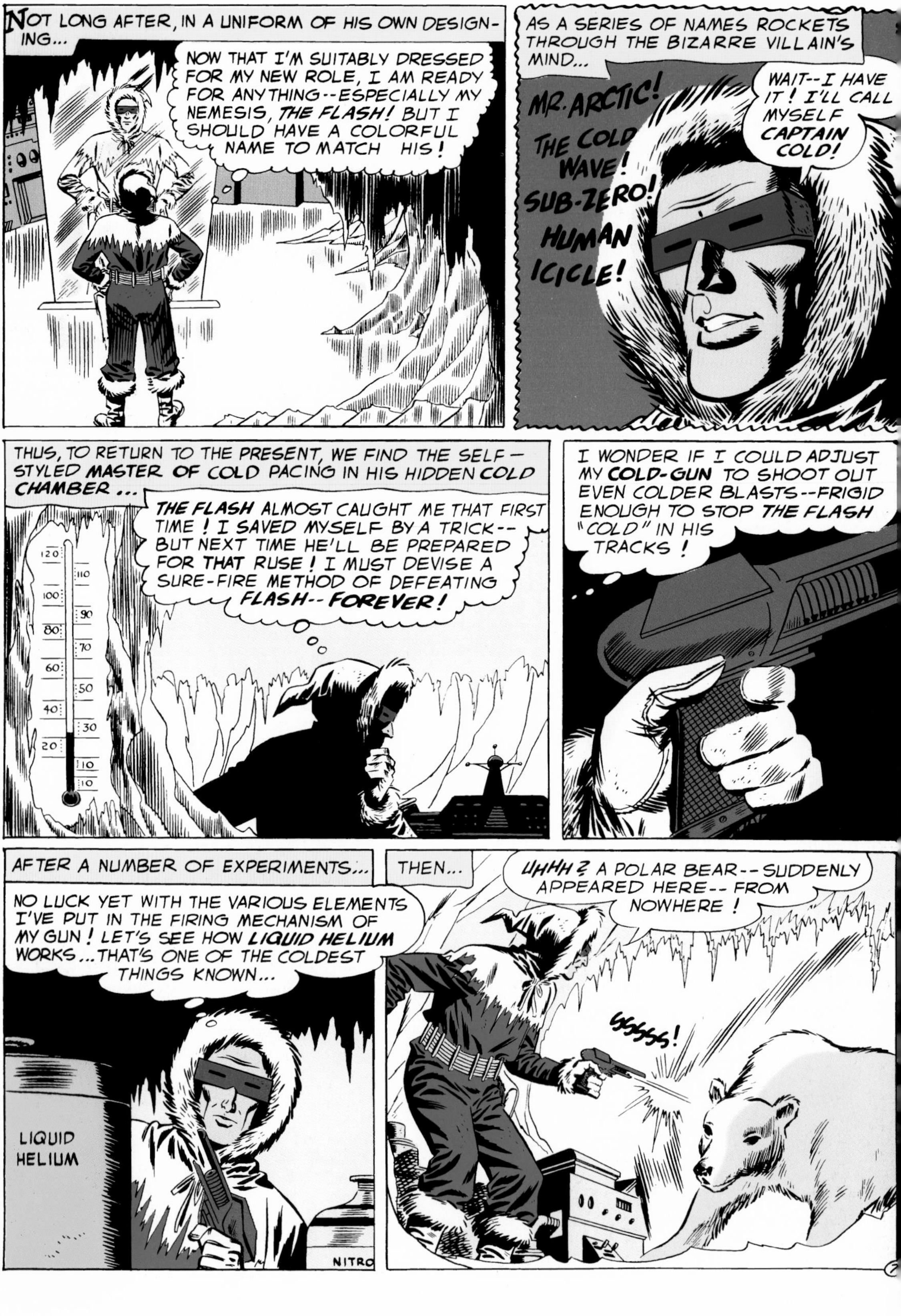
NOT LONG AFTER, IN A UNIFORM OF HIS OWN DESIGNING...
NOW THAT I'M SUITABLY DRESSED FOR MY NEW ROLE, I AM READY FOR ANYTHING--ESPECIALLY MY NEMESIS, THE FLASH! BUT I SHOULD HAVE A COLORFUL NAME TO MATCH HIS!
AS A SERIES OF NAMES ROCKETS THROUGH THE BIZARRE VILLAIN'S MIND...
MR. ARCTIC!
THE COLD WAVE!
SUB-ZERO!
HUMAN ICICLE!
WAIT--I HAVE IT! I'LL CALL MYSELF CAPTAIN COLD!
THUS, TO RETURN TO THE PRESENT, WE FIND THE SELF-STYLED MASTER OF COLD PACING IN HIS HIDDEN COLD CHAMBER...
THE FLASH ALMOST CAUGHT ME THAT FIRST TIME! I SAVED MYSELF BY A TRICK--BUT NEXT TIME HE'LL BE PREPARED FOR THAT RUSE! I MUST DEVISE A SURE-FIRE METHOD OF DEFEATING FLASH--FOREVER!
I WONDER IF I COULD ADJUST MY COLD-GUN TO SHOOT OUT EVEN COLDER BLASTS--FRIGID ENOUGH TO STOP THE FLASH "COLD" IN HIS TRACKS!
AFTER A NUMBER OF EXPERIMENTS...
NO LUCK YET WITH THE VARIOUS ELEMENTS I'VE PUT IN THE FIRING MECHANISM OF MY GUN! LET'S SEE HOW LIQUID HELIUM WORKS...THAT'S ONE OF THE COLDEST THINGS KNOWN...
LIQUID HELIUM
NITRO
THEN...
UHHH? A POLAR BEAR--SUDDENLY APPEARED HERE--FROM NOWHERE!
SSSSSS!

AS THE BEAR RUSHES AT THE BEWILDERED CRIMINAL...

THE BEAR WENT RIGHT **THROUGH** ME! IT WAS ONLY A **MIRAGE**--CAUSED BY THE FIRING OF MY LIQUID HELIUM **COLD-GUN!**

MY GUN SHOOTS OUT **ABSOLUTE ZERO** COLD-- MINUS *460°* FAHRENHEIT! AND JUST LIKE INTENSE HEAT CAUSES STRANGE MIRAGES ON THE DESERT, INTENSE COLD CAUSES EVEN MORE FANTASTIC MIRAGES!

AS THE MINUTES GO BY, **CAPTAIN COLD** WATCHES THE ODD ILLUSION WEAKEN...

THE BEAR-- IT'S FADING!

FADING FASTER NOW!

GONE! BUT IT LASTED **LONG ENOUGH! NOW** I HAVE THE PERFECT WEAPON TO USE AGAINST THE FLASH!

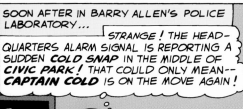

SOON AFTER IN BARRY ALLEN'S POLICE LABORATORY...

STRANGE! THE HEAD-QUARTERS ALARM SIGNAL IS REPORTING A SUDDEN **COLD SNAP** IN THE MIDDLE OF CIVIC PARK! THAT COULD ONLY MEAN-- **CAPTAIN COLD** IS ON THE MOVE AGAIN!

BZZZZZ! BZZZZ!

AND SO IS **THE FLASH,** AS HE SPEEDS TO *CIVIC PARK...*

CAPTAIN COLD MUST BE HERE SOMEWHERE!

IMAGINE! THE LAKE FROZE SOLID-- IN JULY!

8

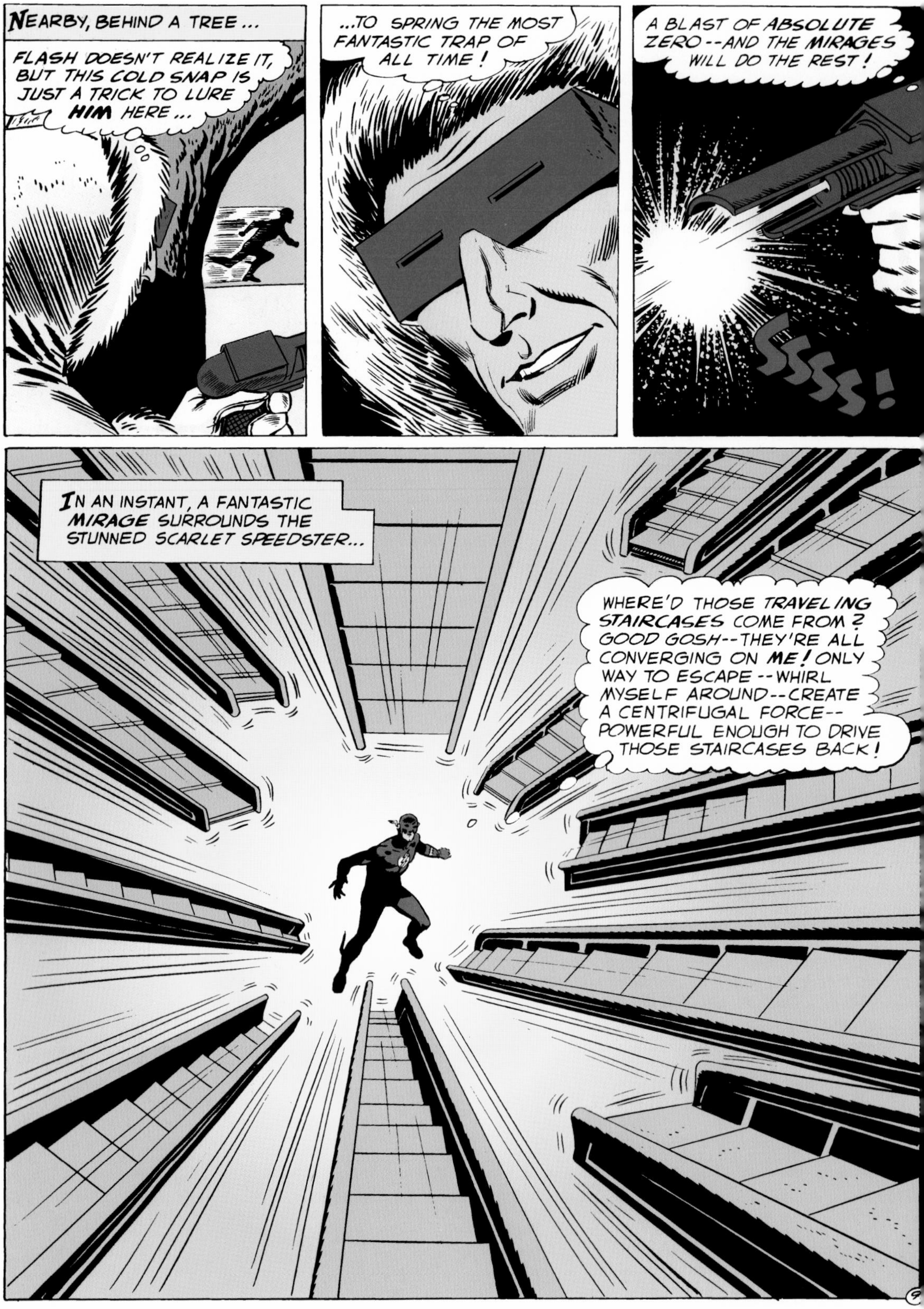
NEARBY, BEHIND A TREE ...
FLASH DOESN'T REALIZE IT, BUT THIS COLD SNAP IS JUST A TRICK TO LURE HIM HERE ...
...TO SPRING THE MOST FANTASTIC TRAP OF ALL TIME!
A BLAST OF ABSOLUTE ZERO --AND THE MIRAGES WILL DO THE REST!
SSSSS!
IN AN INSTANT, A FANTASTIC MIRAGE SURROUNDS THE STUNNED SCARLET SPEEDSTER...
WHERE'D THOSE TRAVELING STAIRCASES COME FROM? GOOD GOSH--THEY'RE ALL CONVERGING ON ME! ONLY WAY TO ESCAPE --WHIRL MYSELF AROUND--CREATE A CENTRIFUGAL FORCE-- POWERFUL ENOUGH TO DRIVE THOSE STAIRCASES BACK!

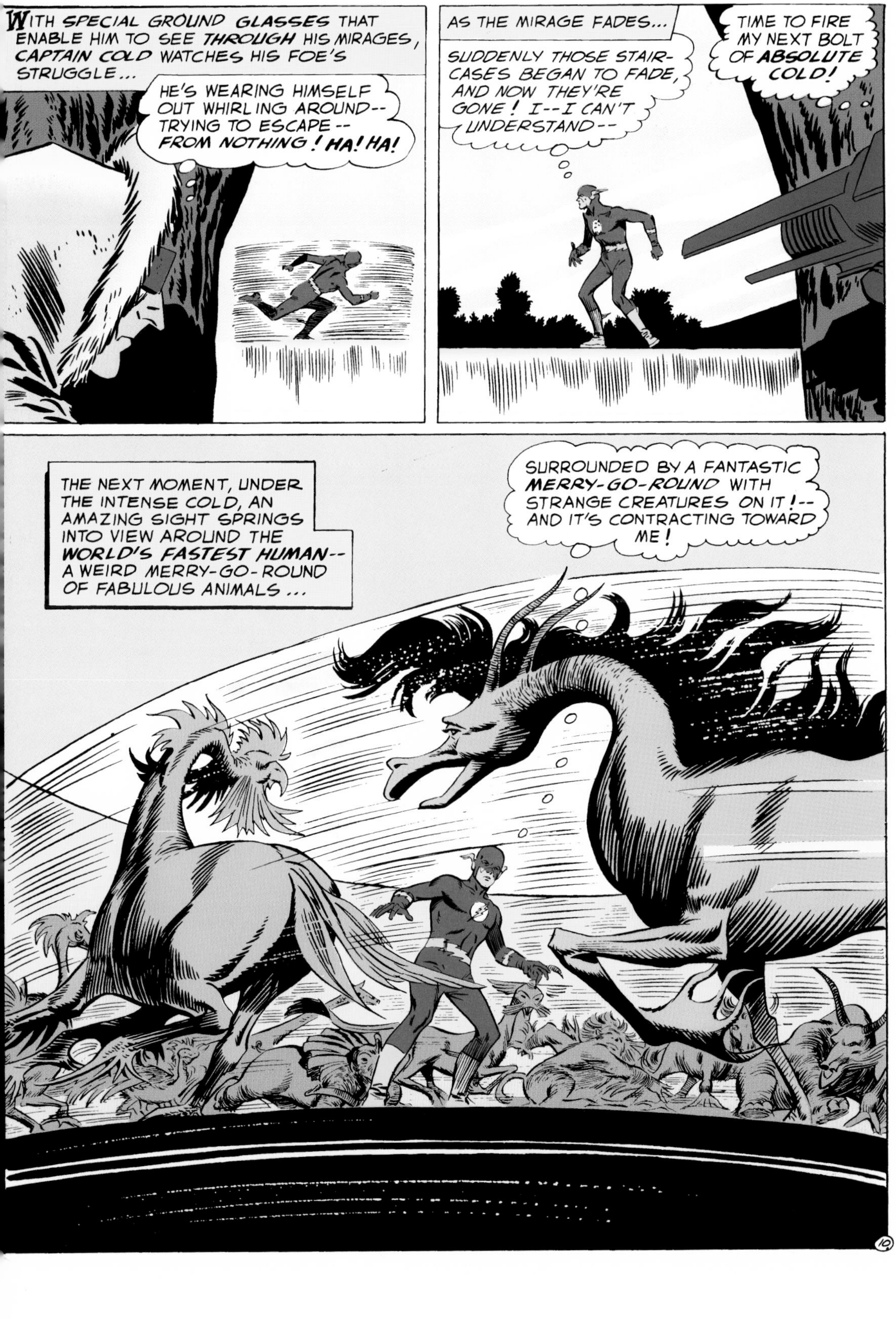
WITH SPECIAL GROUND GLASSES THAT ENABLE HIM TO SEE THROUGH HIS MIRAGES, CAPTAIN COLD WATCHES HIS FOE'S STRUGGLE...
HE'S WEARING HIMSELF OUT WHIRLING AROUND-- TRYING TO ESCAPE -- FROM NOTHING! HA! HA!
AS THE MIRAGE FADES...
SUDDENLY THOSE STAIR-CASES BEGAN TO FADE, AND NOW THEY'RE GONE! I--I CAN'T UNDERSTAND--
TIME TO FIRE MY NEXT BOLT OF ABSOLUTE COLD!
THE NEXT MOMENT, UNDER THE INTENSE COLD, AN AMAZING SIGHT SPRINGS INTO VIEW AROUND THE WORLD'S FASTEST HUMAN-- A WEIRD MERRY-GO-ROUND OF FABULOUS ANIMALS...
SURROUNDED BY A FANTASTIC MERRY-GO-ROUND WITH STRANGE CREATURES ON IT!-- AND IT'S CONTRACTING TOWARD ME!
10

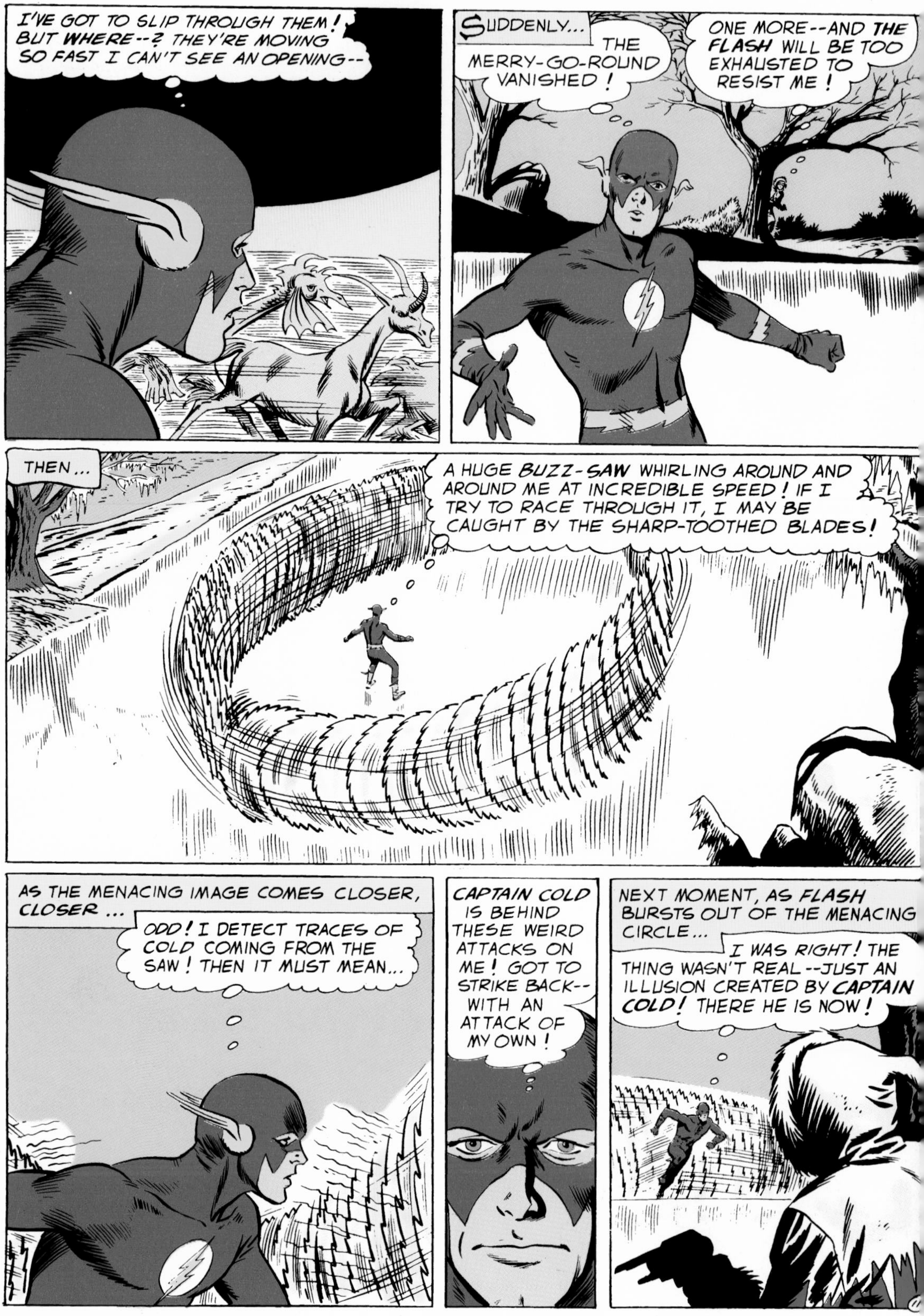

I'VE GOT TO SLIP THROUGH THEM! BUT WHERE--? THEY'RE MOVING SO FAST I CAN'T SEE AN OPENING--
SUDDENLY...
THE MERRY-GO-ROUND VANISHED!
ONE MORE--AND THE FLASH WILL BE TOO EXHAUSTED TO RESIST ME!
THEN...
A HUGE BUZZ-SAW WHIRLING AROUND AND AROUND ME AT INCREDIBLE SPEED! IF I TRY TO RACE THROUGH IT, I MAY BE CAUGHT BY THE SHARP-TOOTHED BLADES!
AS THE MENACING IMAGE COMES CLOSER, CLOSER ...
ODD! I DETECT TRACES OF COLD COMING FROM THE SAW! THEN IT MUST MEAN...
CAPTAIN COLD IS BEHIND THESE WEIRD ATTACKS ON ME! GOT TO STRIKE BACK--WITH AN ATTACK OF MY OWN!
NEXT MOMENT, AS FLASH BURSTS OUT OF THE MENACING CIRCLE...
I WAS RIGHT! THE THING WASN'T REAL--JUST AN ILLUSION CREATED BY CAPTAIN COLD! THERE HE IS NOW!

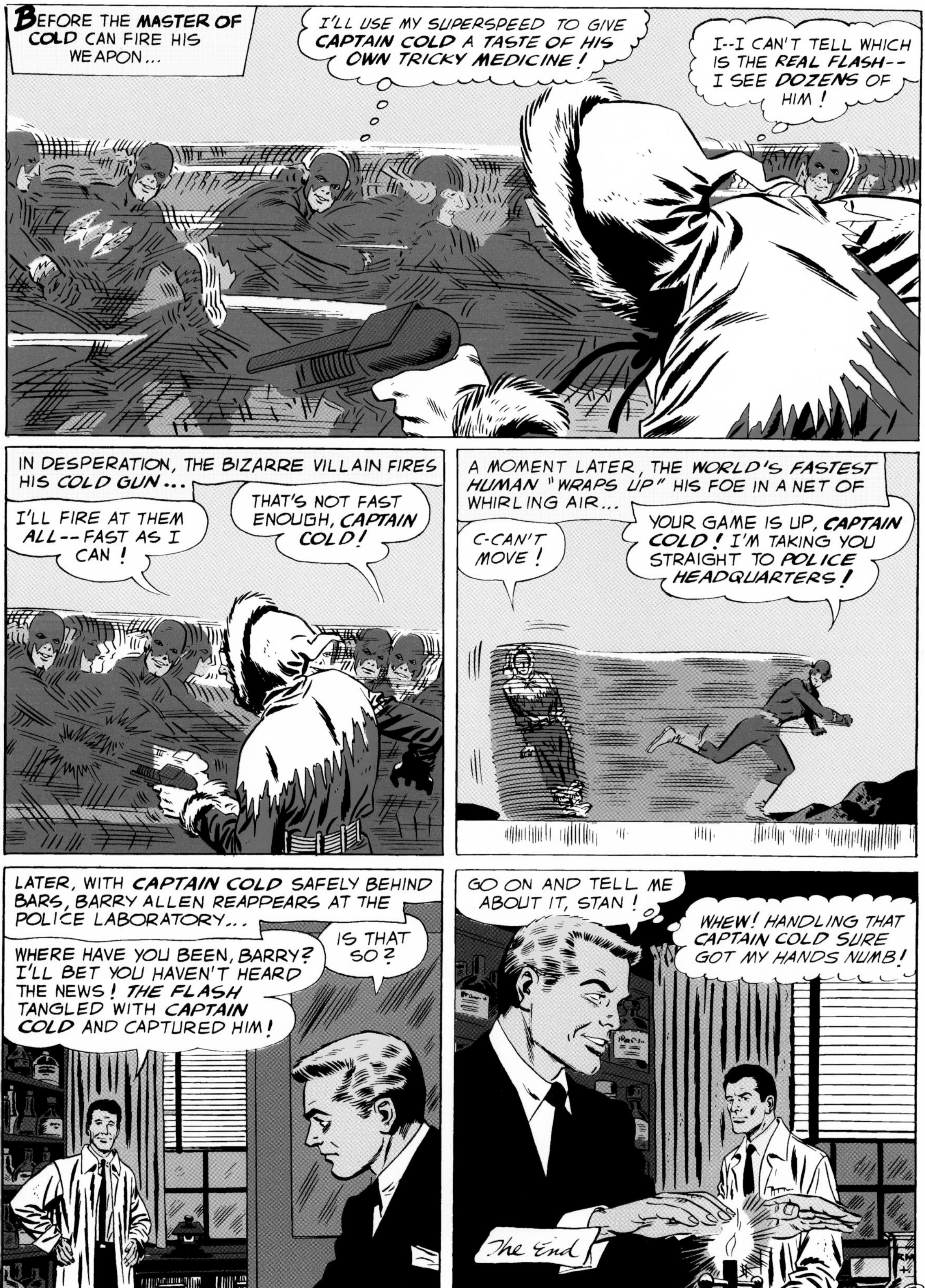
BEFORE THE MASTER OF COLD CAN FIRE HIS WEAPON...
I'LL USE MY SUPERSPEED TO GIVE CAPTAIN COLD A TASTE OF HIS OWN TRICKY MEDICINE!
I--I CAN'T TELL WHICH IS THE REAL FLASH-- I SEE DOZENS OF HIM!
IN DESPERATION, THE BIZARRE VILLAIN FIRES HIS COLD GUN...
I'LL FIRE AT THEM ALL--FAST AS I CAN!
THAT'S NOT FAST ENOUGH, CAPTAIN COLD!
A MOMENT LATER, THE WORLD'S FASTEST HUMAN "WRAPS UP" HIS FOE IN A NET OF WHIRLING AIR...
C-CAN'T MOVE!
YOUR GAME IS UP, CAPTAIN COLD! I'M TAKING YOU STRAIGHT TO POLICE HEADQUARTERS!
LATER, WITH CAPTAIN COLD SAFELY BEHIND BARS, BARRY ALLEN REAPPEARS AT THE POLICE LABORATORY...
WHERE HAVE YOU BEEN, BARRY? I'LL BET YOU HAVEN'T HEARD THE NEWS! THE FLASH TANGLED WITH CAPTAIN COLD AND CAPTURED HIM!
IS THAT SO?
GO ON AND TELL ME ABOUT IT, STAN!
WHEW! HANDLING THAT CAPTAIN COLD SURE GOT MY HANDS NUMB!
The End
12

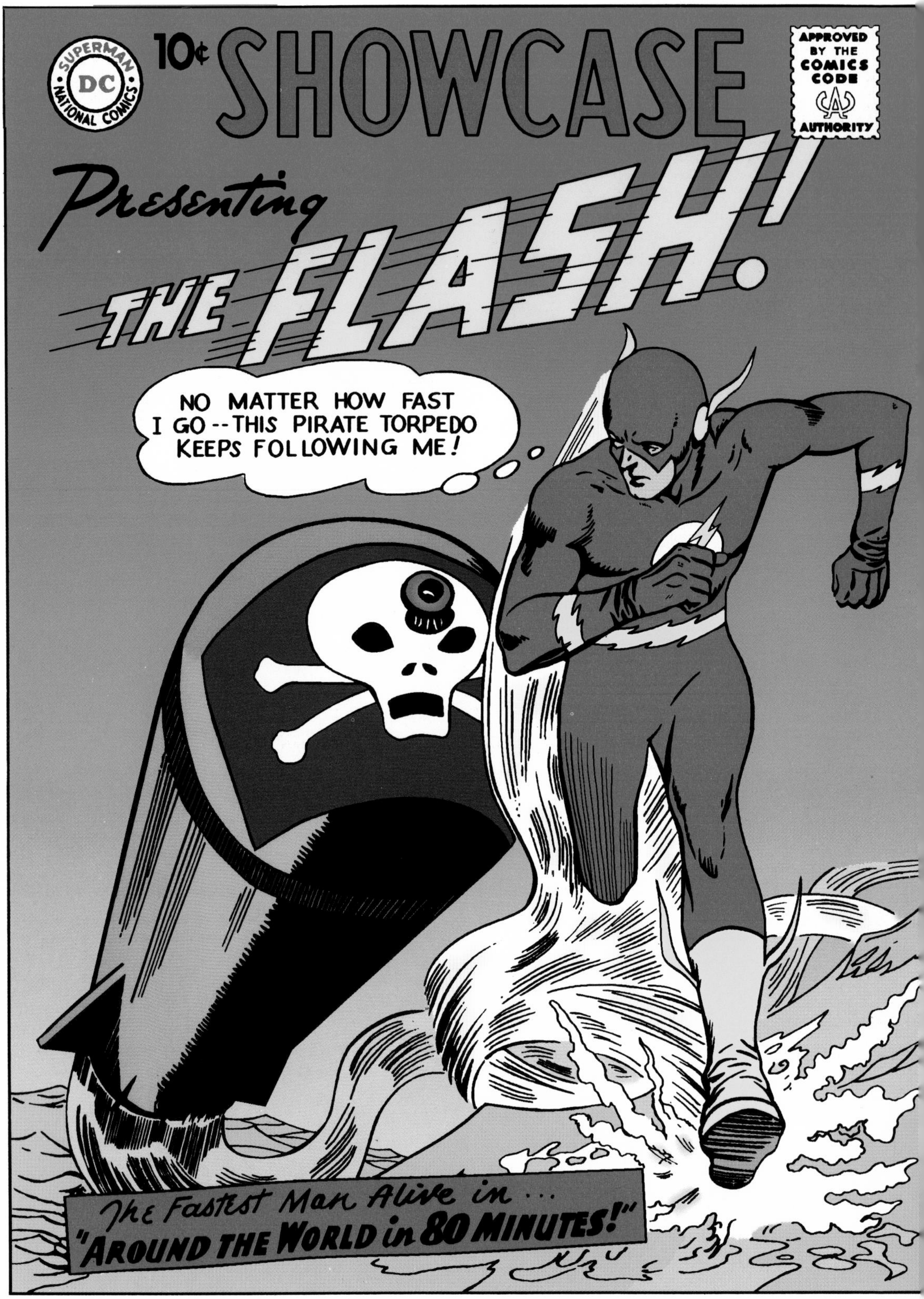
SUPERMAN DC NATIONAL COMICS
10¢
SHOWCASE
APPROVED BY THE COMICS CODE AUTHORITY
Presenting
THE FLASH!
NO MATTER HOW FAST I GO--THIS PIRATE TORPEDO KEEPS FOLLOWING ME!
The Fastest Man Alive in...
"AROUND THE WORLD in 80 MINUTES!"

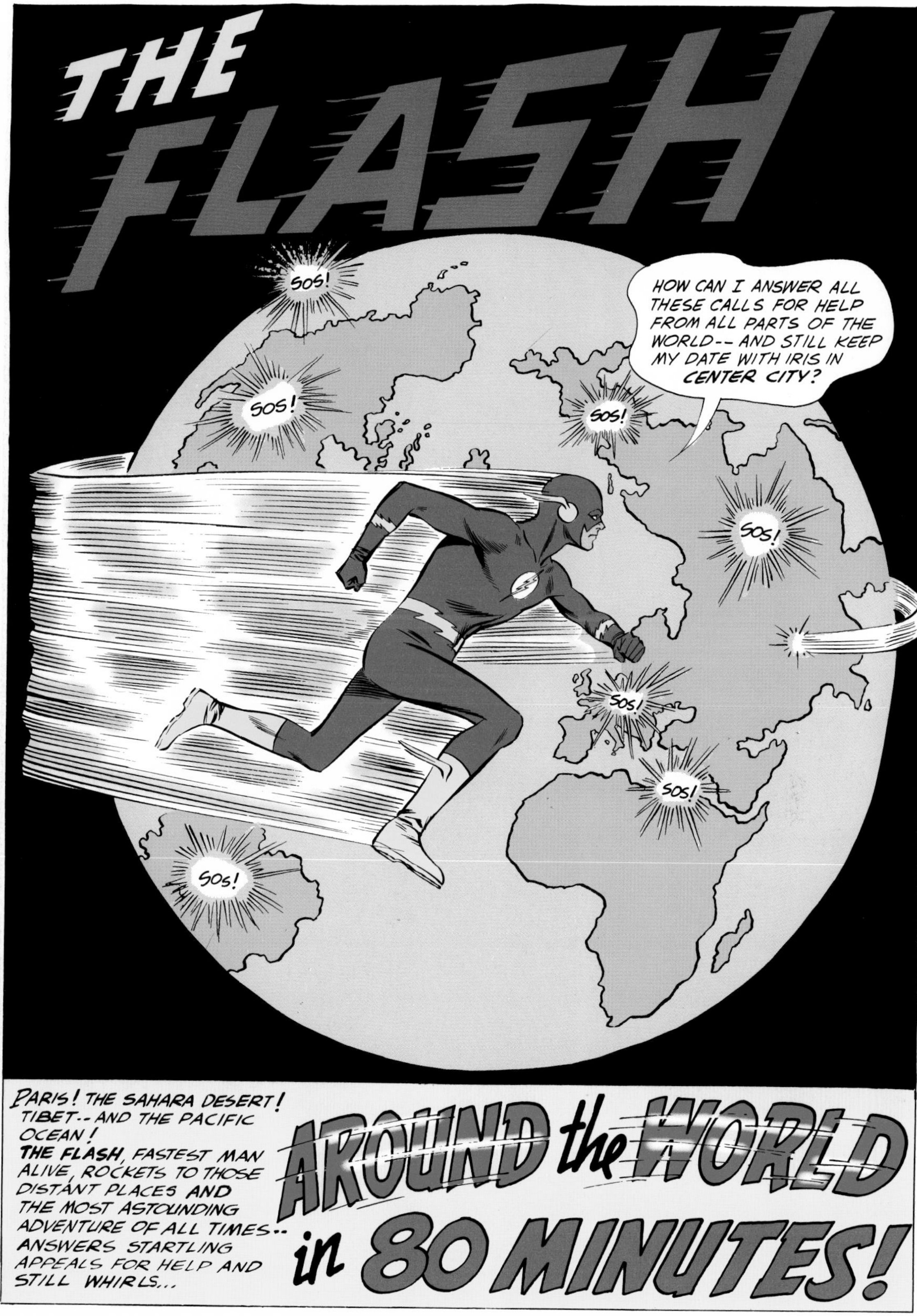
THE FLASH
SOS!
SOS!
SOS!
SOS!
SOS!
SOS!
SOS!
HOW CAN I ANSWER ALL THESE CALLS FOR HELP FROM ALL PARTS OF THE WORLD-- AND STILL KEEP MY DATE WITH IRIS IN CENTER CITY?
PARIS! THE SAHARA DESERT! TIBET-- AND THE PACIFIC OCEAN! THE FLASH, FASTEST MAN ALIVE, ROCKETS TO THOSE DISTANT PLACES AND THE MOST ASTOUNDING ADVENTURE OF ALL TIMES-- ANSWERS STARTLING APPEALS FOR HELP AND STILL WHIRLS...
AROUND the WORLD in 80 MINUTES!

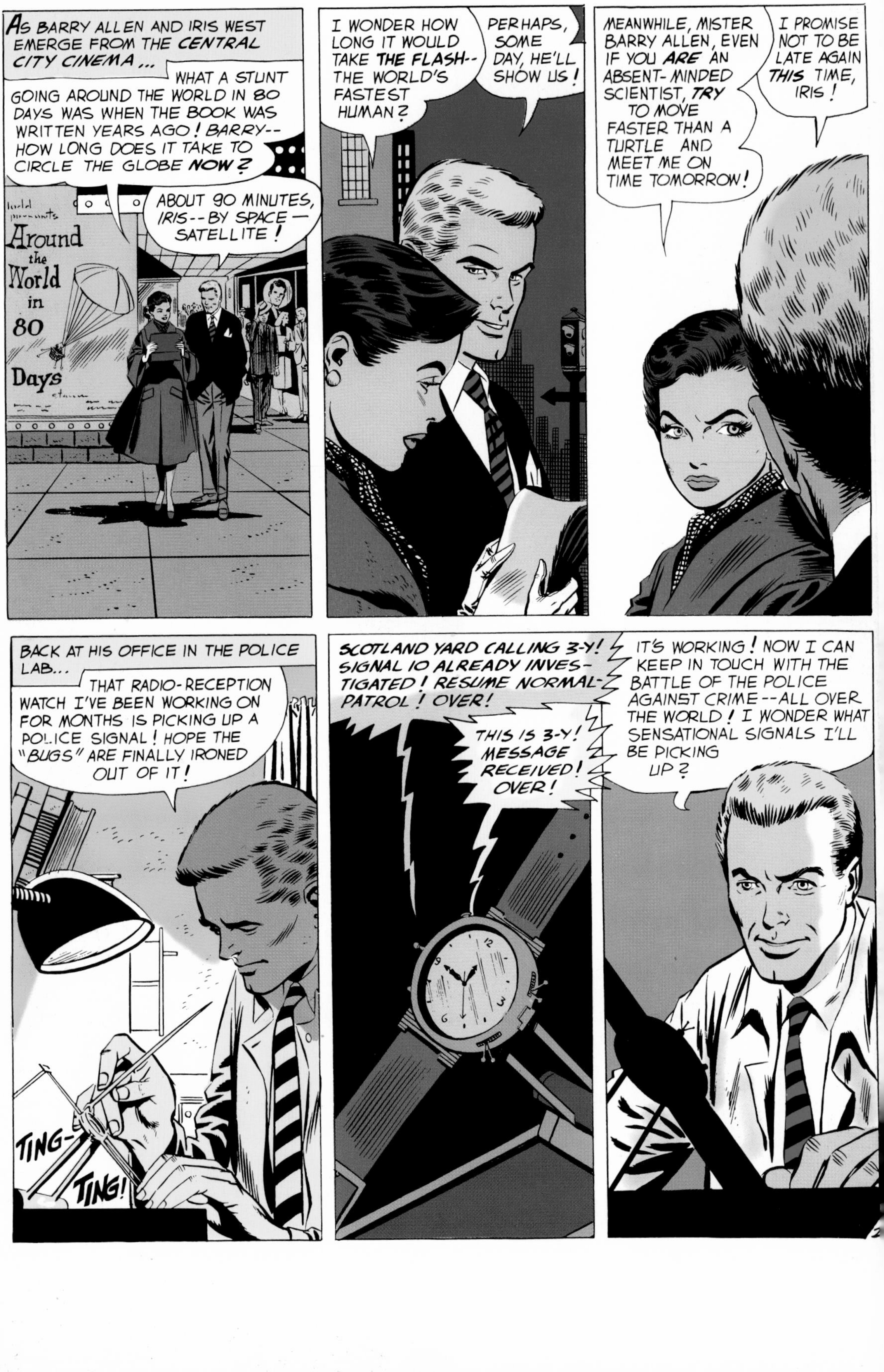
AS BARRY ALLEN AND IRIS WEST EMERGE FROM THE CENTRAL CITY CINEMA...
WHAT A STUNT GOING AROUND THE WORLD IN 80 DAYS WAS WHEN THE BOOK WAS WRITTEN YEARS AGO! BARRY-- HOW LONG DOES IT TAKE TO CIRCLE THE GLOBE NOW?
ABOUT 90 MINUTES, IRIS--BY SPACE-SATELLITE!
Around the World in 80 Days
I WONDER HOW LONG IT WOULD TAKE THE FLASH-- THE WORLD'S FASTEST HUMAN?
PERHAPS, SOME DAY, HE'LL SHOW US!
MEANWHILE, MISTER BARRY ALLEN, EVEN IF YOU ARE AN ABSENT-MINDED SCIENTIST, TRY TO MOVE FASTER THAN A TURTLE AND MEET ME ON TIME TOMORROW!
I PROMISE NOT TO BE LATE AGAIN THIS TIME, IRIS!
BACK AT HIS OFFICE IN THE POLICE LAB...
THAT RADIO-RECEPTION WATCH I'VE BEEN WORKING ON FOR MONTHS IS PICKING UP A POLICE SIGNAL! HOPE THE "BUGS" ARE FINALLY IRONED OUT OF IT!
TING-TING!
SCOTLAND YARD CALLING 3-Y! SIGNAL 10 ALREADY INVESTIGATED! RESUME NORMAL PATROL! OVER!
THIS IS 3-Y! MESSAGE RECEIVED! OVER!
IT'S WORKING! NOW I CAN KEEP IN TOUCH WITH THE BATTLE OF THE POLICE AGAINST CRIME--ALL OVER THE WORLD! I WONDER WHAT SENSATIONAL SIGNALS I'LL BE PICKING UP?

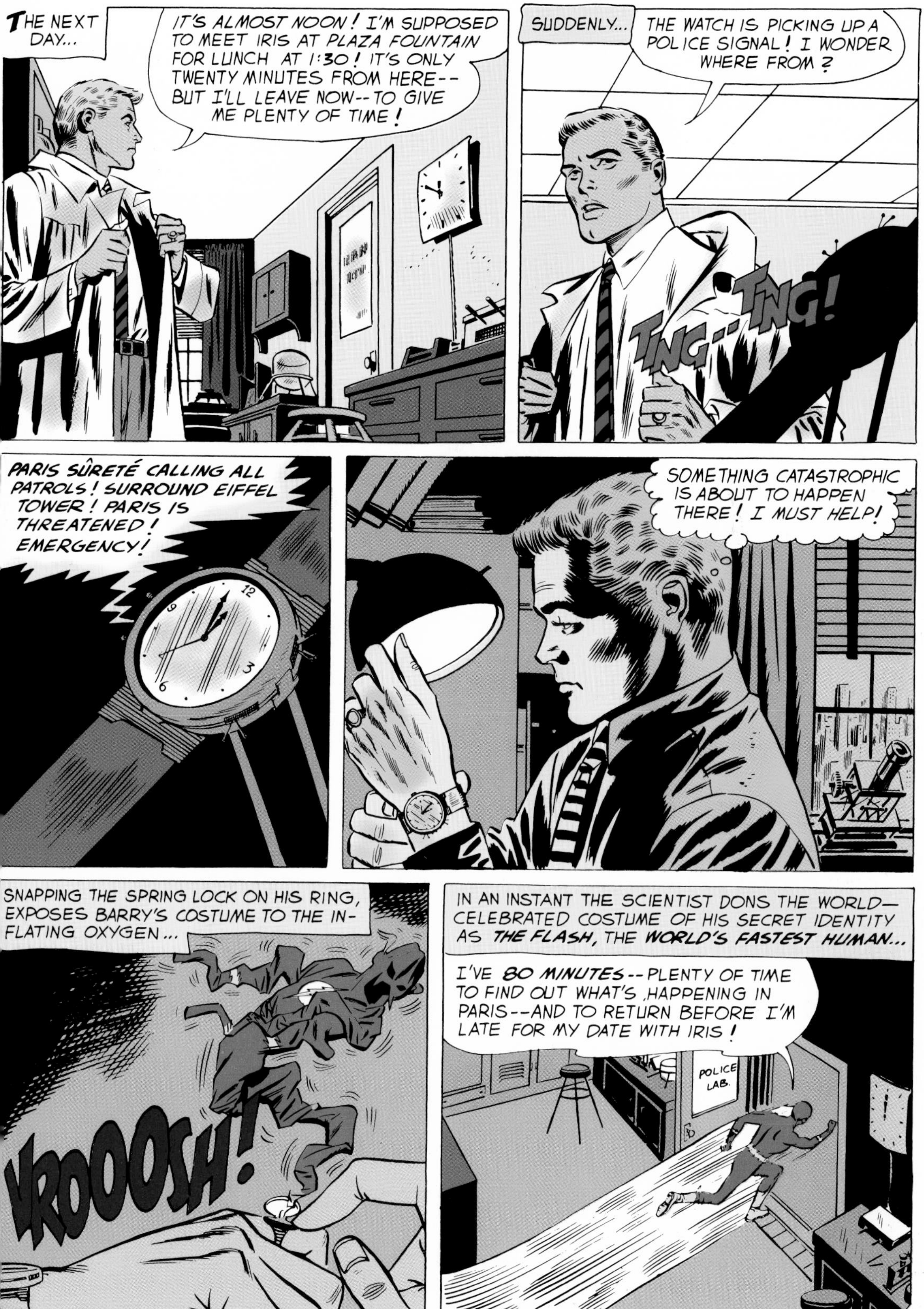
THE NEXT DAY...
IT'S ALMOST NOON! I'M SUPPOSED TO MEET IRIS AT PLAZA FOUNTAIN FOR LUNCH AT 1:30! IT'S ONLY TWENTY MINUTES FROM HERE--BUT I'LL LEAVE NOW--TO GIVE ME PLENTY OF TIME!
SUDDENLY...
THE WATCH IS PICKING UP A POLICE SIGNAL! I WONDER WHERE FROM?
TING..TING!
PARIS SÛRETÉ CALLING ALL PATROLS! SURROUND EIFFEL TOWER! PARIS IS THREATENED! EMERGENCY!
SOMETHING CATASTROPHIC IS ABOUT TO HAPPEN THERE! I MUST HELP!
SNAPPING THE SPRING LOCK ON HIS RING, EXPOSES BARRY'S COSTUME TO THE IN-FLATING OXYGEN...
VROOOSH!
IN AN INSTANT THE SCIENTIST DONS THE WORLD-CELEBRATED COSTUME OF HIS SECRET IDENTITY AS THE FLASH, THE WORLD'S FASTEST HUMAN...
I'VE 80 MINUTES--PLENTY OF TIME TO FIND OUT WHAT'S HAPPENING IN PARIS--AND TO RETURN BEFORE I'M LATE FOR MY DATE WITH IRIS!
POLICE LAB.
3

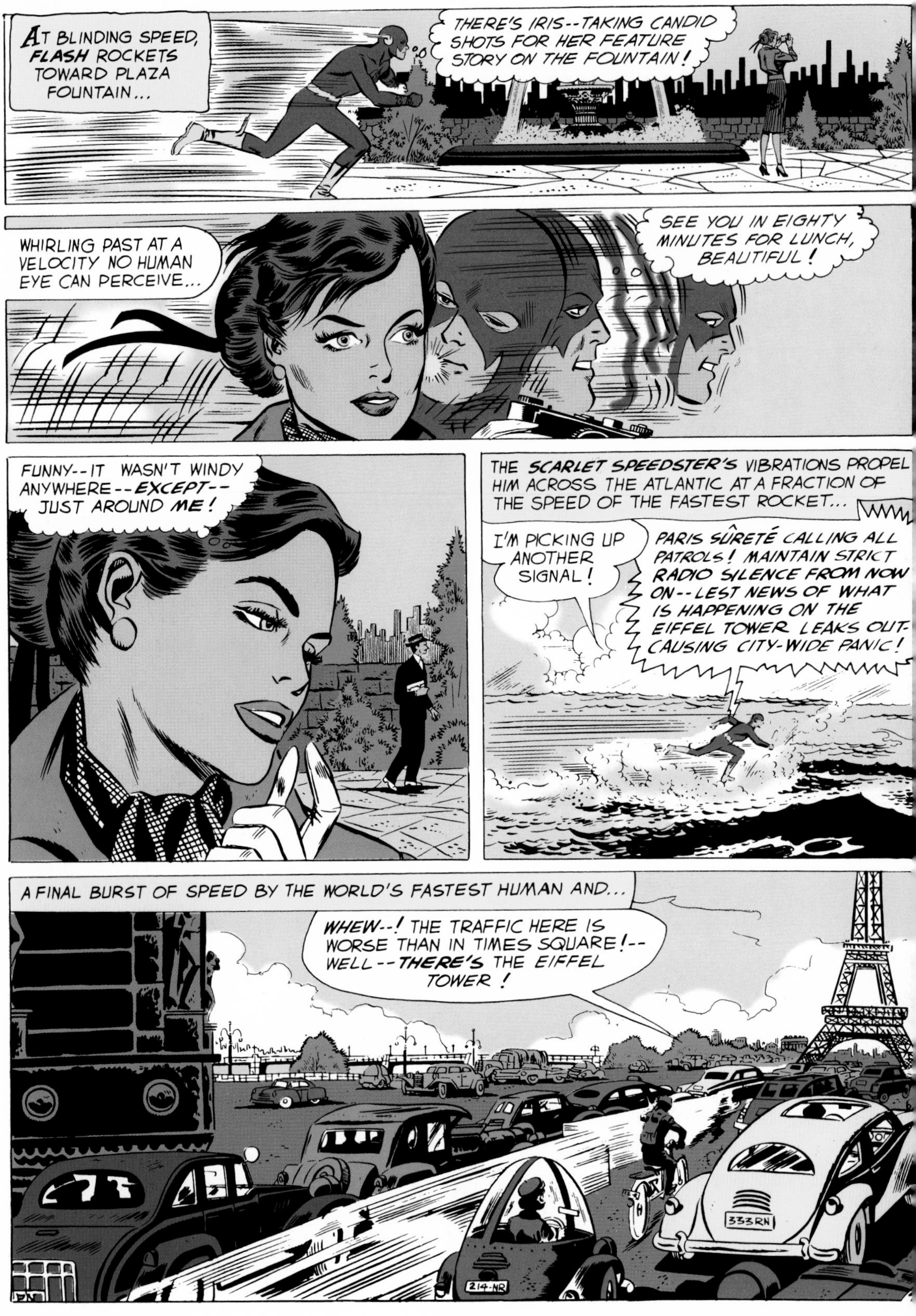
AT BLINDING SPEED, FLASH ROCKETS TOWARD PLAZA FOUNTAIN...
THERE'S IRIS--TAKING CANDID SHOTS FOR HER FEATURE STORY ON THE FOUNTAIN!
WHIRLING PAST AT A VELOCITY NO HUMAN EYE CAN PERCEIVE...
SEE YOU IN EIGHTY MINUTES FOR LUNCH, BEAUTIFUL!
FUNNY--IT WASN'T WINDY ANYWHERE--EXCEPT--JUST AROUND ME!
THE SCARLET SPEEDSTER'S VIBRATIONS PROPEL HIM ACROSS THE ATLANTIC AT A FRACTION OF THE SPEED OF THE FASTEST ROCKET...
I'M PICKING UP ANOTHER SIGNAL!
PARIS SÛRETÉ CALLING ALL PATROLS! MAINTAIN STRICT RADIO SILENCE FROM NOW ON--LEST NEWS OF WHAT IS HAPPENING ON THE EIFFEL TOWER LEAKS OUT-CAUSING CITY-WIDE PANIC!
A FINAL BURST OF SPEED BY THE WORLD'S FASTEST HUMAN AND...
WHEW--! THE TRAFFIC HERE IS WORSE THAN IN TIMES SQUARE!--WELL--THERE'S THE EIFFEL TOWER!
333RN
214-NR

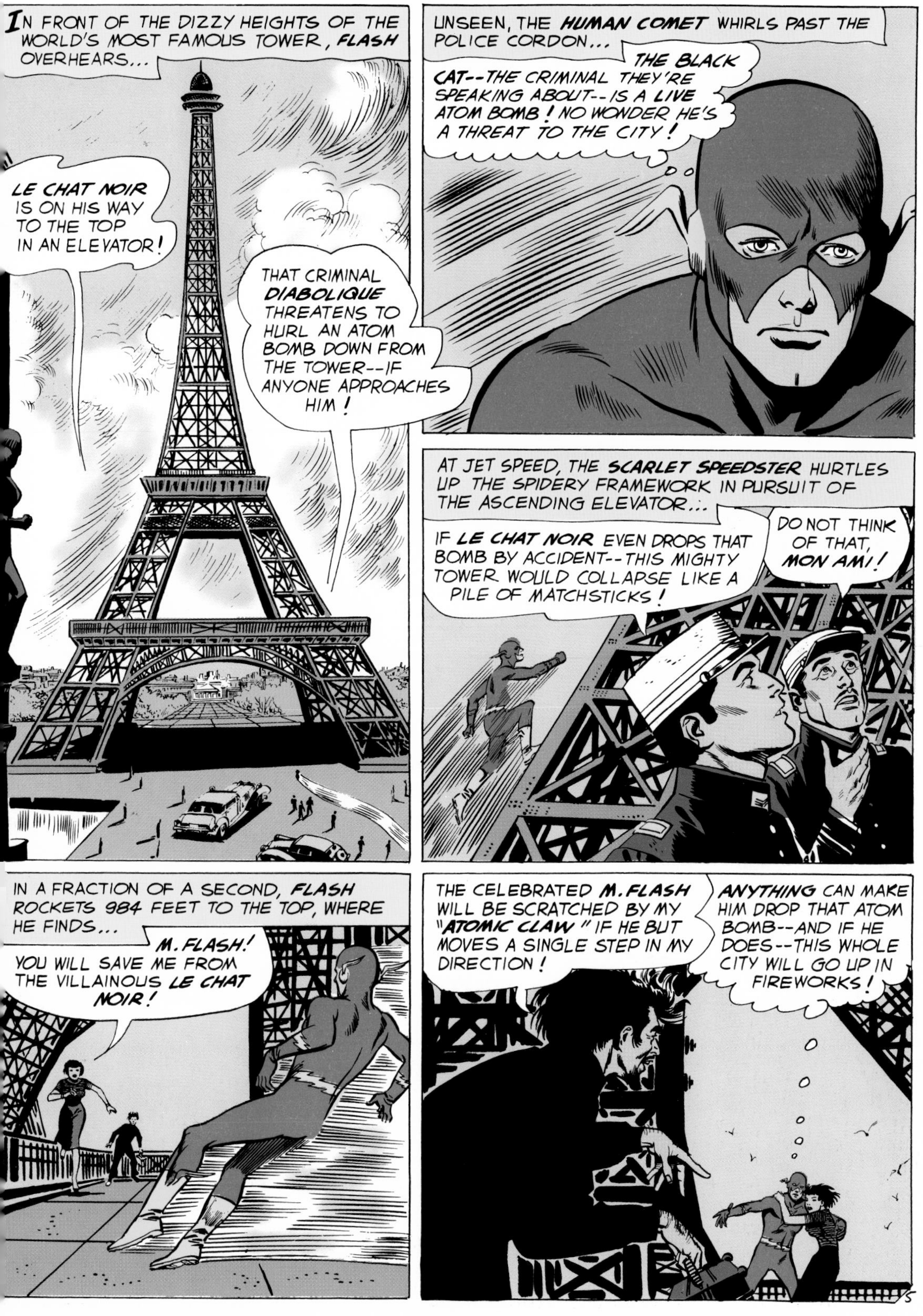
IN FRONT OF THE DIZZY HEIGHTS OF THE WORLD'S MOST FAMOUS TOWER, FLASH OVERHEARS...
LE CHAT NOIR IS ON HIS WAY TO THE TOP IN AN ELEVATOR!
THAT CRIMINAL DIABOLIQUE THREATENS TO HURL AN ATOM BOMB DOWN FROM THE TOWER--IF ANYONE APPROACHES HIM!
UNSEEN, THE HUMAN COMET WHIRLS PAST THE POLICE CORDON...
THE BLACK CAT--THE CRIMINAL THEY'RE SPEAKING ABOUT--IS A LIVE ATOM BOMB! NO WONDER HE'S A THREAT TO THE CITY!
AT JET SPEED, THE SCARLET SPEEDSTER HURTLES UP THE SPIDERY FRAMEWORK IN PURSUIT OF THE ASCENDING ELEVATOR...
IF LE CHAT NOIR EVEN DROPS THAT BOMB BY ACCIDENT--THIS MIGHTY TOWER WOULD COLLAPSE LIKE A PILE OF MATCHSTICKS!
DO NOT THINK OF THAT, MON AMI!
IN A FRACTION OF A SECOND, FLASH ROCKETS 984 FEET TO THE TOP, WHERE HE FINDS...
M. FLASH! YOU WILL SAVE ME FROM THE VILLAINOUS LE CHAT NOIR!
THE CELEBRATED M. FLASH WILL BE SCRATCHED BY MY "ATOMIC CLAW" IF HE BUT MOVES A SINGLE STEP IN MY DIRECTION!
ANYTHING CAN MAKE HIM DROP THAT ATOM BOMB--AND IF HE DOES--THIS WHOLE CITY WILL GO UP IN FIREWORKS!

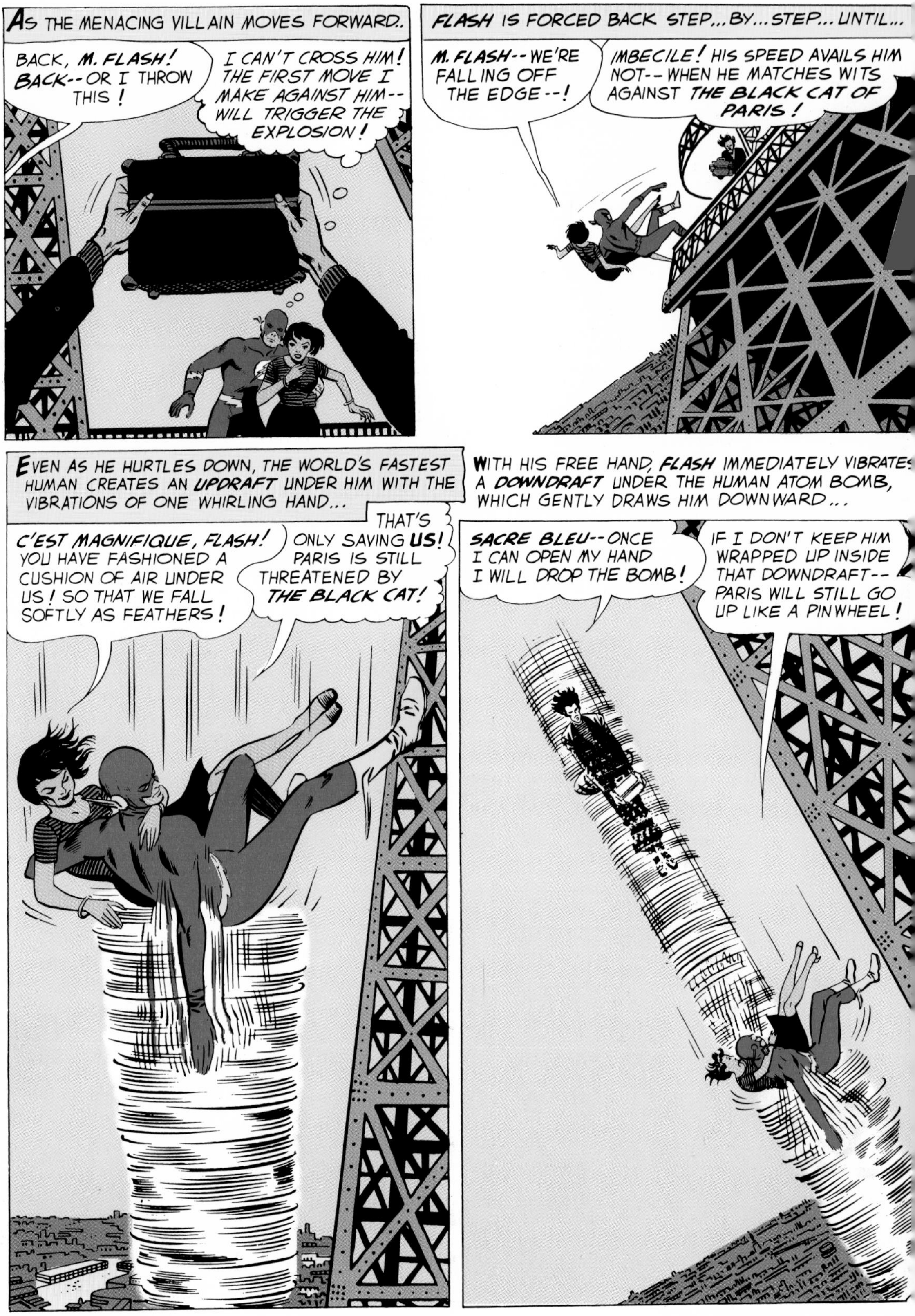
AS THE MENACING VILLAIN MOVES FORWARD.
BACK, M. FLASH! BACK--OR I THROW THIS!
I CAN'T CROSS HIM! THE FIRST MOVE I MAKE AGAINST HIM--WILL TRIGGER THE EXPLOSION!
FLASH IS FORCED BACK STEP... BY... STEP... UNTIL...
M. FLASH--WE'RE FALLING OFF THE EDGE--!
IMBECILE! HIS SPEED AVAILS HIM NOT--WHEN HE MATCHES WITS AGAINST THE BLACK CAT OF PARIS!
EVEN AS HE HURTLES DOWN, THE WORLD'S FASTEST HUMAN CREATES AN UPDRAFT UNDER HIM WITH THE VIBRATIONS OF ONE WHIRLING HAND...
C'EST MAGNIFIQUE, FLASH! YOU HAVE FASHIONED A CUSHION OF AIR UNDER US! SO THAT WE FALL SOFTLY AS FEATHERS!
THAT'S ONLY SAVING US! PARIS IS STILL THREATENED BY THE BLACK CAT!
WITH HIS FREE HAND, FLASH IMMEDIATELY VIBRATES A DOWNDRAFT UNDER THE HUMAN ATOM BOMB, WHICH GENTLY DRAWS HIM DOWNWARD...
SACRE BLEU--ONCE I CAN OPEN MY HAND I WILL DROP THE BOMB!
IF I DON'T KEEP HIM WRAPPED UP INSIDE THAT DOWNDRAFT--PARIS WILL STILL GO UP LIKE A PINWHEEL!

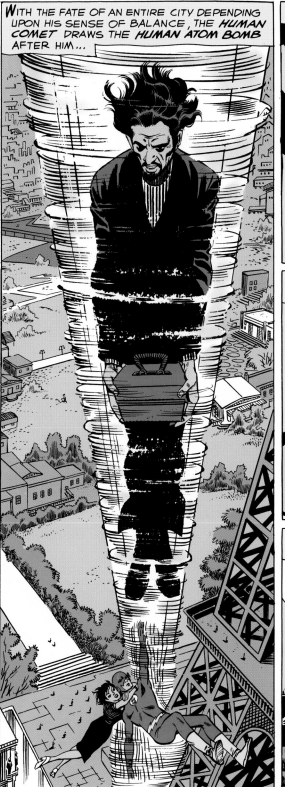

WITH THE FATE OF AN ENTIRE CITY DEPENDING UPON HIS SENSE OF BALANCE, THE *HUMAN COMET* DRAWS THE *HUMAN ATOM BOMB* AFTER HIM...

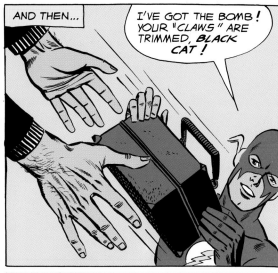

AND THEN...

I'VE GOT THE BOMB! YOUR "CLAWS" ARE TRIMMED, *BLACK CAT!*

AS THE CRIMINAL IS LED AWAY AND THE BOMB IS DISARMED...

M. FLASH -- ON BEHALF OF ALL PARIS -- I THANK YOU!

SUDDENLY, AS NEARBY *NOTRE DAME* TOLLS THE HOUR...

MY LUNCHEON DATE WITH IRIS -- CAN'T BE LATE AGAIN -- GOT TO BREEZE BACK ACROSS THE ATLANTIC!

BONG! BONG! BONG!

SUDDENLY, THE RADIO WATCH AGAIN PICKS UP A POLICE SIGNAL...

DESERT PATROL K-3 CALLING CAIRO POLICE H.Q.! HAVE TRAILED MISSING PRINCESS TARA TO KHUFU PYRAMID! WILL INVES--

AGAIN THE *WORLD'S FASTEST HUMAN* ROCKETS OFF...

THE MESSAGE WAS CUT OFF! THAT PATROL IS IN TROUBLE! I'VE GOT TO HELP THE PRINCESS!

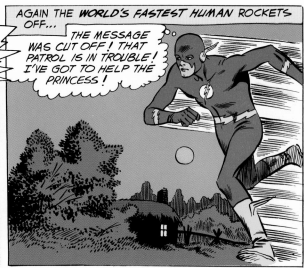

MOMENTS LATER, THE *SCARLET SPEEDSTER* WHIRLS TOWARD AN ANCIENT SPECTACLE...

HELP!

A CALL FOR HELP FROM ATOP THE PYRAMID! IT MUST BE COMING FROM THE PRINCESS!

AS *FLASH* REACHES THE BASE OF THE PYRAMID, HE STARTS TO RACE UP THE HUGE BLOCKS OF STONE...

IT IS *FLASH*! TREMBLE, *EL CLAW*! HE WILL SWEEP OVER YOU LIKE THE WIND OF THE DESERT!

EL FLASH DOES NOT KNOW THE SECRET WAY UP HERE, PRINCESS TARA! HE WILL SPEND THE REST OF HIS LIFE RUNNING IN THE SAME PLACE! YOU SHALL SEE!

AT THAT MOMENT, THE *WORLD'S FASTEST HUMAN* DISCOVERS TO HIS DISMAY THAT...

THE BLOCKS HAVE BEEN COATED WITH OIL!

THE FASTER I GO-- THE QUICKER I SLIP BACK!

I'M PRACTICALLY STANDING IN ONE SPOT!

ATOP THE PYRAMID, THE CUNNING BANDIT CHIEF LAUGHS AT *FLASH'S* DILEMMA...

YOUR CHAMPION IS AS HELPLESS AS A GOAT STUCK IN TAR, PRINCESS TARA! NOW, TELL ME WHERE YOU HID THE JEWELS YOU WERE TAKING TO BAGDAD!

NO--NO-- I WAS SELLING THEM FOR MONEY TO BE USED FOR A CHILDREN'S HOSPITAL IN OUR TOWN!

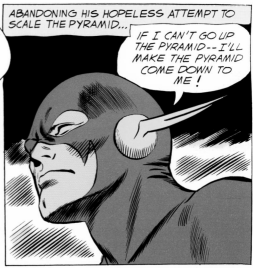

ABANDONING HIS HOPELESS ATTEMPT TO SCALE THE PYRAMID...

IF I CAN'T GO UP THE PYRAMID--I'LL MAKE THE PYRAMID COME DOWN TO ME!

WHIRLING AROUND THE PYRAMID AT INCREDIBLE SPEED, *FLASH'S* VIBRATIONS TUMBLE THE HUGE ROCKS FROM THEIR PLACES...

RRRUMBLE!

DEFTLY HE REACHES OUT...

YOU ARE SWIFTER THAN THE DESERT HAWK, *EL FLASH!*

NOT ONLY HAVE YOU SWEPT THE BANDITS OFF THEIR FEET, HANDSOME ONE-- BUT ME TOO!

BUT, THE *HUMAN COMET'S* JOB IS NOT FINISHED, FOR, AS HE RACES AROUND THE GIGANTIC HEAP OF BLOCKS...

AND WHAT TOOK YEARS TO BUILD-- HE ERECTS IN A FEW SECONDS!...

LEAVING THE BANDITS IN THE HANDS OF THE ARRIVING DESERT POLICE...

MUST YOU DEPART SO SOON, *FLASH* OF MY HEART?

SORRY, *PRINCESS!* I HAVE A LUNCHEON DATE IN *CENTRAL CITY!* I'VE GOT ABOUT FORTY MINUTES TO GET BACK ACROSS THE OCEAN AND...

SUDDENLY, *FLASH'S* WATCH BROADCASTS ANOTHER APPEAL...

LOOKOUT STATION AT MT. EVEREST CALLING! WE ARE IN THE PATH OF A GIGANTIC AVALANCHE! ALL IS LOST-- UNLESS--

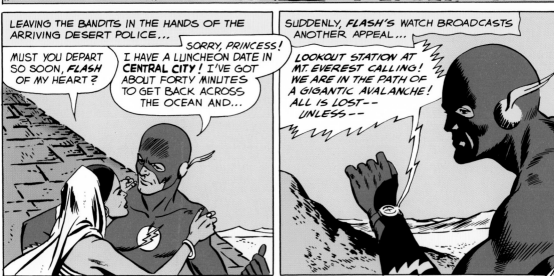

10

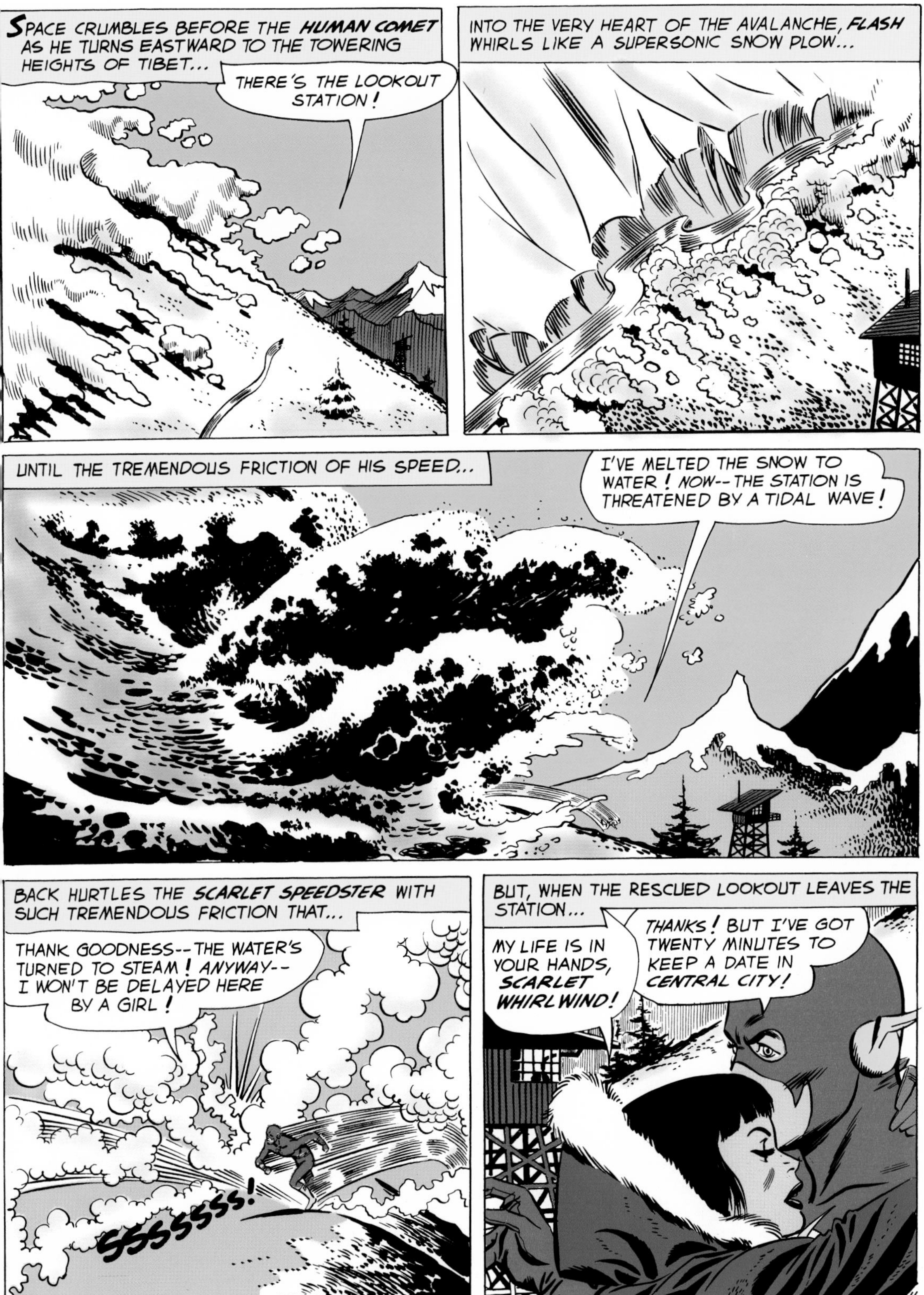
SPACE CRUMBLES BEFORE THE HUMAN COMET AS HE TURNS EASTWARD TO THE TOWERING HEIGHTS OF TIBET...
THERE'S THE LOOKOUT STATION!
INTO THE VERY HEART OF THE AVALANCHE, FLASH WHIRLS LIKE A SUPERSONIC SNOW PLOW...
UNTIL THE TREMENDOUS FRICTION OF HIS SPEED...
I'VE MELTED THE SNOW TO WATER! NOW--THE STATION IS THREATENED BY A TIDAL WAVE!
BACK HURTLES THE SCARLET SPEEDSTER WITH SUCH TREMENDOUS FRICTION THAT...
THANK GOODNESS--THE WATER'S TURNED TO STEAM! ANYWAY--I WON'T BE DELAYED HERE BY A GIRL!
SSSSSSS!
BUT, WHEN THE RESCUED LOOKOUT LEAVES THE STATION...
MY LIFE IS IN YOUR HANDS, SCARLET WHIRLWIND!
THANKS! BUT I'VE GOT TWENTY MINUTES TO KEEP A DATE IN CENTRAL CITY!
11

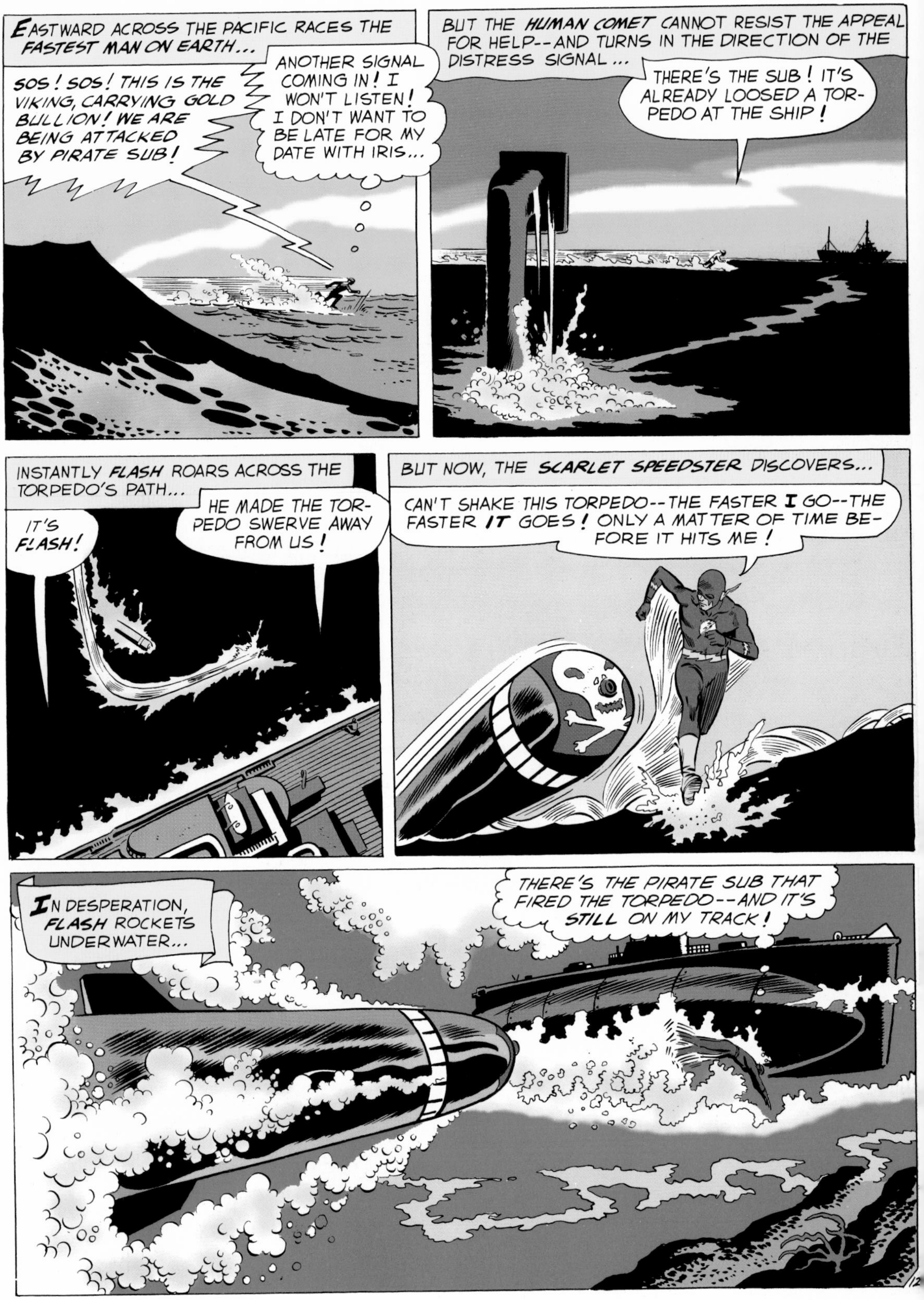

EASTWARD ACROSS THE PACIFIC RACES THE FASTEST MAN ON EARTH...
SOS! SOS! THIS IS THE VIKING, CARRYING GOLD BULLION! WE ARE BEING ATTACKED BY PIRATE SUB!
ANOTHER SIGNAL COMING IN! I WON'T LISTEN! I DON'T WANT TO BE LATE FOR MY DATE WITH IRIS...
BUT THE HUMAN COMET CANNOT RESIST THE APPEAL FOR HELP--AND TURNS IN THE DIRECTION OF THE DISTRESS SIGNAL...
THERE'S THE SUB! IT'S ALREADY LOOSED A TORPEDO AT THE SHIP!
INSTANTLY FLASH ROARS ACROSS THE TORPEDO'S PATH...
IT'S FLASH!
HE MADE THE TORPEDO SWERVE AWAY FROM US!
BUT NOW, THE SCARLET SPEEDSTER DISCOVERS...
CAN'T SHAKE THIS TORPEDO--THE FASTER I GO--THE FASTER IT GOES! ONLY A MATTER OF TIME BEFORE IT HITS ME!
IN DESPERATION, FLASH ROCKETS UNDERWATER...
THERE'S THE PIRATE SUB THAT FIRED THE TORPEDO--AND IT'S STILL ON MY TRACK!

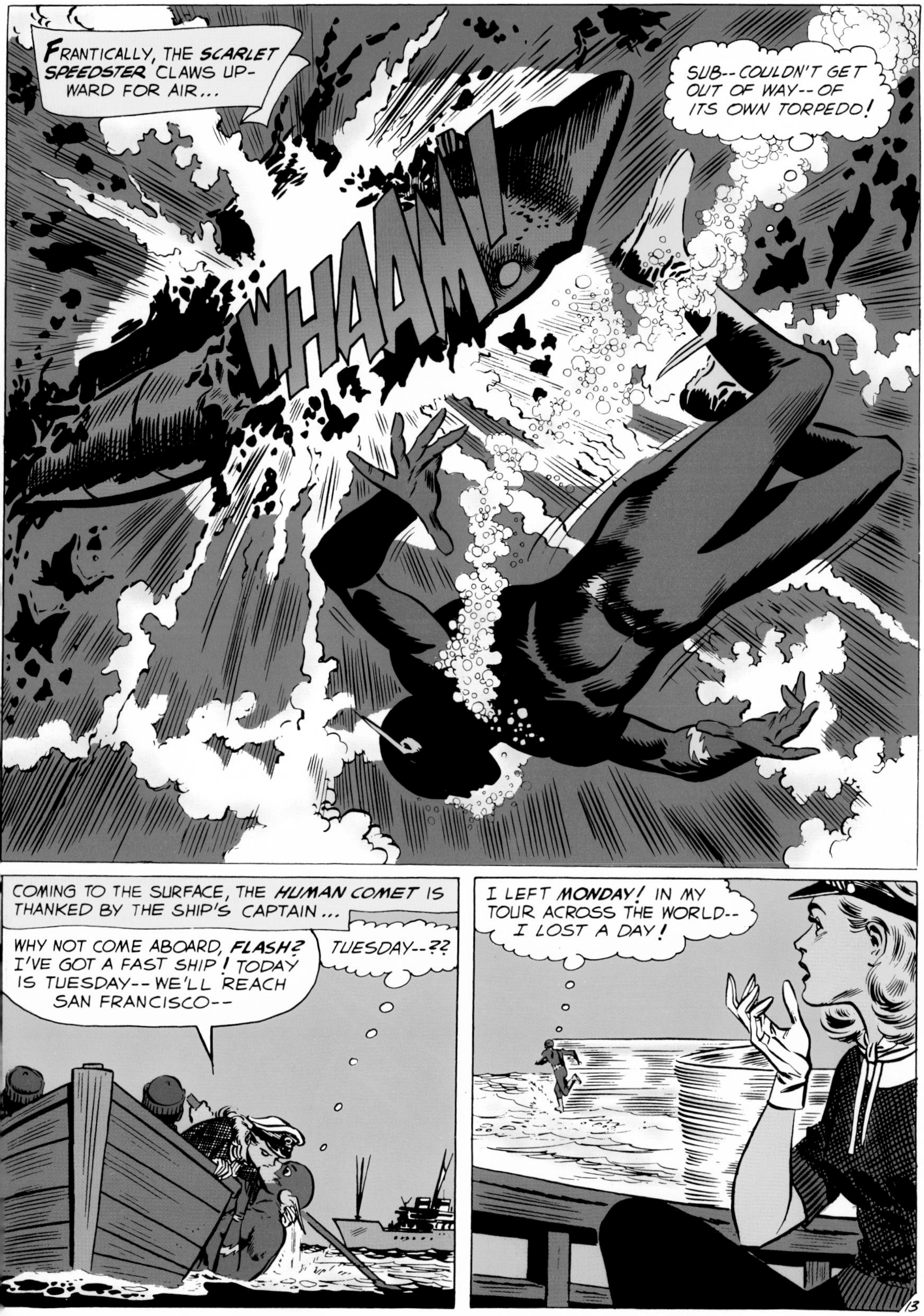
FRANTICALLY, THE SCARLET SPEEDSTER CLAWS UPWARD FOR AIR...
SUB--COULDN'T GET OUT OF WAY--OF ITS OWN TORPEDO!
WHAAM!
COMING TO THE SURFACE, THE HUMAN COMET IS THANKED BY THE SHIP'S CAPTAIN...
WHY NOT COME ABOARD, FLASH? I'VE GOT A FAST SHIP! TODAY IS TUESDAY--WE'LL REACH SAN FRANCISCO--
TUESDAY--??
I LEFT MONDAY! IN MY TOUR ACROSS THE WORLD--I LOST A DAY!
13

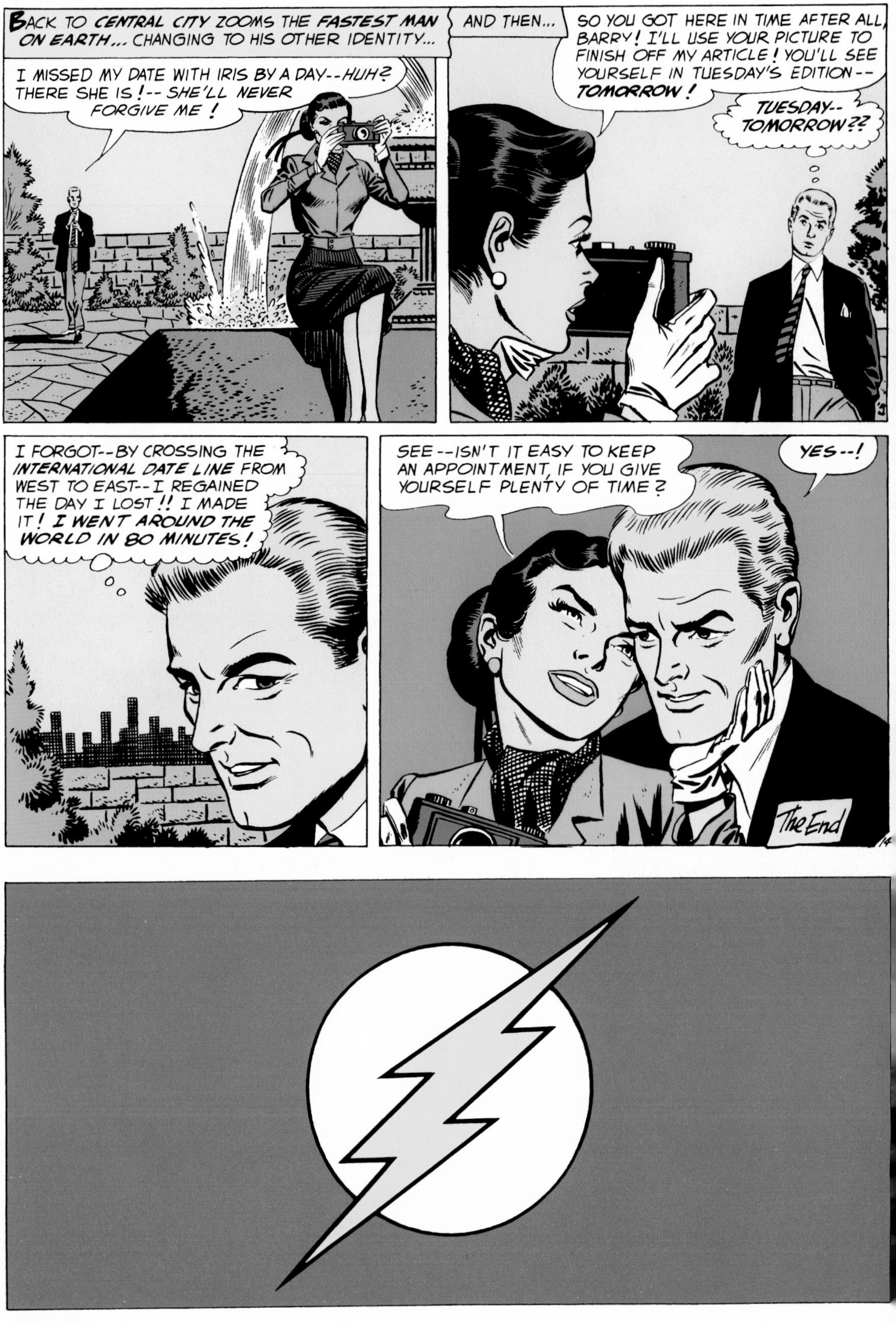
BACK TO CENTRAL CITY ZOOMS THE FASTEST MAN ON EARTH... CHANGING TO HIS OTHER IDENTITY...
I MISSED MY DATE WITH IRIS BY A DAY--HUH? THERE SHE IS!-- SHE'LL NEVER FORGIVE ME!
AND THEN...
SO YOU GOT HERE IN TIME AFTER ALL, BARRY! I'LL USE YOUR PICTURE TO FINISH OFF MY ARTICLE! YOU'LL SEE YOURSELF IN TUESDAY'S EDITION-- TOMORROW!
TUESDAY-- TOMORROW??
I FORGOT--BY CROSSING THE INTERNATIONAL DATE LINE FROM WEST TO EAST--I REGAINED THE DAY I LOST!! I MADE IT! I WENT AROUND THE WORLD IN 80 MINUTES!
SEE--ISN'T IT EASY TO KEEP AN APPOINTMENT, IF YOU GIVE YOURSELF PLENTY OF TIME?
YES--!
The End
14

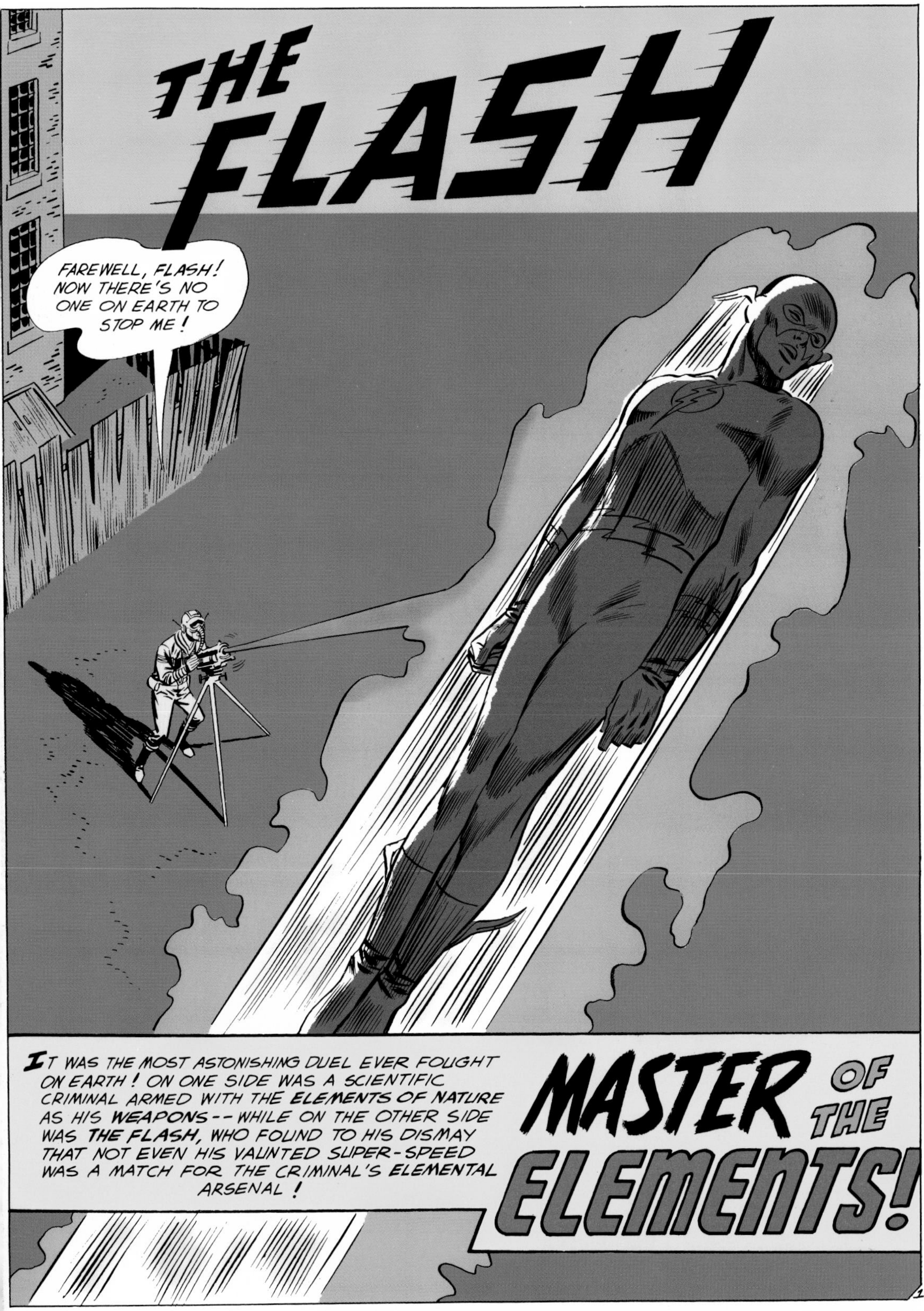
THE FLASH
FAREWELL, FLASH! NOW THERE'S NO ONE ON EARTH TO STOP ME!
IT WAS THE MOST ASTONISHING DUEL EVER FOUGHT ON EARTH! ON ONE SIDE WAS A SCIENTIFIC CRIMINAL ARMED WITH THE ELEMENTS OF NATURE AS HIS WEAPONS -- WHILE ON THE OTHER SIDE WAS THE FLASH, WHO FOUND TO HIS DISMAY THAT NOT EVEN HIS VAUNTED SUPER-SPEED WAS A MATCH FOR THE CRIMINAL'S ELEMENTAL ARSENAL!
MASTER OF THE ELEMENTS!
1

IN THE FASHIONABLE *PALLADIUM JEWELRY STORE* IN CENTRAL CITY, CLERKS AND CUSTOMERS ALIKE STARE AGHAST...

W-WHAT IS IT?

WHO IS IT?

INTO THE EXCLUSIVE SHOP A FANTASTIC FIGURE HAS STEPPED...

YOU ARE ABOUT TO WITNESS A MOMENTOUS EVENT-- THE INITIAL ROBBERY OF *MR. ELEMENT!* I DELIBERATELY CHOSE AS MY VICTIM A PLACE NAMED FOR ONE OF MY FAVORITE ELEMENTS--*PALLADIUM!*

ARGON, RADON--KEEP THEM COVERED--WHILE I PROCEED TO AMASS OUR GLITTERING LOOT!

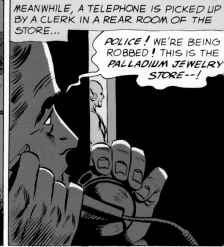

MEANWHILE, A TELEPHONE IS PICKED UP BY A CLERK IN A REAR ROOM OF THE STORE...

POLICE! WE'RE BEING ROBBED! THIS IS THE *PALLADIUM JEWELRY STORE*--!

AND NOT FAR AWAY, BARRY ALLEN, POLICE LABORATORY SCIENTIST, GOES TO MEET HIS DATE, REPORTER IRIS WEST...

THERE'S BARRY-- LATE AGAIN! HE'S THE SLOWEST THING ON TWO FEET!

I'M LATE, BUT I CAN'T PUT ON A BURST OF SPEED NOW, OR IRIS WOULD GUESS I'M *THE FLASH!* EH?

...ROBBERY AT THE PALLADIUM *JEWELRY STORE!* PROCEED AT ONCE--!

...STRANGELY-GARBED GANG...

THAT SOUNDS LIKE A JOB FOR *THE FLASH!* BUT HOW CAN THE *FLASH* APPEAR-- WHILE IRIS IS WATCHING ME?

A ROBBERY AT THE *PALLADIUM!* I'VE GOT TO GET OVER THERE AND COVER IT FOR MY PAPER! COME ON, BARRY! FOR ONCE IN YOUR LIFE-- *HURRY UP!*

UH--ALL RIGHT, IRIS!

BUT AS THE *"SLOW AND LAZY"* SCIENTIST LAGS BEHIND...

THIS COULD MEAN A SCOOP FOR *PICTURE NEWS!*

I'VE *GOT* TO CHANGE TO MY *FLASH* UNIFORM AND GET GOING! AND I THINK I KNOW HOW TO DO IT WITHOUT AROUSING IRIS'S SUS- PICIONS...

IN A TWINKLING, BARRY SETS UP A SMALL WHIRLWIND BY RAPIDLY CIRCLING...

THE DUST OF THE CITY WHIRLED AT SUPER-SPEED MAKES A CONVENIENT SCREEN! IT'LL LAST JUST LONG ENOUGH FOR MY PURPOSE--

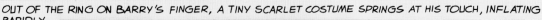

OUT OF THE RING ON BARRY'S FINGER, A TINY SCARLET COSTUME SPRINGS AT HIS TOUCH, INFLATING RAPIDLY...

3

THEN, A SPLIT-INSTANT LATER...

ODD HOW THAT WIND CAME UP WHEN IT WAS SO STILL...! GOSH! WHERE'S BARRY? I GUESS I WENT TOO FAST FOR THAT SLOWPOKE--!

SOON, AT THE *PALLADIUM*...

MR. ELEMENT! LOOK-- IT'S *THE FLASH!*

WHAT DELAYED YOU, *FLASH?* I'VE BEEN EXPECTING YOU!

BUT THEN, AS THE *SCARLET SPEEDSTER* ATTEMPTS TO REACH HIS TANTALIZING NEW FOE, A MYSTERIOUS FORCE RESTRAINS HIM...

YOU'VE NEGLECTED *ONE ELEMENT* IN YOUR CALCULATIONS, *FLASH!* FAREWELL!

WHAT'S HOLDING ME BACK? I CAN'T MOVE--YET THERE DOESN'T SEEM TO BE ANYTHING HERE--!

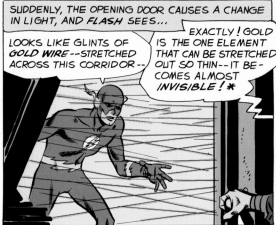

SUDDENLY, THE OPENING DOOR CAUSES A CHANGE IN LIGHT, AND *FLASH* SEES...

LOOKS LIKE GLINTS OF *GOLD WIRE*--STRETCHED ACROSS THIS CORRIDOR--

EXACTLY! GOLD IS THE ONE ELEMENT THAT CAN BE STRETCHED OUT SO THIN--IT BECOMES ALMOST *INVISIBLE!* *

*EDITOR'S NOTE: THIS QUALITY IS DUE TO THE SCIENTIFIC FACT THAT GOLD HAS THE GREATEST MALLEABILITY OF ALL ELEMENTS!

AND WHEN THE *FASTEST MAN ALIVE* AT LAST BURSTS THROUGH THE *GOLDEN BARRIER*...

GONE! MR. ELEMENT SEEMS TO HAVE BESTED ME THIS TIME! BUT I HAVE A STRONG HUNCH WE'LL MEET AGAIN *SOON!*

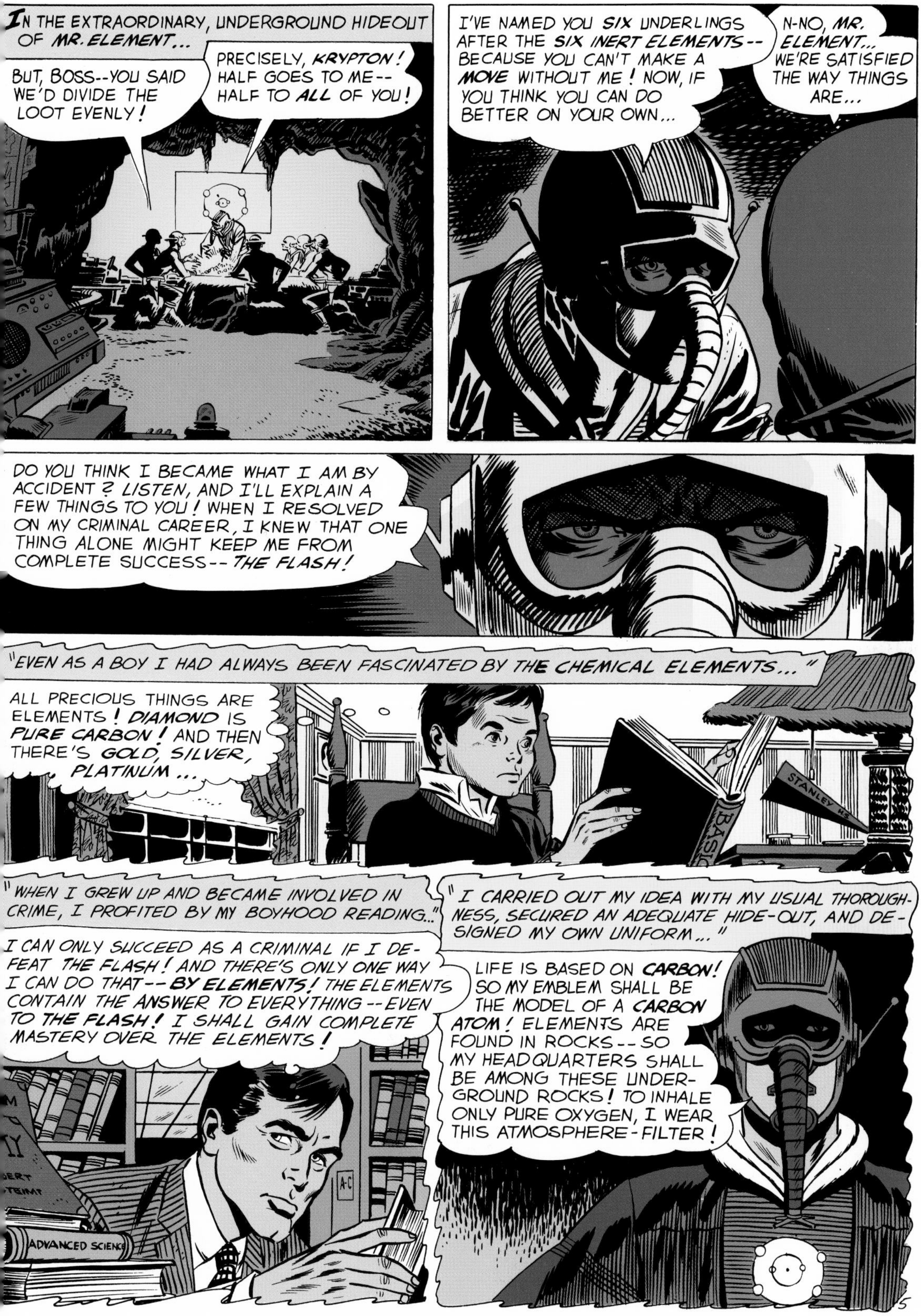
IN THE EXTRAORDINARY, UNDERGROUND HIDEOUT OF MR. ELEMENT...
BUT, BOSS--YOU SAID WE'D DIVIDE THE LOOT EVENLY!
PRECISELY, KRYPTON! HALF GOES TO ME--HALF TO ALL OF YOU!
I'VE NAMED YOU SIX UNDERLINGS AFTER THE SIX INERT ELEMENTS--BECAUSE YOU CAN'T MAKE A MOVE WITHOUT ME! NOW, IF YOU THINK YOU CAN DO BETTER ON YOUR OWN...
N-NO, MR. ELEMENT... WE'RE SATISFIED THE WAY THINGS ARE...
DO YOU THINK I BECAME WHAT I AM BY ACCIDENT? LISTEN, AND I'LL EXPLAIN A FEW THINGS TO YOU! WHEN I RESOLVED ON MY CRIMINAL CAREER, I KNEW THAT ONE THING ALONE MIGHT KEEP ME FROM COMPLETE SUCCESS--THE FLASH!
"EVEN AS A BOY I HAD ALWAYS BEEN FASCINATED BY THE CHEMICAL ELEMENTS..."
ALL PRECIOUS THINGS ARE ELEMENTS! DIAMOND IS PURE CARBON! AND THEN THERE'S GOLD, SILVER, PLATINUM...
STANLEY HS
BASIC
"WHEN I GREW UP AND BECAME INVOLVED IN CRIME, I PROFITED BY MY BOYHOOD READING..."
I CAN ONLY SUCCEED AS A CRIMINAL IF I DEFEAT THE FLASH! AND THERE'S ONLY ONE WAY I CAN DO THAT--BY ELEMENTS! THE ELEMENTS CONTAIN THE ANSWER TO EVERYTHING--EVEN TO THE FLASH! I SHALL GAIN COMPLETE MASTERY OVER THE ELEMENTS!
ADVANCED SCIENCE
A-C
"I CARRIED OUT MY IDEA WITH MY USUAL THOROUGHNESS, SECURED AN ADEQUATE HIDE-OUT, AND DESIGNED MY OWN UNIFORM..."
LIFE IS BASED ON CARBON! SO MY EMBLEM SHALL BE THE MODEL OF A CARBON ATOM! ELEMENTS ARE FOUND IN ROCKS--SO MY HEADQUARTERS SHALL BE AMONG THESE UNDERGROUND ROCKS! TO INHALE ONLY PURE OXYGEN, I WEAR THIS ATMOSPHERE-FILTER!
5

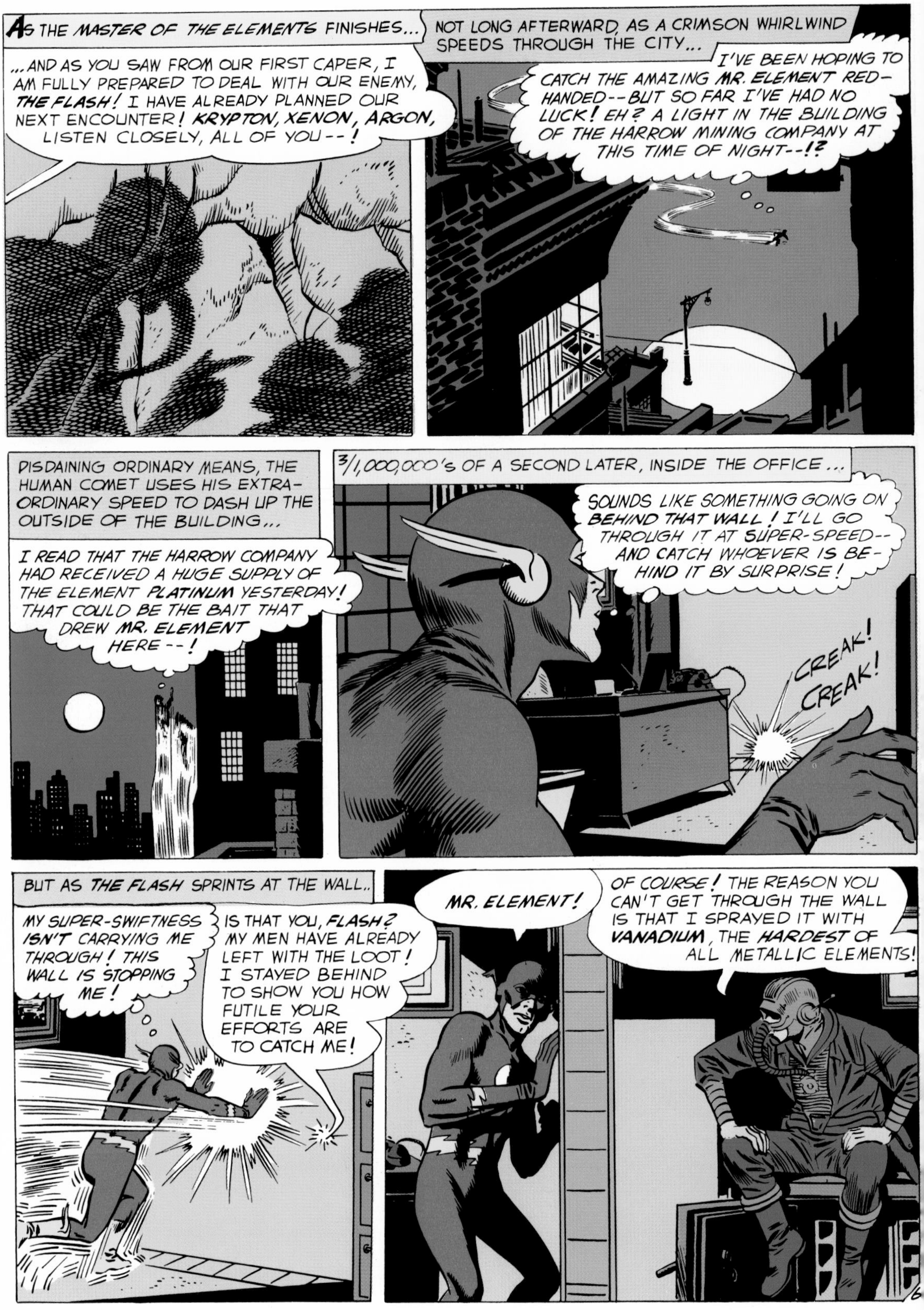
AS THE MASTER OF THE ELEMENTS FINISHES...
...AND AS YOU SAW FROM OUR FIRST CAPER, I AM FULLY PREPARED TO DEAL WITH OUR ENEMY, THE FLASH! I HAVE ALREADY PLANNED OUR NEXT ENCOUNTER! KRYPTON, XENON, ARGON, LISTEN CLOSELY, ALL OF YOU--!
NOT LONG AFTERWARD, AS A CRIMSON WHIRLWIND SPEEDS THROUGH THE CITY...
I'VE BEEN HOPING TO CATCH THE AMAZING MR. ELEMENT RED-HANDED--BUT SO FAR I'VE HAD NO LUCK! EH? A LIGHT IN THE BUILDING OF THE HARROW MINING COMPANY AT THIS TIME OF NIGHT--!?
DISDAINING ORDINARY MEANS, THE HUMAN COMET USES HIS EXTRA-ORDINARY SPEED TO DASH UP THE OUTSIDE OF THE BUILDING...
I READ THAT THE HARROW COMPANY HAD RECEIVED A HUGE SUPPLY OF THE ELEMENT PLATINUM YESTERDAY! THAT COULD BE THE BAIT THAT DREW MR. ELEMENT HERE--!
3/1,000,000'S OF A SECOND LATER, INSIDE THE OFFICE...
SOUNDS LIKE SOMETHING GOING ON BEHIND THAT WALL! I'LL GO THROUGH IT AT SUPER-SPEED--AND CATCH WHOEVER IS BE-HIND IT BY SURPRISE!
CREAK! CREAK!
BUT AS THE FLASH SPRINTS AT THE WALL...
MY SUPER-SWIFTNESS ISN'T CARRYING ME THROUGH! THIS WALL IS STOPPING ME!
IS THAT YOU, FLASH? MY MEN HAVE ALREADY LEFT WITH THE LOOT! I STAYED BEHIND TO SHOW YOU HOW FUTILE YOUR EFFORTS ARE TO CATCH ME!
MR. ELEMENT!
OF COURSE! THE REASON YOU CAN'T GET THROUGH THE WALL IS THAT I SPRAYED IT WITH VANADIUM, THE HARDEST OF ALL METALLIC ELEMENTS!
6

I'M LEAVING NOW, FLASH! SEE YOU AT MY NEXT JOB!

THERE MUST BE A WAY FOR ME TO GET AT HIM! WAIT--!

HEAT--INTENSE HEAT--CAN MELT ANY METAL! BY RAPIDLY RUBBING MY HEAT-PROOF GLOVE AGAINST THIS VANADIUM, THE HEAT RAISED BY THE FRICTION WILL MELT THE METAL!

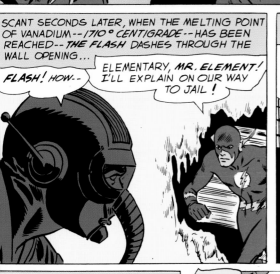

SCANT SECONDS LATER, WHEN THE MELTING POINT OF VANADIUM--1710° CENTIGRADE--HAS BEEN REACHED--THE FLASH DASHES THROUGH THE WALL OPENING...

FLASH! HOW--

ELEMENTARY, MR. ELEMENT! I'LL EXPLAIN ON OUR WAY TO JAIL!

AS THE SURPRISED CRIMINAL IS HUSTLED OFF TOWARD POLICE HEADQUARTERS...

AFTER I GET YOU BEHIND IRON BARS, MR. ELEMENT, I'M GOING AFTER YOUR HENCHMEN--AND PUT THEM WITH YOU!

YOU HAVEN'T GOT ME THERE YET, FLASH...

SUDDENLY, CROSSING CENTRAL RIVER BRIDGE...

EH? WHAT'S THAT YOU DROPPED--

WAIT A MOMENT, FLASH...AND I'LL EXPLAIN...

THEN...

UHH! EXPLOSION--!

OF COURSE! WHAT ELSE DID YOU EXPECT WHEN MY SPECIAL SODIUM PELLET HIT WATER? THE ELEMENT SODIUM EXPLODES IN CONTACT WITH WATER!

POW!

7

WHEN *THE FLASH* RECOVERS...

GONE! I HAD *MR. ELEMENT*-- AND HE SLIPPED THROUGH MY FINGERS!

AS THE DAYS GO BY, AND THE *MASTER OF ELEMENTS* SHOWS INCREASING DARING IN HIS FORAYS...

I WAS LUCKY THE OTHER NIGHT... SINCE THEN, WHATEVER SECTION OF TOWN I COVER, *MR. ELEMENT* MANAGES TO APPEAR SOME-WHERE ELSE!

MR. ELEMENT STRIKES AT BANK!

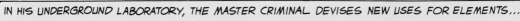

IN HIS UNDERGROUND LABORATORY, THE MASTER CRIMINAL DEVISES NEW USES FOR ELEMENTS...

MY SPECIAL LIQUID MAKES *IRON* RUST SO FAST--THAT I CAN STICK MY HAND RIGHT THROUGH THIS THICK SAFE!

THIS SPECIAL *MAGNESIUM* FLARE WILL PREVENT ANYONE FROM SEEING WHAT I'M DOING!

BULLETS BOUNCE OFF THIS SUPER-GLASS--MADE WITH THE ELEMENT *SILICON!* I'LL USE IT ON MY GETAWAY CAR!

BWEE!

BAM!

IN A RESTAURANT ONE EVENING, *IRIS WEST* FINALLY CORNERS *BARRY ALLEN...*

BARRY, WHAT IS THE MATTER WITH YOU LATELY? YOUR MIND SEEMS A MILLION MILES AWAY...

IT'S JUST SOMETHING I CAN'T TALK ABOUT--EH?

WHAT ARE YOU SO JUMPY ABOUT? IT'S JUST SOME FIREWORKS...

THEY'RE FORMING *LETTERS*--LIKE A *NEON* SIGN-- AN *ELEMENT* THAT MUST MEAN --

THEN AS THE ENTIRE CITY LOOKS UP, AN INCREDIBLE MESSAGE APPEARS IN THE SKY...

Flash When we meet again Tonight, it will be the last time For you! Mr. Element!

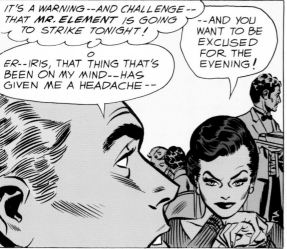

IT'S A WARNING--AND CHALLENGE-- THAT *MR. ELEMENT* IS GOING TO STRIKE TONIGHT!

--AND YOU WANT TO BE EXCUSED FOR THE EVENING!

ER--IRIS, THAT THING THAT'S BEEN ON MY MIND--HAS GIVEN ME A HEADACHE--

ALL RIGHT, TAKE ME HOME! I'LL GIVE YOU AN *IRON* TONIC...

UGH! SHE DOESN'T KNOW WHAT SHE'S SAYING! EVEN THE NAME OF AN ELEMENT--LIKE *IRON*-- MAKES ME WINCE!

AS THE *SCARLET SPEEDSTER* ONCE AGAIN SCOURS THE CITY FOR HIS FOE...

IT SHOULDN'T TAKE LONG TO FIND *MR. ELEMENT*--NOT AFTER HURLING THAT CHALLENGE AT ME!

SURE ENOUGH, FLASH SOON SPIES HIS QUARRY...

AH! THE CONTEST IS ABOUT TO *BEGIN*-- WITH EVERY ELEMENT STACKED IN MY FAVOR!

9

THEN, AS THE **WORLD'S FASTEST HUMAN** HURTLES TOWARD HIS ARCHENEMY...

UH? WHAT'S HAPPENING TO ME?

I'M USING AN ELEMENT OF **SPEED** TO DEFEAT YOU, **FLASH**...

I HAVE DISCOVERED THIS **NEW ELEMENT**-- THAT I CALL **ELEMENTO!** IT IS A FORM OF **MAGNETIC LIGHT**--

THE LIGHT BEAM'S HOLDING ME IN A MAGNETIC GRIP-- PROPELLING ME FASTER AND FASTER ...

THEN, AS **MR. ELEMENT** SHOOTS HIS **ELEMENTO** BEAM SKYWARD...

FAREWELL, **FLASH!** NOW THERE'S NO ONE ON EARTH TO STOP ME!

INTO SPACE SPEEDS THE HELPLESS **FLASH**...

STILL ACCELERATING! IF I ATTAIN **ESCAPE VELOCITY,** * I'LL **NEVER** BE ABLE TO GET BACK TO EARTH!

* Editor's Note-- **ESCAPE VELOCITY-- SEVEN MILES A SECOND-- IS THE SPEED NECESSARY FOR AN OBJECT TO BREAK LOOSE FROM THE GRAVITATIONAL PULL OF EARTH!**

I'M HEADING IN THE DIRECTION OF THE MOON! IF I HIT IT, IT'LL BE MY FINISH! IF I MISS IT, I'LL CONTINUE TRAVELING THROUGH SPACE FOREVER!

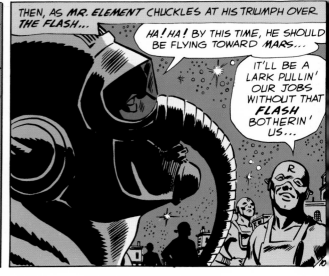

THEN, AS **MR. ELEMENT** CHUCKLES AT HIS TRIUMPH OVER THE **FLASH**...

HA! HA! BY THIS TIME, HE SHOULD BE FLYING TOWARD **MARS**...

IT'LL BE A LARK PULLIN' OUR JOBS WITHOUT THAT **FLASH** BOTHERIN' US...

SUDDENLY, FROM OUT OF SPACE...

BOSS-- LOOK!

F-FLASH!?

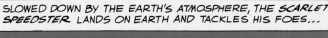

SLOWED DOWN BY THE EARTH'S ATMOSPHERE, THE *SCARLET SPEEDSTER* LANDS ON EARTH AND TACKLES HIS FOES...

AS THE DISGRUNTLED *MASTER OF THE ELEMENTS* AND HIS MINIONS ARE RENDERED UNARMED AND HELPLESS...

FLASH, YOU HAVE DEFEATED ME! BUT TELL ME-- *HOW* DID YOU MANAGE TO AVOID DISASTER IN SPACE?

AS I HURTLED OFF THE EARTH, I REALIZED THAT THERE WERE *THREE* POSSIBLE THINGS THAT COULD HAPPEN TO ME...

"FIRST--I COULD HAVE A FATAL COLLISION WITH THE MOON..."

"THE SECOND POSSIBILITY WAS BYPASSING THE MOON AND TRAVELING FOREVER THROUGH SPACE..."

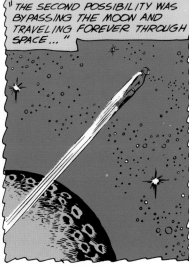

THAT WOULD HAVE MEANT MY FINISH TOO! BUT AS I SPED TOWARD THE MOON I REALIZED THAT THERE WAS *ANOTHER* POSSIBILITY! I MIGHT MAKE A *CURVE* AROUND THE MOON-- THE WAY A *COMET CIRCLES THE SUN!*

11

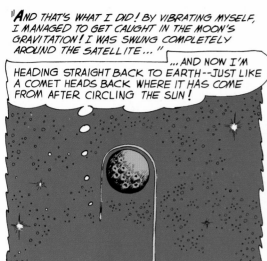

"*AND THAT'S WHAT I DID!* BY VIBRATING MYSELF, I MANAGED TO GET CAUGHT IN THE *MOON'S GRAVITATION!* I WAS SWUNG COMPLETELY AROUND THE SATELLITE..."

...AND NOW I'M HEADING STRAIGHT BACK TO EARTH--JUST LIKE A *COMET* HEADS BACK WHERE IT HAS COME FROM AFTER CIRCLING THE SUN!

OF COURSE, TRAVELING AT THE *SPEED OF LIGHT*, THIS ENTIRE OCCURRENCE LASTED LESS THAN A *MINUTE*-- AND BY HOLDING MY BREATH IN AIRLESS SPACE, I MANAGED TO *SURVIVE!* NOW, MR. ELEMENT-- OFF TO JAIL!

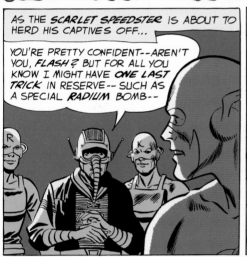

AS THE *SCARLET SPEEDSTER* IS ABOUT TO HERD HIS CAPTIVES OFF...

YOU'RE PRETTY CONFIDENT--AREN'T YOU, *FLASH?* BUT FOR ALL YOU KNOW I MIGHT HAVE *ONE LAST TRICK* IN RESERVE-- SUCH AS A SPECIAL *RADIUM BOMB*--

--WORKED BY THE HANDS OF--*EH?* MY WRISTWATCH--?!

LOOKING FOR THIS, *MR. ELE-MENT?* I NOTICED THE *PECULIAR GLOW* OF THIS DIAL, SO I REMOVED IT FROM YOUR WRIST AT SUPER-SPEED A FEW MOMENTS AGO!

NEXT EVENING, AS BARRY (*THE FLASH*) ALLEN VISITS IRIS...

WELL, THE CAPTURE OF *MR. ELEMENT* MADE A GOOD STORY FOR MY PAPER, BARRY! BUT I SURE WISH I KNEW HOW *THE FLASH* HANDLED AN AMAZING VILLAIN LIKE THAT! OF COURSE, A STICK-IN-THE-MUD LIKE YOU...

...WOULDN'T KNOW ANY-THING ABOUT THAT!

WELL, I GUESS THERE'S AN *ELEMENT* OF TRUTH IN WHAT YOU SAY, IRIS!

FLASH CAPTURES MR. ELEMENT!

RE·19-15   *The End*

DAILY PRESS

FLASH CAPTURES MR. ELEMENT!

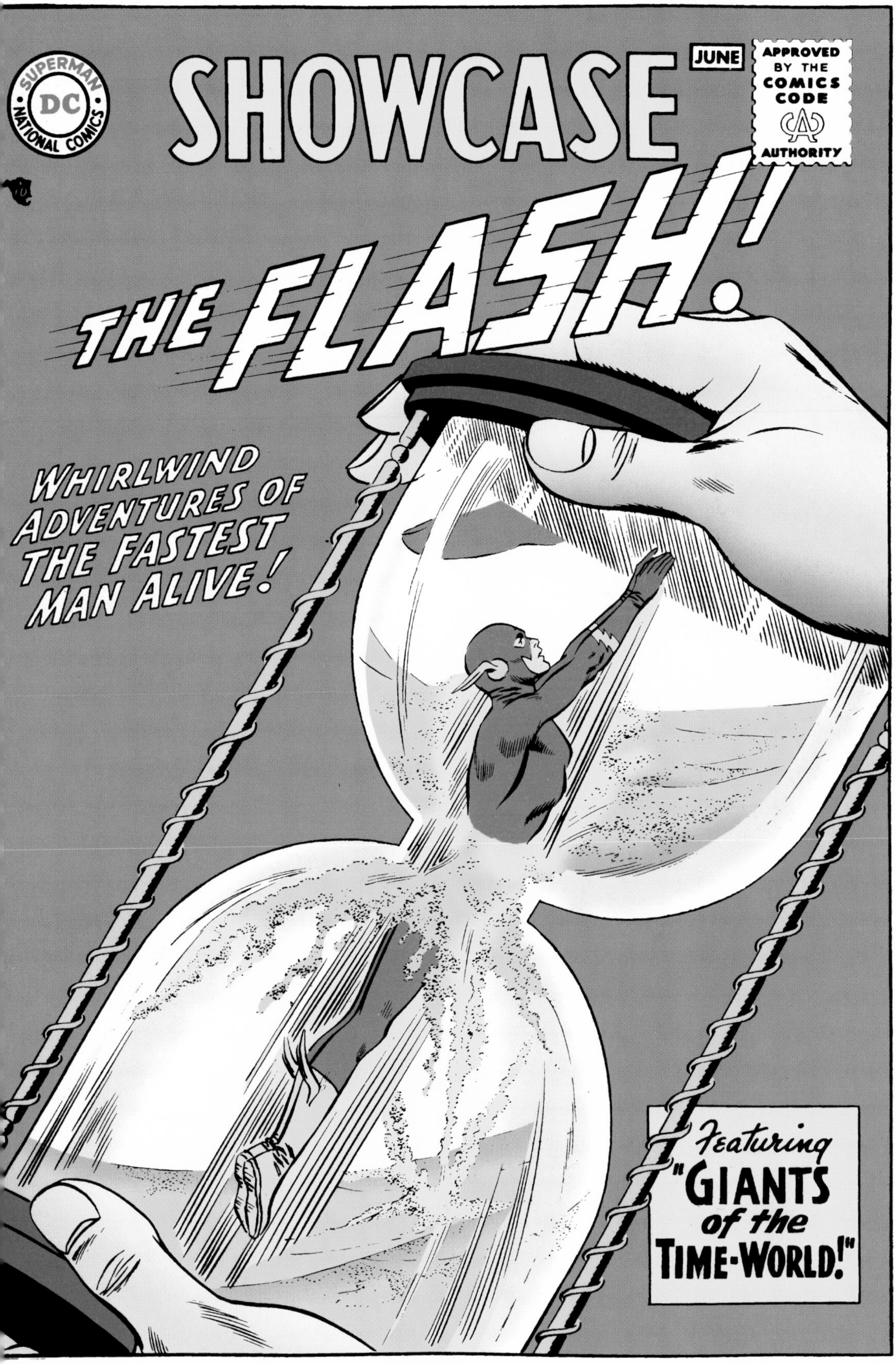
SUPERMAN DC NATIONAL COMICS
SHOWCASE
JUNE
APPROVED BY THE COMICS CODE AUTHORITY
THE FLASH!
WHIRLWIND ADVENTURES OF THE FASTEST MAN ALIVE!
Featuring "GIANTS of the TIME-WORLD!"

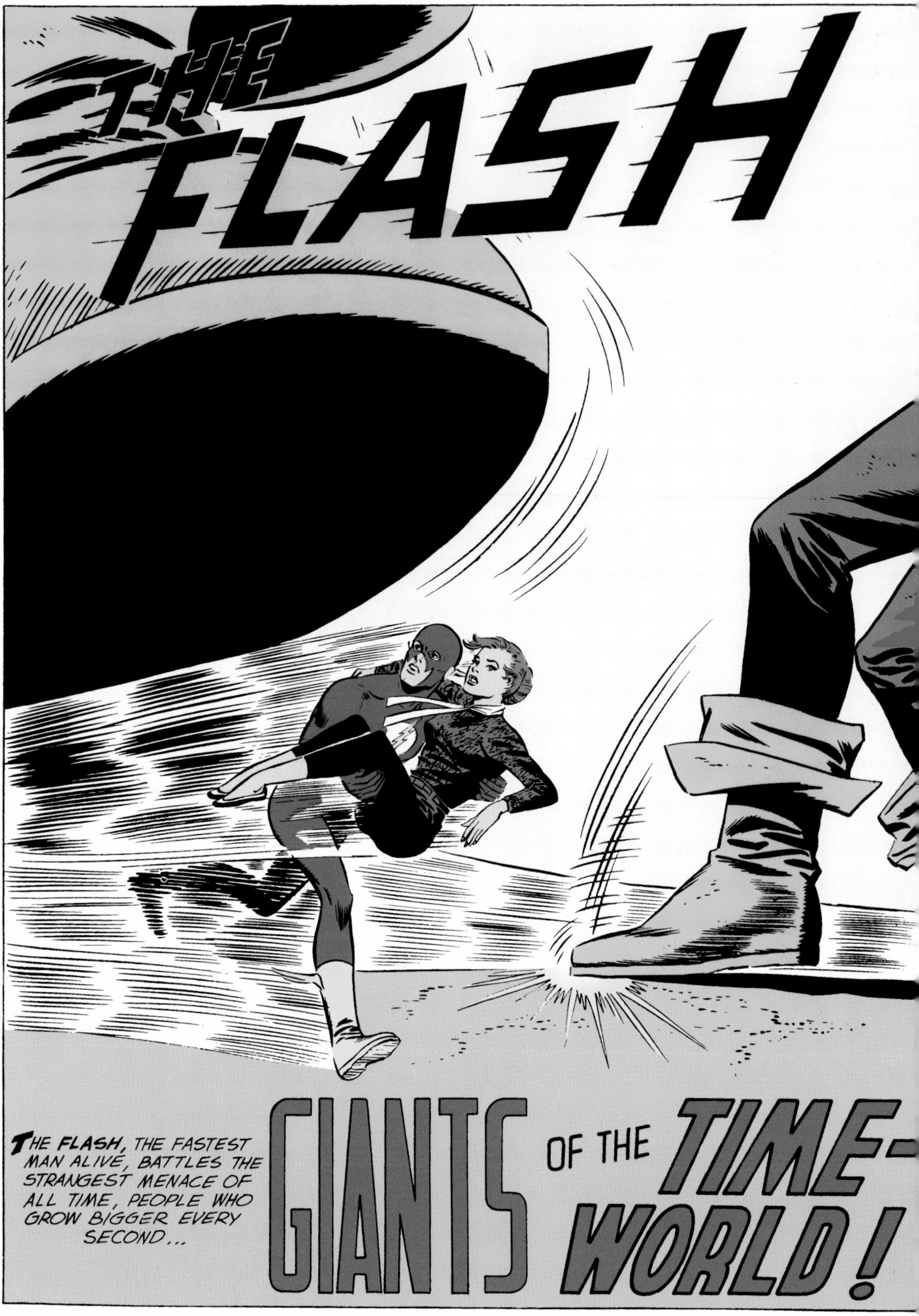
THE FLASH
THE FLASH, THE FASTEST MAN ALIVE, BATTLES THE STRANGEST MENACE OF ALL TIME, PEOPLE WHO GROW BIGGER EVERY SECOND...
GIANTS OF THE TIME-WORLD!

IN CENTRAL CITY, IRIS WEST, *PICTURE NEWS* PHOTOGRAPHER, IMPATIENTLY GREETS HER BOY FRIEND...

BARRY ALLEN! YOU MOVE SO SLOWLY-- I DOUBT WHETHER YOU'D WIN A RACE WITH A TURTLE! COME ON--YOU KNOW IT'S HARD TO GET A TABLE AT PARDY'S FROM ONE O'CLOCK ON!

I WONDER WHY I PUT UP WITH YOUR SLOWNESS, BARRY--WHEN THE MAN I ADMIRE MOST IS *THE FLASH*-- THE FASTEST MAN ALIVE!

JUST THEN...

GLASS OF WATER'S FALLING OFF THAT TRAY!

WITH A SPEED UNDETECTABLE TO ANY HUMAN EYE, THE POLICE SCIENTIST'S HAND HURTLES OUT...

VOOOSH!

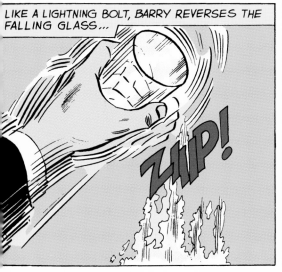

LIKE A LIGHTNING BOLT, BARRY REVERSES THE FALLING GLASS...

ZIIP!

AND CATCHES THE FALLING WATER BEFORE IT REACHES THE FLOOR...

VROOOOOOOSH!

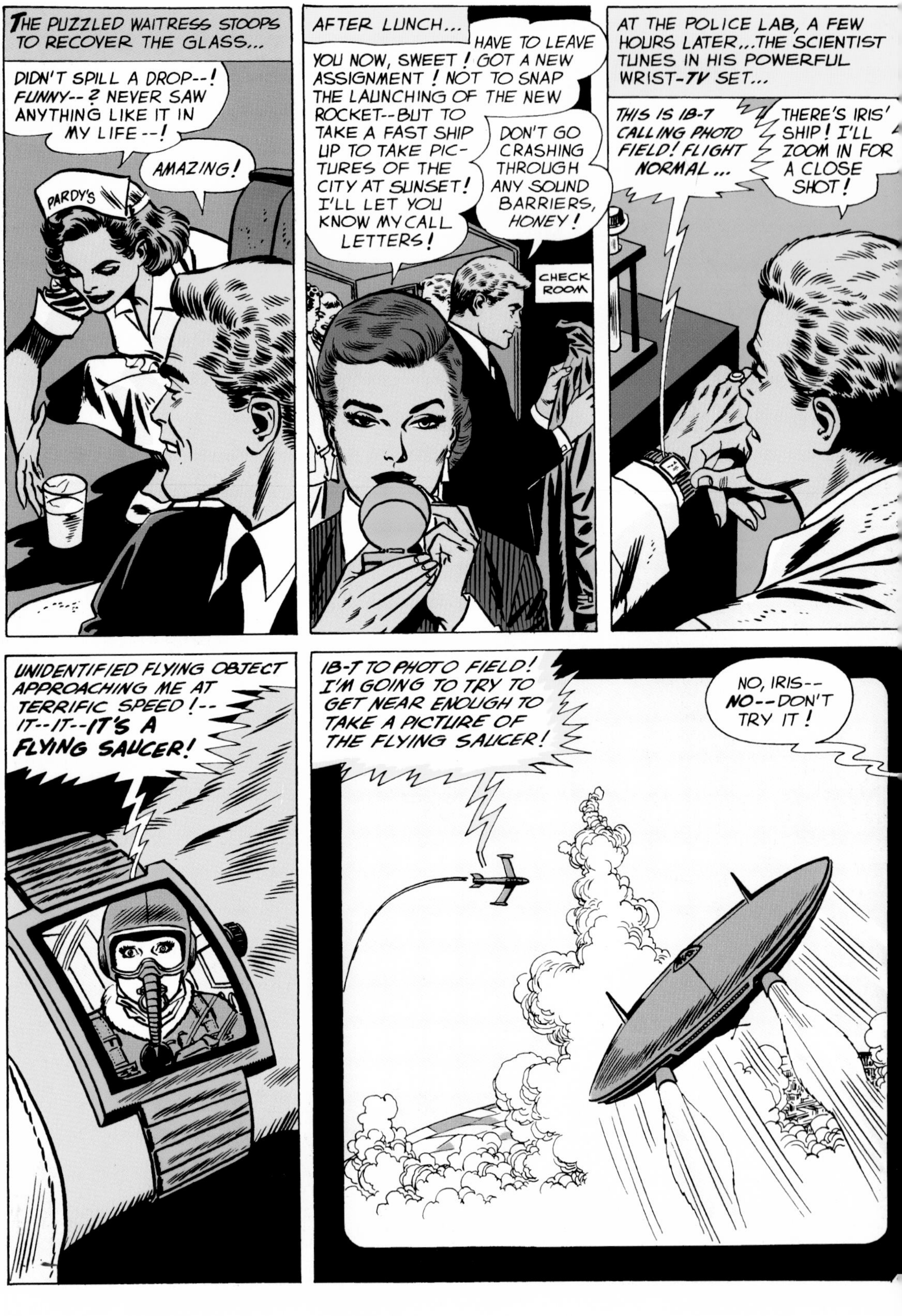
THE PUZZLED WAITRESS STOOPS TO RECOVER THE GLASS...
DIDN'T SPILL A DROP--! FUNNY--? NEVER SAW ANYTHING LIKE IT IN MY LIFE--!
AMAZING!
PARDY'S
AFTER LUNCH...
HAVE TO LEAVE YOU NOW, SWEET! GOT A NEW ASSIGNMENT! NOT TO SNAP THE LAUNCHING OF THE NEW ROCKET--BUT TO TAKE A FAST SHIP UP TO TAKE PICTURES OF THE CITY AT SUNSET! I'LL LET YOU KNOW MY CALL LETTERS!
DON'T GO CRASHING THROUGH ANY SOUND BARRIERS, HONEY!
CHECK ROOM
AT THE POLICE LAB, A FEW HOURS LATER...THE SCIENTIST TUNES IN HIS POWERFUL WRIST-TV SET...
THIS IS IB-7 CALLING PHOTO FIELD! FLIGHT NORMAL...
THERE'S IRIS' SHIP! I'LL ZOOM IN FOR A CLOSE SHOT!
UNIDENTIFIED FLYING OBJECT APPROACHING ME AT TERRIFIC SPEED!--IT--IT--IT'S A FLYING SAUCER!
IB-7 TO PHOTO FIELD! I'M GOING TO TRY TO GET NEAR ENOUGH TO TAKE A PICTURE OF THE FLYING SAUCER!
NO, IRIS--NO--DON'T TRY IT!

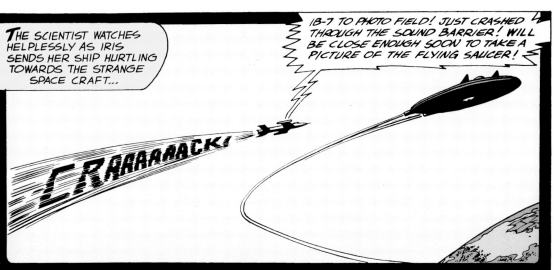

THE SCIENTIST WATCHES HELPLESSLY AS IRIS SENDS HER SHIP HURTLING TOWARDS THE STRANGE SPACE CRAFT...

1B-7 TO PHOTO FIELD! JUST CRASHED THROUGH THE SOUND BARRIER! WILL BE CLOSE ENOUGH SOON TO TAKE A PICTURE OF THE FLYING SAUCER!

CRRAAAAACK!

WHEN YOU HEAR THE CLICK OF THE SHUTTER--LITTLE IRIS WEST WILL GET THE PICTURE OF THE CENTURY!

AT THAT MOMENT... A BLAZE OF LIGHT ERUPTS AROUND THE DARING PHOTOGRAPHER'S PLANE AND...

POOOOF!

IN BARRY'S LAB...

SHE'S GONE--*SHE'S GONE*! BUT-- THAT SAUCER'S STILL UP THERE! GOT TO TRY TO GET TO HER IN TIME!

THE SCIENTIST SNAPS THE SPRING LOCK ON HIS RING, AND A FAMOUS SCARLET COSTUME STARTS EXPANDING IN THE INFLATING OXYGEN...

ONLY ONE MAN IN THE WORLD FAST ENOUGH TO MAKE THE ATTEMPT--*THE FLASH!*

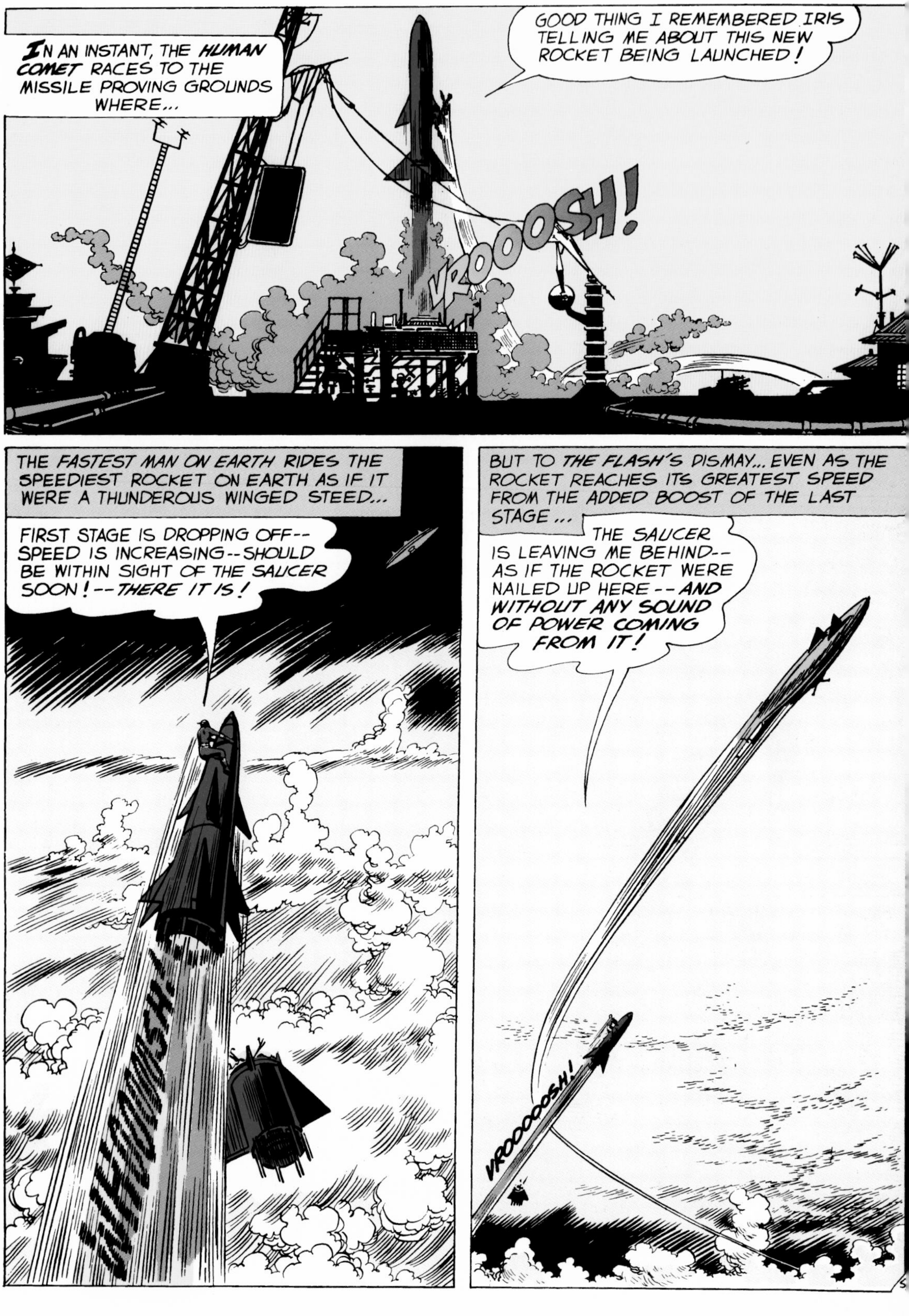
IN AN INSTANT, THE HUMAN COMET RACES TO THE MISSILE PROVING GROUNDS WHERE...
GOOD THING I REMEMBERED IRIS TELLING ME ABOUT THIS NEW ROCKET BEING LAUNCHED!
VROOOOSH!
THE FASTEST MAN ON EARTH RIDES THE SPEEDIEST ROCKET ON EARTH AS IF IT WERE A THUNDEROUS WINGED STEED...
FIRST STAGE IS DROPPING OFF-- SPEED IS INCREASING--SHOULD BE WITHIN SIGHT OF THE SAUCER SOON!--THERE IT IS!
BUT TO THE FLASH'S DISMAY... EVEN AS THE ROCKET REACHES ITS GREATEST SPEED FROM THE ADDED BOOST OF THE LAST STAGE...
THE SAUCER IS LEAVING ME BEHIND-- AS IF THE ROCKET WERE NAILED UP HERE--AND WITHOUT ANY SOUND OF POWER COMING FROM IT!

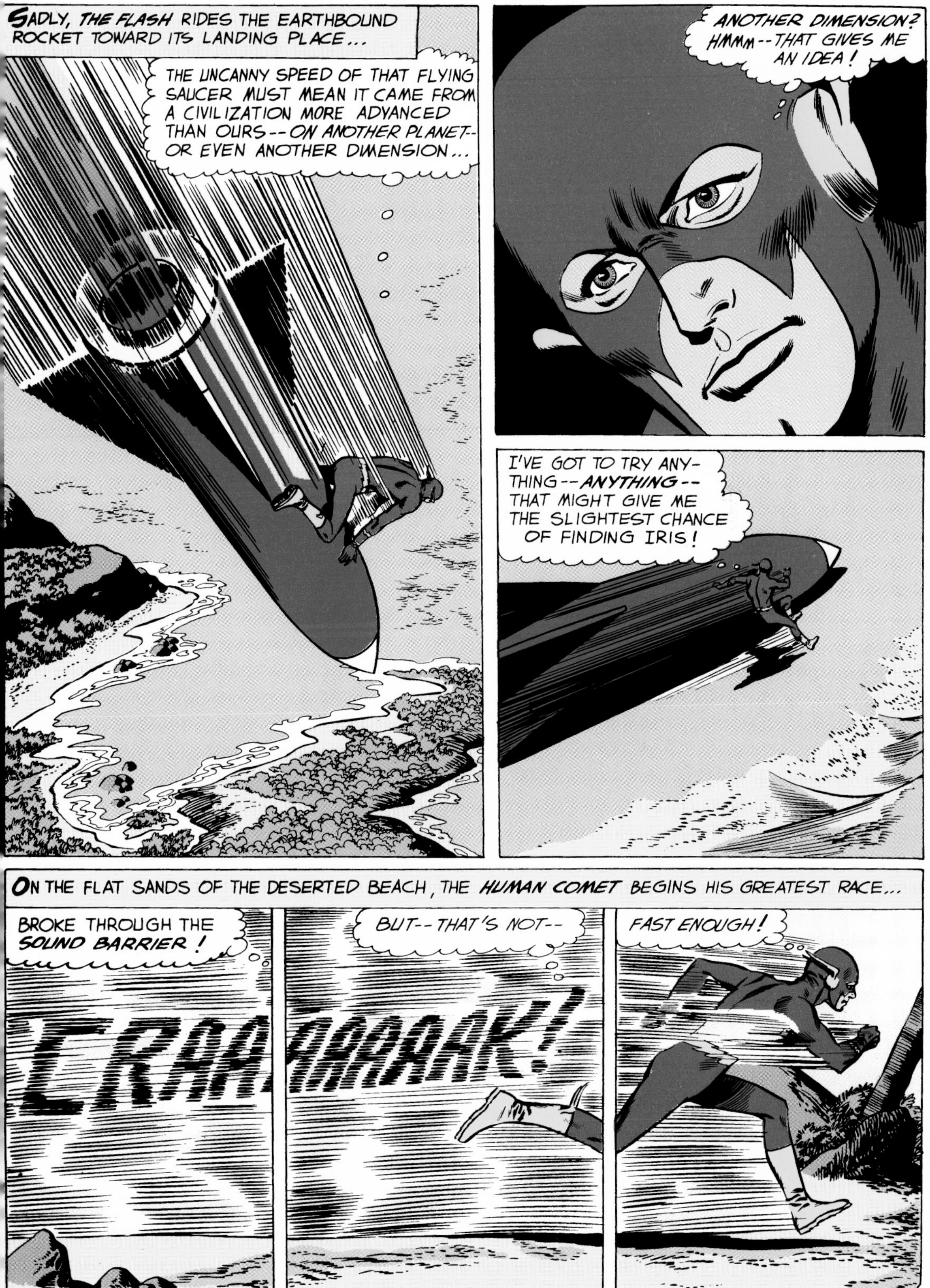
SADLY, THE FLASH RIDES THE EARTHBOUND ROCKET TOWARD ITS LANDING PLACE...
THE UNCANNY SPEED OF THAT FLYING SAUCER MUST MEAN IT CAME FROM A CIVILIZATION MORE ADVANCED THAN OURS--ON ANOTHER PLANET--OR EVEN ANOTHER DIMENSION...
ANOTHER DIMENSION? HMMM--THAT GIVES ME AN IDEA!
I'VE GOT TO TRY ANYTHING--ANYTHING--THAT MIGHT GIVE ME THE SLIGHTEST CHANCE OF FINDING IRIS!
ON THE FLAT SANDS OF THE DESERTED BEACH, THE HUMAN COMET BEGINS HIS GREATEST RACE...
BROKE THROUGH THE SOUND BARRIER!
CRAAAARRAAK!
BUT--THAT'S NOT--
FAST ENOUGH!
6

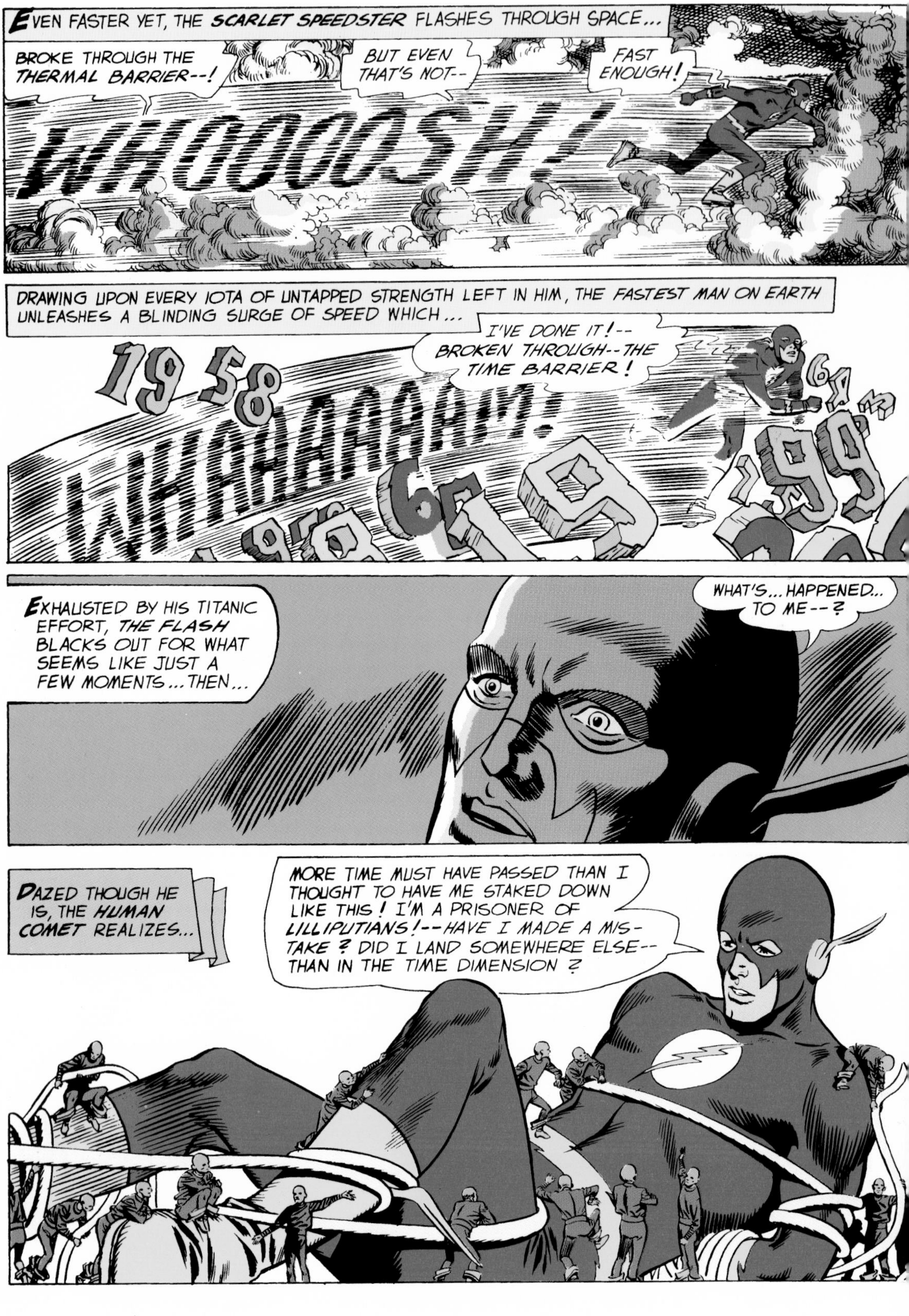
EVEN FASTER YET, THE SCARLET SPEEDSTER FLASHES THROUGH SPACE...
BROKE THROUGH THE THERMAL BARRIER--!
BUT EVEN THAT'S NOT--
FAST ENOUGH!
WHOOOOSH!
DRAWING UPON EVERY IOTA OF UNTAPPED STRENGTH LEFT IN HIM, THE FASTEST MAN ON EARTH UNLEASHES A BLINDING SURGE OF SPEED WHICH...
I'VE DONE IT!-- BROKEN THROUGH--THE TIME BARRIER!
1958
WHAAAAAAM!
EXHAUSTED BY HIS TITANIC EFFORT, THE FLASH BLACKS OUT FOR WHAT SEEMS LIKE JUST A FEW MOMENTS...THEN...
WHAT'S...HAPPENED... TO ME--?
DAZED THOUGH HE IS, THE HUMAN COMET REALIZES...
MORE TIME MUST HAVE PASSED THAN I THOUGHT TO HAVE ME STAKED DOWN LIKE THIS! I'M A PRISONER OF LILLIPUTIANS!--HAVE I MADE A MIS-TAKE? DID I LAND SOMEWHERE ELSE--THAN IN THE TIME DIMENSION?

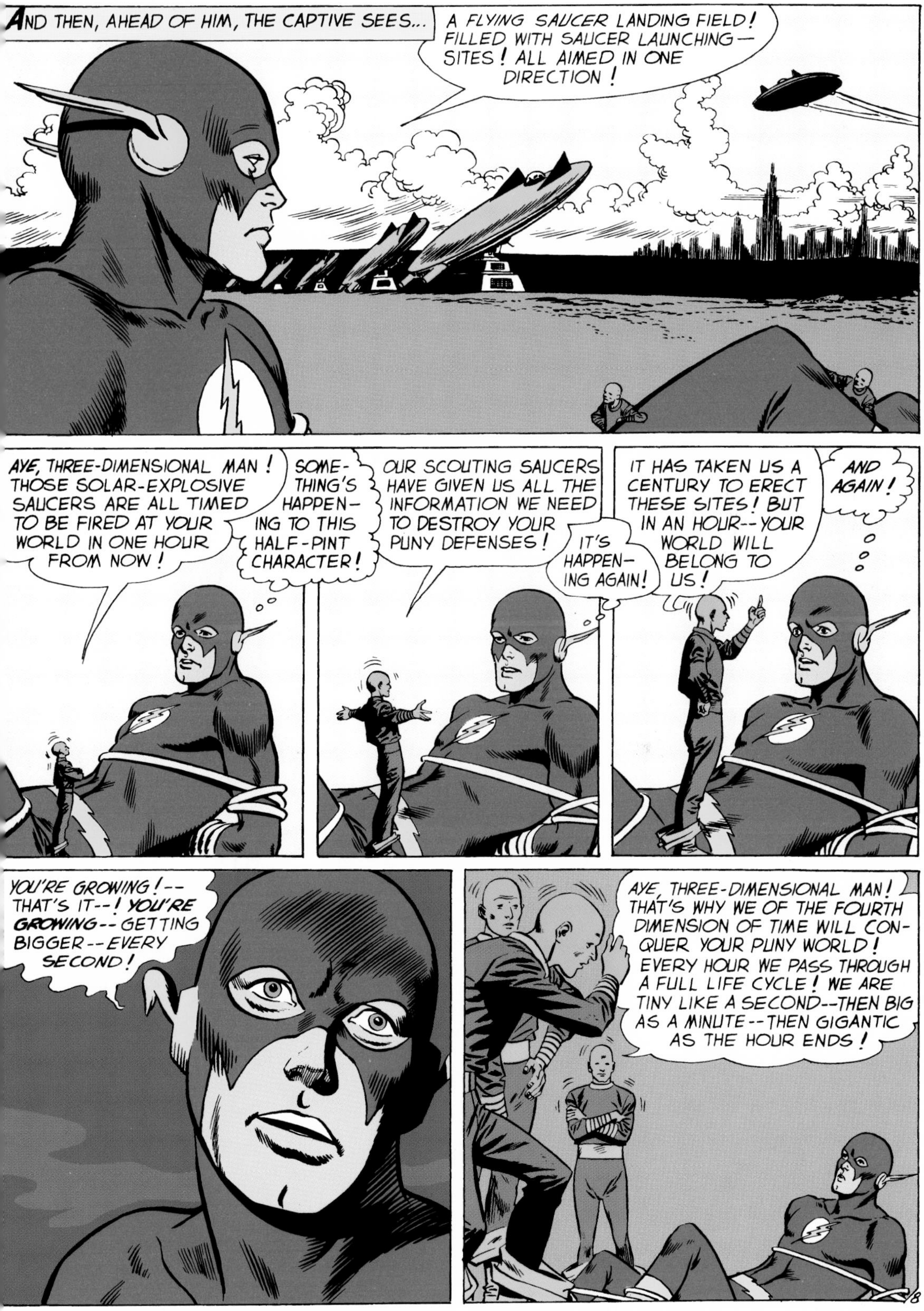
AND THEN, AHEAD OF HIM, THE CAPTIVE SEES...
A FLYING SAUCER LANDING FIELD! FILLED WITH SAUCER LAUNCHING-SITES! ALL AIMED IN ONE DIRECTION!
AYE, THREE-DIMENSIONAL MAN! THOSE SOLAR-EXPLOSIVE SAUCERS ARE ALL TIMED TO BE FIRED AT YOUR WORLD IN ONE HOUR FROM NOW!
SOMETHING'S HAPPENING TO THIS HALF-PINT CHARACTER!
OUR SCOUTING SAUCERS HAVE GIVEN US ALL THE INFORMATION WE NEED TO DESTROY YOUR PUNY DEFENSES!
IT'S HAPPENING AGAIN!
IT HAS TAKEN US A CENTURY TO ERECT THESE SITES! BUT IN AN HOUR--YOUR WORLD WILL BELONG TO US!
AND AGAIN!
YOU'RE GROWING!--THAT'S IT--! YOU'RE GROWING--GETTING BIGGER--EVERY SECOND!
AYE, THREE-DIMENSIONAL MAN! THAT'S WHY WE OF THE FOURTH DIMENSION OF TIME WILL CONQUER YOUR PUNY WORLD! EVERY HOUR WE PASS THROUGH A FULL LIFE CYCLE! WE ARE TINY LIKE A SECOND--THEN BIG AS A MINUTE--THEN GIGANTIC AS THE HOUR ENDS!
8

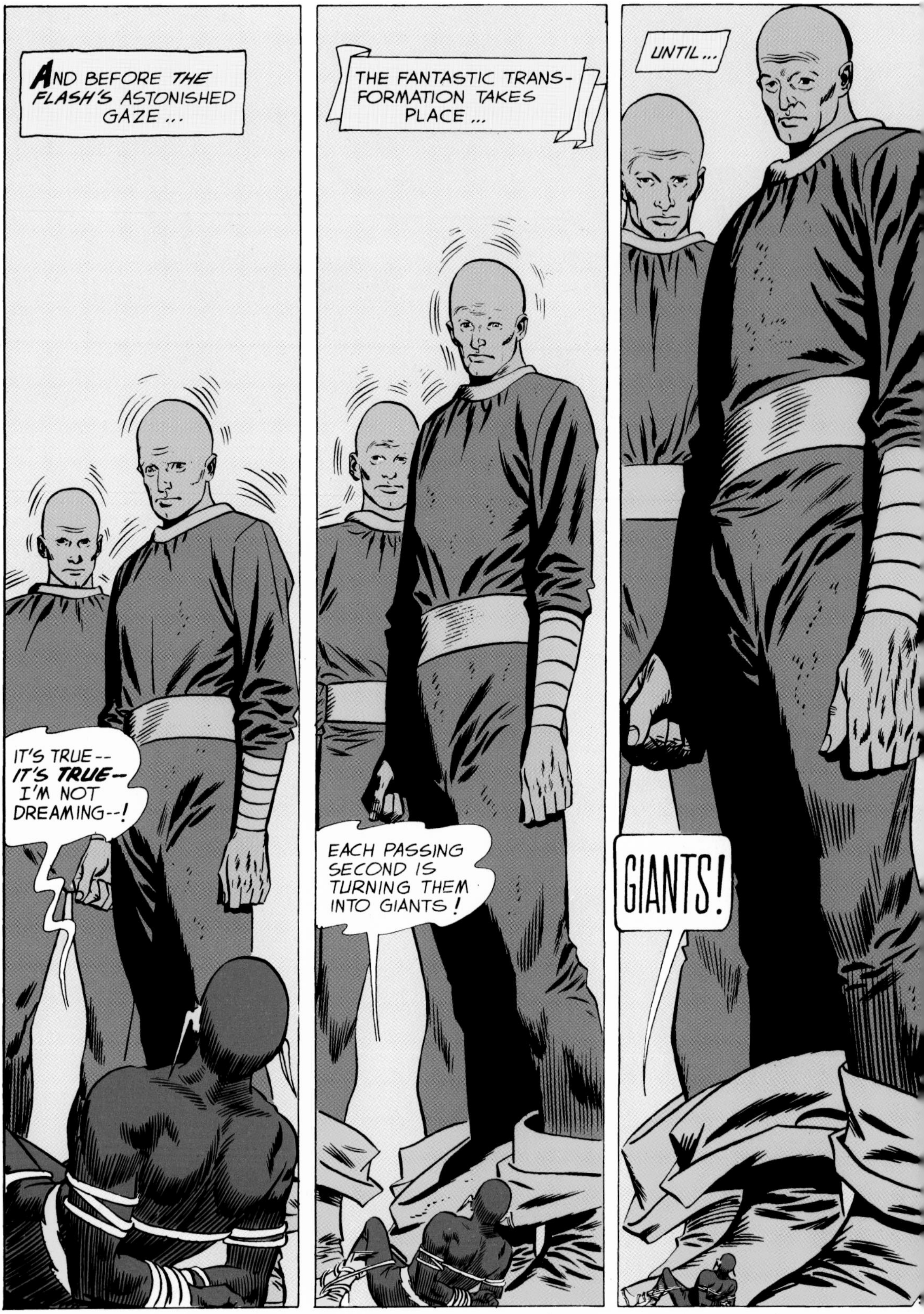
AND BEFORE THE FLASH'S ASTONISHED GAZE ...
IT'S TRUE -- IT'S TRUE -- I'M NOT DREAMING--!
THE FANTASTIC TRANSFORMATION TAKES PLACE ...
EACH PASSING SECOND IS TURNING THEM INTO GIANTS!
UNTIL ...
GIANTS!

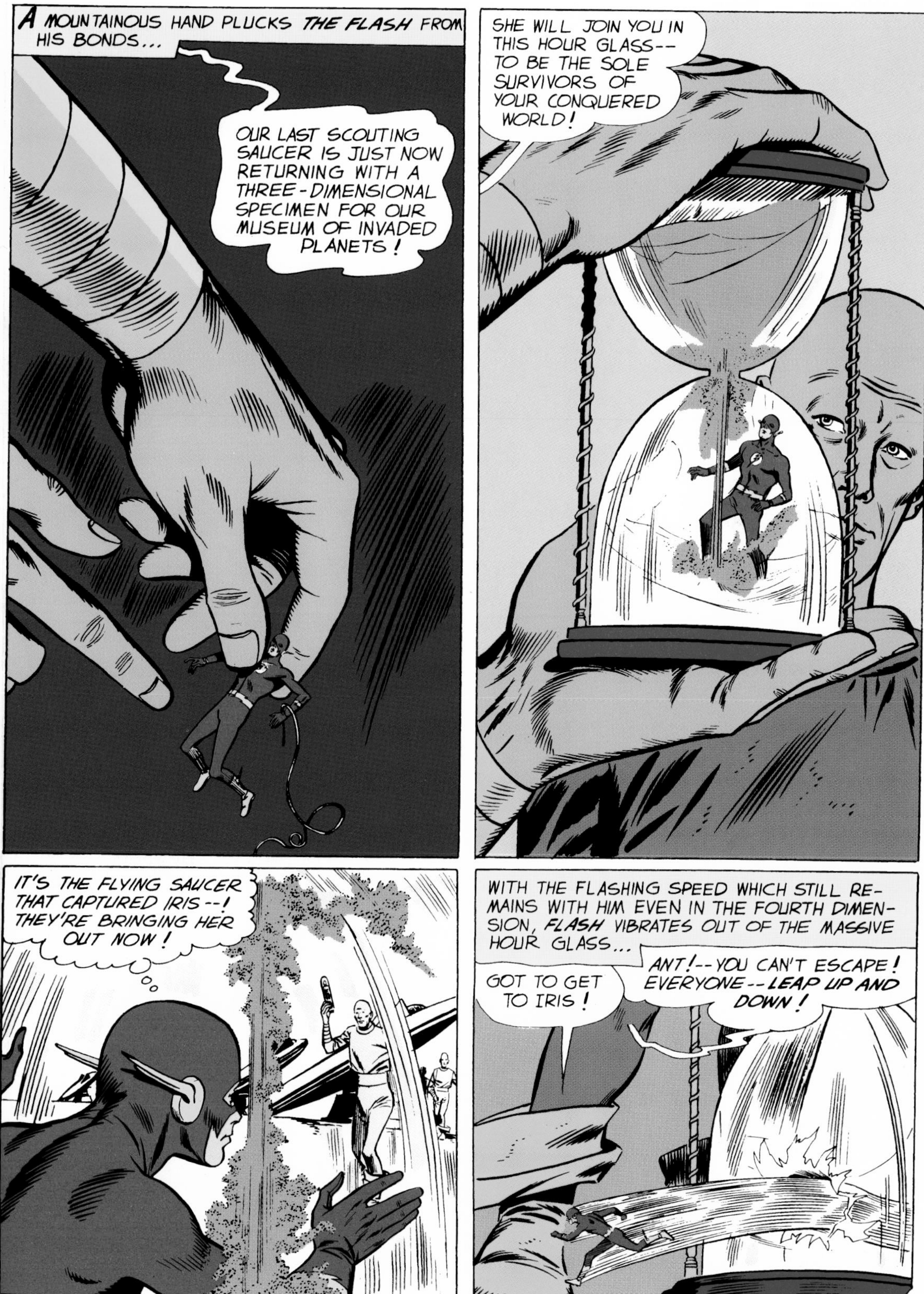
A MOUNTAINOUS HAND PLUCKS THE FLASH FROM HIS BONDS...
OUR LAST SCOUTING SAUCER IS JUST NOW RETURNING WITH A THREE-DIMENSIONAL SPECIMEN FOR OUR MUSEUM OF INVADED PLANETS!
SHE WILL JOIN YOU IN THIS HOUR GLASS--TO BE THE SOLE SURVIVORS OF YOUR CONQUERED WORLD!
IT'S THE FLYING SAUCER THAT CAPTURED IRIS--! THEY'RE BRINGING HER OUT NOW!
WITH THE FLASHING SPEED WHICH STILL REMAINS WITH HIM EVEN IN THE FOURTH DIMENSION, FLASH VIBRATES OUT OF THE MASSIVE HOUR GLASS...
GOT TO GET TO IRIS!
ANT!--YOU CAN'T ESCAPE! EVERYONE--LEAP UP AND DOWN!
10

SUDDENLY, THE GROUND BENEATH *THE FLASH* QUIVERS AND SHAKES AS...

ON M-M-M-ME!

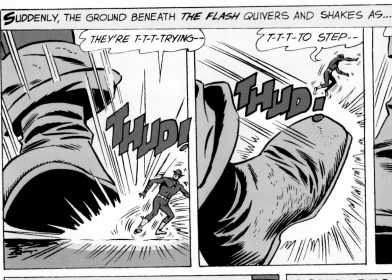

THEY'RE T-T-T-TRYING--

T-T-T-TO STEP--

THUD!

THUD!

THUD!

WITH BREATHLESS DARING...THE *SCARLET SPEEDSTER* HURLS HIMSELF UPWARD...

GROUND'S NO PLACE FOR ME! I'LL HOP INTO THIS CHARACTER'S BOOT CUFF!

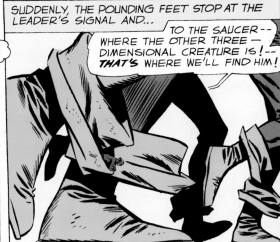

SUDDENLY, THE POUNDING FEET STOP AT THE LEADER'S SIGNAL AND...

TO THE SAUCER-- WHERE THE OTHER THREE-- DIMENSIONAL CREATURE IS!-- *THAT'S* WHERE WE'LL FIND HIM!

STAND HERE! HE'S SURE TO TRY TO RESCUE HIS FELLOW PRISONER--THEN-- WE'LL HAVE HIM!

THERE'S IRIS--OUT OF REACH! HOW CAN I MAKE THAT MAN-MOUNTAIN SET HER DOWN?

DESPERATELY, THE HUMAN COMET LEAPS ONTO THE GIANT'S BOOT...

ONLY A MATTER OF MOMENTS--BEFORE THEY SPOT ME!

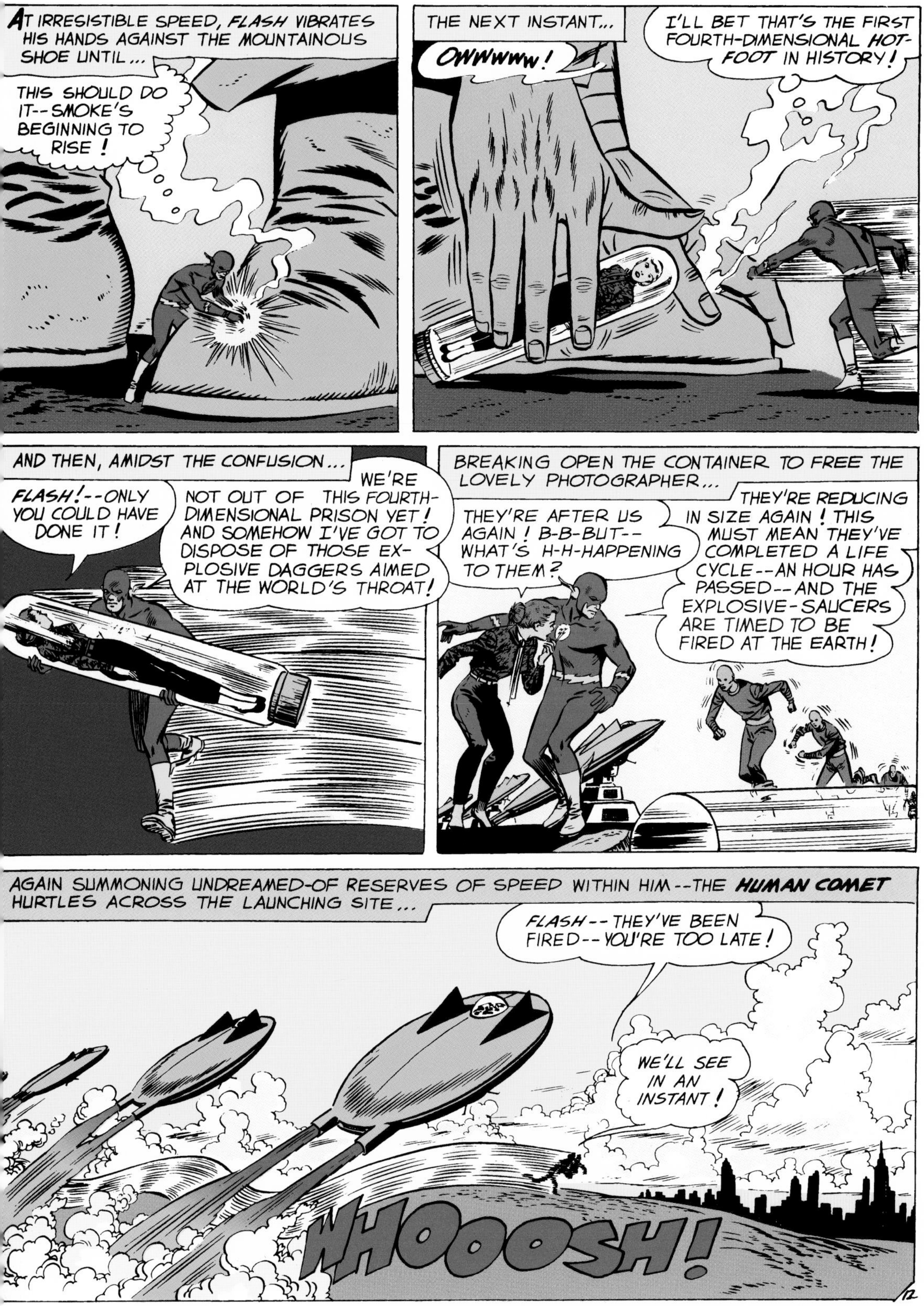
AT IRRESISTIBLE SPEED, FLASH VIBRATES HIS HANDS AGAINST THE MOUNTAINOUS SHOE UNTIL...
THIS SHOULD DO IT--SMOKE'S BEGINNING TO RISE!
THE NEXT INSTANT...
OWWWWW!
I'LL BET THAT'S THE FIRST FOURTH-DIMENSIONAL HOT-FOOT IN HISTORY!
AND THEN, AMIDST THE CONFUSION...
FLASH!--ONLY YOU COULD HAVE DONE IT!
WE'RE NOT OUT OF THIS FOURTH-DIMENSIONAL PRISON YET! AND SOMEHOW I'VE GOT TO DISPOSE OF THOSE EX-PLOSIVE DAGGERS AIMED AT THE WORLD'S THROAT!
BREAKING OPEN THE CONTAINER TO FREE THE LOVELY PHOTOGRAPHER...
THEY'RE AFTER US AGAIN! B-B-BUT--WHAT'S H-H-HAPPENING TO THEM?
THEY'RE REDUCING IN SIZE AGAIN! THIS MUST MEAN THEY'VE COMPLETED A LIFE CYCLE--AN HOUR HAS PASSED--AND THE EXPLOSIVE-SAUCERS ARE TIMED TO BE FIRED AT THE EARTH!
AGAIN SUMMONING UNDREAMED-OF RESERVES OF SPEED WITHIN HIM--THE HUMAN COMET HURTLES ACROSS THE LAUNCHING SITE...
FLASH--THEY'VE BEEN FIRED--YOU'RE TOO LATE!
WE'LL SEE IN AN INSTANT!
WHOOOSH!
12

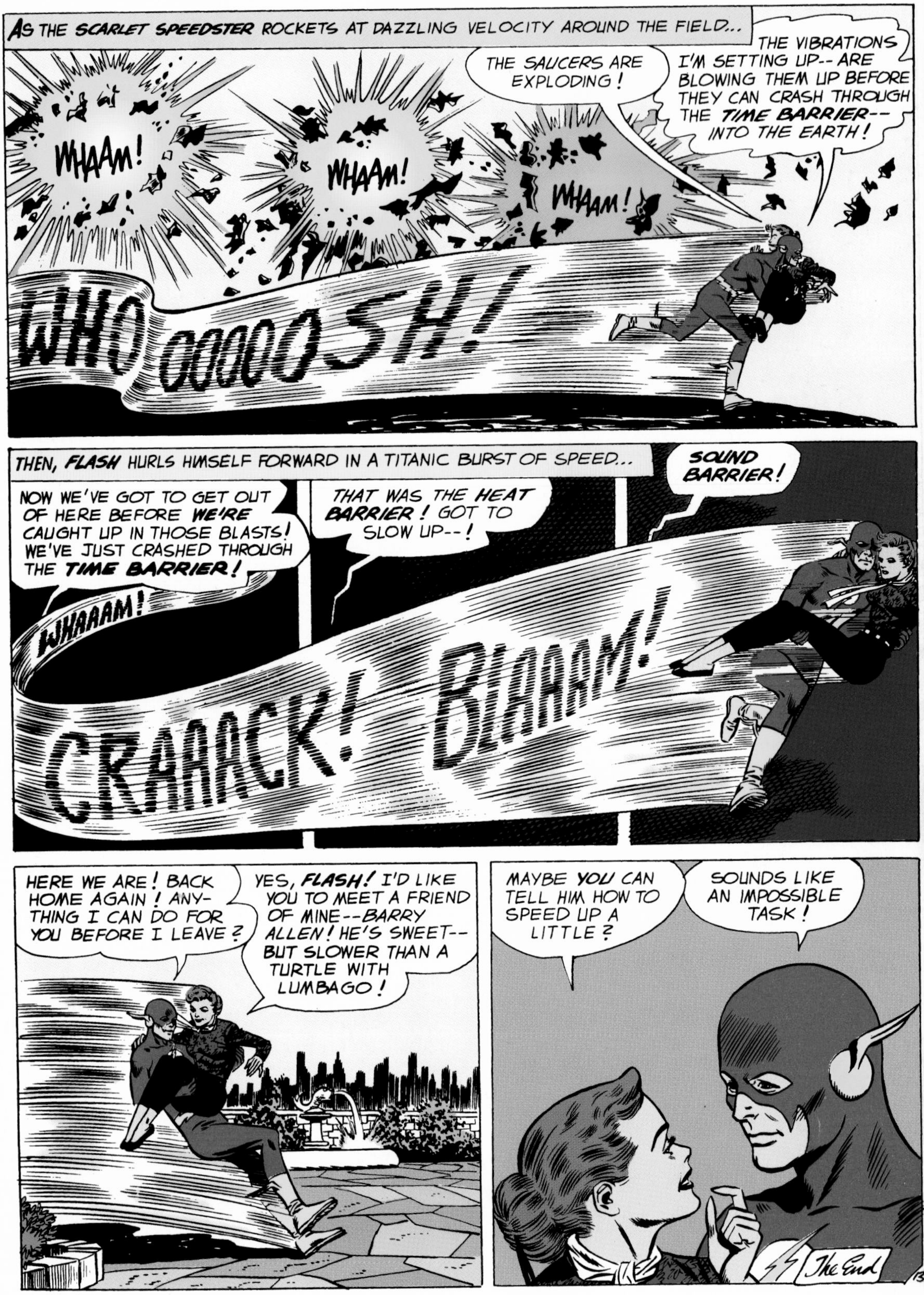
AS THE SCARLET SPEEDSTER ROCKETS AT DAZZLING VELOCITY AROUND THE FIELD...
THE SAUCERS ARE EXPLODING!
THE VIBRATIONS I'M SETTING UP-- ARE BLOWING THEM UP BEFORE THEY CAN CRASH THROUGH THE TIME BARRIER-- INTO THE EARTH!
WHAAM!
WHAAM!
WHAAM!
WHOOOOOOSH!
THEN, FLASH HURLS HIMSELF FORWARD IN A TITANIC BURST OF SPEED...
NOW WE'VE GOT TO GET OUT OF HERE BEFORE WE'RE CAUGHT UP IN THOSE BLASTS! WE'VE JUST CRASHED THROUGH THE TIME BARRIER!
THAT WAS THE HEAT BARRIER! GOT TO SLOW UP--!
SOUND BARRIER!
WHAAAM!
CRAAACK! BLAAAM!
HERE WE ARE! BACK HOME AGAIN! ANY-THING I CAN DO FOR YOU BEFORE I LEAVE?
YES, FLASH! I'D LIKE YOU TO MEET A FRIEND OF MINE--BARRY ALLEN! HE'S SWEET-- BUT SLOWER THAN A TURTLE WITH LUMBAGO!
MAYBE YOU CAN TELL HIM HOW TO SPEED UP A LITTLE?
SOUNDS LIKE AN IMPOSSIBLE TASK!
The End
13

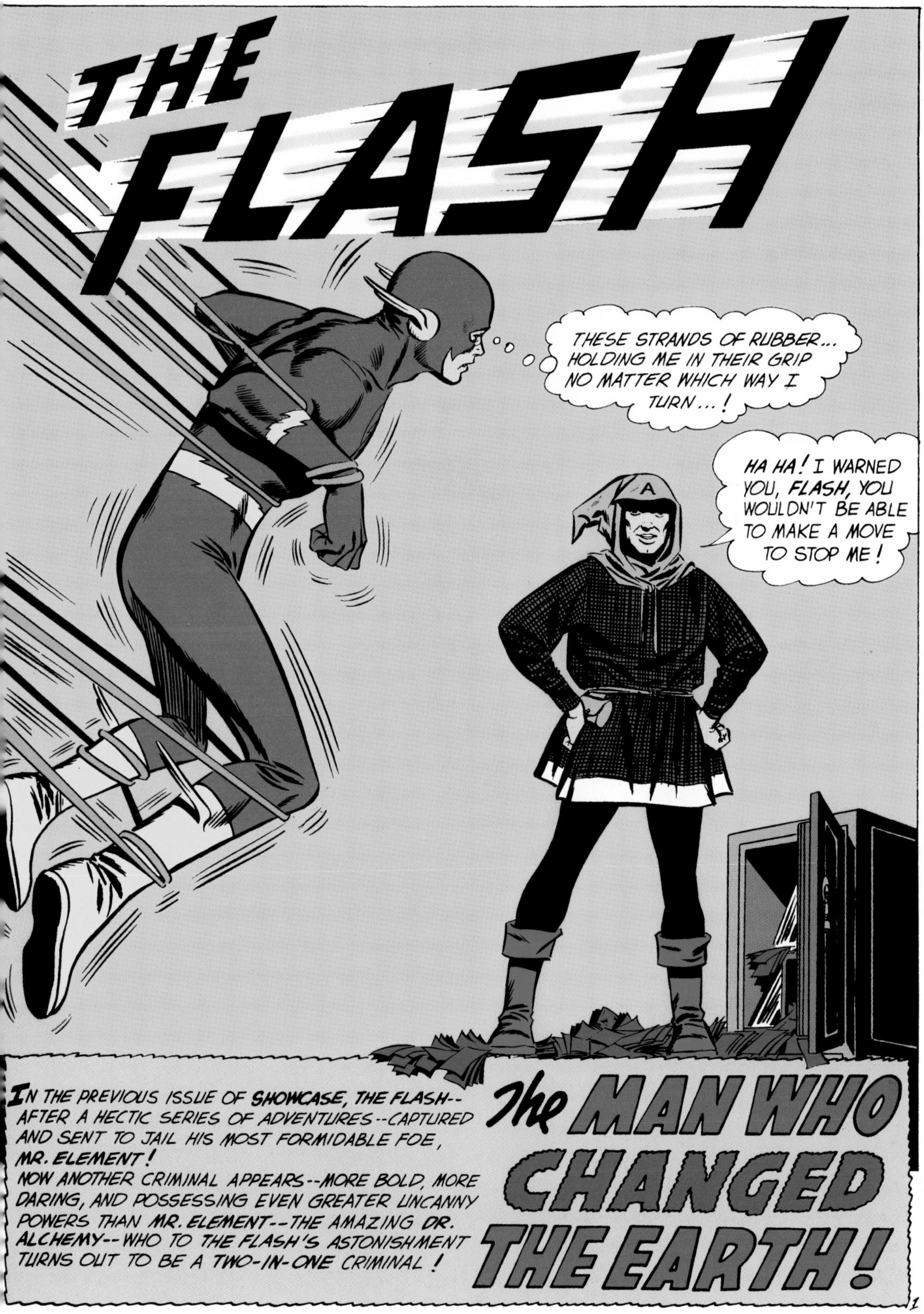
THE FLASH
THESE STRANDS OF RUBBER... HOLDING ME IN THEIR GRIP NO MATTER WHICH WAY I TURN... !
HA HA! I WARNED YOU, FLASH, YOU WOULDN'T BE ABLE TO MAKE A MOVE TO STOP ME!
IN THE PREVIOUS ISSUE OF SHOWCASE, THE FLASH-- AFTER A HECTIC SERIES OF ADVENTURES--CAPTURED AND SENT TO JAIL HIS MOST FORMIDABLE FOE, MR. ELEMENT!
NOW ANOTHER CRIMINAL APPEARS--MORE BOLD, MORE DARING, AND POSSESSING EVEN GREATER UNCANNY POWERS THAN MR. ELEMENT--THE AMAZING DR. ALCHEMY--WHO TO THE FLASH'S ASTONISHMENT TURNS OUT TO BE A TWO-IN-ONE CRIMINAL!
The MAN WHO CHANGED THE EARTH!
1

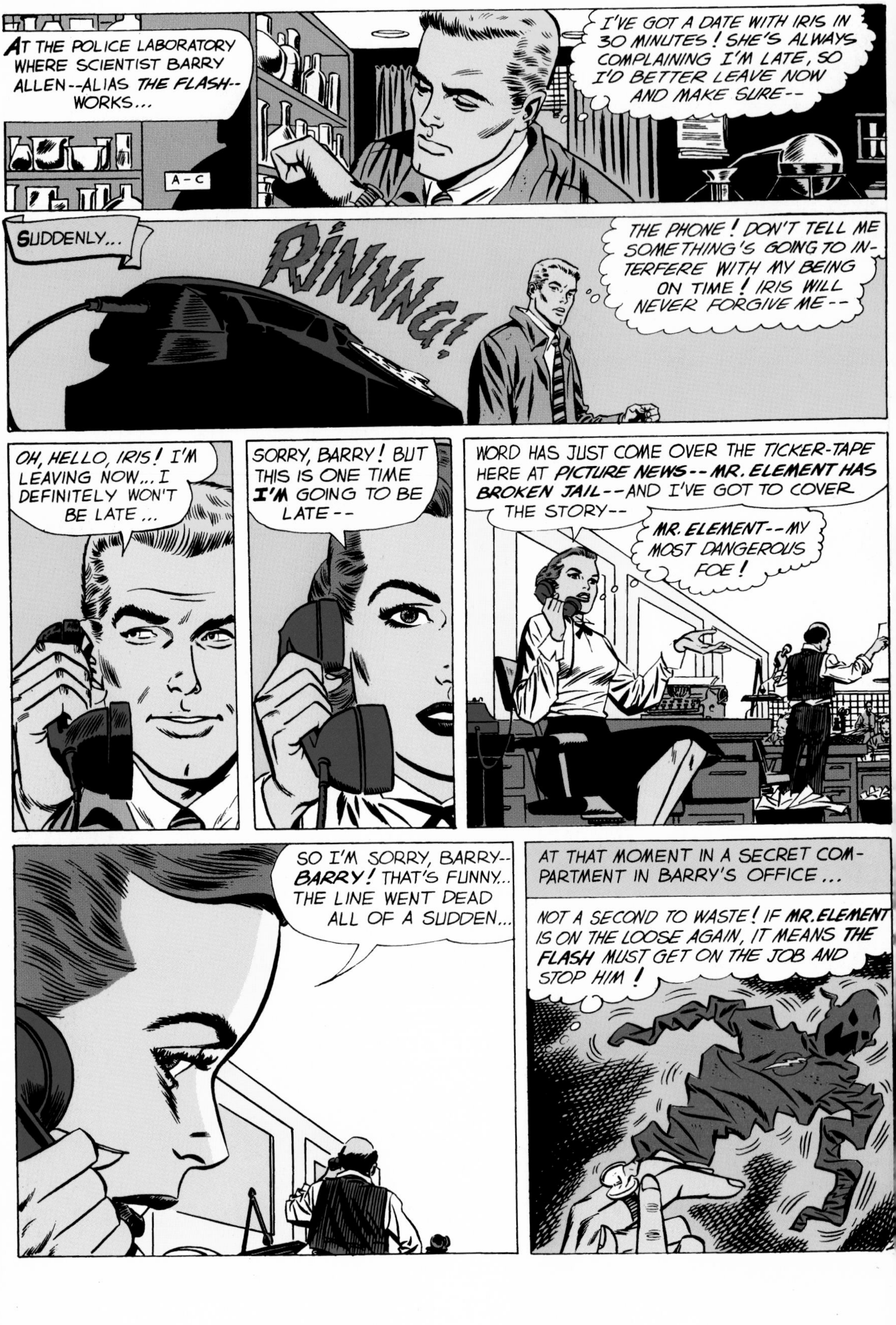
AT THE POLICE LABORATORY WHERE SCIENTIST BARRY ALLEN--ALIAS THE FLASH--WORKS...
I'VE GOT A DATE WITH IRIS IN 30 MINUTES! SHE'S ALWAYS COMPLAINING I'M LATE, SO I'D BETTER LEAVE NOW AND MAKE SURE--
A-C
SUDDENLY...
RINNNG!
THE PHONE! DON'T TELL ME SOMETHING'S GOING TO INTERFERE WITH MY BEING ON TIME! IRIS WILL NEVER FORGIVE ME--
OH, HELLO, IRIS! I'M LEAVING NOW... I DEFINITELY WON'T BE LATE...
SORRY, BARRY! BUT THIS IS ONE TIME I'M GOING TO BE LATE--
WORD HAS JUST COME OVER THE TICKER-TAPE HERE AT PICTURE NEWS--MR. ELEMENT HAS BROKEN JAIL--AND I'VE GOT TO COVER THE STORY--
MR. ELEMENT--MY MOST DANGEROUS FOE!
SO I'M SORRY, BARRY--BARRY! THAT'S FUNNY... THE LINE WENT DEAD ALL OF A SUDDEN...
AT THAT MOMENT IN A SECRET COMPARTMENT IN BARRY'S OFFICE...
NOT A SECOND TO WASTE! IF MR. ELEMENT IS ON THE LOOSE AGAIN, IT MEANS THE FLASH MUST GET ON THE JOB AND STOP HIM!

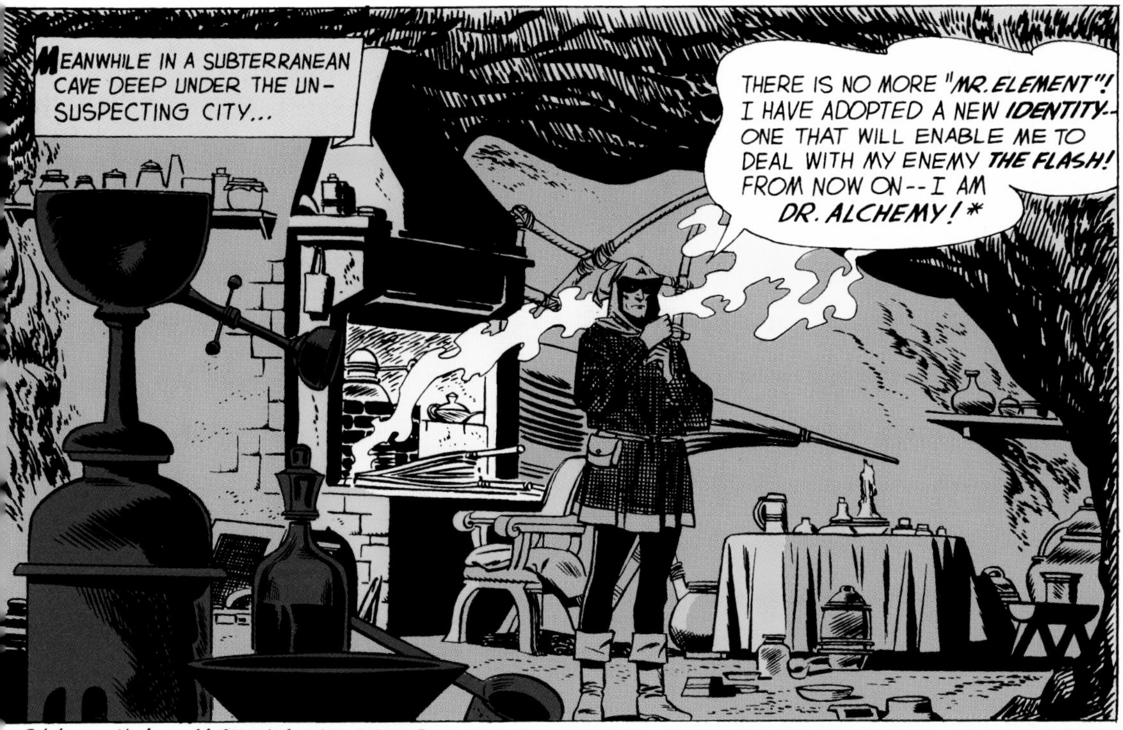
MEANWHILE IN A SUBTERRANEAN CAVE DEEP UNDER THE UN-SUSPECTING CITY...
THERE IS NO MORE "MR. ELEMENT"! I HAVE ADOPTED A NEW IDENTITY-- ONE THAT WILL ENABLE ME TO DEAL WITH MY ENEMY THE FLASH! FROM NOW ON--I AM DR. ALCHEMY! *

*Editor's Note: ALCHEMY WAS AN EARLY AND MYSTERIOUS FORM OF SCIENCE WHICH CONCENTRATED ON CHANGING CERTAIN ELEMENTS INTO OTHER, MORE VALUABLE ELEMENTS!

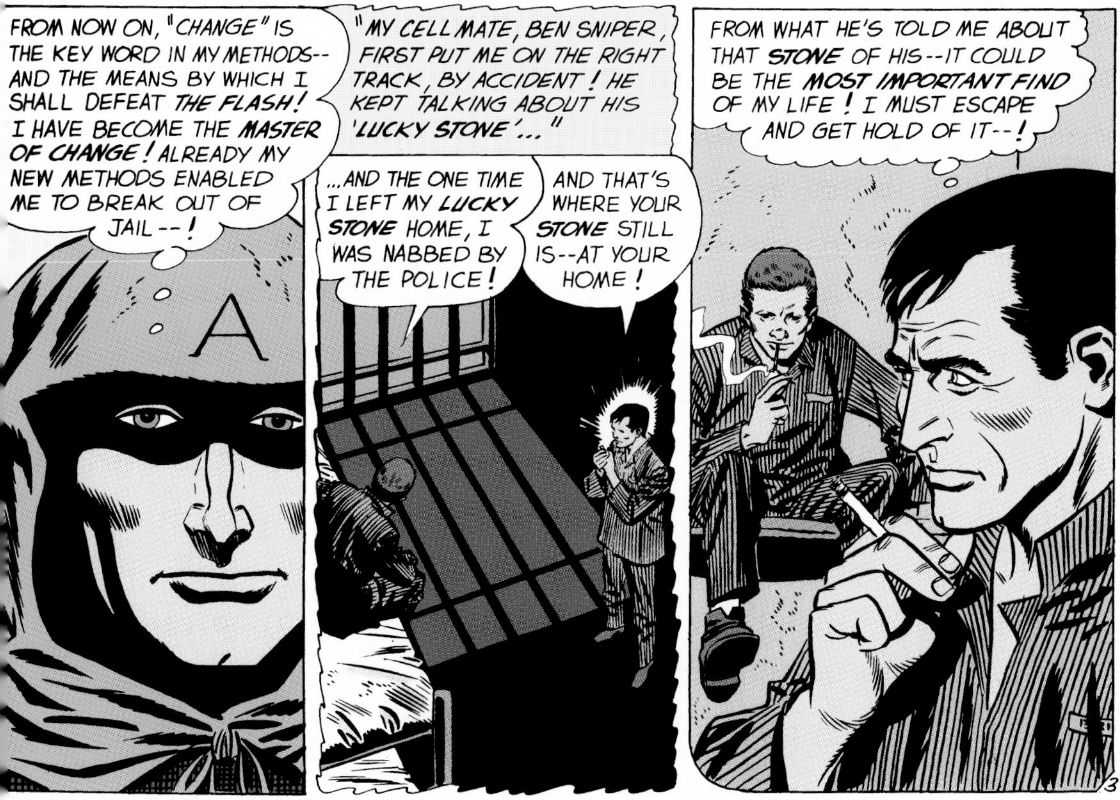
FROM NOW ON, "CHANGE" IS THE KEY WORD IN MY METHODS-- AND THE MEANS BY WHICH I SHALL DEFEAT THE FLASH! I HAVE BECOME THE MASTER OF CHANGE! ALREADY MY NEW METHODS ENABLED ME TO BREAK OUT OF JAIL--!
"MY CELL MATE, BEN SNIPER, FIRST PUT ME ON THE RIGHT TRACK, BY ACCIDENT! HE KEPT TALKING ABOUT HIS 'LUCKY STONE'..."
...AND THE ONE TIME I LEFT MY LUCKY STONE HOME, I WAS NABBED BY THE POLICE!
AND THAT'S WHERE YOUR STONE STILL IS--AT YOUR HOME!
FROM WHAT HE'S TOLD ME ABOUT THAT STONE OF HIS--IT COULD BE THE MOST IMPORTANT FIND OF MY LIFE! I MUST ESCAPE AND GET HOLD OF IT--!
3

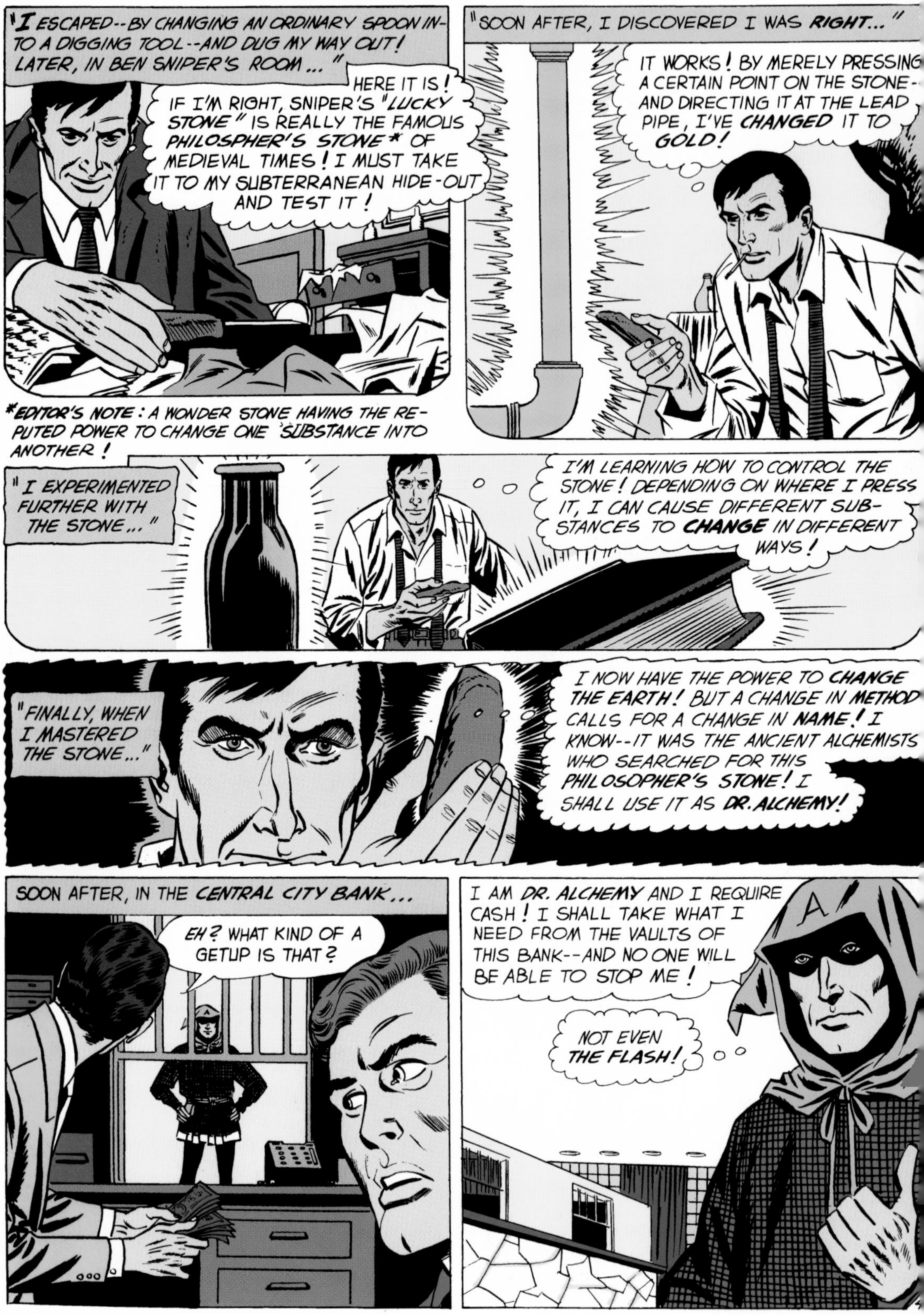
"I ESCAPED--BY CHANGING AN ORDINARY SPOON INTO A DIGGING TOOL--AND DUG MY WAY OUT! LATER, IN BEN SNIPER'S ROOM..."
HERE IT IS! IF I'M RIGHT, SNIPER'S "LUCKY STONE" IS REALLY THE FAMOUS PHILOSPHER'S STONE* OF MEDIEVAL TIMES! I MUST TAKE IT TO MY SUBTERRANEAN HIDE-OUT AND TEST IT!
*EDITOR'S NOTE: A WONDER STONE HAVING THE REPUTED POWER TO CHANGE ONE SUBSTANCE INTO ANOTHER!
"SOON AFTER, I DISCOVERED I WAS RIGHT..."
IT WORKS! BY MERELY PRESSING A CERTAIN POINT ON THE STONE--AND DIRECTING IT AT THE LEAD PIPE, I'VE CHANGED IT TO GOLD!
"I EXPERIMENTED FURTHER WITH THE STONE..."
I'M LEARNING HOW TO CONTROL THE STONE! DEPENDING ON WHERE I PRESS IT, I CAN CAUSE DIFFERENT SUBSTANCES TO CHANGE IN DIFFERENT WAYS!
"FINALLY, WHEN I MASTERED THE STONE..."
I NOW HAVE THE POWER TO CHANGE THE EARTH! BUT A CHANGE IN METHOD CALLS FOR A CHANGE IN NAME! I KNOW--IT WAS THE ANCIENT ALCHEMISTS WHO SEARCHED FOR THIS PHILOSOPHER'S STONE! I SHALL USE IT AS DR. ALCHEMY!
SOON AFTER, IN THE CENTRAL CITY BANK...
EH? WHAT KIND OF A GETUP IS THAT?
I AM DR. ALCHEMY AND I REQUIRE CASH! I SHALL TAKE WHAT I NEED FROM THE VAULTS OF THIS BANK--AND NO ONE WILL BE ABLE TO STOP ME!
NOT EVEN THE FLASH!

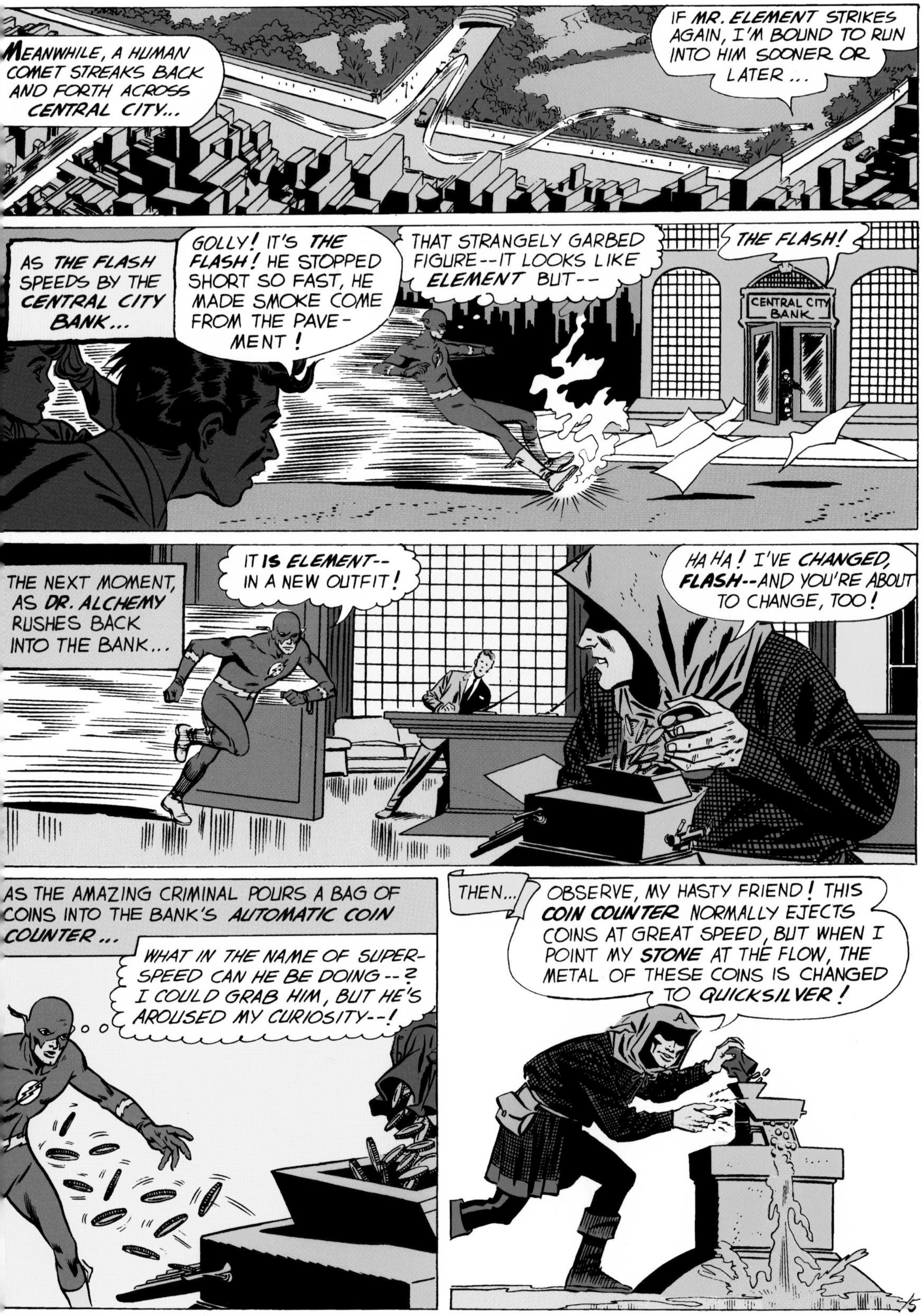
MEANWHILE, A HUMAN COMET STREAKS BACK AND FORTH ACROSS CENTRAL CITY...
IF MR. ELEMENT STRIKES AGAIN, I'M BOUND TO RUN INTO HIM SOONER OR LATER...
AS THE FLASH SPEEDS BY THE CENTRAL CITY BANK...
GOLLY! IT'S THE FLASH! HE STOPPED SHORT SO FAST, HE MADE SMOKE COME FROM THE PAVEMENT!
THAT STRANGELY GARBED FIGURE--IT LOOKS LIKE ELEMENT BUT--
THE FLASH!
CENTRAL CITY BANK
THE NEXT MOMENT, AS DR. ALCHEMY RUSHES BACK INTO THE BANK...
IT IS ELEMENT-- IN A NEW OUTFIT!
HA HA! I'VE CHANGED, FLASH--AND YOU'RE ABOUT TO CHANGE, TOO!
AS THE AMAZING CRIMINAL POURS A BAG OF COINS INTO THE BANK'S AUTOMATIC COIN COUNTER...
WHAT IN THE NAME OF SUPER-SPEED CAN HE BE DOING--? I COULD GRAB HIM, BUT HE'S AROUSED MY CURIOSITY--!
THEN...
OBSERVE, MY HASTY FRIEND! THIS COIN COUNTER NORMALLY EJECTS COINS AT GREAT SPEED, BUT WHEN I POINT MY STONE AT THE FLOW, THE METAL OF THESE COINS IS CHANGED TO QUICKSILVER!
5

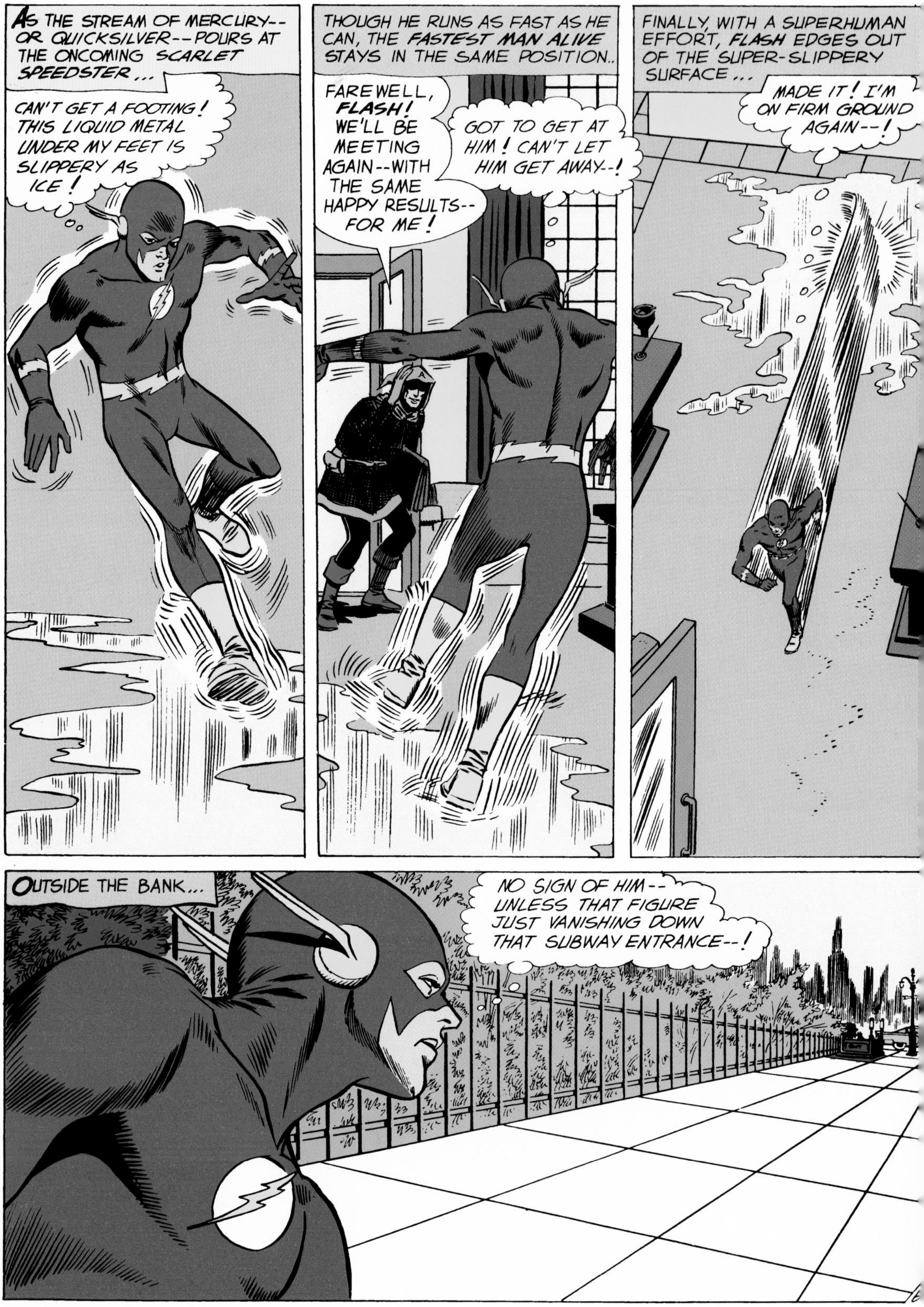
AS THE STREAM OF MERCURY--OR QUICKSILVER--POURS AT THE ONCOMING SCARLET SPEEDSTER...
CAN'T GET A FOOTING! THIS LIQUID METAL UNDER MY FEET IS SLIPPERY AS ICE!
THOUGH HE RUNS AS FAST AS HE CAN, THE FASTEST MAN ALIVE STAYS IN THE SAME POSITION..
FAREWELL, FLASH! WE'LL BE MEETING AGAIN--WITH THE SAME HAPPY RESULTS--FOR ME!
GOT TO GET AT HIM! CAN'T LET HIM GET AWAY--!
FINALLY, WITH A SUPERHUMAN EFFORT, FLASH EDGES OUT OF THE SUPER-SLIPPERY SURFACE...
MADE IT! I'M ON FIRM GROUND AGAIN--!
OUTSIDE THE BANK...
NO SIGN OF HIM--UNLESS THAT FIGURE JUST VANISHING DOWN THAT SUBWAY ENTRANCE--!

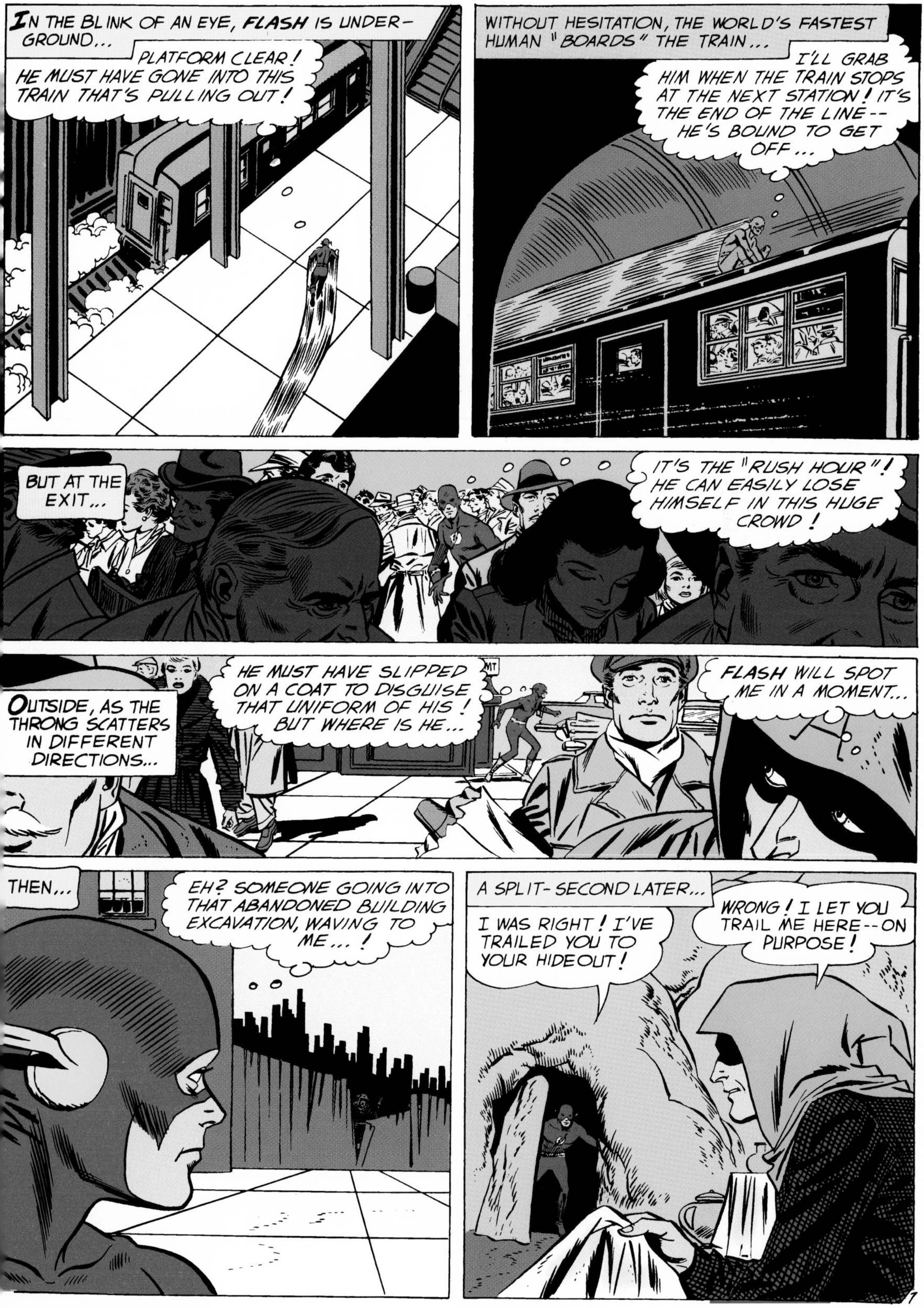
IN THE BLINK OF AN EYE, FLASH IS UNDERGROUND...
PLATFORM CLEAR! HE MUST HAVE GONE INTO THIS TRAIN THAT'S PULLING OUT!
WITHOUT HESITATION, THE WORLD'S FASTEST HUMAN "BOARDS" THE TRAIN...
I'LL GRAB HIM WHEN THE TRAIN STOPS AT THE NEXT STATION! IT'S THE END OF THE LINE-- HE'S BOUND TO GET OFF...
BUT AT THE EXIT...
IT'S THE "RUSH HOUR"! HE CAN EASILY LOSE HIMSELF IN THIS HUGE CROWD!
OUTSIDE, AS THE THRONG SCATTERS IN DIFFERENT DIRECTIONS...
HE MUST HAVE SLIPPED ON A COAT TO DISGUISE THAT UNIFORM OF HIS! BUT WHERE IS HE...
FLASH WILL SPOT ME IN A MOMENT...
THEN...
EH? SOMEONE GOING INTO THAT ABANDONED BUILDING EXCAVATION, WAVING TO ME...!
A SPLIT-SECOND LATER...
I WAS RIGHT! I'VE TRAILED YOU TO YOUR HIDEOUT!
WRONG! I LET YOU TRAIL ME HERE--ON PURPOSE!
7

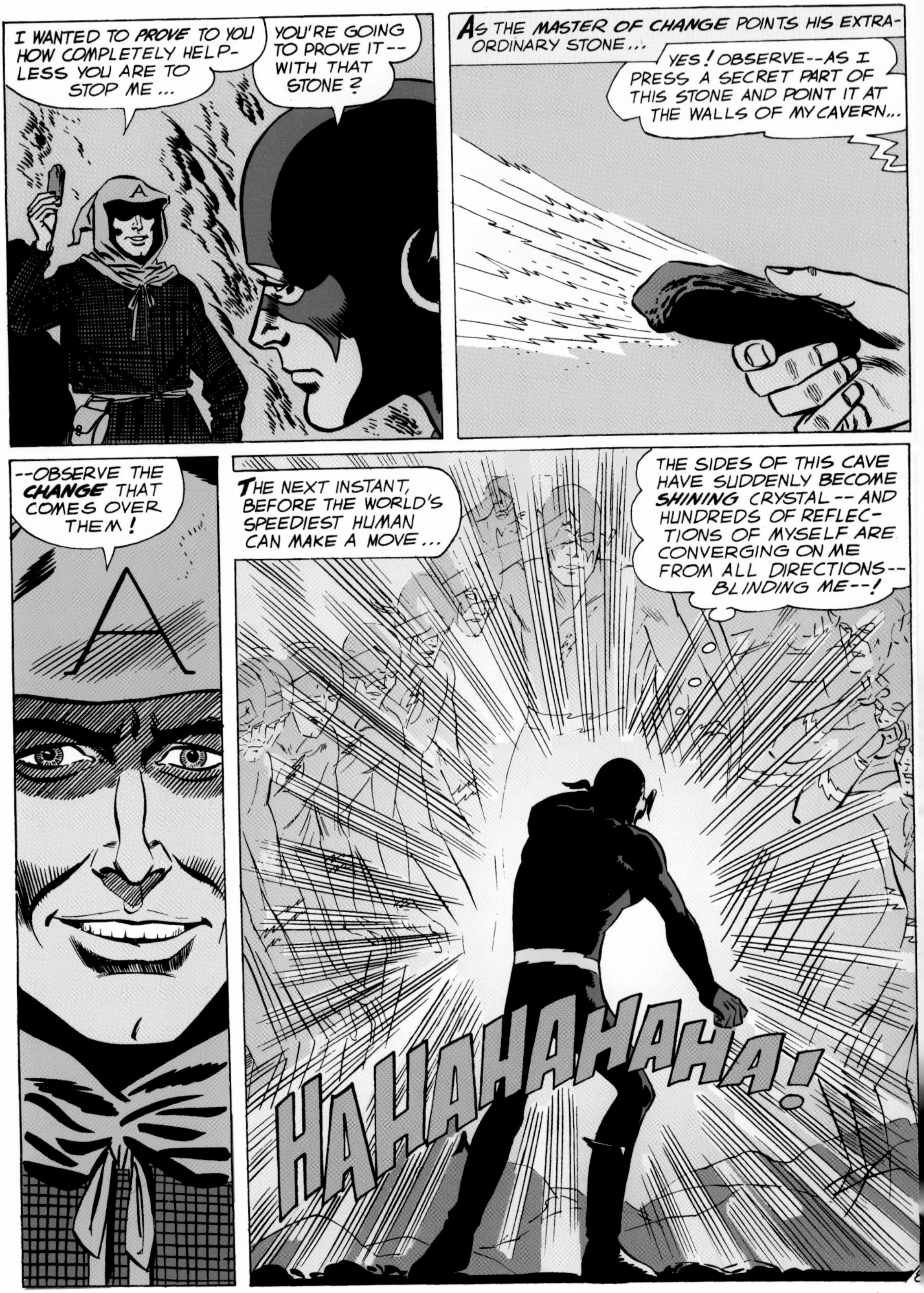
I WANTED TO PROVE TO YOU HOW COMPLETELY HELP-LESS YOU ARE TO STOP ME ...
YOU'RE GOING TO PROVE IT -- WITH THAT STONE ?
AS THE MASTER OF CHANGE POINTS HIS EXTRA-ORDINARY STONE ...
YES ! OBSERVE--AS I PRESS A SECRET PART OF THIS STONE AND POINT IT AT THE WALLS OF MY CAVERN...
--OBSERVE THE CHANGE THAT COMES OVER THEM !
THE NEXT INSTANT, BEFORE THE WORLD'S SPEEDIEST HUMAN CAN MAKE A MOVE ...
THE SIDES OF THIS CAVE HAVE SUDDENLY BECOME SHINING CRYSTAL -- AND HUNDREDS OF REFLEC-TIONS OF MYSELF ARE CONVERGING ON ME FROM ALL DIRECTIONS-- BLINDING ME--!
HAHAHAHAHAHA !

MY FOE'S DISAPPEARED! AND THIS GLARE FROM THE CRYSTALS IS PREVENTING ME FROM FINDING THE WAY OUT--!

ON AN INSPIRATION, THE *FASTEST MAN ALIVE* PICKS UP A PIECE OF ROCK AT HIS FEET AND...

MY ONLY CHANCE IS TO BREAK THESE SHINY SURFACES -- TO CUT DOWN THE GLARE--!

CRAAAAK!

IN A TWINKLING, *FLASH* CARRIES OUT HIS PLAN...

IT'S WORKING...

CRACK!

WITH THE GLARE REDUCED...

KRRRACK!

...I CAN SEE THE DOOR I CAME IN NOW!

AN INSTANT LATER...

HE'S THE MOST DIS-APPEARING MAN I'VE EVER COME UP AGAINST! HE'S PROVED HIS BOAST-- FOR THE TIME BEING!

THE FOLLOWING DAY, BACK AT THE POLICE TECHNICAL LABORATORY...

DR. ALCHEMY! SO THAT'S THE *NEW* NAME OF MY *OLD* FOE!

DR. ALCHEMY ROBS BANK!

9

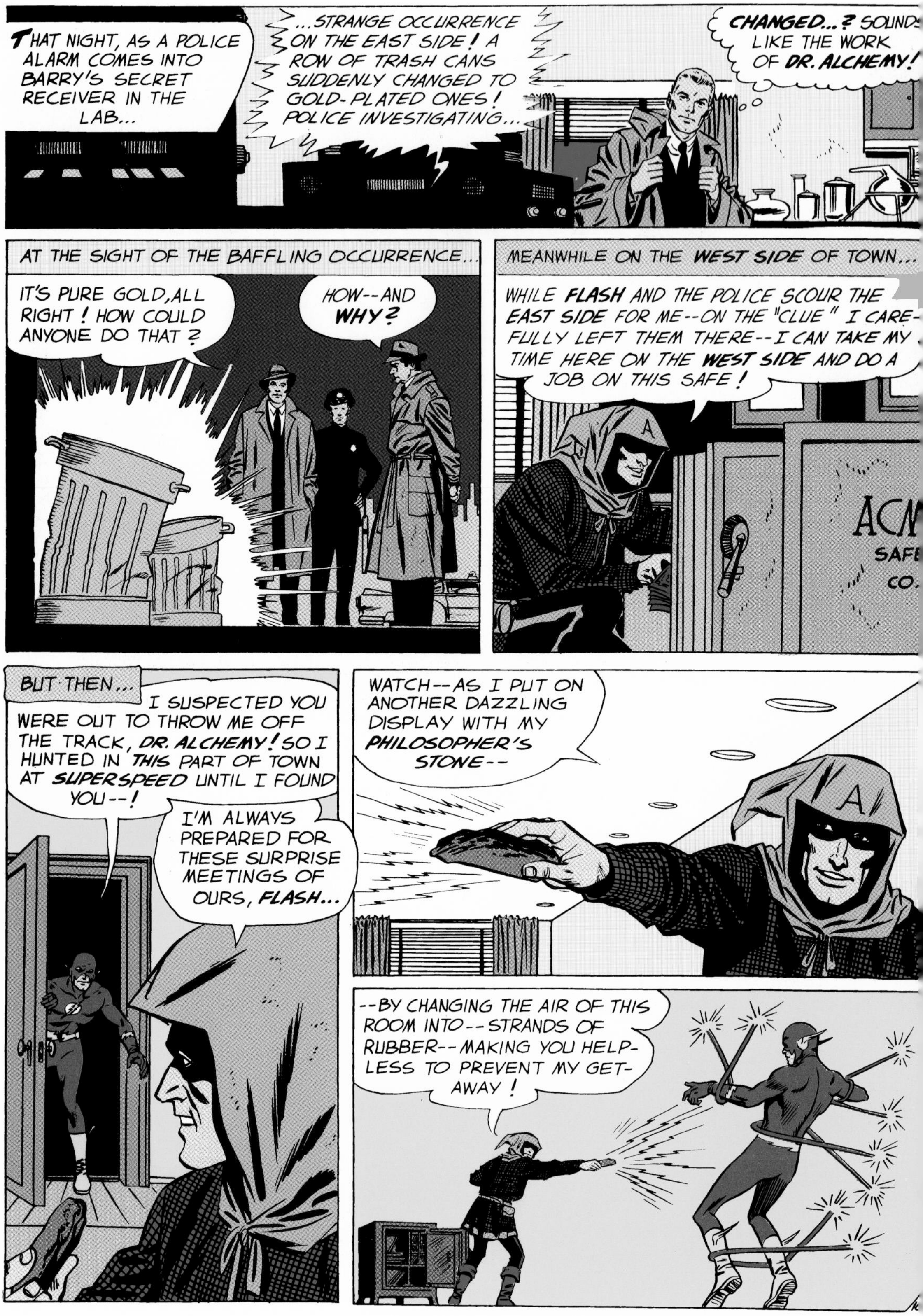
THAT NIGHT, AS A POLICE ALARM COMES INTO BARRY'S SECRET RECEIVER IN THE LAB...
...STRANGE OCCURRENCE ON THE EAST SIDE! A ROW OF TRASH CANS SUDDENLY CHANGED TO GOLD-PLATED ONES! POLICE INVESTIGATING...
CHANGED...? SOUNDS LIKE THE WORK OF DR. ALCHEMY!
AT THE SIGHT OF THE BAFFLING OCCURRENCE...
IT'S PURE GOLD, ALL RIGHT! HOW COULD ANYONE DO THAT?
HOW--AND WHY?
MEANWHILE ON THE WEST SIDE OF TOWN...
WHILE FLASH AND THE POLICE SCOUR THE EAST SIDE FOR ME--ON THE "CLUE" I CAREFULLY LEFT THEM THERE--I CAN TAKE MY TIME HERE ON THE WEST SIDE AND DO A JOB ON THIS SAFE!
BUT THEN...
I SUSPECTED YOU WERE OUT TO THROW ME OFF THE TRACK, DR. ALCHEMY! SO I HUNTED IN THIS PART OF TOWN AT SUPERSPEED UNTIL I FOUND YOU--!
I'M ALWAYS PREPARED FOR THESE SURPRISE MEETINGS OF OURS, FLASH...
WATCH--AS I PUT ON ANOTHER DAZZLING DISPLAY WITH MY PHILOSOPHER'S STONE--
--BY CHANGING THE AIR OF THIS ROOM INTO--STRANDS OF RUBBER--MAKING YOU HELPLESS TO PREVENT MY GETAWAY!

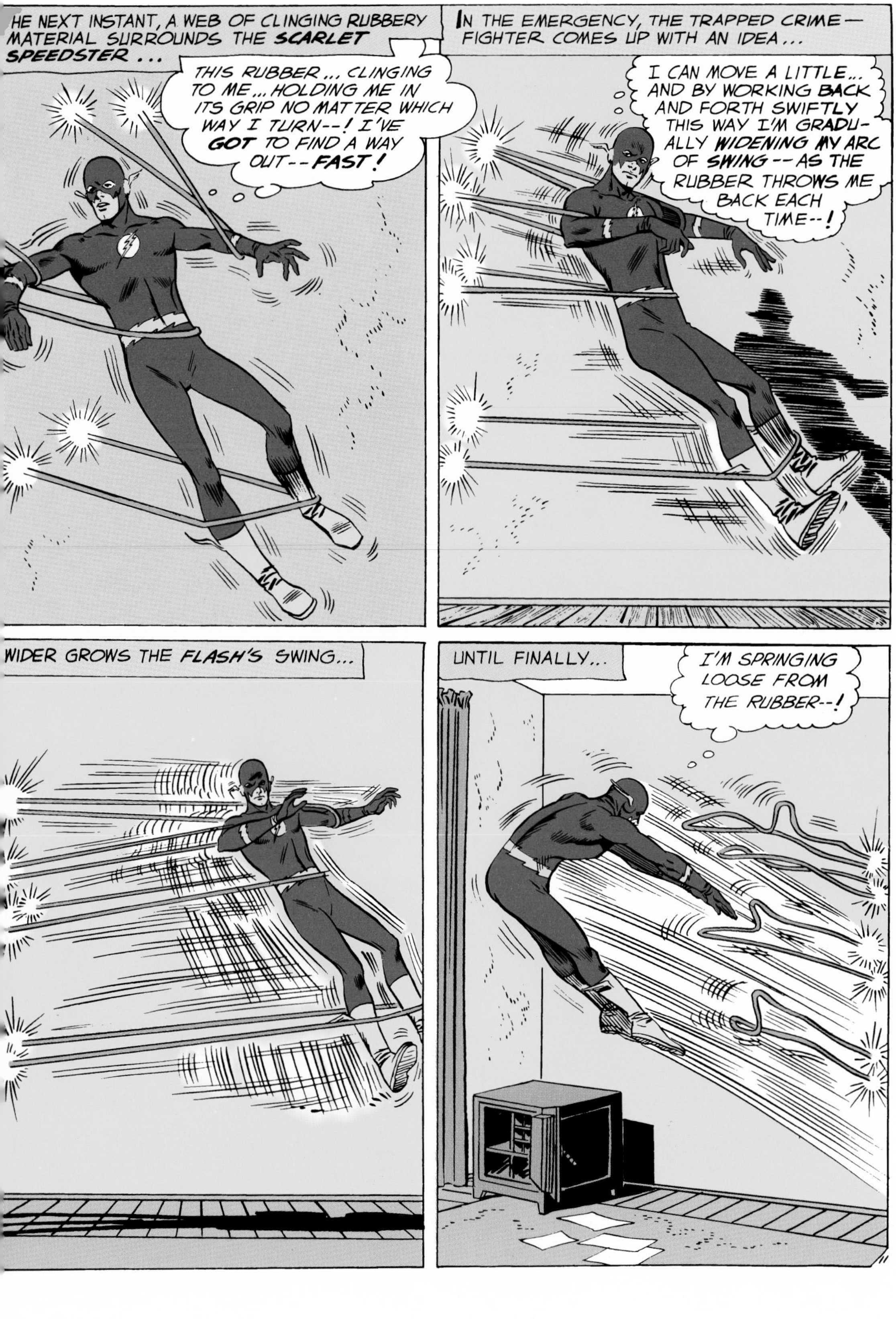
HE NEXT INSTANT, A WEB OF CLINGING RUBBERY MATERIAL SURROUNDS THE SCARLET SPEEDSTER ...
THIS RUBBER... CLINGING TO ME... HOLDING ME IN ITS GRIP NO MATTER WHICH WAY I TURN--! I'VE GOT TO FIND A WAY OUT--FAST!
IN THE EMERGENCY, THE TRAPPED CRIME-FIGHTER COMES UP WITH AN IDEA...
I CAN MOVE A LITTLE... AND BY WORKING BACK AND FORTH SWIFTLY THIS WAY I'M GRADUALLY WIDENING MY ARC OF SWING--AS THE RUBBER THROWS ME BACK EACH TIME--!
WIDER GROWS THE FLASH'S SWING...
UNTIL FINALLY...
I'M SPRINGING LOOSE FROM THE RUBBER--!

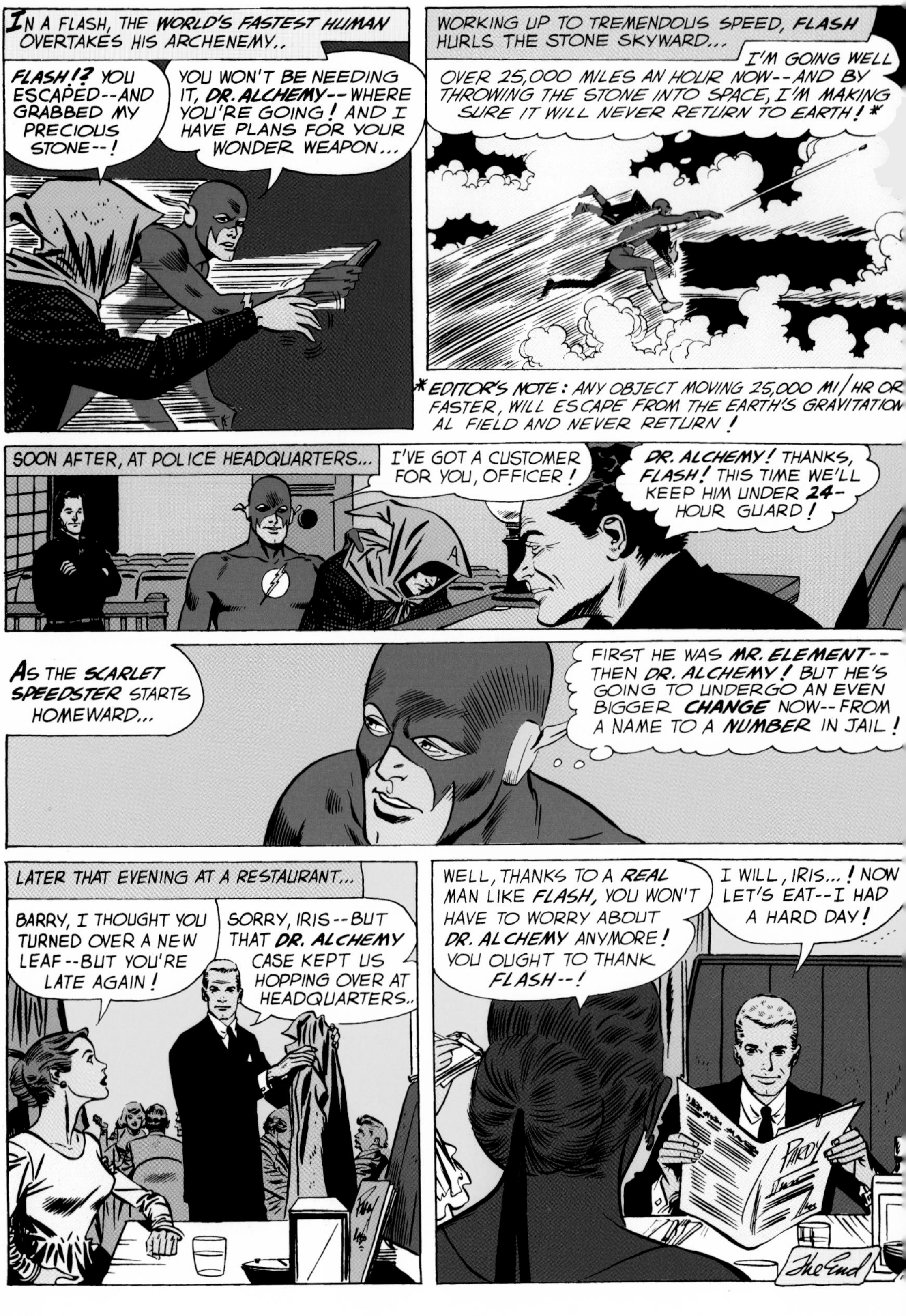
IN A FLASH, THE WORLD'S FASTEST HUMAN OVERTAKES HIS ARCHENEMY..
FLASH!? YOU ESCAPED--AND GRABBED MY PRECIOUS STONE--!
YOU WON'T BE NEEDING IT, DR. ALCHEMY--WHERE YOU'RE GOING! AND I HAVE PLANS FOR YOUR WONDER WEAPON...
WORKING UP TO TREMENDOUS SPEED, FLASH HURLS THE STONE SKYWARD...
I'M GOING WELL OVER 25,000 MILES AN HOUR NOW--AND BY THROWING THE STONE INTO SPACE, I'M MAKING SURE IT WILL NEVER RETURN TO EARTH! *
*EDITOR'S NOTE: ANY OBJECT MOVING 25,000 MI/HR OR FASTER, WILL ESCAPE FROM THE EARTH'S GRAVITATIONAL FIELD AND NEVER RETURN!
SOON AFTER, AT POLICE HEADQUARTERS...
I'VE GOT A CUSTOMER FOR YOU, OFFICER!
DR. ALCHEMY! THANKS, FLASH! THIS TIME WE'LL KEEP HIM UNDER 24-HOUR GUARD!
AS THE SCARLET SPEEDSTER STARTS HOMEWARD...
FIRST HE WAS MR. ELEMENT--THEN DR. ALCHEMY! BUT HE'S GOING TO UNDERGO AN EVEN BIGGER CHANGE NOW--FROM A NAME TO A NUMBER IN JAIL!
LATER THAT EVENING AT A RESTAURANT...
BARRY, I THOUGHT YOU TURNED OVER A NEW LEAF--BUT YOU'RE LATE AGAIN!
SORRY, IRIS--BUT THAT DR. ALCHEMY CASE KEPT US HOPPING OVER AT HEADQUARTERS..
WELL, THANKS TO A REAL MAN LIKE FLASH, YOU WON'T HAVE TO WORRY ABOUT DR. ALCHEMY ANYMORE! YOU OUGHT TO THANK FLASH--!
I WILL, IRIS...! NOW LET'S EAT--I HAD A HARD DAY!
The End

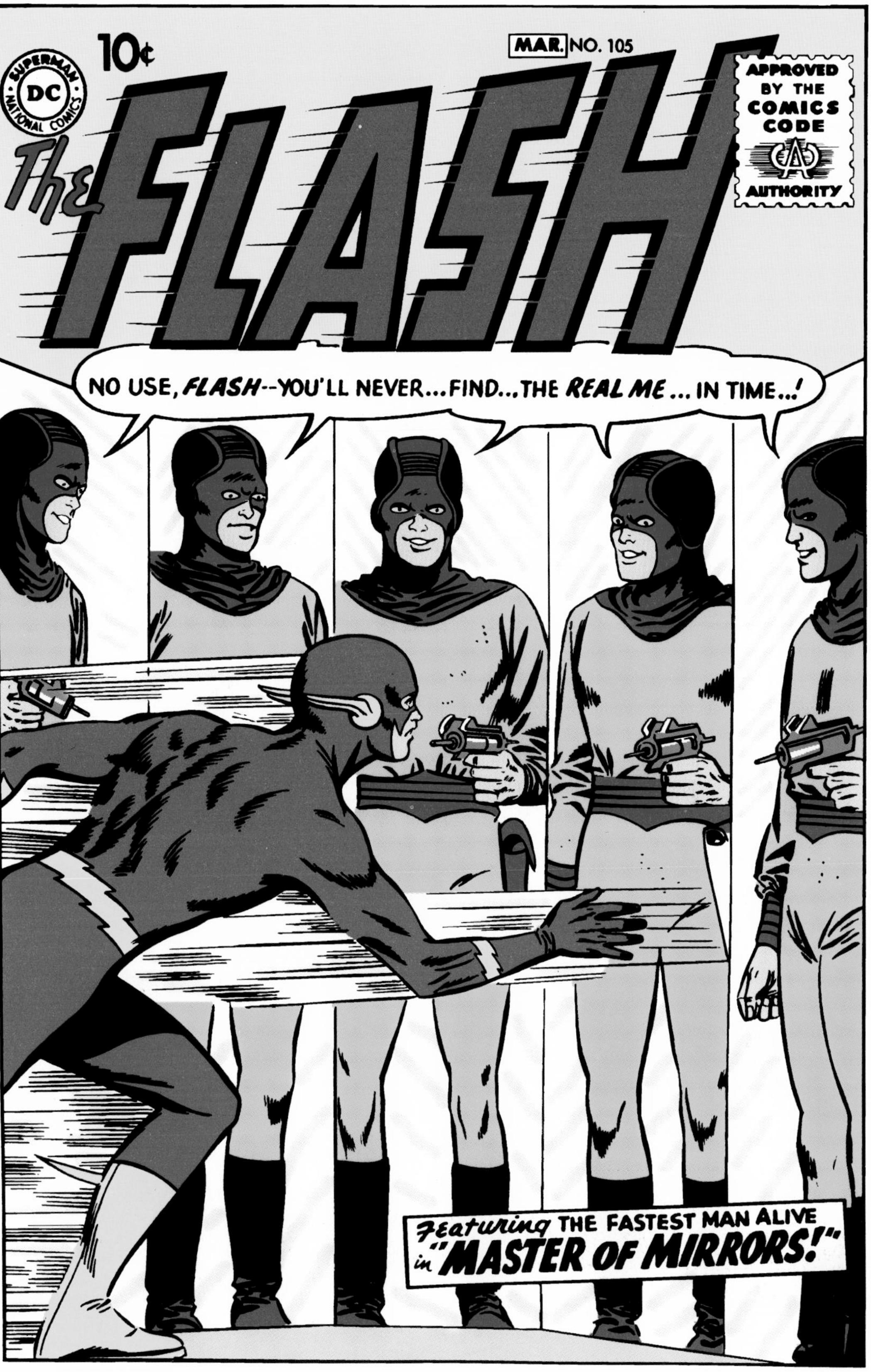
10¢
MAR. NO. 105
SUPERMAN DC NATIONAL COMICS
APPROVED BY THE COMICS CODE AUTHORITY
The FLASH
NO USE, FLASH--YOU'LL NEVER...FIND...THE REAL ME ... IN TIME...!
Featuring THE FASTEST MAN ALIVE
in "MASTER OF MIRRORS!"

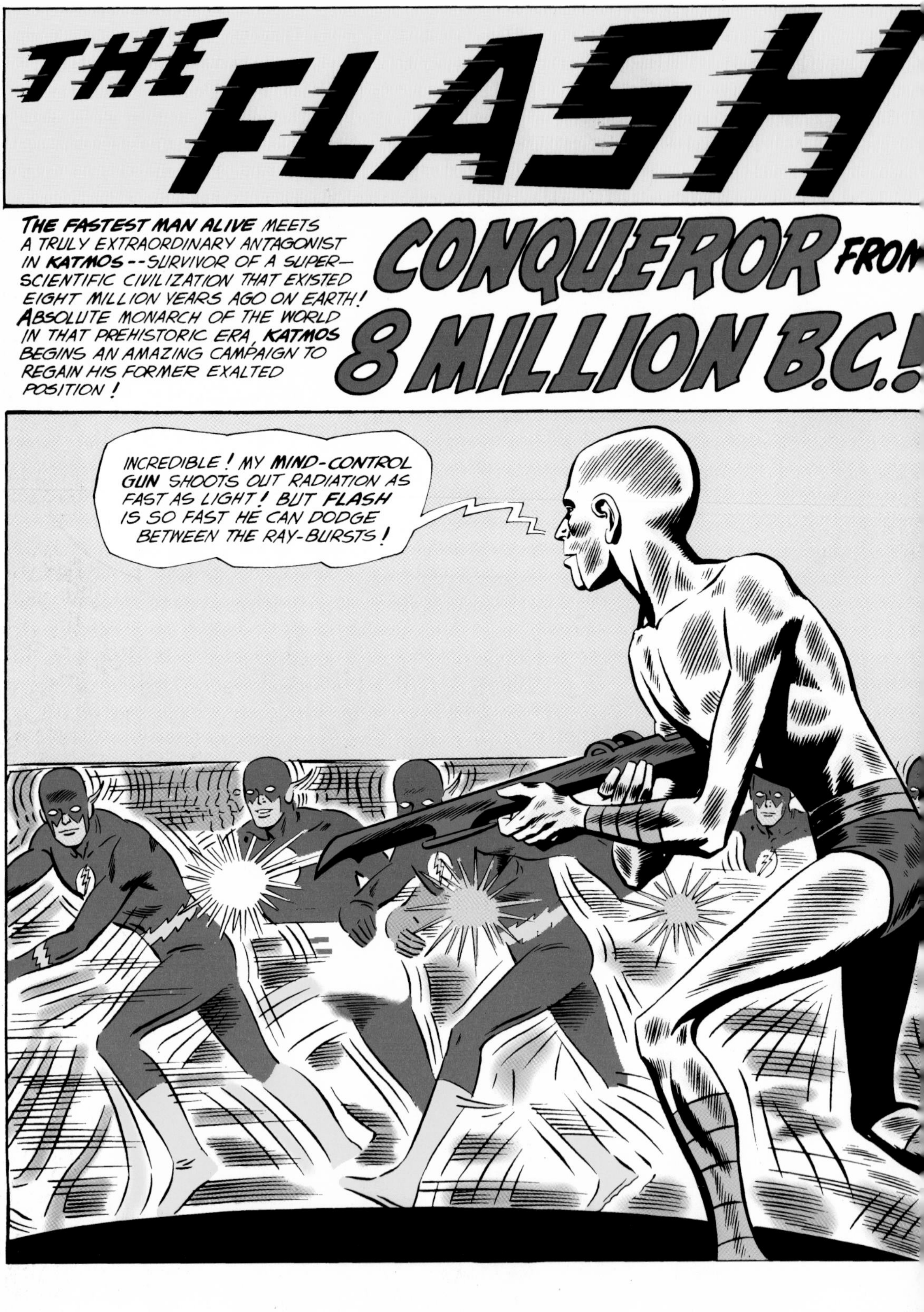
THE FLASH
THE FASTEST MAN ALIVE MEETS A TRULY EXTRAORDINARY ANTAGONIST IN KATMOS--SURVIVOR OF A SUPER-SCIENTIFIC CIVILIZATION THAT EXISTED EIGHT MILLION YEARS AGO ON EARTH! ABSOLUTE MONARCH OF THE WORLD IN THAT PREHISTORIC ERA, KATMOS BEGINS AN AMAZING CAMPAIGN TO REGAIN HIS FORMER EXALTED POSITION!
CONQUEROR FROM 8 MILLION B.C.!
INCREDIBLE! MY MIND-CONTROL GUN SHOOTS OUT RADIATION AS FAST AS LIGHT! BUT FLASH IS SO FAST HE CAN DODGE BETWEEN THE RAY-BURSTS!

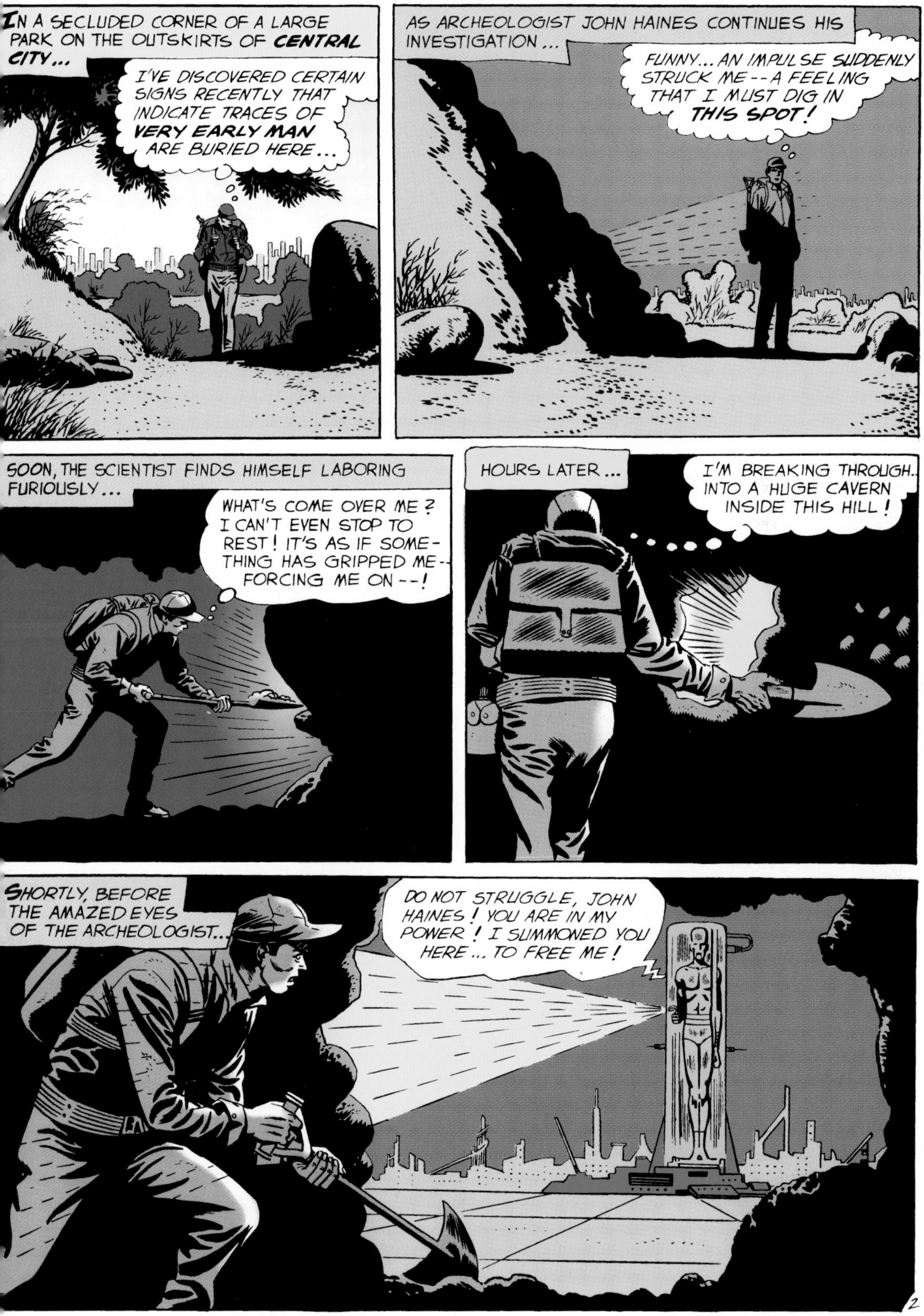

IN A SECLUDED CORNER OF A LARGE PARK ON THE OUTSKIRTS OF CENTRAL CITY...
I'VE DISCOVERED CERTAIN SIGNS RECENTLY THAT INDICATE TRACES OF VERY EARLY MAN ARE BURIED HERE...
AS ARCHEOLOGIST JOHN HAINES CONTINUES HIS INVESTIGATION...
FUNNY... AN IMPULSE SUDDENLY STRUCK ME -- A FEELING THAT I MUST DIG IN THIS SPOT!
SOON, THE SCIENTIST FINDS HIMSELF LABORING FURIOUSLY...
WHAT'S COME OVER ME? I CAN'T EVEN STOP TO REST! IT'S AS IF SOMETHING HAS GRIPPED ME-- FORCING ME ON --!
HOURS LATER...
I'M BREAKING THROUGH.. INTO A HUGE CAVERN INSIDE THIS HILL!
SHORTLY, BEFORE THE AMAZED EYES OF THE ARCHEOLOGIST...
DO NOT STRUGGLE, JOHN HAINES! YOU ARE IN MY POWER! I SUMMONED YOU HERE... TO FREE ME!
2

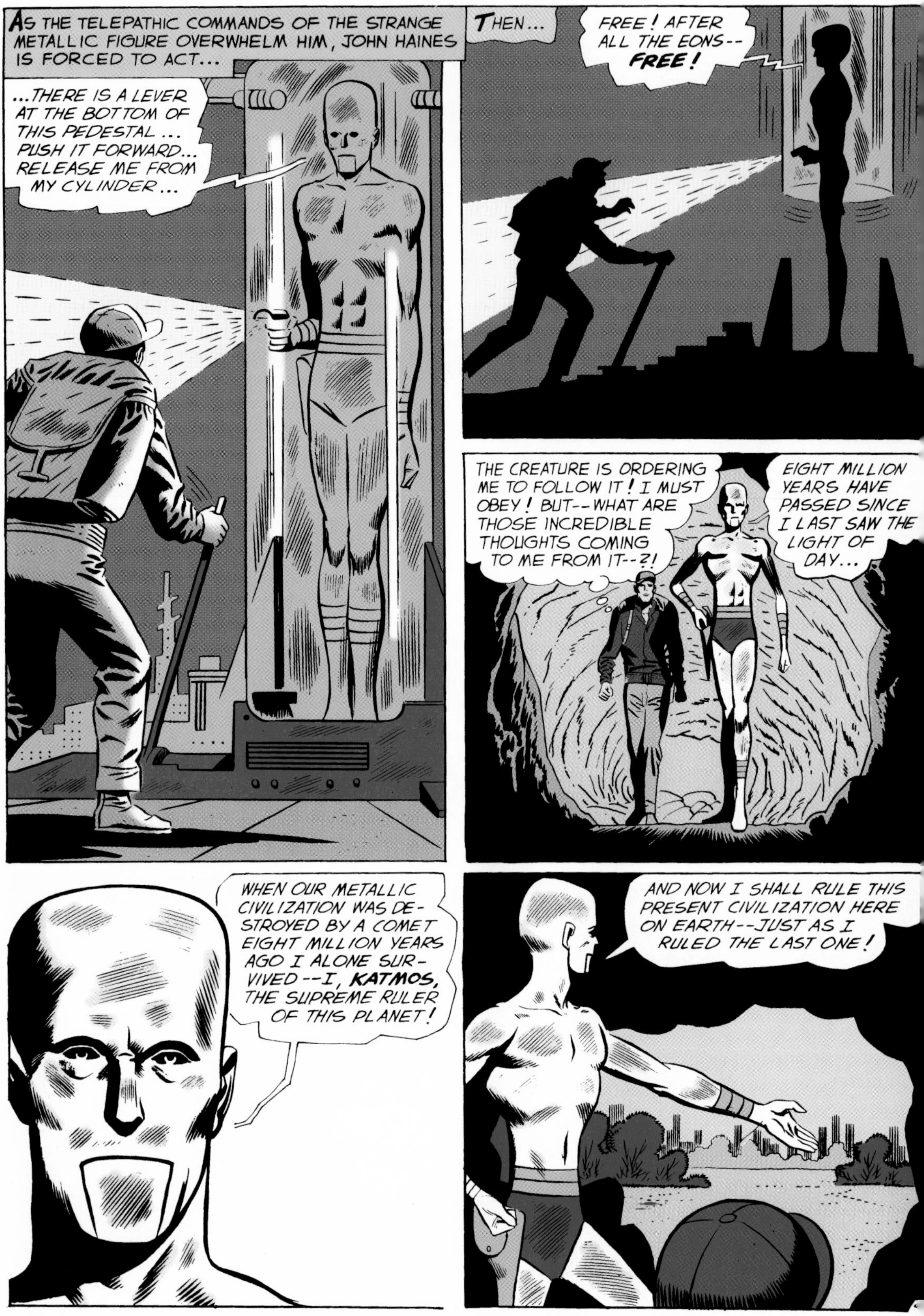
AS THE TELEPATHIC COMMANDS OF THE STRANGE METALLIC FIGURE OVERWHELM HIM, JOHN HAINES IS FORCED TO ACT...
...THERE IS A LEVER AT THE BOTTOM OF THIS PEDESTAL ... PUSH IT FORWARD... RELEASE ME FROM MY CYLINDER...
THEN...
FREE! AFTER ALL THE EONS-- FREE!
THE CREATURE IS ORDERING ME TO FOLLOW IT! I MUST OBEY! BUT--WHAT ARE THOSE INCREDIBLE THOUGHTS COMING TO ME FROM IT--?!
EIGHT MILLION YEARS HAVE PASSED SINCE I LAST SAW THE LIGHT OF DAY...
WHEN OUR METALLIC CIVILIZATION WAS DESTROYED BY A COMET EIGHT MILLION YEARS AGO I ALONE SURVIVED--I, KATMOS, THE SUPREME RULER OF THIS PLANET!
AND NOW I SHALL RULE THIS PRESENT CIVILIZATION HERE ON EARTH--JUST AS I RULED THE LAST ONE!

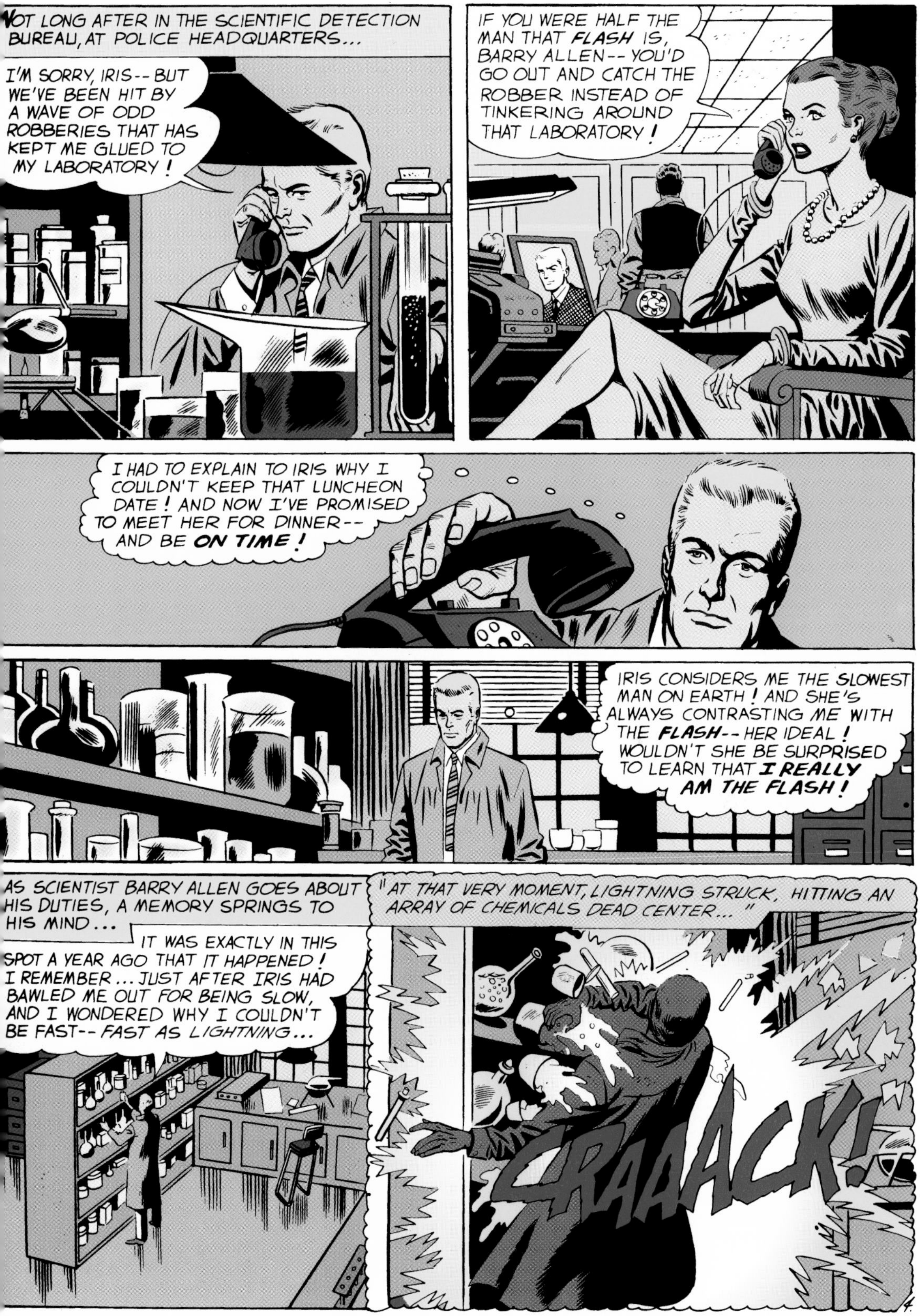
NOT LONG AFTER IN THE SCIENTIFIC DETECTION BUREAU, AT POLICE HEADQUARTERS...
I'M SORRY, IRIS-- BUT WE'VE BEEN HIT BY A WAVE OF ODD ROBBERIES THAT HAS KEPT ME GLUED TO MY LABORATORY!
IF YOU WERE HALF THE MAN THAT FLASH IS, BARRY ALLEN-- YOU'D GO OUT AND CATCH THE ROBBER INSTEAD OF TINKERING AROUND THAT LABORATORY!
I HAD TO EXPLAIN TO IRIS WHY I COULDN'T KEEP THAT LUNCHEON DATE! AND NOW I'VE PROMISED TO MEET HER FOR DINNER-- AND BE ON TIME!
IRIS CONSIDERS ME THE SLOWEST MAN ON EARTH! AND SHE'S ALWAYS CONTRASTING ME WITH THE FLASH-- HER IDEAL! WOULDN'T SHE BE SURPRISED TO LEARN THAT I REALLY AM THE FLASH!
AS SCIENTIST BARRY ALLEN GOES ABOUT HIS DUTIES, A MEMORY SPRINGS TO HIS MIND...
IT WAS EXACTLY IN THIS SPOT A YEAR AGO THAT IT HAPPENED! I REMEMBER... JUST AFTER IRIS HAD BAWLED ME OUT FOR BEING SLOW, AND I WONDERED WHY I COULDN'T BE FAST-- FAST AS LIGHTNING...
"AT THAT VERY MOMENT, LIGHTNING STRUCK, HITTING AN ARRAY OF CHEMICALS DEAD CENTER..."
CRAAACK!
4.

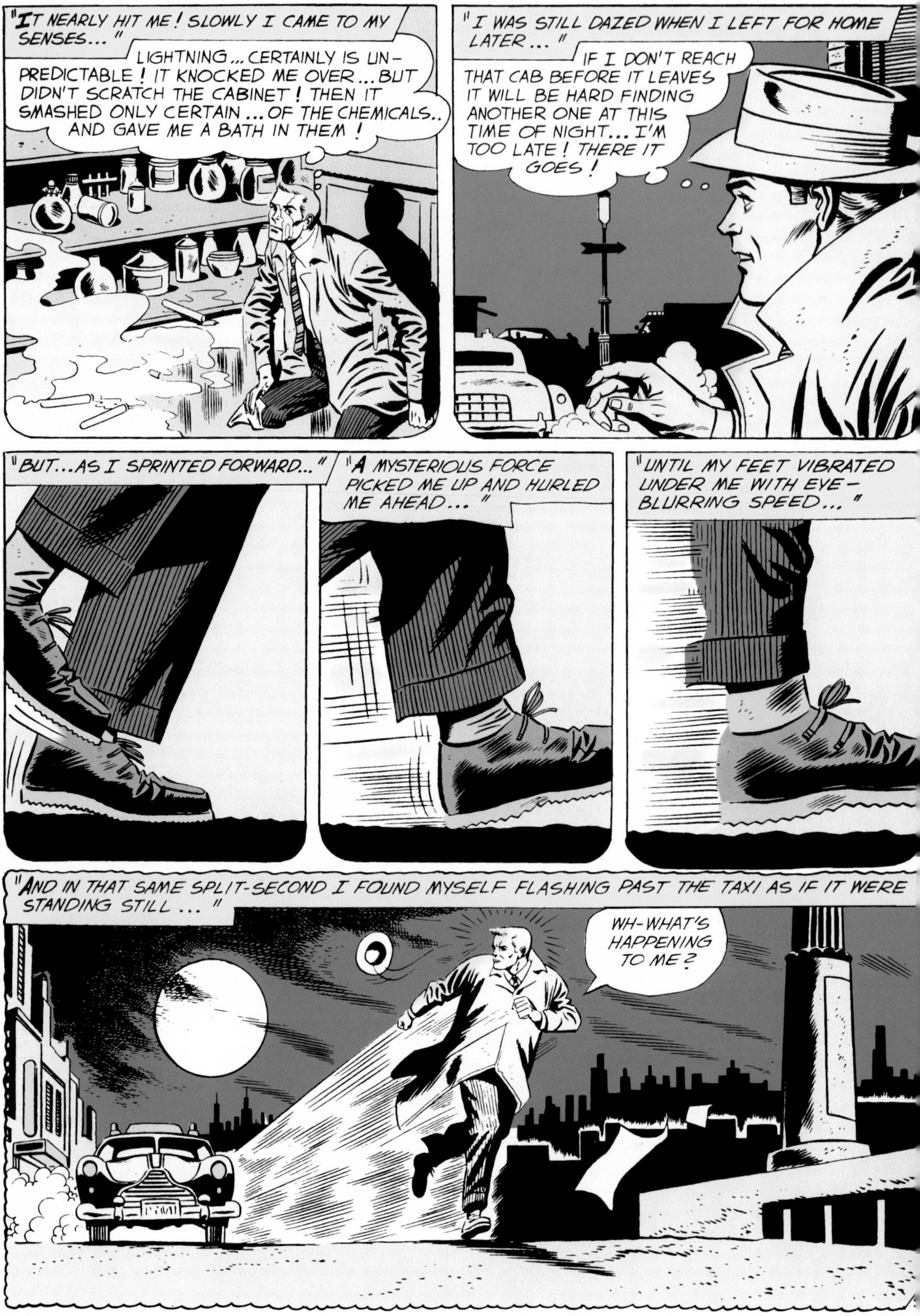
"IT NEARLY HIT ME! SLOWLY I CAME TO MY SENSES..."
LIGHTNING... CERTAINLY IS UN-PREDICTABLE! IT KNOCKED ME OVER... BUT DIDN'T SCRATCH THE CABINET! THEN IT SMASHED ONLY CERTAIN... OF THE CHEMICALS.. AND GAVE ME A BATH IN THEM!
"I WAS STILL DAZED WHEN I LEFT FOR HOME LATER..."
IF I DON'T REACH THAT CAB BEFORE IT LEAVES IT WILL BE HARD FINDING ANOTHER ONE AT THIS TIME OF NIGHT... I'M TOO LATE! THERE IT GOES!
"BUT...AS I SPRINTED FORWARD..."
"A MYSTERIOUS FORCE PICKED ME UP AND HURLED ME AHEAD..."
"UNTIL MY FEET VIBRATED UNDER ME WITH EYE-BLURRING SPEED..."
"AND IN THAT SAME SPLIT-SECOND I FOUND MYSELF FLASHING PAST THE TAXI AS IF IT WERE STANDING STILL..."
WH-WHAT'S HAPPENING TO ME?

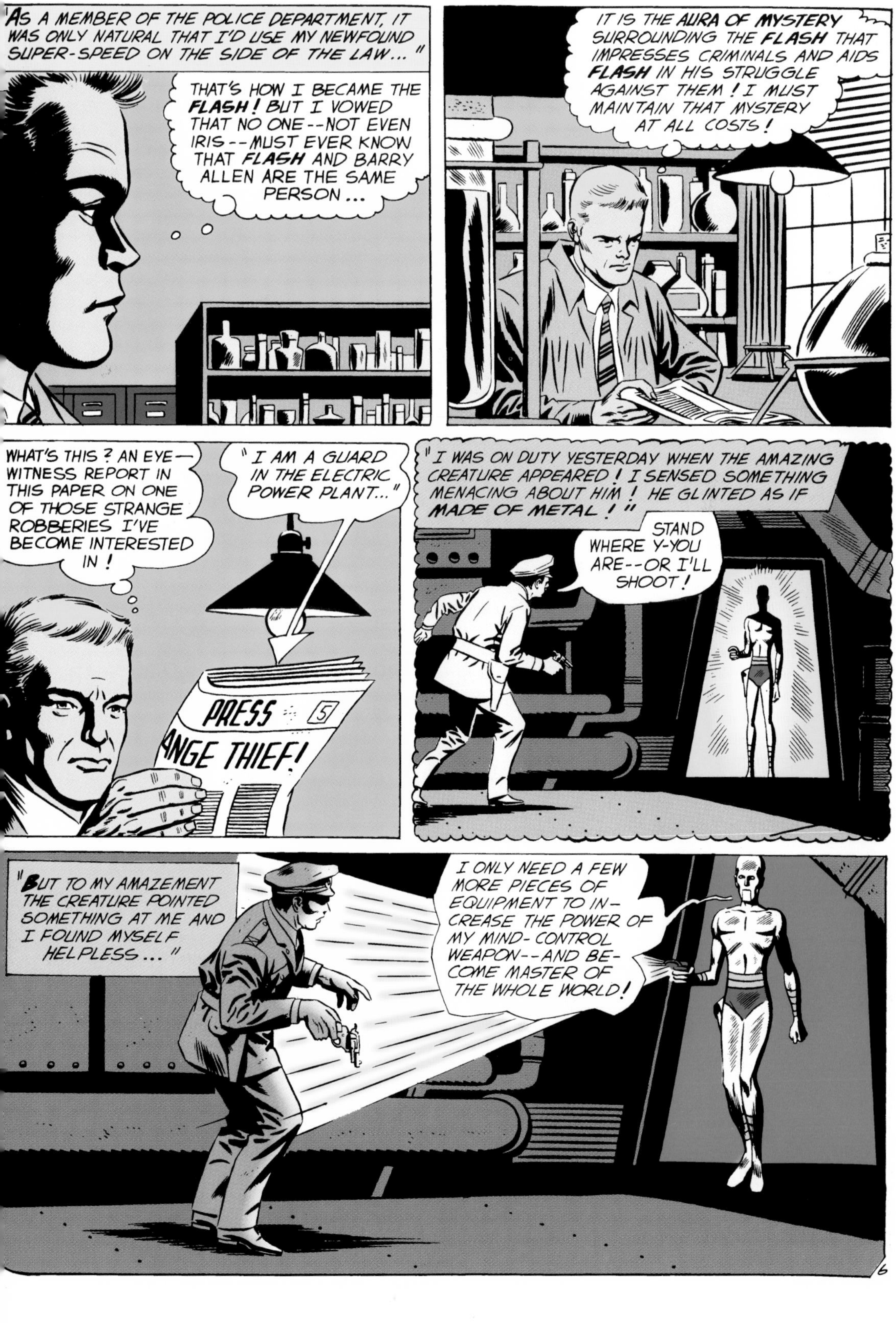
"AS A MEMBER OF THE POLICE DEPARTMENT, IT WAS ONLY NATURAL THAT I'D USE MY NEWFOUND SUPER-SPEED ON THE SIDE OF THE LAW..."
THAT'S HOW I BECAME THE FLASH! BUT I VOWED THAT NO ONE--NOT EVEN IRIS--MUST EVER KNOW THAT FLASH AND BARRY ALLEN ARE THE SAME PERSON...
IT IS THE AURA OF MYSTERY SURROUNDING THE FLASH THAT IMPRESSES CRIMINALS AND AIDS FLASH IN HIS STRUGGLE AGAINST THEM! I MUST MAINTAIN THAT MYSTERY AT ALL COSTS!
WHAT'S THIS? AN EYE-WITNESS REPORT IN THIS PAPER ON ONE OF THOSE STRANGE ROBBERIES I'VE BECOME INTERESTED IN!
"I AM A GUARD IN THE ELECTRIC POWER PLANT..."
PRESS 5
ANGE THIEF!
"I WAS ON DUTY YESTERDAY WHEN THE AMAZING CREATURE APPEARED! I SENSED SOMETHING MENACING ABOUT HIM! HE GLINTED AS IF MADE OF METAL!"
STAND WHERE Y-YOU ARE--OR I'LL SHOOT!
"BUT TO MY AMAZEMENT THE CREATURE POINTED SOMETHING AT ME AND I FOUND MYSELF HELPLESS..."
I ONLY NEED A FEW MORE PIECES OF EQUIPMENT TO INCREASE THE POWER OF MY MIND-CONTROL WEAPON--AND BECOME MASTER OF THE WHOLE WORLD!
6

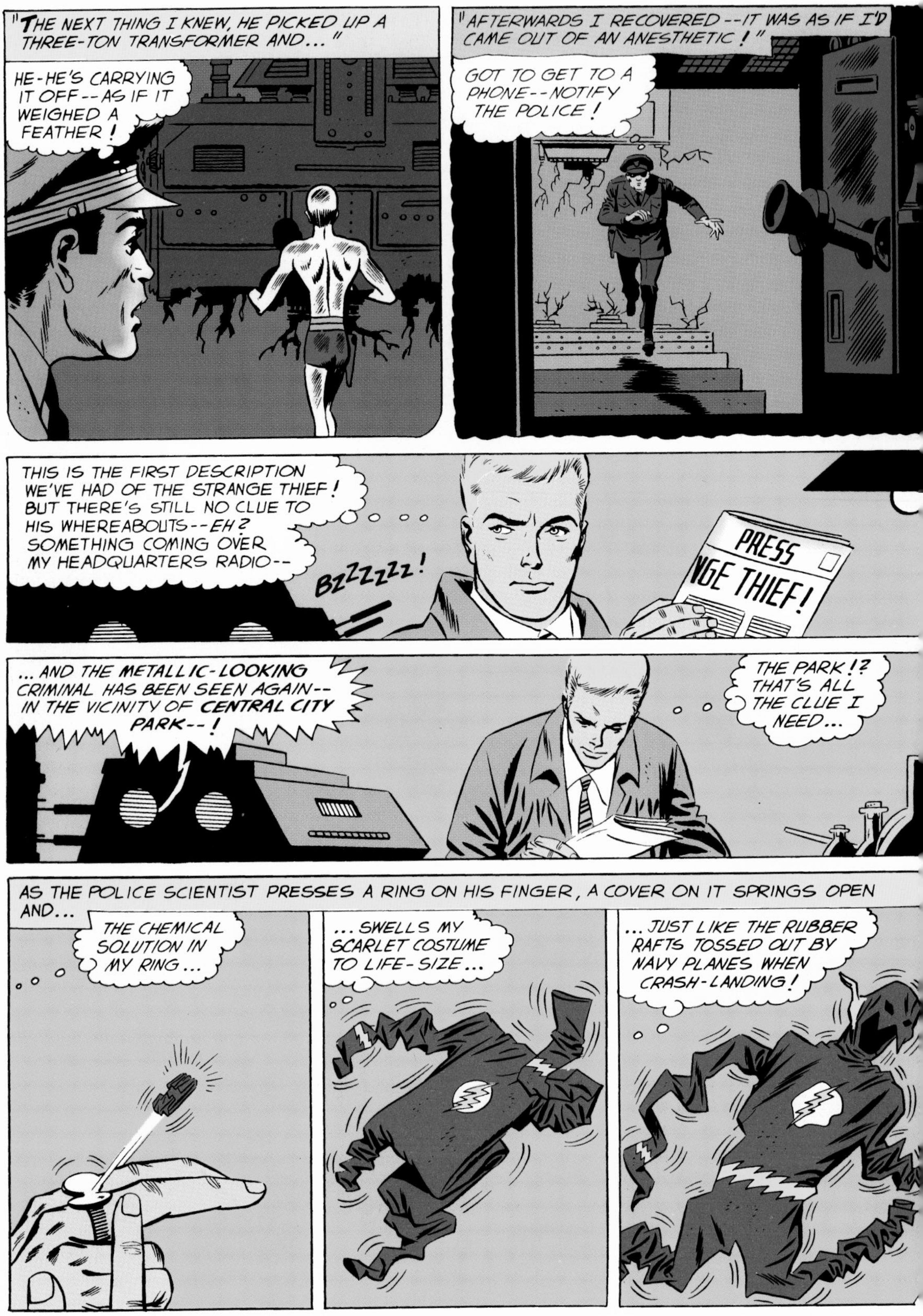
"THE NEXT THING I KNEW, HE PICKED UP A THREE-TON TRANSFORMER AND..."
HE-HE'S CARRYING IT OFF--AS IF IT WEIGHED A FEATHER!
"AFTERWARDS I RECOVERED--IT WAS AS IF I'D CAME OUT OF AN ANESTHETIC!"
GOT TO GET TO A PHONE--NOTIFY THE POLICE!
THIS IS THE FIRST DESCRIPTION WE'VE HAD OF THE STRANGE THIEF! BUT THERE'S STILL NO CLUE TO HIS WHEREABOUTS--EH? SOMETHING COMING OVER MY HEADQUARTERS RADIO--
BZZZZZZ!
PRESS
NGE THIEF!
...AND THE METALLIC-LOOKING CRIMINAL HAS BEEN SEEN AGAIN--IN THE VICINITY OF CENTRAL CITY PARK--!
THE PARK!? THAT'S ALL THE CLUE I NEED...
AS THE POLICE SCIENTIST PRESSES A RING ON HIS FINGER, A COVER ON IT SPRINGS OPEN AND...
THE CHEMICAL SOLUTION IN MY RING...
...SWELLS MY SCARLET COSTUME TO LIFE-SIZE...
...JUST LIKE THE RUBBER RAFTS TOSSED OUT BY NAVY PLANES WHEN CRASH-LANDING!

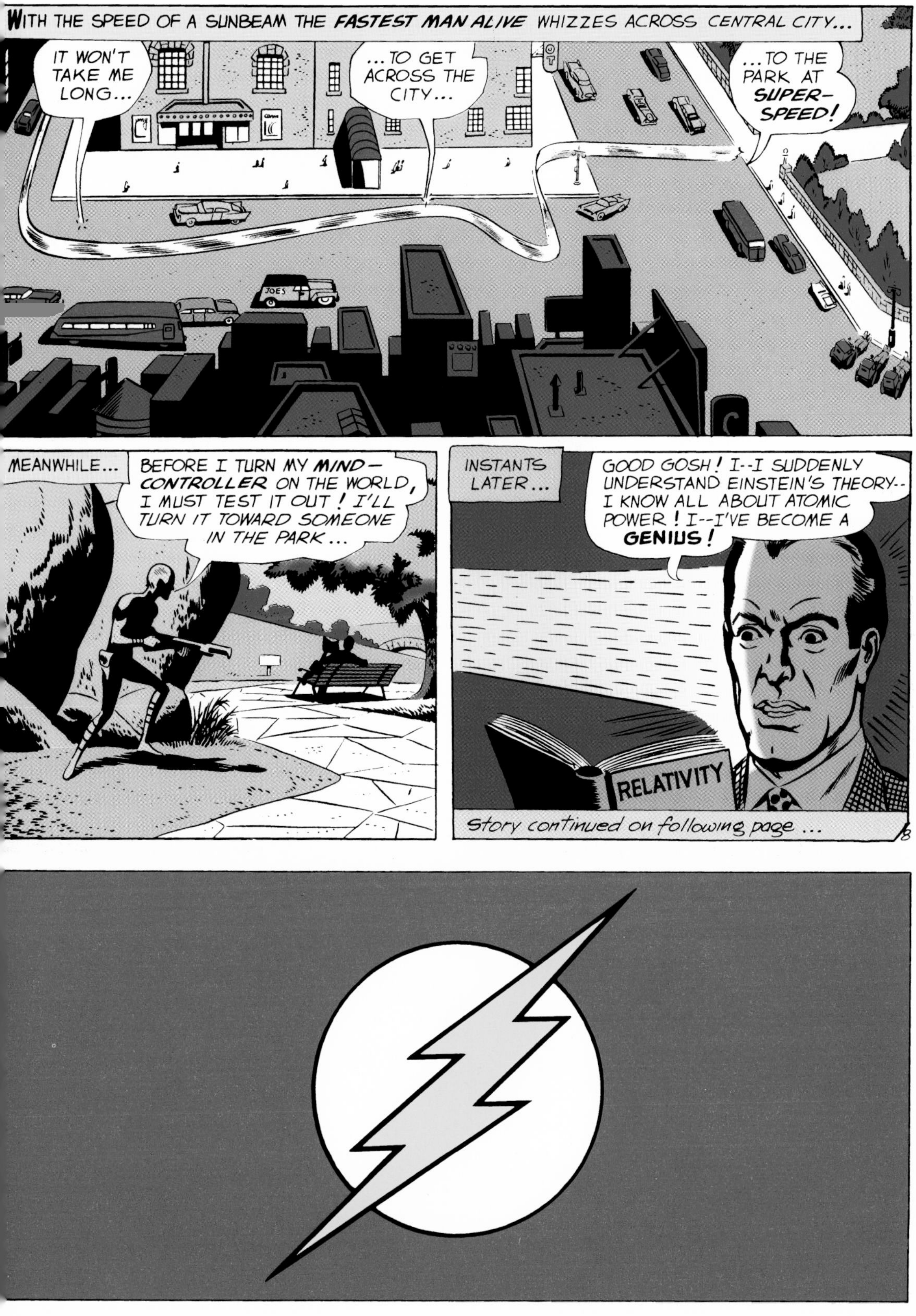
WITH THE SPEED OF A SUNBEAM THE FASTEST MAN ALIVE WHIZZES ACROSS CENTRAL CITY...
IT WON'T TAKE ME LONG...
...TO GET ACROSS THE CITY...
...TO THE PARK AT SUPER-SPEED!
JOES
MEANWHILE...
BEFORE I TURN MY MIND-CONTROLLER ON THE WORLD, I MUST TEST IT OUT! I'LL TURN IT TOWARD SOMEONE IN THE PARK...
INSTANTS LATER...
GOOD GOSH! I--I SUDDENLY UNDERSTAND EINSTEIN'S THEORY--I KNOW ALL ABOUT ATOMIC POWER! I--I'VE BECOME A GENIUS!
RELATIVITY
Story continued on following page ...
8

MY WEAPON NEEDS ADJUSTMENT! INSTEAD OF TURNING THESE PEOPLE INTO MIND-SLAVES-- IT MAKES GENIUSES OUT OF THEM! I CAN'T ALLOW *THAT* TO HAPPEN!

WHAT'S THAT--?

CONTINUED...

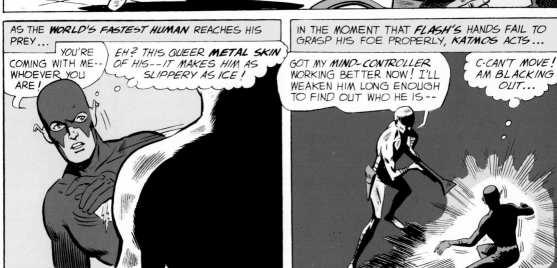

AS THE *WORLD'S FASTEST HUMAN* REACHES HIS PREY...

YOU'RE COMING WITH ME-- WHOEVER YOU ARE!

EH? THIS QUEER *METAL SKIN* OF HIS--IT MAKES HIM AS SLIPPERY AS ICE!

IN THE MOMENT THAT *FLASH'S* HANDS FAIL TO GRASP HIS FOE PROPERLY, *KATMOS* ACTS...

GOT MY *MIND-CONTROLLER* WORKING BETTER NOW! I'LL WEAKEN HIM LONG ENOUGH TO FIND OUT WHO HE IS--

C-CAN'T MOVE! AM BLACKING OUT...

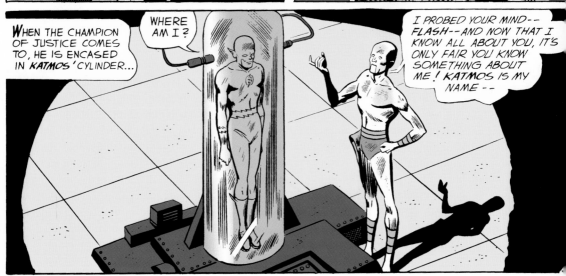

WHEN THE CHAMPION OF JUSTICE COMES TO, HE IS ENCASED IN *KATMOS'* CYLINDER...

WHERE AM I?

I PROBED YOUR MIND-- FLASH--AND NOW THAT I KNOW ALL ABOUT YOU, IT'S ONLY FAIR YOU KNOW SOMETHING ABOUT ME! *KATMOS* IS MY NAME--

MY RACE WAS DIFFERENT FROM YOURS, *FLASH!* A RACE BASED ON *IRON* ATOMS--AS YOUR FORM OF LIFE IS BASED ON *CARBON!* BUT EIGHT MILLION YEARS AGO OUR RACE PERISHED--DUE TO A COMET! I ALONE SURVIVED-- BY THE SCIENCE OF SUSPENDED ANIMATION--!

NOW, AS I PLANNED, I HAVE COME TO LIFE AGAIN...TO TAKE OVER RULE OF EARTH ONCE MORE! YOU ARE MY BIGGEST THREAT, *FLASH!* AND SO I SHALL DISPOSE OF YOU AS I DISPOSED OF MY ENEMIES IN MY TIME! I HAVE MADE AN OPENING IN THE CAVERN ROOF ABOVE...

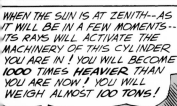

WHEN THE SUN IS AT ZENITH--AS IT WILL BE IN A FEW MOMENTS-- ITS RAYS WILL ACTIVATE THE MACHINERY OF THIS CYLINDER YOU ARE IN! YOU WILL BECOME *1000* TIMES *HEAVIER* THAN YOU ARE NOW! YOU WILL WEIGH ALMOST *100 TONS!*

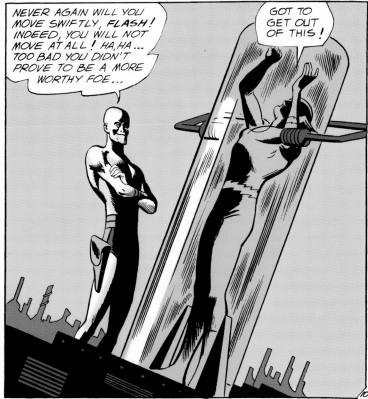

NEVER AGAIN WILL YOU MOVE SWIFTLY, *FLASH!* INDEED, YOU WILL NOT MOVE AT ALL! HA,HA... TOO BAD YOU DIDN'T PROVE TO BE A MORE WORTHY FOE...

GOT TO GET OUT OF THIS!

10

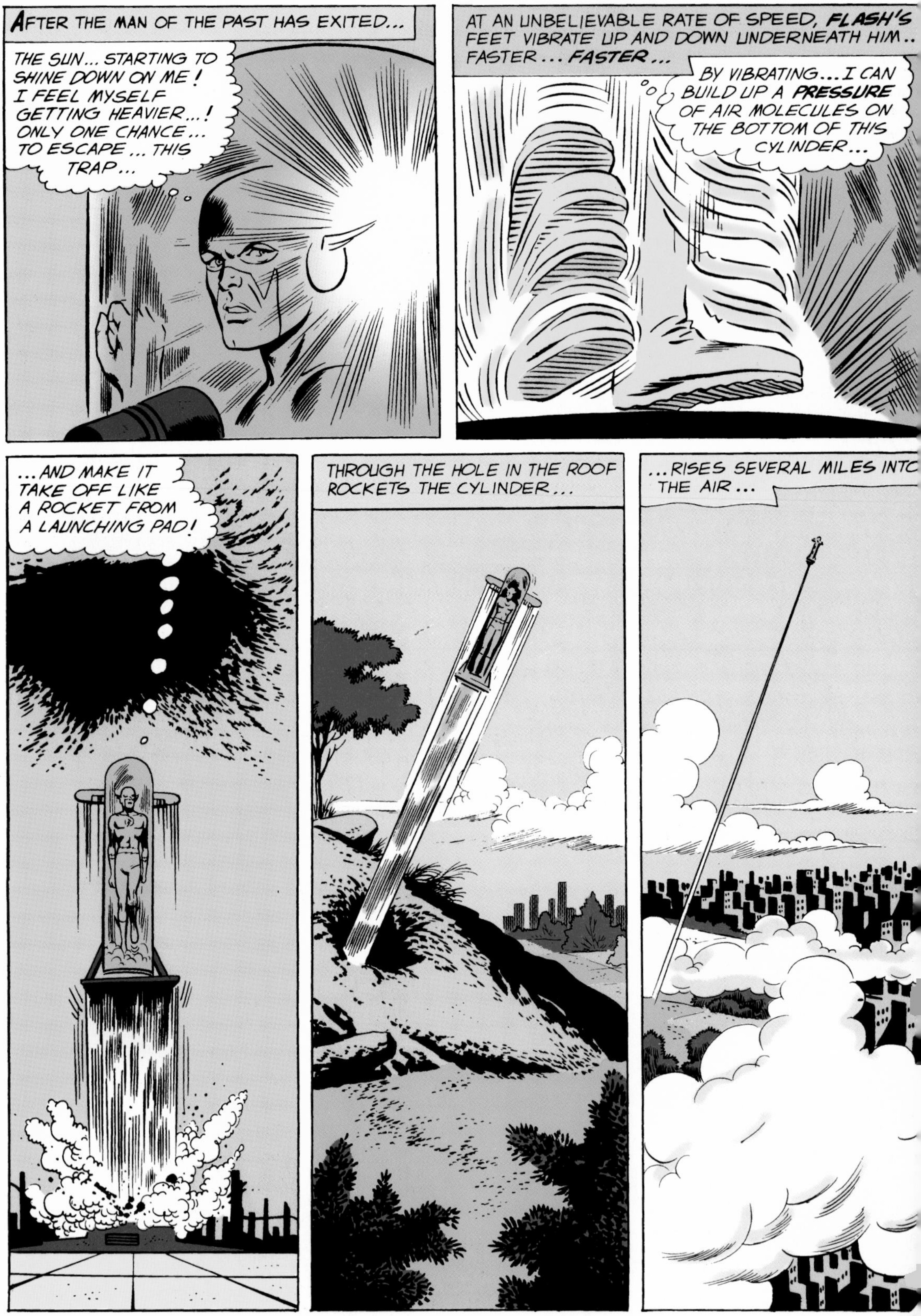
AFTER THE MAN OF THE PAST HAS EXITED...
THE SUN... STARTING TO SHINE DOWN ON ME! I FEEL MYSELF GETTING HEAVIER...! ONLY ONE CHANCE... TO ESCAPE... THIS TRAP...
AT AN UNBELIEVABLE RATE OF SPEED, FLASH'S FEET VIBRATE UP AND DOWN UNDERNEATH HIM.. FASTER... FASTER...
BY VIBRATING... I CAN BUILD UP A PRESSURE OF AIR MOLECULES ON THE BOTTOM OF THIS CYLINDER...
...AND MAKE IT TAKE OFF LIKE A ROCKET FROM A LAUNCHING PAD!
THROUGH THE HOLE IN THE ROOF ROCKETS THE CYLINDER...
...RISES SEVERAL MILES INTO THE AIR...

...THEN FALLS BACK TO EARTH...

FREE! NOW TO TAKE CARE OF KATMOS!

UNBELIEVABLE! FLASH ESCAPED MY SUN-TRAP!

AS **KATMOS** TURNS HIS WEAPON ON THE **SCARLET SPEEDSTER**...

FLASH SHALL BE THE FIRST VICTIM OF THE FULL POWER OF MY **MIND-CONTROLLER**! AS SOON AS THE RAYS HIT HIM, HE WILL BECOME A MINDLESS PAWN!

SSSST!

BUT AS BURSTS OF RADIATION SHOOT OUT...

EH? MY RADIATION ISN'T HITTING HIM! WITH THAT INCREDIBLE SPEED, HE'S DODGING BETWEEN THE **RAY-BURSTS** I'M SHOOTING OUT AT HIM!

SSSST!

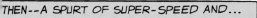

THEN--A SPURT OF SUPER-SPEED AND...

THIS TIME I WON'T MAKE ANY MISTAKE! I'LL KNOCK HIM OUT-- **BEFORE** I TRY TO GRAB HIM!

THAT EVENING, WITH **KATMOS** IN JAIL AND ARCHEOLOGIST JOHN HAINES RECOVERING FROM HIS EXPERIENCE, BARRY ALLEN KEEPS A DINNER DATE WITH IRIS WEST...

EXTRA! FLASH CAPTURES PREHISTORIC THIEF!

AREN'T YOU GOING TO BUY A COPY, BARRY-- AND READ MY EXCLUSIVE INTERVIEW WITH THE FLASH?

LATER, IRIS! ALL I'M INTERESTED IN NOW IS A **LEISURELY** DINNER!

The End

/12

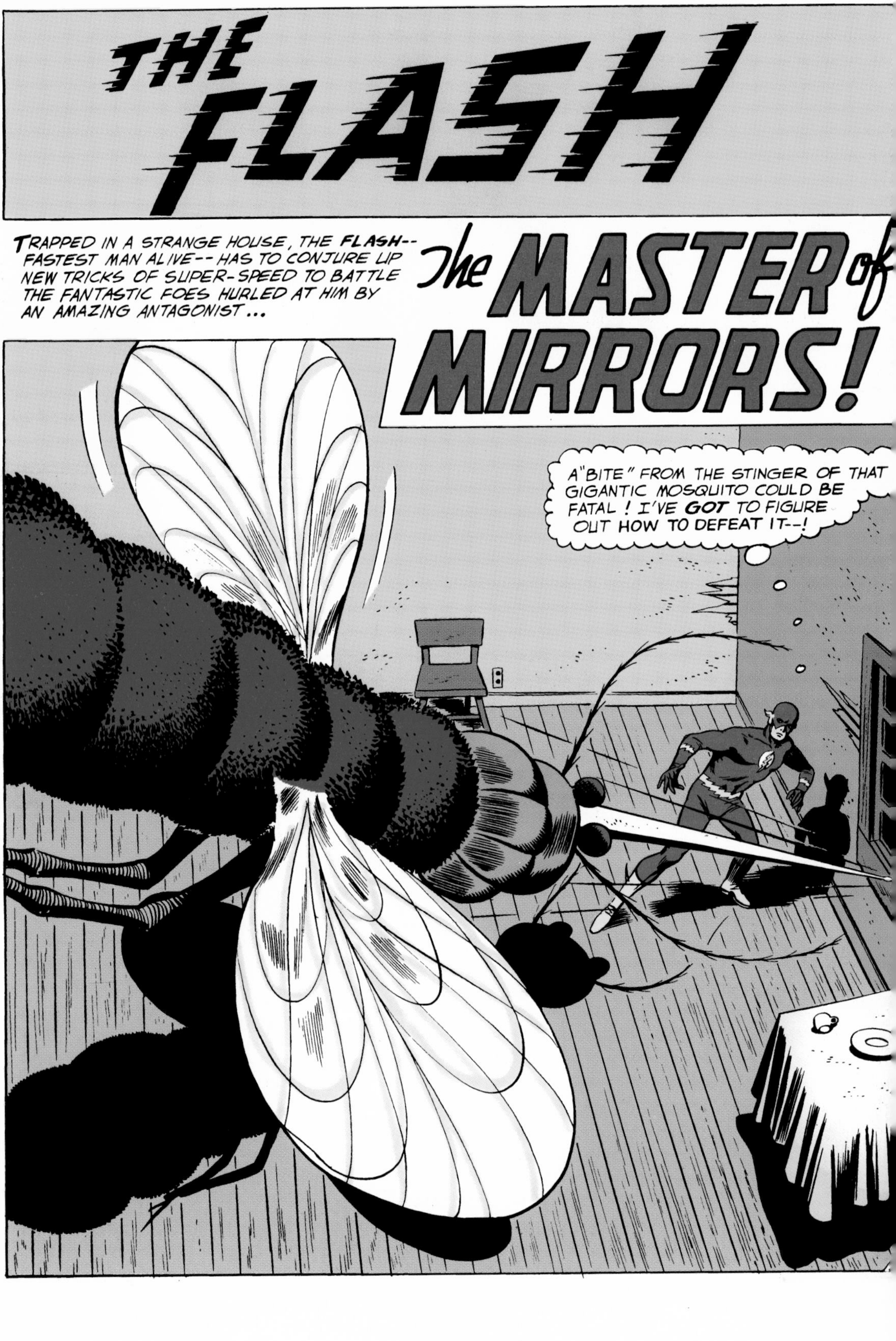
THE FLASH
TRAPPED IN A STRANGE HOUSE, THE FLASH-- FASTEST MAN ALIVE-- HAS TO CONJURE UP NEW TRICKS OF SUPER-SPEED TO BATTLE THE FANTASTIC FOES HURLED AT HIM BY AN AMAZING ANTAGONIST...
The MASTER of MIRRORS!
A "BITE" FROM THE STINGER OF THAT GIGANTIC MOSQUITO COULD BE FATAL! I'VE GOT TO FIGURE OUT HOW TO DEFEAT IT--!

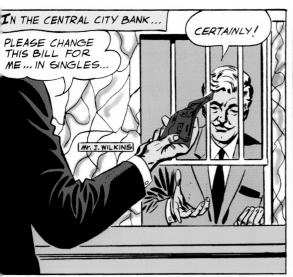

IN THE CENTRAL CITY BANK...

PLEASE CHANGE THIS BILL FOR ME... IN SINGLES...

CERTAINLY!

Mr. J. WILKINS

AS THE TELLER EXAMINES THE BILL, THE VISITOR PEERS AT HIM WITH CURIOUS INTENTNESS...

NOW TO NONCHALANTLY TAKE OUT MY CIGARETTE CASE...

...AND SECRETLY CAPTURE THE TELLER'S IMAGE IN THE CASE'S MIRROR!

MOMENTS LATER...

CAUGHT HIS REFLECTION FROM ALL ANGLES! GOT TO GET IT TO MY "DEVELOPING ROOM"...!

SOON, IN AN ISOLATED HOUSE OUTSIDE THE CITY...

I'LL SLIP INTO MY SPECIAL UNIFORM AND GO TO WORK! SCIENCE WOULD GIVE A GOOD DEAL TO KNOW HOW THIS "CAMERA MIRROR" OF MINE CAPTURES AN IMAGE -- *AND HOLDS IT!* BUT THAT'S ONLY THE SIMPLEST PART OF THE TRICKS I CAN DO-- *WITH MIRRORS!*

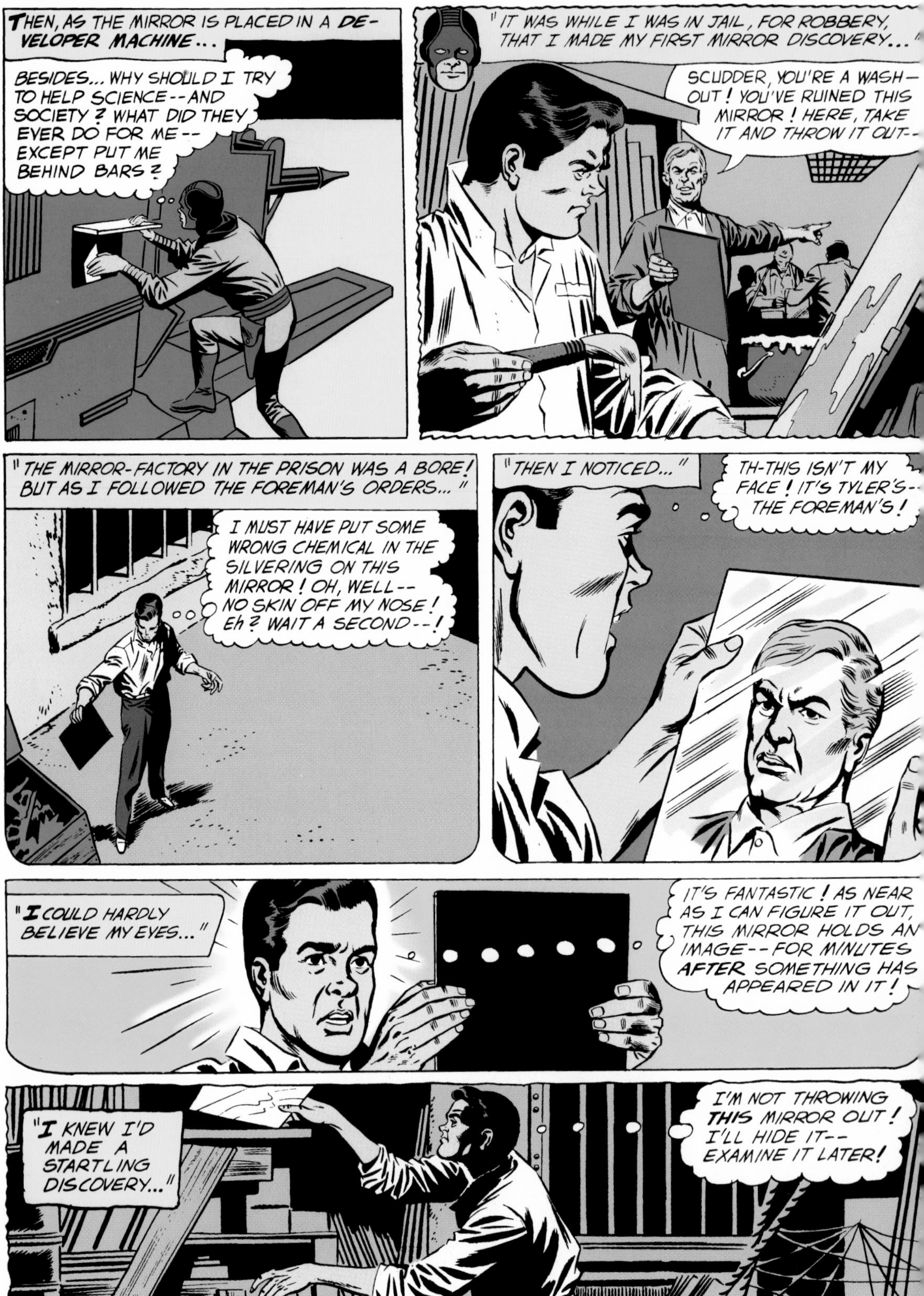
THEN, AS THE MIRROR IS PLACED IN A DEVELOPER MACHINE...
BESIDES... WHY SHOULD I TRY TO HELP SCIENCE--AND SOCIETY? WHAT DID THEY EVER DO FOR ME--EXCEPT PUT ME BEHIND BARS?
"IT WAS WHILE I WAS IN JAIL, FOR ROBBERY, THAT I MADE MY FIRST MIRROR DISCOVERY..."
SCUDDER, YOU'RE A WASH-OUT! YOU'VE RUINED THIS MIRROR! HERE, TAKE IT AND THROW IT OUT--
"THE MIRROR-FACTORY IN THE PRISON WAS A BORE! BUT AS I FOLLOWED THE FOREMAN'S ORDERS..."
I MUST HAVE PUT SOME WRONG CHEMICAL IN THE SILVERING ON THIS MIRROR! OH, WELL--NO SKIN OFF MY NOSE! Eh? WAIT A SECOND--!
"THEN I NOTICED..."
TH-THIS ISN'T MY FACE! IT'S TYLER'S--THE FOREMAN'S!
"I COULD HARDLY BELIEVE MY EYES..."
IT'S FANTASTIC! AS NEAR AS I CAN FIGURE IT OUT, THIS MIRROR HOLDS AN IMAGE--FOR MINUTES AFTER SOMETHING HAS APPEARED IN IT!
"I KNEW I'D MADE A STARTLING DISCOVERY..."
I'M NOT THROWING THIS MIRROR OUT! I'LL HIDE IT--EXAMINE IT LATER!

THAT WAS THE START OF MY AMAZING MIRROR DISCOVERIES! SINCE MY RELEASE FROM JAIL, I'VE NOT ONLY PERFECTED MY IMAGE-CAPTURING MIRRORS--

I'VE EVEN FIGURED OUT HOW TO *"DEVELOP"* THE CAPTURED IMAGES IN THREE DIMENSIONS-- LIKE I'M DOING NOW--!

THE NEXT MOMENT...

IT'S COMING THROUGH...

A LITTLE MORE *"DEVELOPING-RAY"* IS MAKING IT CLEARER...

AH--A PERFECT *"PRINT"*!

THE BANK TELLER'S OWN MOTHER WOULDN'T KNOW HIM FROM THIS LIFESIZE *MIRROR-IMAGE*!

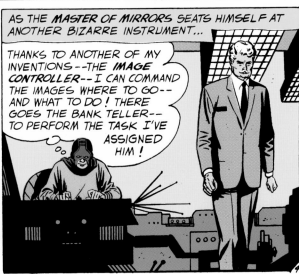

AS THE *MASTER OF MIRRORS* SEATS HIMSELF AT ANOTHER BIZARRE INSTRUMENT...

THANKS TO ANOTHER OF MY INVENTIONS--THE *IMAGE CONTROLLER*--I CAN COMMAND THE IMAGES WHERE TO GO-- AND WHAT TO DO! THERE GOES THE BANK TELLER-- TO PERFORM THE TASK I'VE ASSIGNED HIM!

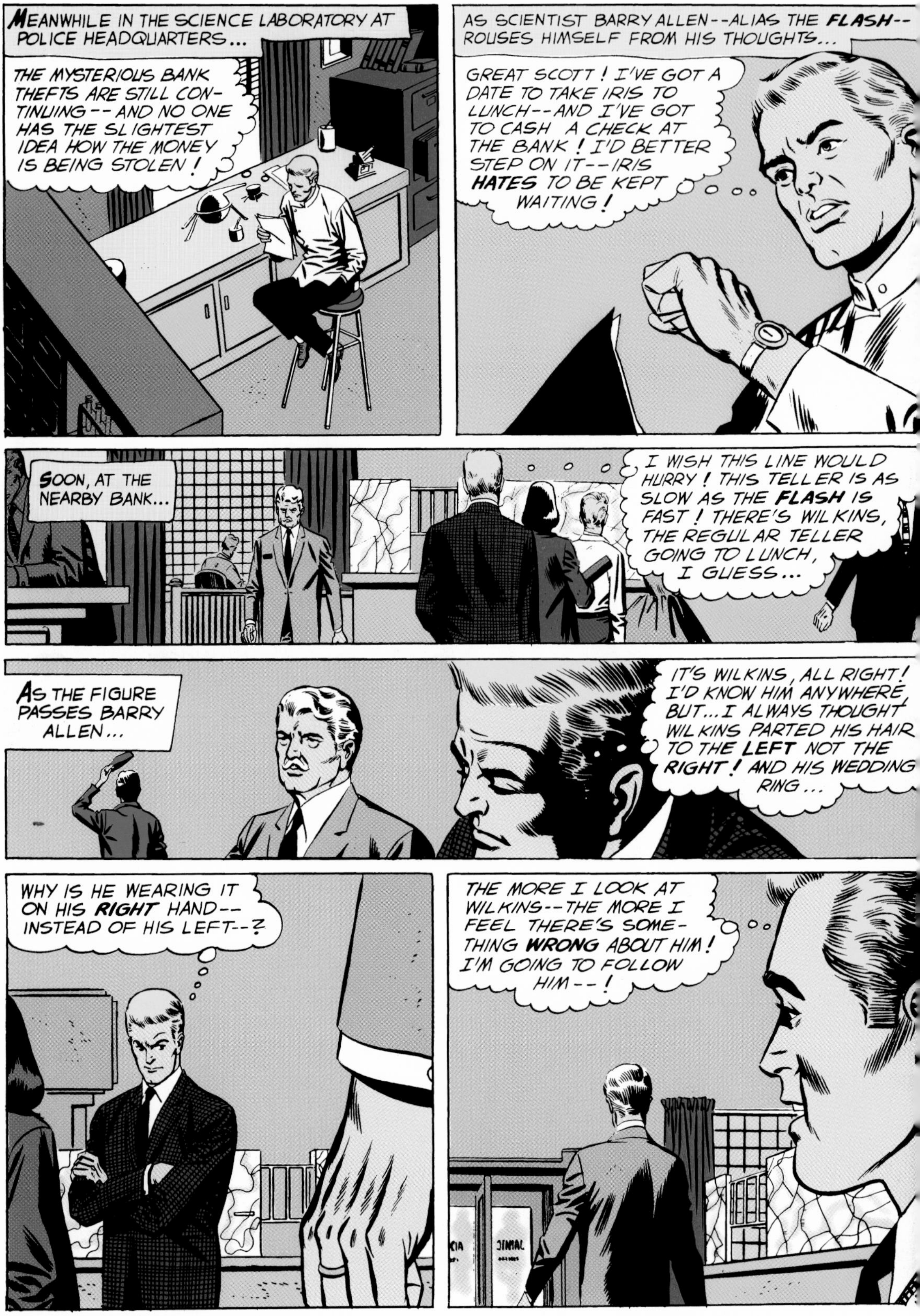
MEANWHILE IN THE SCIENCE LABORATORY AT POLICE HEADQUARTERS...
THE MYSTERIOUS BANK THEFTS ARE STILL CON-TINUING -- AND NO ONE HAS THE SLIGHTEST IDEA HOW THE MONEY IS BEING STOLEN!
AS SCIENTIST BARRY ALLEN--ALIAS THE FLASH--ROUSES HIMSELF FROM HIS THOUGHTS...
GREAT SCOTT! I'VE GOT A DATE TO TAKE IRIS TO LUNCH--AND I'VE GOT TO CASH A CHECK AT THE BANK! I'D BETTER STEP ON IT--IRIS HATES TO BE KEPT WAITING!
SOON, AT THE NEARBY BANK...
I WISH THIS LINE WOULD HURRY! THIS TELLER IS AS SLOW AS THE FLASH IS FAST! THERE'S WILKINS, THE REGULAR TELLER GOING TO LUNCH, I GUESS...
AS THE FIGURE PASSES BARRY ALLEN...
IT'S WILKINS, ALL RIGHT! I'D KNOW HIM ANYWHERE, BUT... I ALWAYS THOUGHT WILKINS PARTED HIS HAIR TO THE LEFT NOT THE RIGHT! AND HIS WEDDING RING...
WHY IS HE WEARING IT ON HIS RIGHT HAND--INSTEAD OF HIS LEFT--?
THE MORE I LOOK AT WILKINS--THE MORE I FEEL THERE'S SOME-THING WRONG ABOUT HIM! I'M GOING TO FOLLOW HIM--!

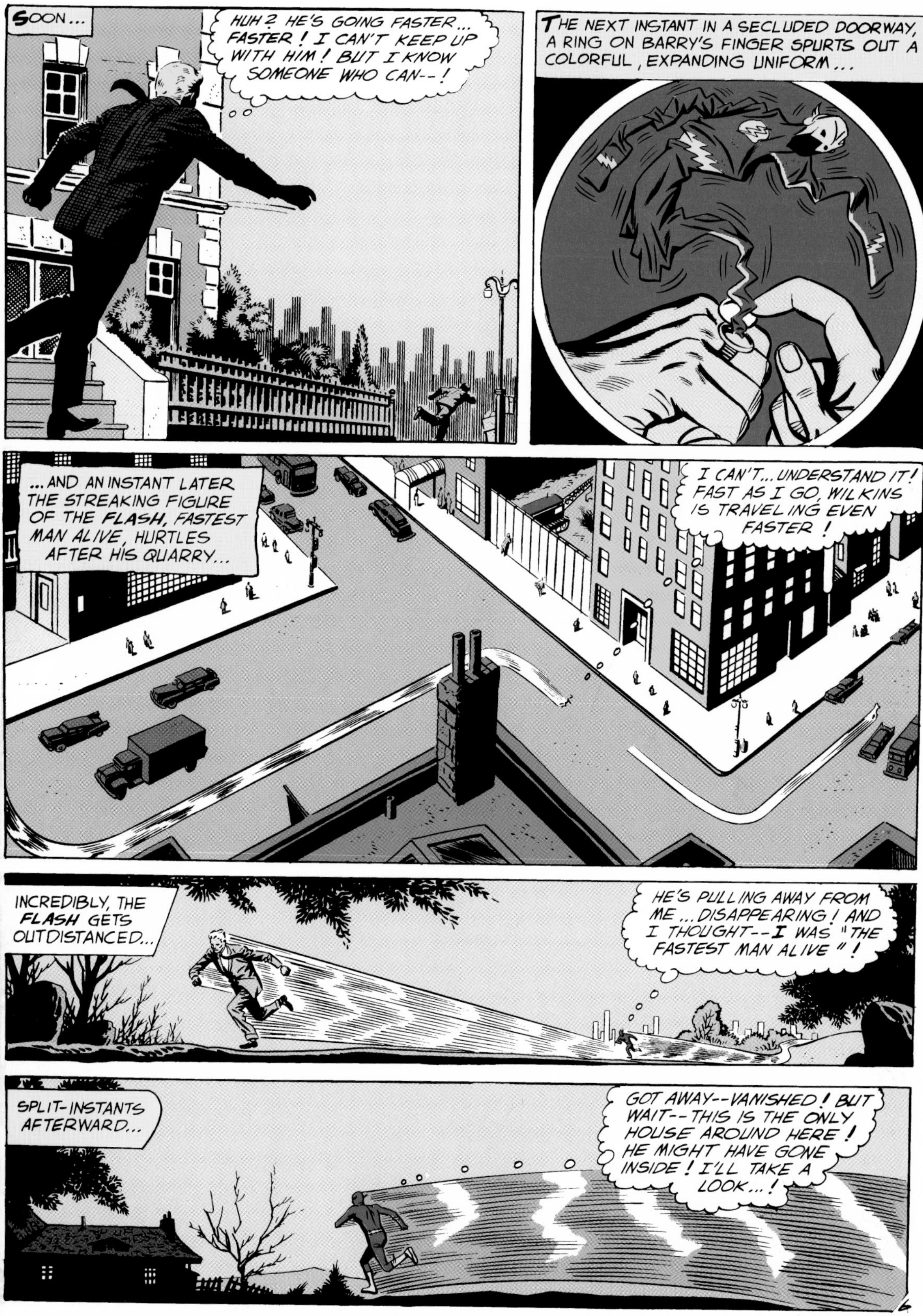
SOON...
HUH? HE'S GOING FASTER... FASTER! I CAN'T KEEP UP WITH HIM! BUT I KNOW SOMEONE WHO CAN--!
THE NEXT INSTANT IN A SECLUDED DOORWAY, A RING ON BARRY'S FINGER SPURTS OUT A COLORFUL, EXPANDING UNIFORM...
...AND AN INSTANT LATER THE STREAKING FIGURE OF THE FLASH, FASTEST MAN ALIVE, HURTLES AFTER HIS QUARRY...
I CAN'T... UNDERSTAND IT! FAST AS I GO, WILKINS IS TRAVELING EVEN FASTER!
INCREDIBLY, THE FLASH GETS OUTDISTANCED...
HE'S PULLING AWAY FROM ME... DISAPPEARING! AND I THOUGHT--I WAS "THE FASTEST MAN ALIVE"!
SPLIT-INSTANTS AFTERWARD...
GOT AWAY--VANISHED! BUT WAIT--THIS IS THE ONLY HOUSE AROUND HERE! HE MIGHT HAVE GONE INSIDE! I'LL TAKE A LOOK...!
6

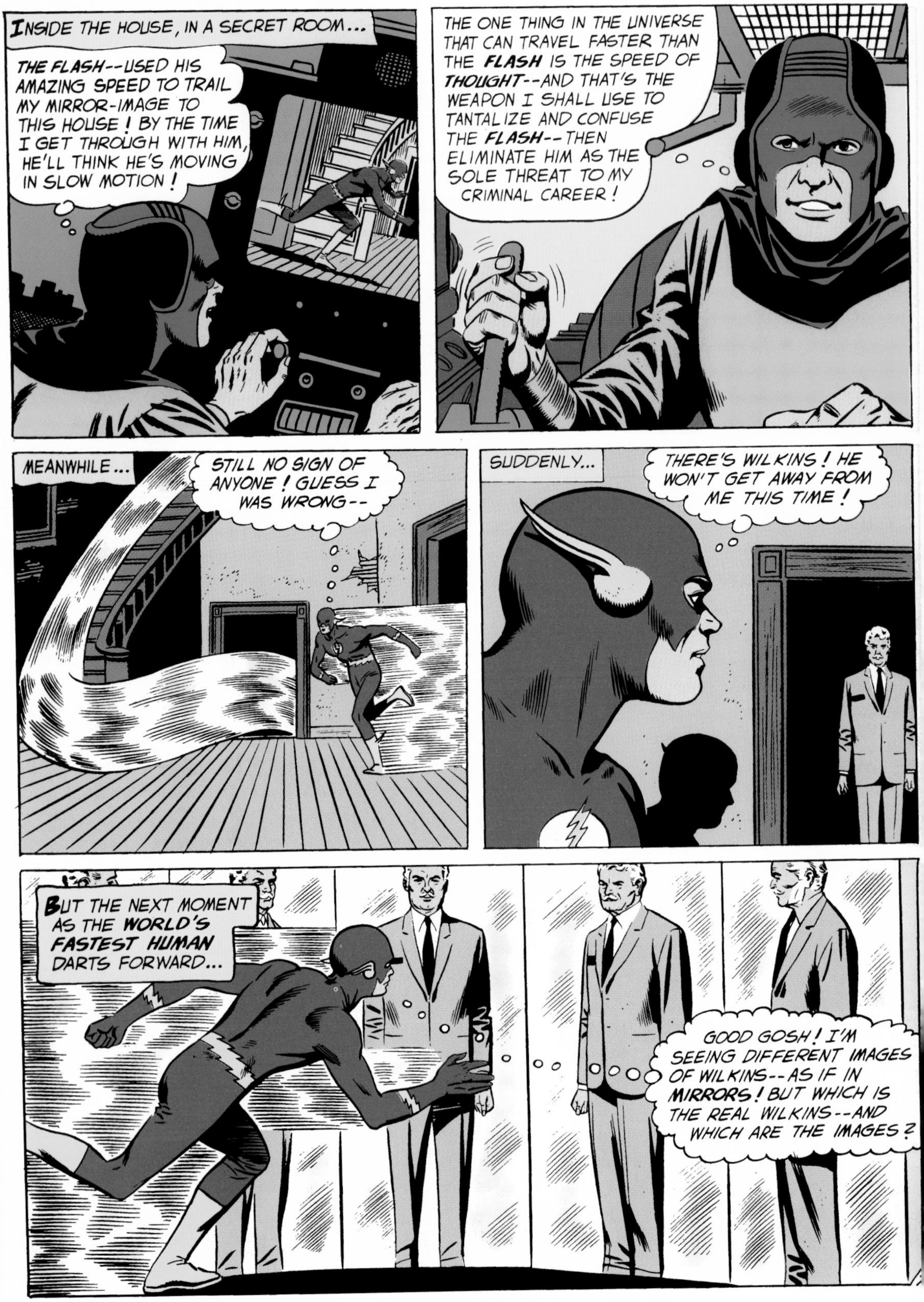
INSIDE THE HOUSE, IN A SECRET ROOM...
THE FLASH--USED HIS AMAZING SPEED TO TRAIL MY MIRROR-IMAGE TO THIS HOUSE! BY THE TIME I GET THROUGH WITH HIM, HE'LL THINK HE'S MOVING IN SLOW MOTION!
THE ONE THING IN THE UNIVERSE THAT CAN TRAVEL FASTER THAN THE FLASH IS THE SPEED OF THOUGHT--AND THAT'S THE WEAPON I SHALL USE TO TANTALIZE AND CONFUSE THE FLASH--THEN ELIMINATE HIM AS THE SOLE THREAT TO MY CRIMINAL CAREER!
MEANWHILE...
STILL NO SIGN OF ANYONE! GUESS I WAS WRONG--
SUDDENLY...
THERE'S WILKINS! HE WON'T GET AWAY FROM ME THIS TIME!
BUT THE NEXT MOMENT AS THE WORLD'S FASTEST HUMAN DARTS FORWARD...
GOOD GOSH! I'M SEEING DIFFERENT IMAGES OF WILKINS--AS IF IN MIRRORS! BUT WHICH IS THE REAL WILKINS--AND WHICH ARE THE IMAGES?

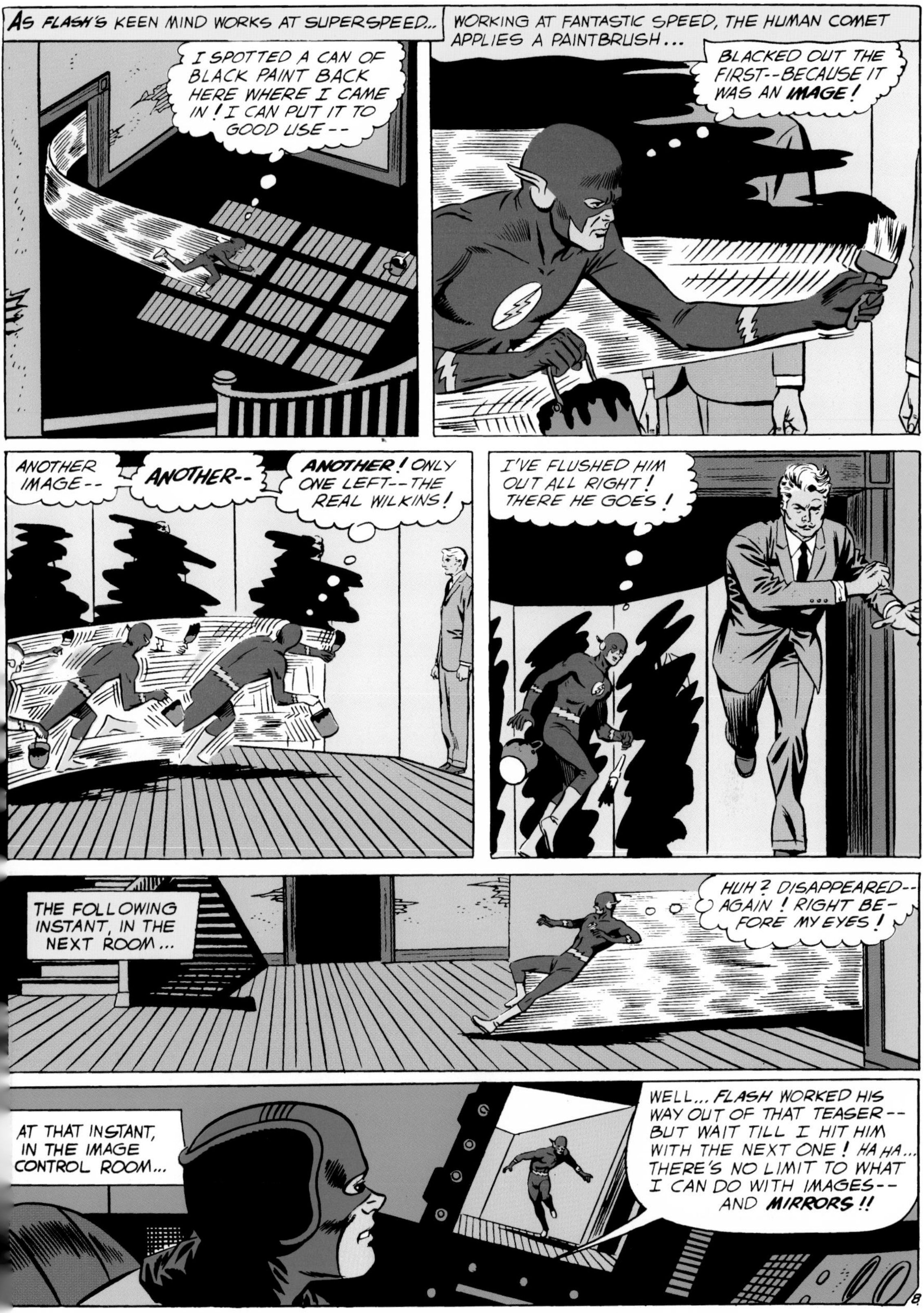
AS FLASH'S KEEN MIND WORKS AT SUPERSPEED...
I SPOTTED A CAN OF BLACK PAINT BACK HERE WHERE I CAME IN! I CAN PUT IT TO GOOD USE--
WORKING AT FANTASTIC SPEED, THE HUMAN COMET APPLIES A PAINTBRUSH...
BLACKED OUT THE FIRST--BECAUSE IT WAS AN IMAGE!
ANOTHER IMAGE--
ANOTHER--
ANOTHER! ONLY ONE LEFT--THE REAL WILKINS!
I'VE FLUSHED HIM OUT ALL RIGHT! THERE HE GOES!
THE FOLLOWING INSTANT, IN THE NEXT ROOM...
HUH? DISAPPEARED--AGAIN! RIGHT BEFORE MY EYES!
AT THAT INSTANT, IN THE IMAGE CONTROL ROOM...
WELL... FLASH WORKED HIS WAY OUT OF THAT TEASER--BUT WAIT TILL I HIT HIM WITH THE NEXT ONE! HA HA... THERE'S NO LIMIT TO WHAT I CAN DO WITH IMAGES--AND MIRRORS!!
8

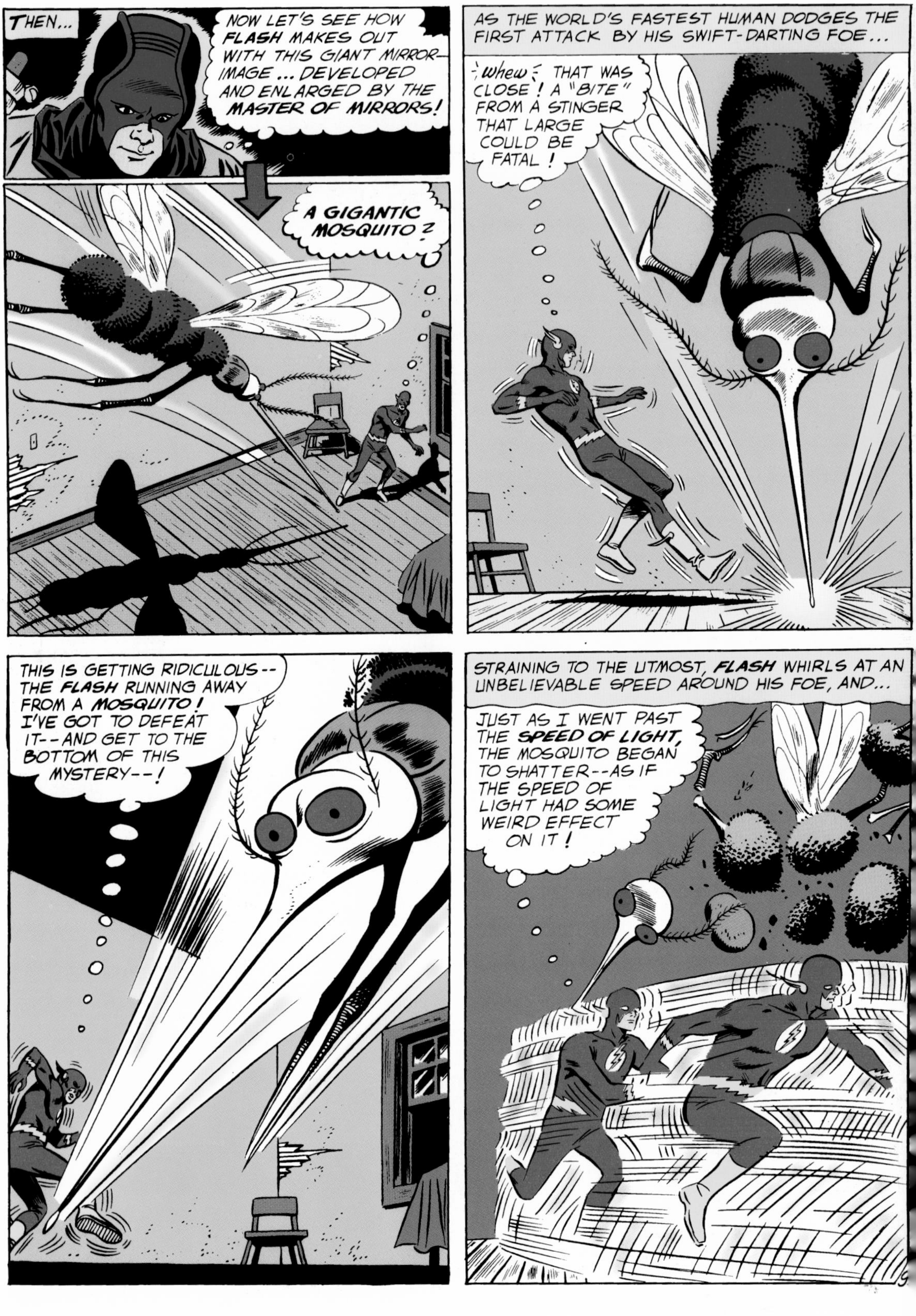
THEN...
NOW LET'S SEE HOW FLASH MAKES OUT WITH THIS GIANT MIRROR-IMAGE ... DEVELOPED AND ENLARGED BY THE MASTER OF MIRRORS!
A GIGANTIC MOSQUITO ?
AS THE WORLD'S FASTEST HUMAN DODGES THE FIRST ATTACK BY HIS SWIFT-DARTING FOE...
-WHEW- THAT WAS CLOSE! A "BITE" FROM A STINGER THAT LARGE COULD BE FATAL!
THIS IS GETTING RIDICULOUS-- THE FLASH RUNNING AWAY FROM A MOSQUITO! I'VE GOT TO DEFEAT IT--AND GET TO THE BOTTOM OF THIS MYSTERY--!
STRAINING TO THE UTMOST, FLASH WHIRLS AT AN UNBELIEVABLE SPEED AROUND HIS FOE, AND...
JUST AS I WENT PAST THE SPEED OF LIGHT, THE MOSQUITO BEGAN TO SHATTER--AS IF THE SPEED OF LIGHT HAD SOME WEIRD EFFECT ON IT!
9

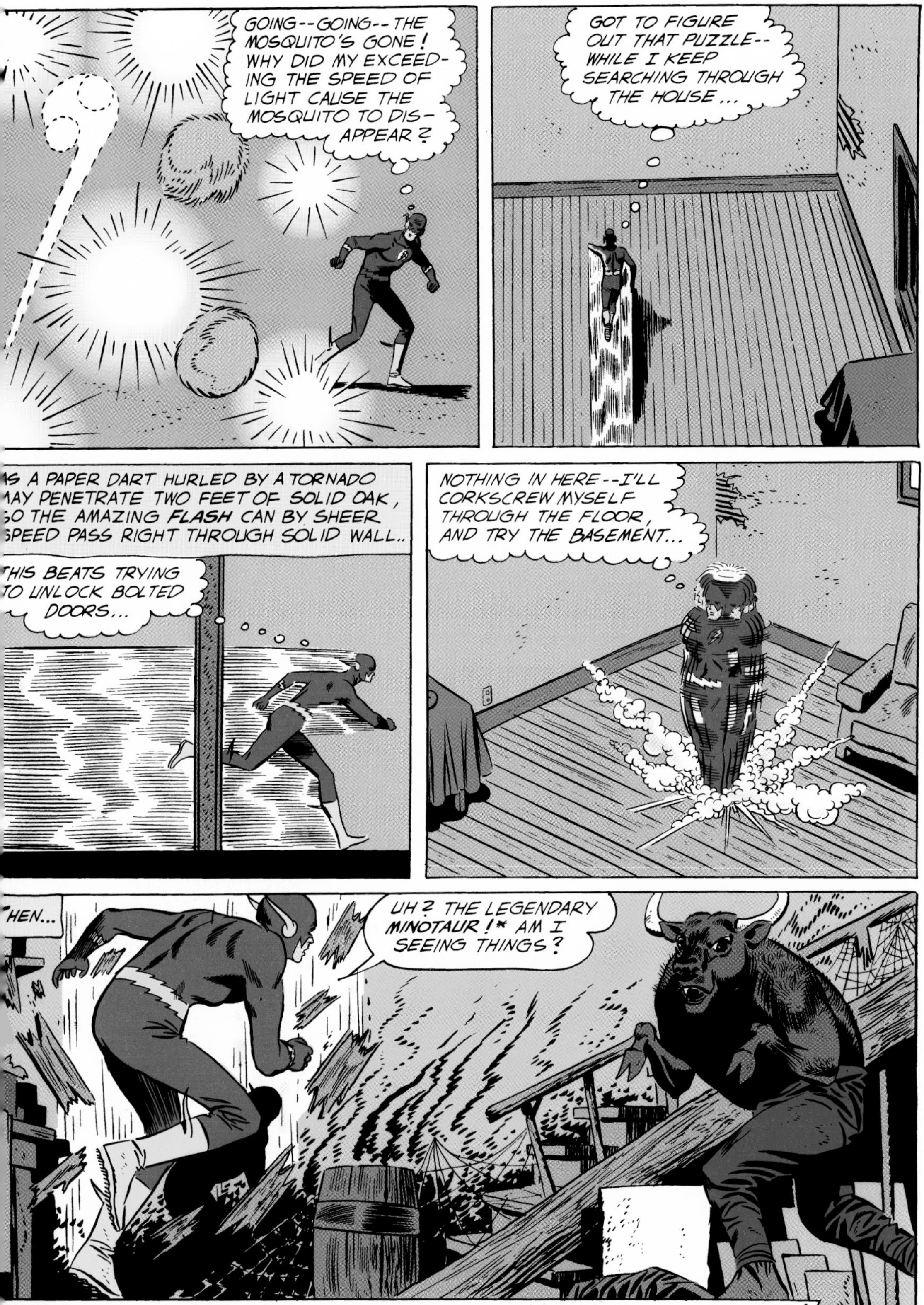
GOING--GOING--THE MOSQUITO'S GONE! WHY DID MY EXCEEDING THE SPEED OF LIGHT CAUSE THE MOSQUITO TO DISAPPEAR?
GOT TO FIGURE OUT THAT PUZZLE--WHILE I KEEP SEARCHING THROUGH THE HOUSE...
AS A PAPER DART HURLED BY A TORNADO MAY PENETRATE TWO FEET OF SOLID OAK, SO THE AMAZING FLASH CAN BY SHEER SPEED PASS RIGHT THROUGH SOLID WALL..
THIS BEATS TRYING TO UNLOCK BOLTED DOORS...
NOTHING IN HERE--I'LL CORKSCREW MYSELF THROUGH THE FLOOR, AND TRY THE BASEMENT...
THEN...
UH? THE LEGENDARY MINOTAUR!* AM I SEEING THINGS?
EDITOR'S NOTE: IN GREEK MYTHOLOGY, THE MINOTAUR WAS A HALF-BULL, HALF-MAN!
10

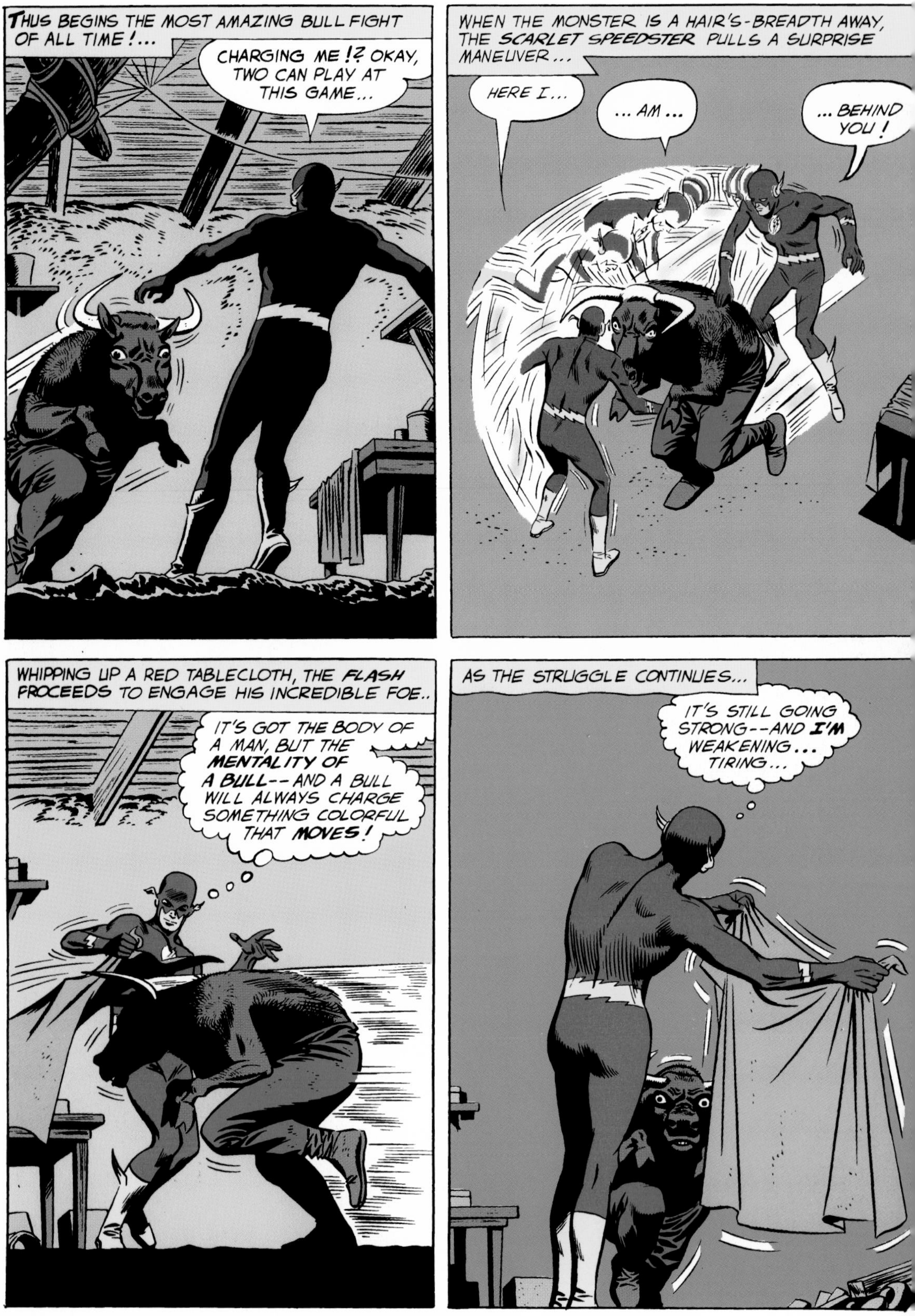
THUS BEGINS THE MOST AMAZING BULL FIGHT OF ALL TIME!...
CHARGING ME!? OKAY, TWO CAN PLAY AT THIS GAME...
WHEN THE MONSTER IS A HAIR'S-BREADTH AWAY, THE SCARLET SPEEDSTER PULLS A SURPRISE MANEUVER...
HERE I...
...AM...
...BEHIND YOU!
WHIPPING UP A RED TABLECLOTH, THE FLASH PROCEEDS TO ENGAGE HIS INCREDIBLE FOE..
IT'S GOT THE BODY OF A MAN, BUT THE MENTALITY OF A BULL--AND A BULL WILL ALWAYS CHARGE SOMETHING COLORFUL THAT MOVES!
AS THE STRUGGLE CONTINUES...
IT'S STILL GOING STRONG--AND I'M WEAKENING... TIRING...

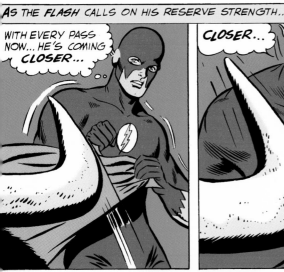

AS THE *FLASH* CALLS ON HIS RESERVE STRENGTH...

WITH EVERY PASS NOW... HE'S COMING *CLOSER*...

CLOSER...

CLOSER!

MY MUSCLES ARE DEAD... LEGS LIKE STUMPS! MY ONLY CHANCE ... SOMETHING I JUST THOUGHT OF -- IN CONNECTION WITH THAT MOSQUITO--

HOTLY PURSUED BY THE *MINOTAUR*, THE EMBATTLED SPEEDSTER HEADS FOR A CERTAIN SPOT IN THE ROOM...

IF I'M RIGHT, THIS CONTEST WILL END IN THE NEXT SECOND! IF NOT, IT WILL BE *MY* END...

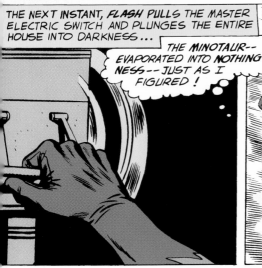

THE NEXT INSTANT, *FLASH* PULLS THE MASTER ELECTRIC SWITCH AND PLUNGES THE ENTIRE HOUSE INTO DARKNESS...

THE MINOTAUR-- EVAPORATED INTO *NOTHINGNESS* -- JUST AS I FIGURED!

NOW THAT I KNOW *HOW* TO ELIMINATE MY STRANGE ADVERSARIES, I'VE GOT TO FIND OUT *WHO* IS DIRECTING THEM!

12

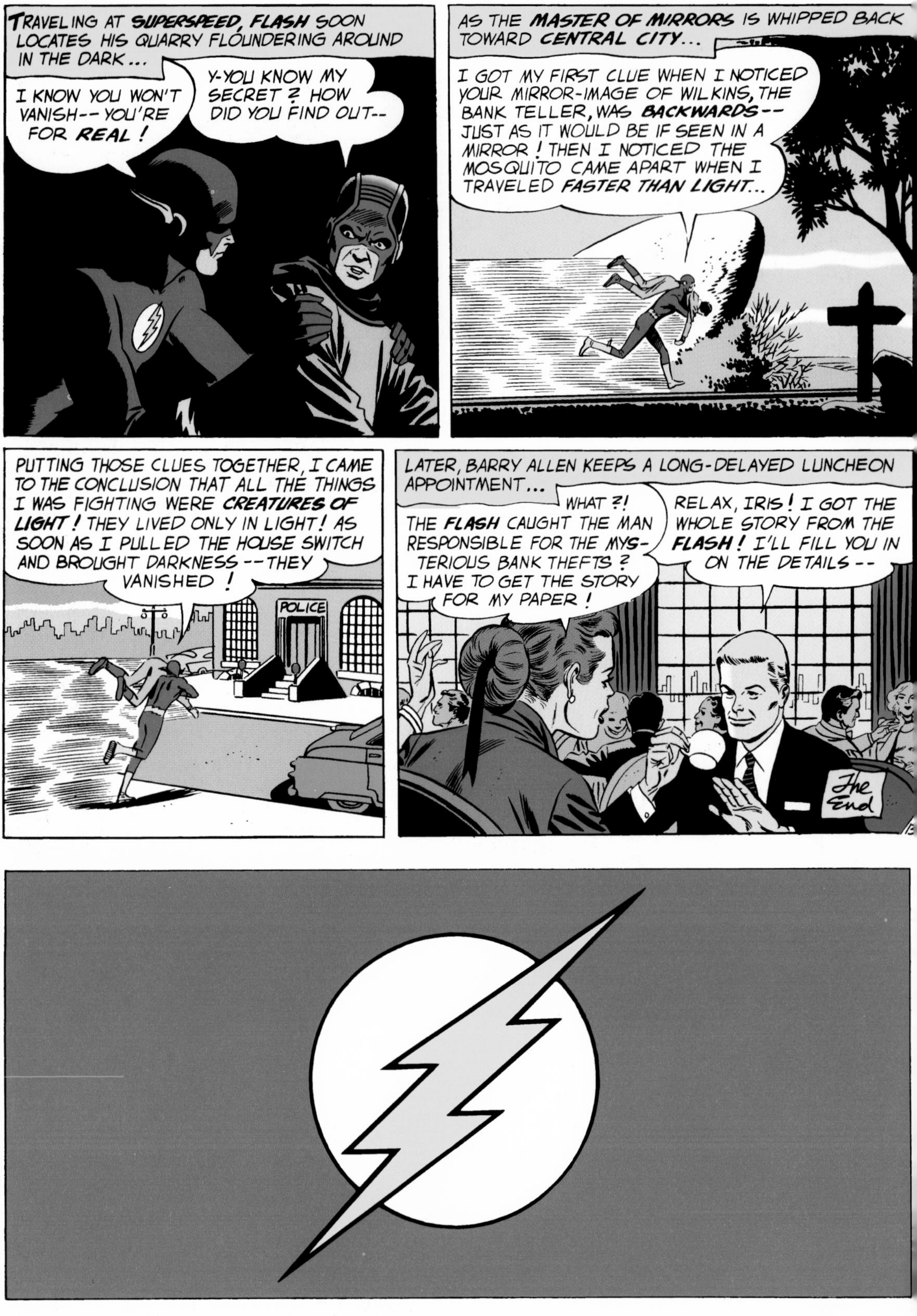
TRAVELING AT SUPERSPEED, FLASH SOON LOCATES HIS QUARRY FLOUNDERING AROUND IN THE DARK...
I KNOW YOU WON'T VANISH-- YOU'RE FOR REAL!
Y-YOU KNOW MY SECRET? HOW DID YOU FIND OUT--
AS THE MASTER OF MIRRORS IS WHIPPED BACK TOWARD CENTRAL CITY...
I GOT MY FIRST CLUE WHEN I NOTICED YOUR MIRROR-IMAGE OF WILKINS, THE BANK TELLER, WAS BACKWARDS-- JUST AS IT WOULD BE IF SEEN IN A MIRROR! THEN I NOTICED THE MOSQUITO CAME APART WHEN I TRAVELED FASTER THAN LIGHT...
PUTTING THOSE CLUES TOGETHER, I CAME TO THE CONCLUSION THAT ALL THE THINGS I WAS FIGHTING WERE CREATURES OF LIGHT! THEY LIVED ONLY IN LIGHT! AS SOON AS I PULLED THE HOUSE SWITCH AND BROUGHT DARKNESS -- THEY VANISHED!
POLICE
LATER, BARRY ALLEN KEEPS A LONG-DELAYED LUNCHEON APPOINTMENT...
WHAT?! THE FLASH CAUGHT THE MAN RESPONSIBLE FOR THE MYSTERIOUS BANK THEFTS? I HAVE TO GET THE STORY FOR MY PAPER!
RELAX, IRIS! I GOT THE WHOLE STORY FROM THE FLASH! I'LL FILL YOU IN ON THE DETAILS --
The End

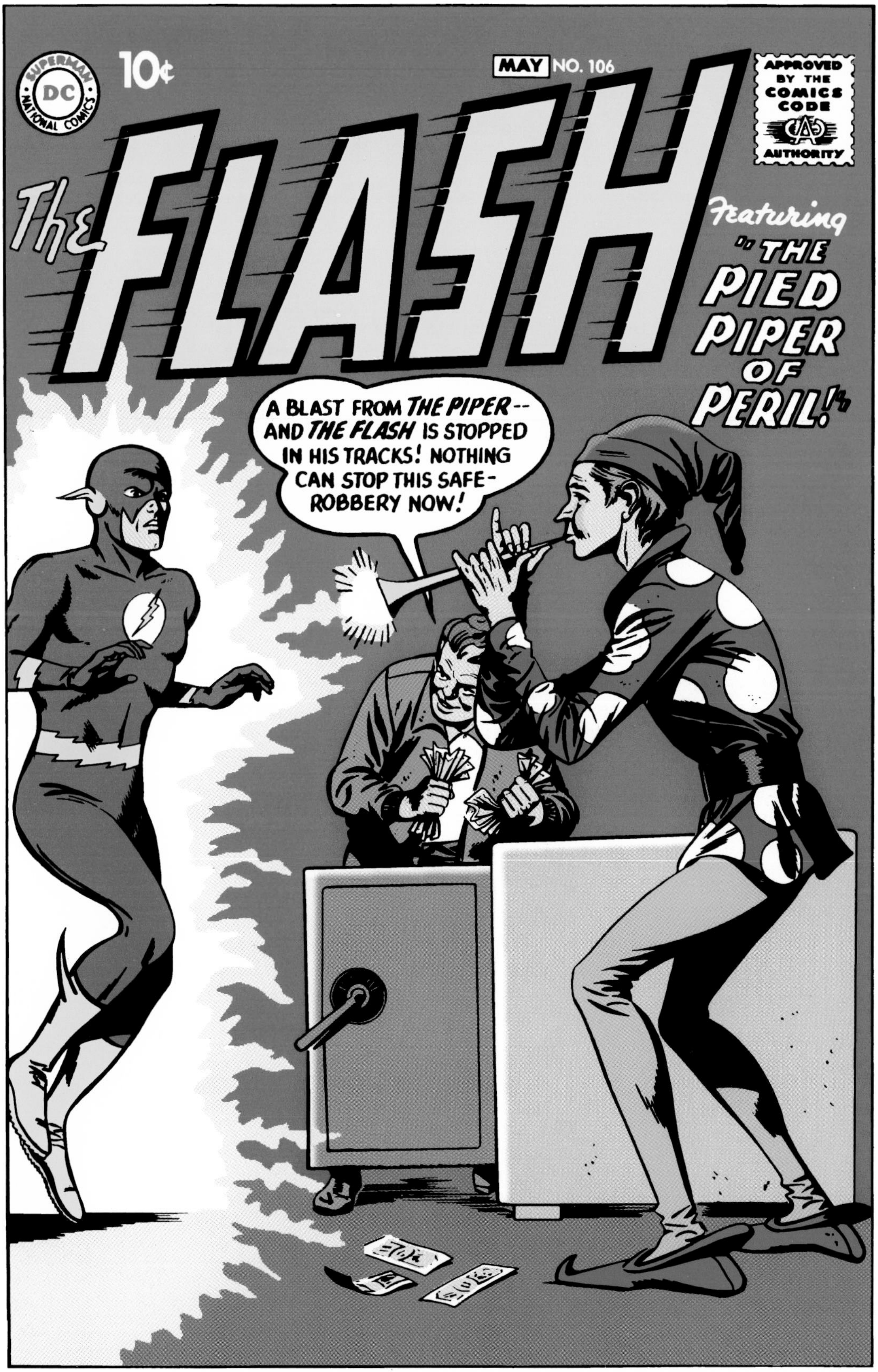
SUPERMAN DC NATIONAL COMICS
10¢
MAY NO. 106
APPROVED BY THE COMICS CODE AUTHORITY
The FLASH
Featuring "THE PIED PIPER OF PERIL!"
A BLAST FROM THE PIPER -- AND THE FLASH IS STOPPED IN HIS TRACKS! NOTHING CAN STOP THIS SAFE-ROBBERY NOW!

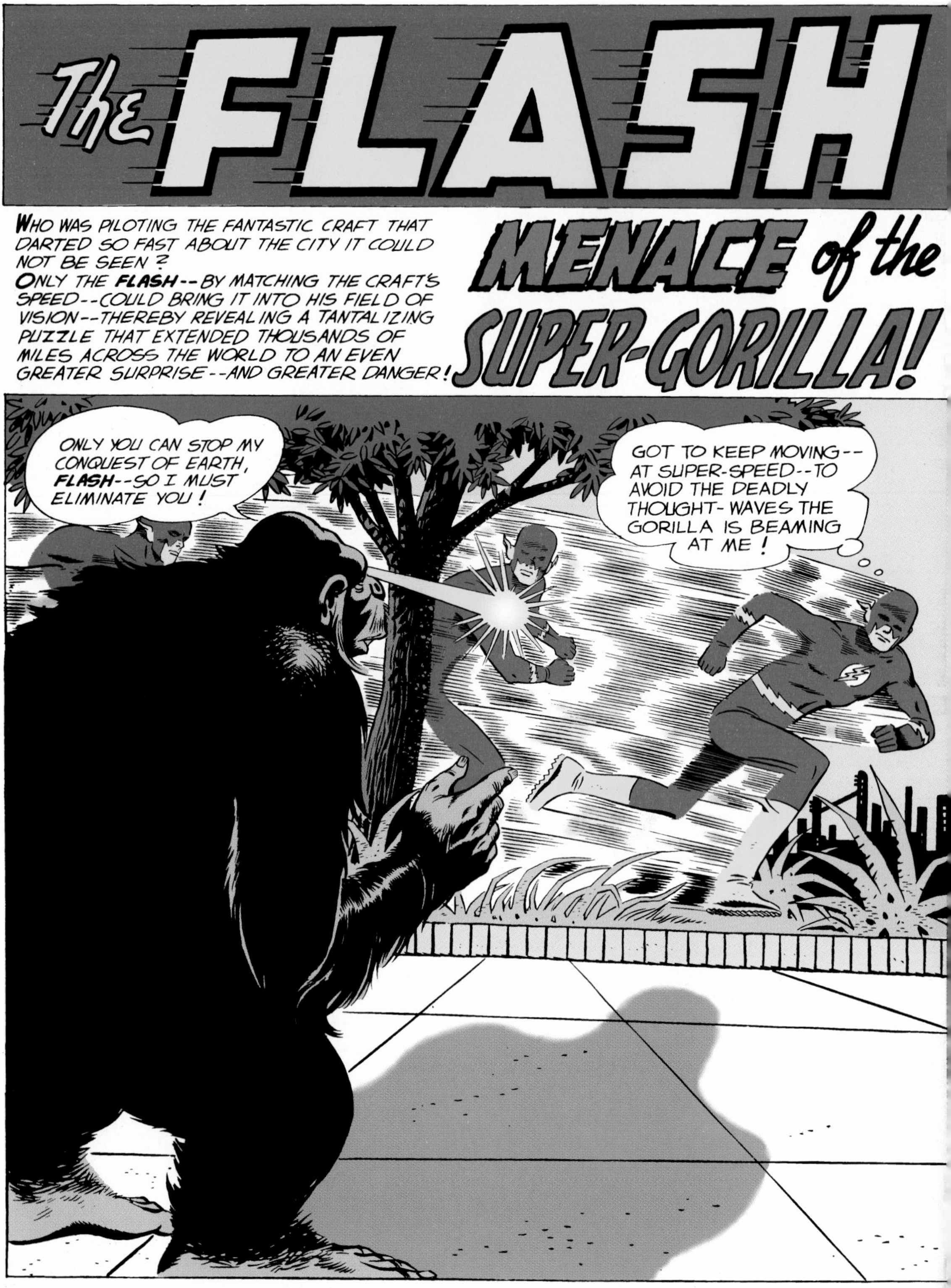
The FLASH
WHO WAS PILOTING THE FANTASTIC CRAFT THAT DARTED SO FAST ABOUT THE CITY IT COULD NOT BE SEEN ? ONLY THE FLASH -- BY MATCHING THE CRAFT'S SPEED--COULD BRING IT INTO HIS FIELD OF VISION--THEREBY REVEALING A TANTALIZING PUZZLE THAT EXTENDED THOUSANDS OF MILES ACROSS THE WORLD TO AN EVEN GREATER SURPRISE--AND GREATER DANGER!
MENACE of the SUPER-GORILLA!
ONLY YOU CAN STOP MY CONQUEST OF EARTH, FLASH--SO I MUST ELIMINATE YOU!
GOT TO KEEP MOVING-- AT SUPER-SPEED--TO AVOID THE DEADLY THOUGHT-WAVES THE GORILLA IS BEAMING AT ME!

FROM THE DEPTHS OF THE DARK CONTINENT OF AFRICA, A STRANGE CRAFT RISES...

IT WHIZZES THROUGH THE AIR AT BREATHTAKING SPEED...

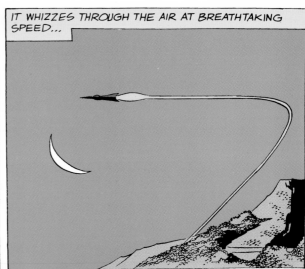

IN THE RADIO ROOM OF A U.S. NAVY PATROL SHIP NEAR THE AFRICAN COAST...

UNIDENTIFIED FLYING OBJECT SHOOTING ACROSS RADAR SCREEN -- AT INCREDIBLE SPEED!

WHEN IT REACHES THE ATLANTIC OCEAN, IT MAKES A SUDDEN DIVE...

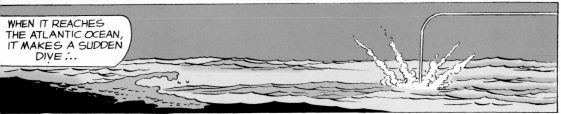

AFTER CROSSING THE ATLANTIC OCEAN **UNDERWATER**, IT PLOWS **UNDERNEATH** THE UNITED STATES -- UNTIL...

NOW UPWARD -- TO MY DESTINATION...

IN **CENTRAL CITY PARK**, WHERE THE ALL-PURPOSE CRAFT HAS EMERGED FROM THE EARTH...

I HAVE ARRIVED -- WITHOUT BEING SEEN! NOW I CAN BEGIN MY **PLAN**...

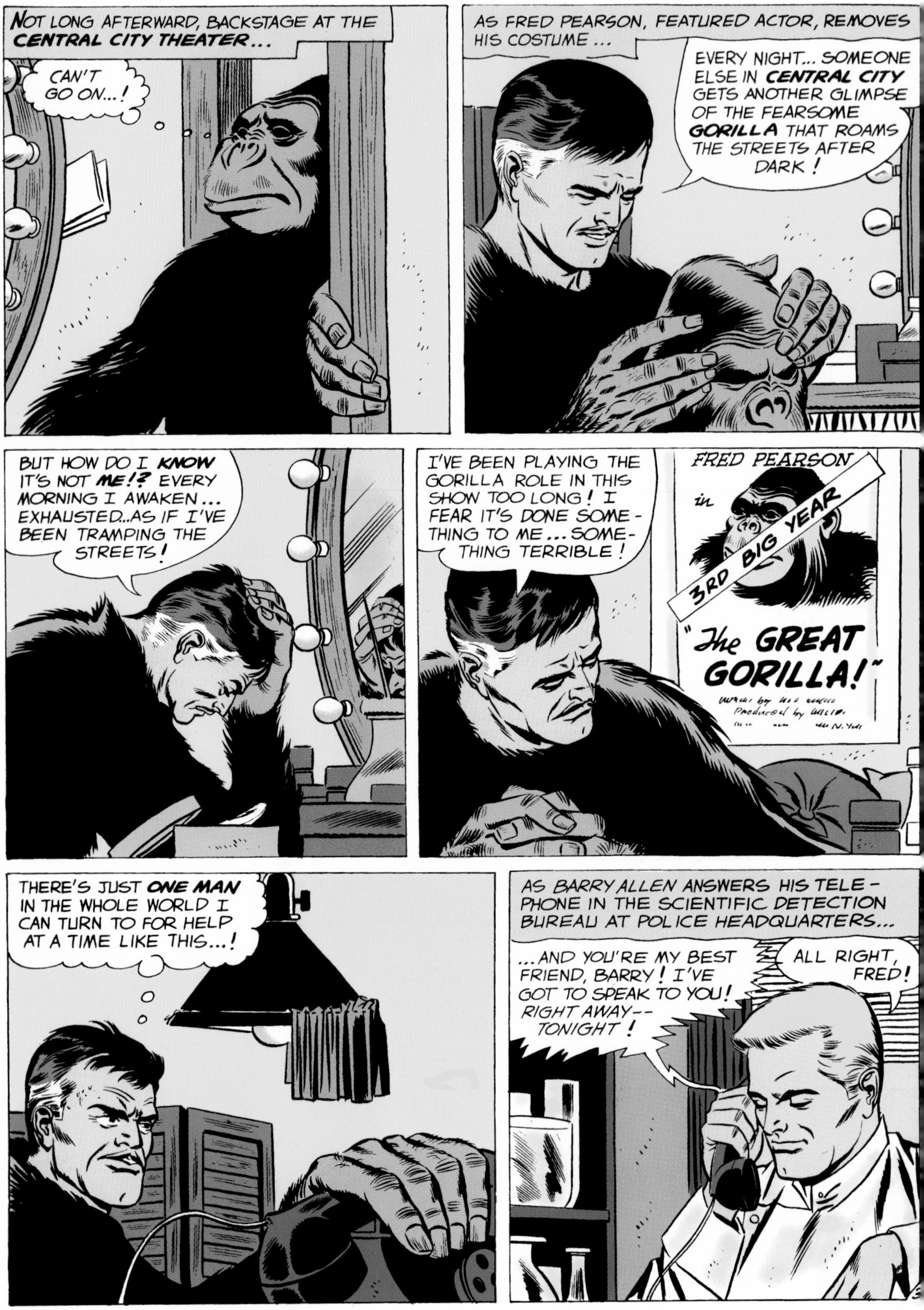
NOT LONG AFTERWARD, BACKSTAGE AT THE CENTRAL CITY THEATER...
CAN'T GO ON...!
AS FRED PEARSON, FEATURED ACTOR, REMOVES HIS COSTUME...
EVERY NIGHT... SOMEONE ELSE IN CENTRAL CITY GETS ANOTHER GLIMPSE OF THE FEARSOME GORILLA THAT ROAMS THE STREETS AFTER DARK!
BUT HOW DO I KNOW IT'S NOT ME!? EVERY MORNING I AWAKEN... EXHAUSTED...AS IF I'VE BEEN TRAMPING THE STREETS!
I'VE BEEN PLAYING THE GORILLA ROLE IN THIS SHOW TOO LONG! I FEAR IT'S DONE SOMETHING TO ME... SOMETHING TERRIBLE!
FRED PEARSON
in
3RD BIG YEAR
"The GREAT GORILLA!"
THERE'S JUST ONE MAN IN THE WHOLE WORLD I CAN TURN TO FOR HELP AT A TIME LIKE THIS...!
AS BARRY ALLEN ANSWERS HIS TELEPHONE IN THE SCIENTIFIC DETECTION BUREAU AT POLICE HEADQUARTERS...
...AND YOU'RE MY BEST FRIEND, BARRY! I'VE GOT TO SPEAK TO YOU! RIGHT AWAY-- TONIGHT!
ALL RIGHT, FRED!

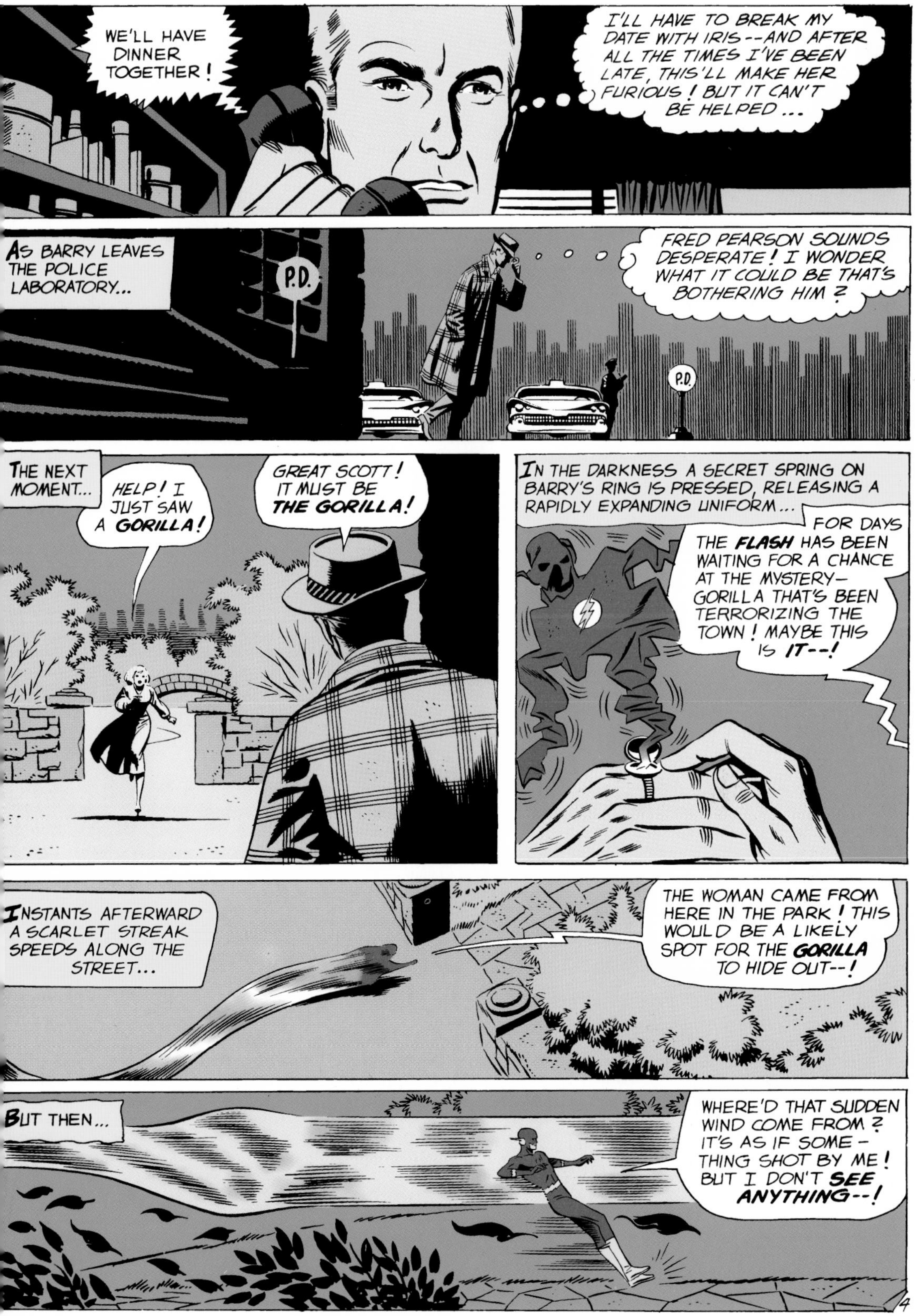
WE'LL HAVE DINNER TOGETHER!
I'LL HAVE TO BREAK MY DATE WITH IRIS--AND AFTER ALL THE TIMES I'VE BEEN LATE, THIS'LL MAKE HER FURIOUS! BUT IT CAN'T BE HELPED...
AS BARRY LEAVES THE POLICE LABORATORY...
P.D.
FRED PEARSON SOUNDS DESPERATE! I WONDER WHAT IT COULD BE THAT'S BOTHERING HIM?
P.D.
THE NEXT MOMENT...
HELP! I JUST SAW A GORILLA!
GREAT SCOTT! IT MUST BE THE GORILLA!
IN THE DARKNESS A SECRET SPRING ON BARRY'S RING IS PRESSED, RELEASING A RAPIDLY EXPANDING UNIFORM...
FOR DAYS THE FLASH HAS BEEN WAITING FOR A CHANCE AT THE MYSTERY-GORILLA THAT'S BEEN TERRORIZING THE TOWN! MAYBE THIS IS IT--!
INSTANTS AFTERWARD A SCARLET STREAK SPEEDS ALONG THE STREET...
THE WOMAN CAME FROM HERE IN THE PARK! THIS WOULD BE A LIKELY SPOT FOR THE GORILLA TO HIDE OUT--!
BUT THEN...
WHERE'D THAT SUDDEN WIND COME FROM? IT'S AS IF SOME-THING SHOT BY ME! BUT I DON'T SEE ANYTHING--!
4

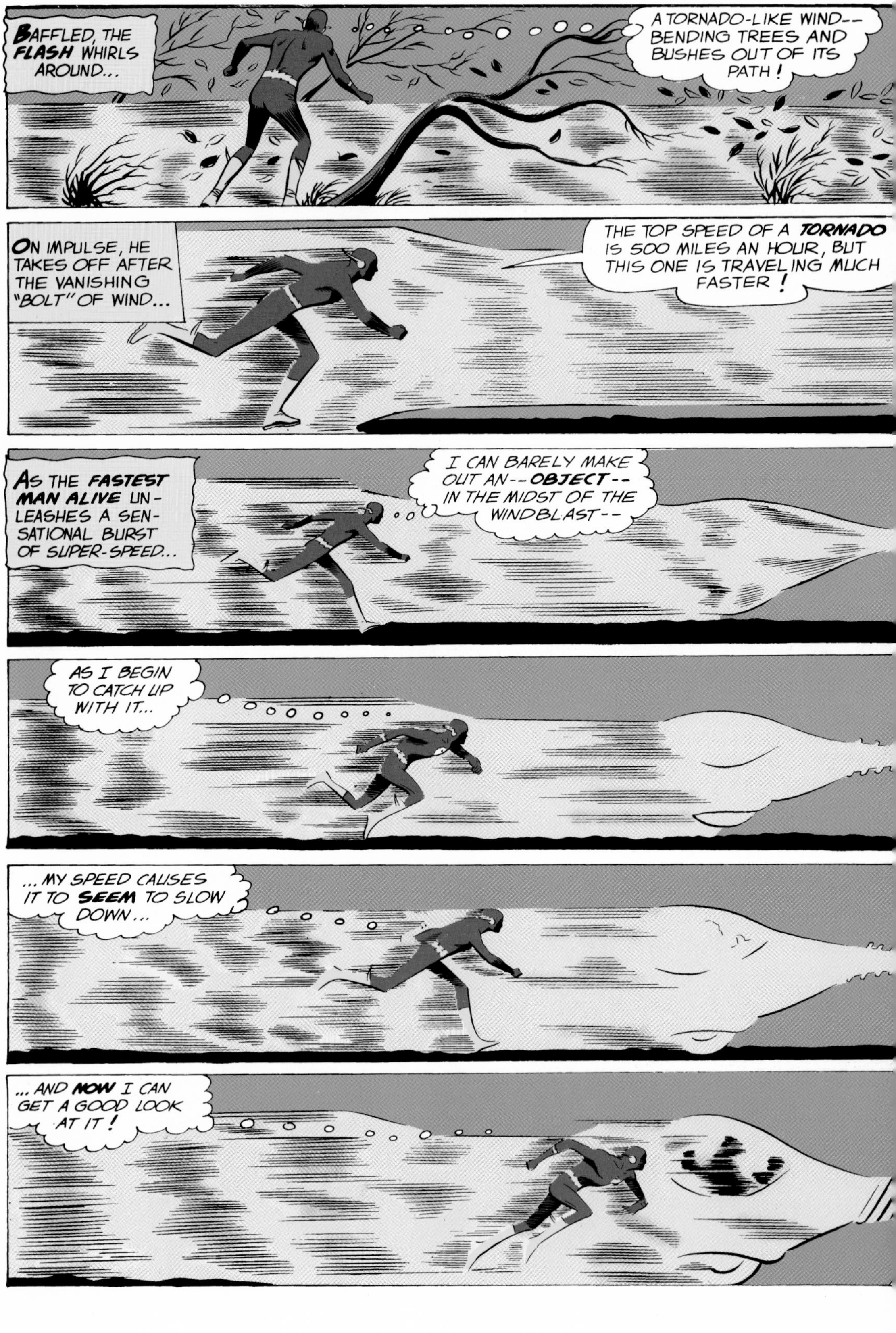
BAFFLED, THE FLASH WHIRLS AROUND...
A TORNADO-LIKE WIND-- BENDING TREES AND BUSHES OUT OF ITS PATH!
ON IMPULSE, HE TAKES OFF AFTER THE VANISHING "BOLT" OF WIND...
THE TOP SPEED OF A TORNADO IS 500 MILES AN HOUR, BUT THIS ONE IS TRAVELING MUCH FASTER!
AS THE FASTEST MAN ALIVE UN-LEASHES A SEN-SATIONAL BURST OF SUPER-SPEED...
I CAN BARELY MAKE OUT AN--OBJECT-- IN THE MIDST OF THE WINDBLAST--
AS I BEGIN TO CATCH UP WITH IT...
...MY SPEED CAUSES IT TO SEEM TO SLOW DOWN...
...AND NOW I CAN GET A GOOD LOOK AT IT!

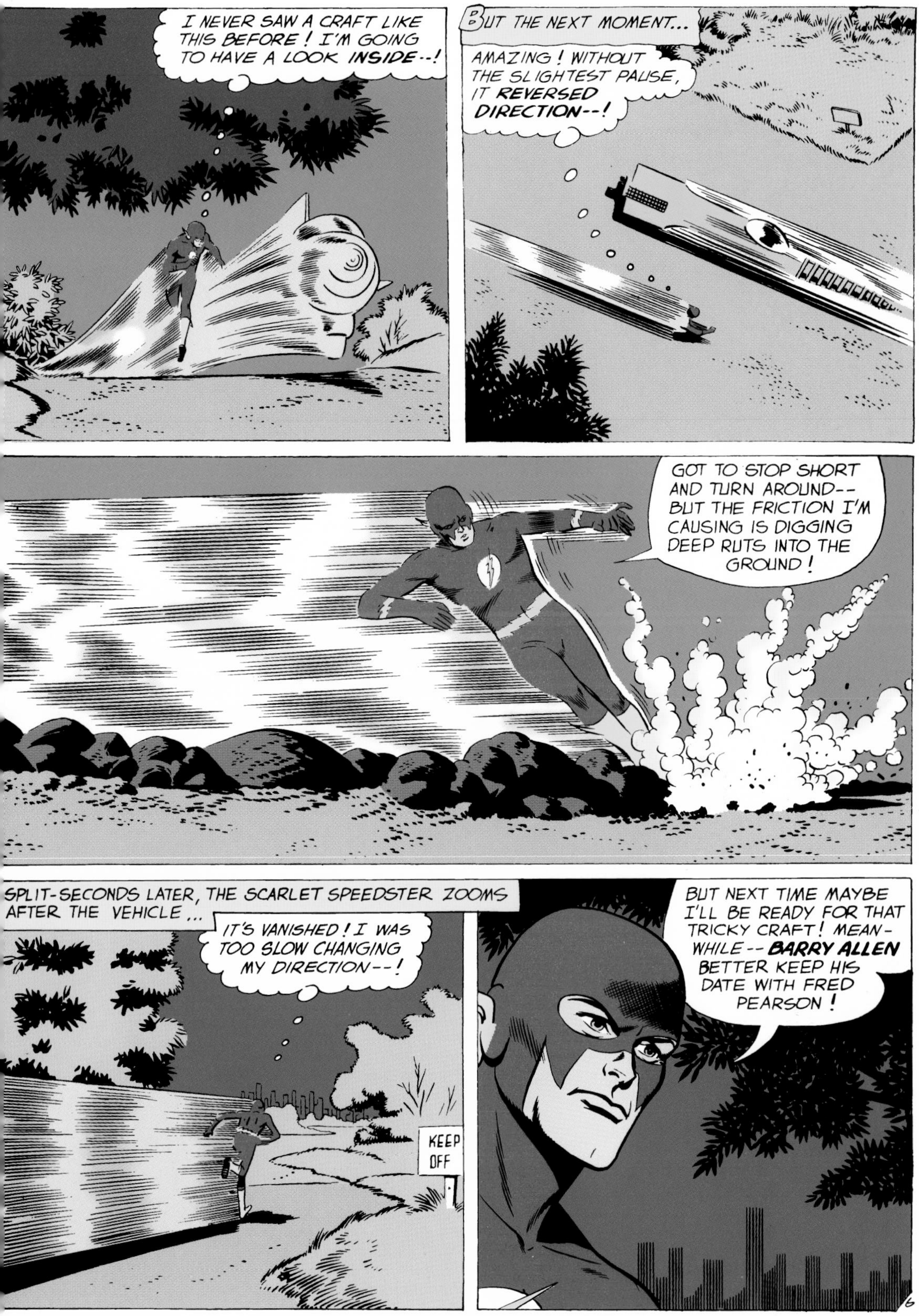
I NEVER SAW A CRAFT LIKE THIS BEFORE! I'M GOING TO HAVE A LOOK INSIDE--!
BUT THE NEXT MOMENT...
AMAZING! WITHOUT THE SLIGHTEST PAUSE, IT REVERSED DIRECTION--!
GOT TO STOP SHORT AND TURN AROUND-- BUT THE FRICTION I'M CAUSING IS DIGGING DEEP RUTS INTO THE GROUND!
SPLIT-SECONDS LATER, THE SCARLET SPEEDSTER ZOOMS AFTER THE VEHICLE...
IT'S VANISHED! I WAS TOO SLOW CHANGING MY DIRECTION--!
KEEP OFF
BUT NEXT TIME MAYBE I'LL BE READY FOR THAT TRICKY CRAFT! MEAN-WHILE-- BARRY ALLEN BETTER KEEP HIS DATE WITH FRED PEARSON!
6

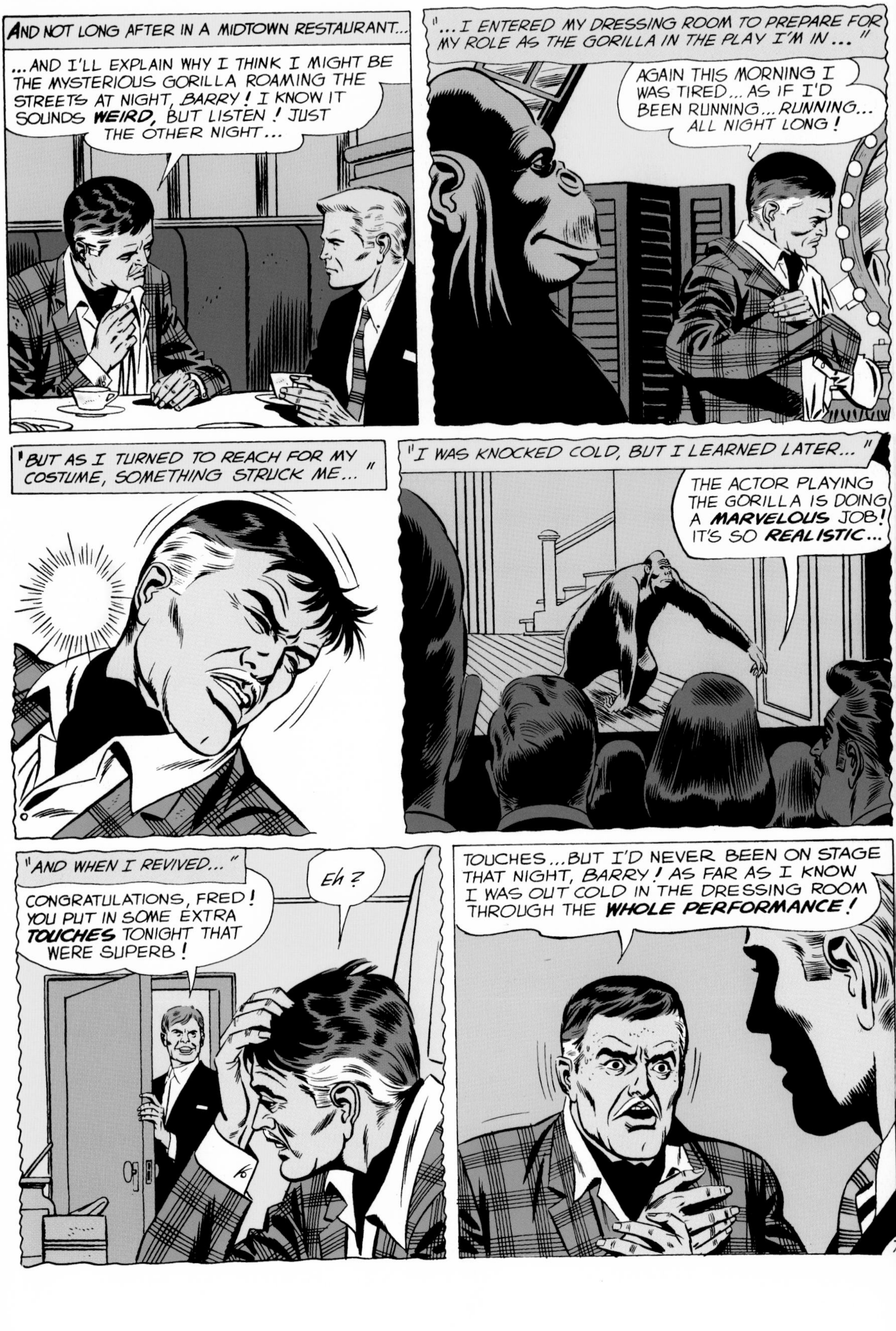
AND NOT LONG AFTER IN A MIDTOWN RESTAURANT...
...AND I'LL EXPLAIN WHY I THINK I MIGHT BE THE MYSTERIOUS GORILLA ROAMING THE STREETS AT NIGHT, BARRY! I KNOW IT SOUNDS WEIRD, BUT LISTEN! JUST THE OTHER NIGHT...
"...I ENTERED MY DRESSING ROOM TO PREPARE FOR MY ROLE AS THE GORILLA IN THE PLAY I'M IN..."
AGAIN THIS MORNING I WAS TIRED... AS IF I'D BEEN RUNNING... RUNNING... ALL NIGHT LONG!
"BUT AS I TURNED TO REACH FOR MY COSTUME, SOMETHING STRUCK ME..."
"I WAS KNOCKED COLD, BUT I LEARNED LATER..."
THE ACTOR PLAYING THE GORILLA IS DOING A MARVELOUS JOB! IT'S SO REALISTIC...
"AND WHEN I REVIVED..."
CONGRATULATIONS, FRED! YOU PUT IN SOME EXTRA TOUCHES TONIGHT THAT WERE SUPERB!
Eh?
TOUCHES...BUT I'D NEVER BEEN ON STAGE THAT NIGHT, BARRY! AS FAR AS I KNOW I WAS OUT COLD IN THE DRESSING ROOM THROUGH THE WHOLE PERFORMANCE!

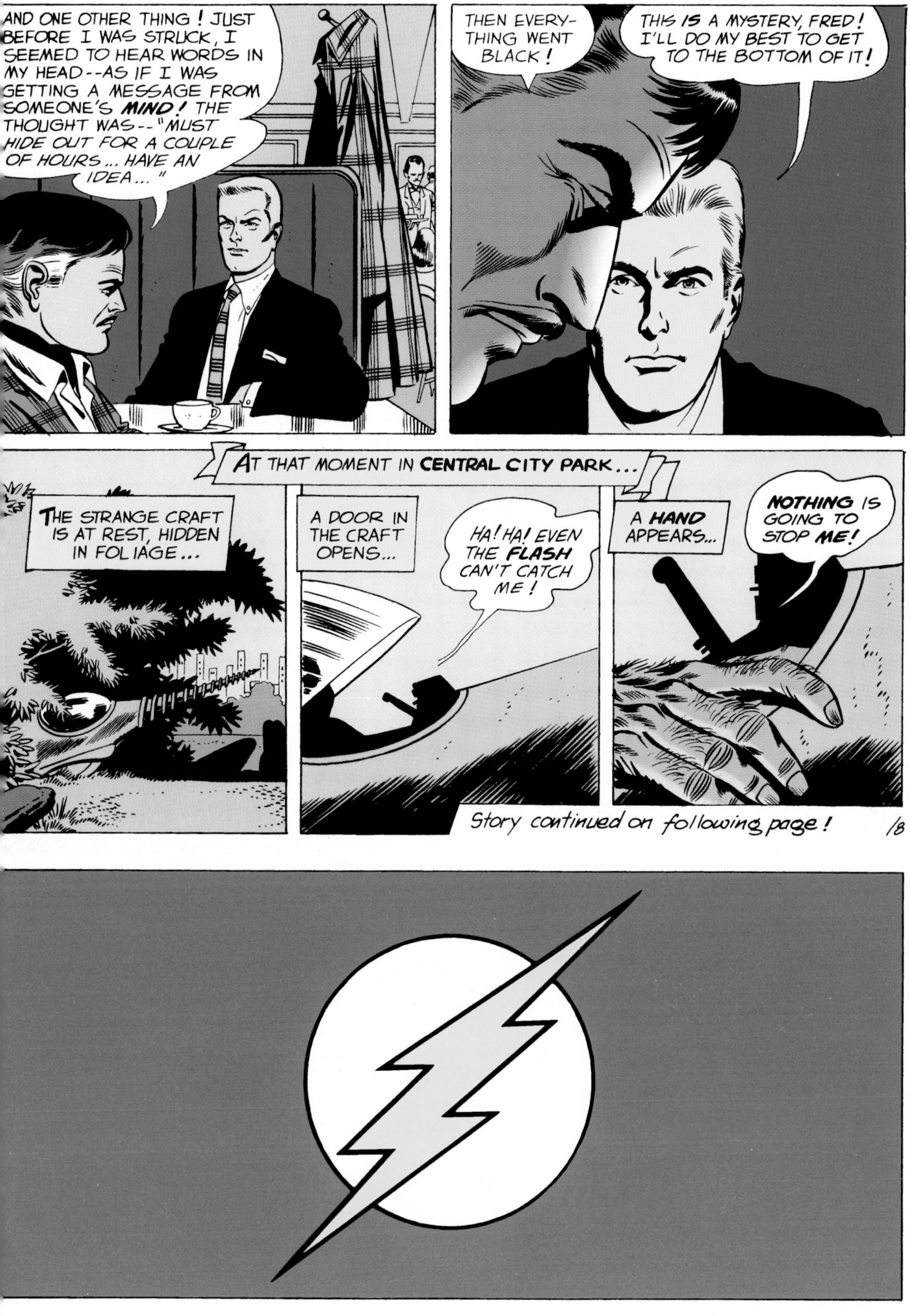
AND ONE OTHER THING! JUST BEFORE I WAS STRUCK, I SEEMED TO HEAR WORDS IN MY HEAD--AS IF I WAS GETTING A MESSAGE FROM SOMEONE'S MIND! THE THOUGHT WAS--"MUST HIDE OUT FOR A COUPLE OF HOURS... HAVE AN IDEA..."
THEN EVERYTHING WENT BLACK!
THIS IS A MYSTERY, FRED! I'LL DO MY BEST TO GET TO THE BOTTOM OF IT!
AT THAT MOMENT IN CENTRAL CITY PARK...
THE STRANGE CRAFT IS AT REST, HIDDEN IN FOLIAGE...
A DOOR IN THE CRAFT OPENS...
HA! HA! EVEN THE FLASH CAN'T CATCH ME!
A HAND APPEARS...
NOTHING IS GOING TO STOP ME!
Story continued on following page!
18

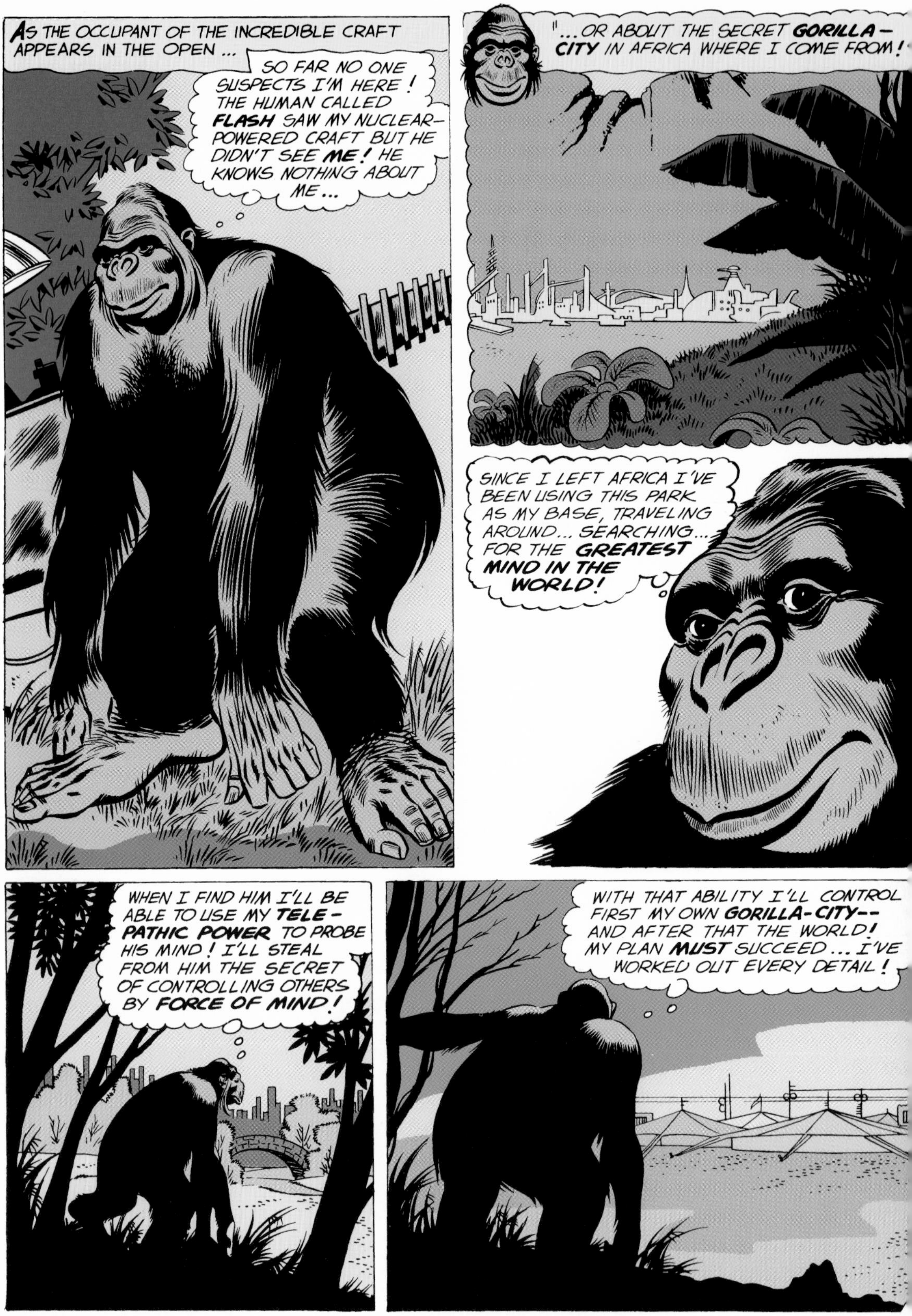
AS THE OCCUPANT OF THE INCREDIBLE CRAFT APPEARS IN THE OPEN ...
SO FAR NO ONE SUSPECTS I'M HERE! THE HUMAN CALLED FLASH SAW MY NUCLEAR-POWERED CRAFT BUT HE DIDN'T SEE ME! HE KNOWS NOTHING ABOUT ME ...
"... OR ABOUT THE SECRET GORILLA-CITY IN AFRICA WHERE I COME FROM!"
SINCE I LEFT AFRICA I'VE BEEN USING THIS PARK AS MY BASE, TRAVELING AROUND... SEARCHING... FOR THE GREATEST MIND IN THE WORLD!
WHEN I FIND HIM I'LL BE ABLE TO USE MY TELE-PATHIC POWER TO PROBE HIS MIND! I'LL STEAL FROM HIM THE SECRET OF CONTROLLING OTHERS BY FORCE OF MIND!
WITH THAT ABILITY I'LL CONTROL FIRST MY OWN GORILLA-CITY-- AND AFTER THAT THE WORLD! MY PLAN MUST SUCCEED ... I'VE WORKED OUT EVERY DETAIL!

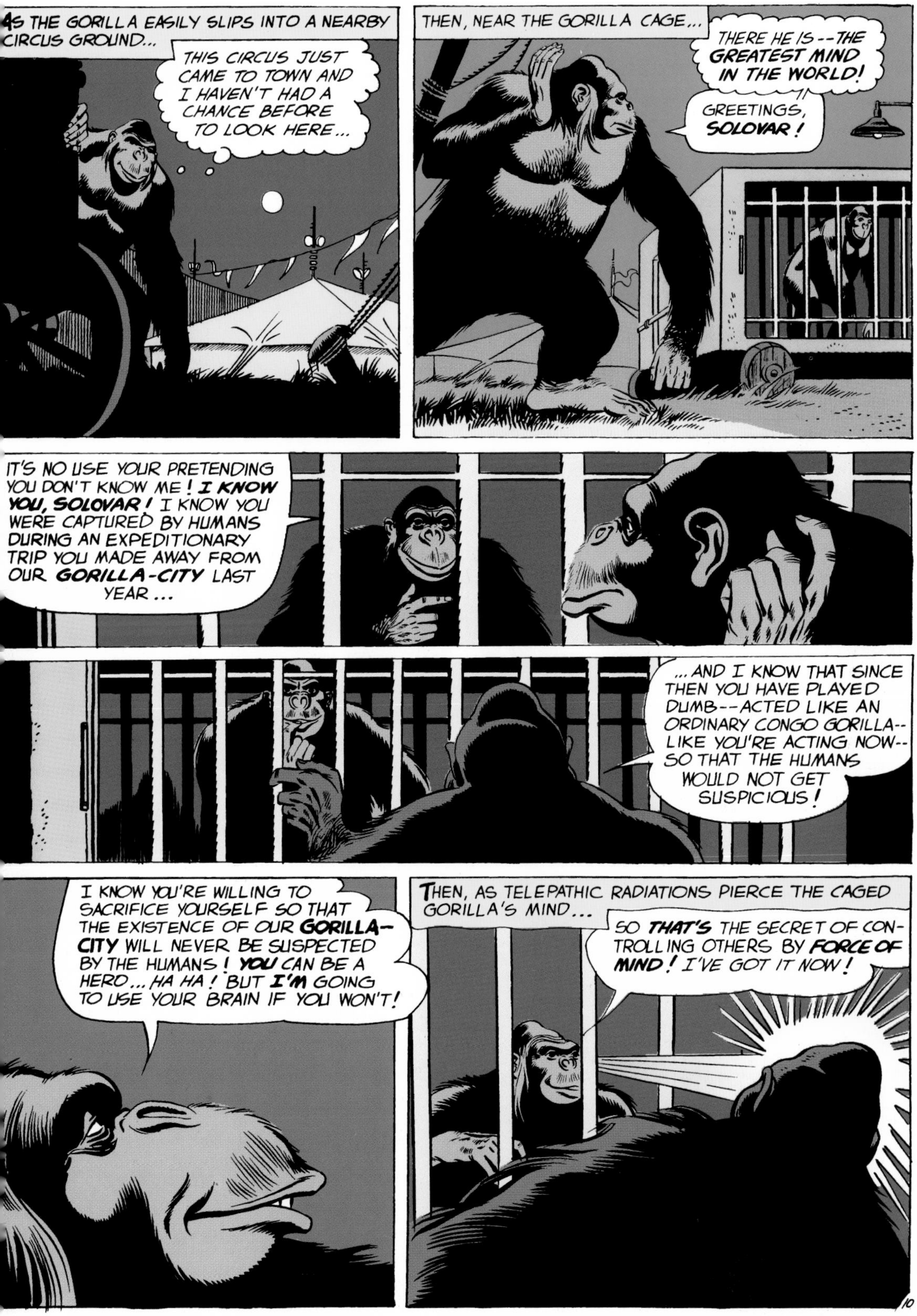
AS THE GORILLA EASILY SLIPS INTO A NEARBY CIRCUS GROUND...
THIS CIRCUS JUST CAME TO TOWN AND I HAVEN'T HAD A CHANCE BEFORE TO LOOK HERE...
THEN, NEAR THE GORILLA CAGE...
THERE HE IS--THE GREATEST MIND IN THE WORLD!
GREETINGS, SOLOVAR!
IT'S NO USE YOUR PRETENDING YOU DON'T KNOW ME! I KNOW YOU, SOLOVAR! I KNOW YOU WERE CAPTURED BY HUMANS DURING AN EXPEDITIONARY TRIP YOU MADE AWAY FROM OUR GORILLA-CITY LAST YEAR...
...AND I KNOW THAT SINCE THEN YOU HAVE PLAYED DUMB--ACTED LIKE AN ORDINARY CONGO GORILLA--LIKE YOU'RE ACTING NOW--SO THAT THE HUMANS WOULD NOT GET SUSPICIOUS!
I KNOW YOU'RE WILLING TO SACRIFICE YOURSELF SO THAT THE EXISTENCE OF OUR GORILLA-CITY WILL NEVER BE SUSPECTED BY THE HUMANS! YOU CAN BE A HERO... HA HA! BUT I'M GOING TO USE YOUR BRAIN IF YOU WON'T!
THEN, AS TELEPATHIC RADIATIONS PIERCE THE CAGED GORILLA'S MIND...
SO THAT'S THE SECRET OF CONTROLLING OTHERS BY FORCE OF MIND! I'VE GOT IT NOW!
10

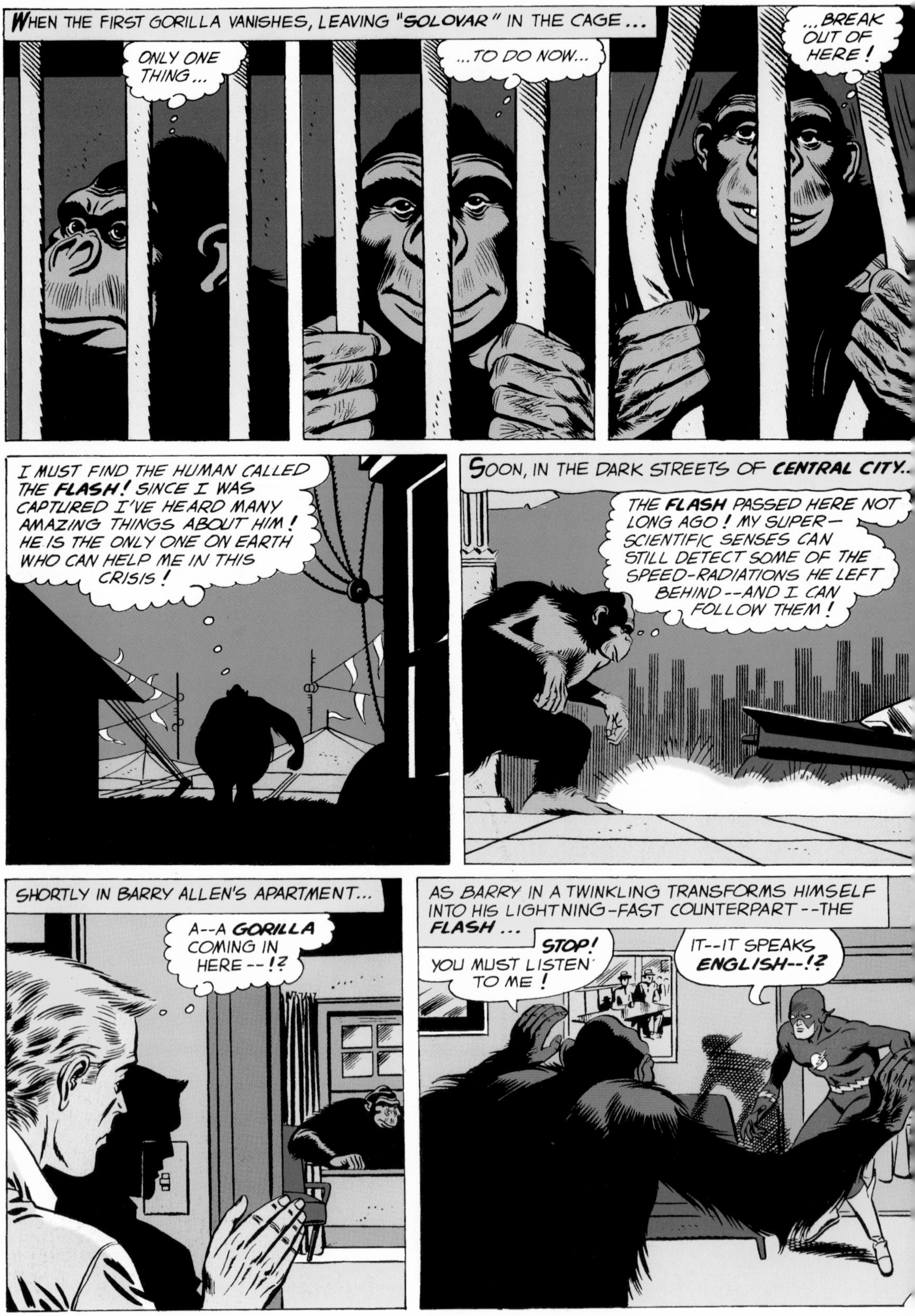
WHEN THE FIRST GORILLA VANISHES, LEAVING "SOLOVAR" IN THE CAGE...
ONLY ONE THING...
...TO DO NOW...
...BREAK OUT OF HERE!
I MUST FIND THE HUMAN CALLED THE FLASH! SINCE I WAS CAPTURED I'VE HEARD MANY AMAZING THINGS ABOUT HIM! HE IS THE ONLY ONE ON EARTH WHO CAN HELP ME IN THIS CRISIS!
SOON, IN THE DARK STREETS OF CENTRAL CITY...
THE FLASH PASSED HERE NOT LONG AGO! MY SUPER-SCIENTIFIC SENSES CAN STILL DETECT SOME OF THE SPEED-RADIATIONS HE LEFT BEHIND--AND I CAN FOLLOW THEM!
SHORTLY IN BARRY ALLEN'S APARTMENT...
A--A GORILLA COMING IN HERE--!?
AS BARRY IN A TWINKLING TRANSFORMS HIMSELF INTO HIS LIGHTNING-FAST COUNTERPART--THE FLASH...
STOP! YOU MUST LISTEN TO ME!
IT--IT SPEAKS ENGLISH--!?

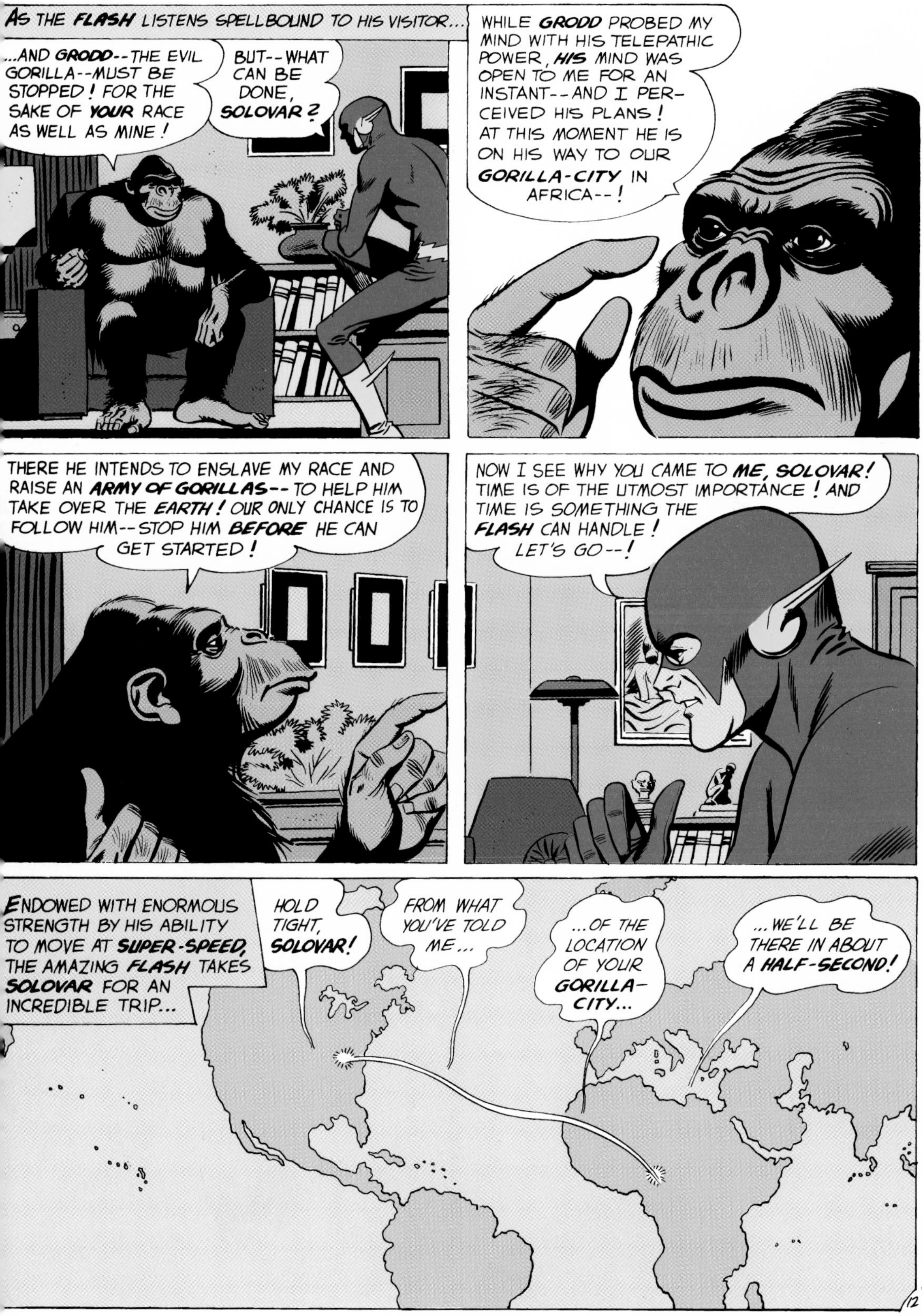
AS THE FLASH LISTENS SPELLBOUND TO HIS VISITOR...
...AND GRODD--THE EVIL GORILLA--MUST BE STOPPED! FOR THE SAKE OF YOUR RACE AS WELL AS MINE!
BUT--WHAT CAN BE DONE, SOLOVAR?
WHILE GRODD PROBED MY MIND WITH HIS TELEPATHIC POWER, HIS MIND WAS OPEN TO ME FOR AN INSTANT--AND I PERCEIVED HIS PLANS! AT THIS MOMENT HE IS ON HIS WAY TO OUR GORILLA-CITY IN AFRICA--!
THERE HE INTENDS TO ENSLAVE MY RACE AND RAISE AN ARMY OF GORILLAS--TO HELP HIM TAKE OVER THE EARTH! OUR ONLY CHANCE IS TO FOLLOW HIM--STOP HIM BEFORE HE CAN GET STARTED!
NOW I SEE WHY YOU CAME TO ME, SOLOVAR! TIME IS OF THE UTMOST IMPORTANCE! AND TIME IS SOMETHING THE FLASH CAN HANDLE! LET'S GO--!
ENDOWED WITH ENORMOUS STRENGTH BY HIS ABILITY TO MOVE AT SUPER-SPEED, THE AMAZING FLASH TAKES SOLOVAR FOR AN INCREDIBLE TRIP...
HOLD TIGHT, SOLOVAR!
FROM WHAT YOU'VE TOLD ME...
...OF THE LOCATION OF YOUR GORILLA-CITY...
...WE'LL BE THERE IN ABOUT A HALF-SECOND!
12

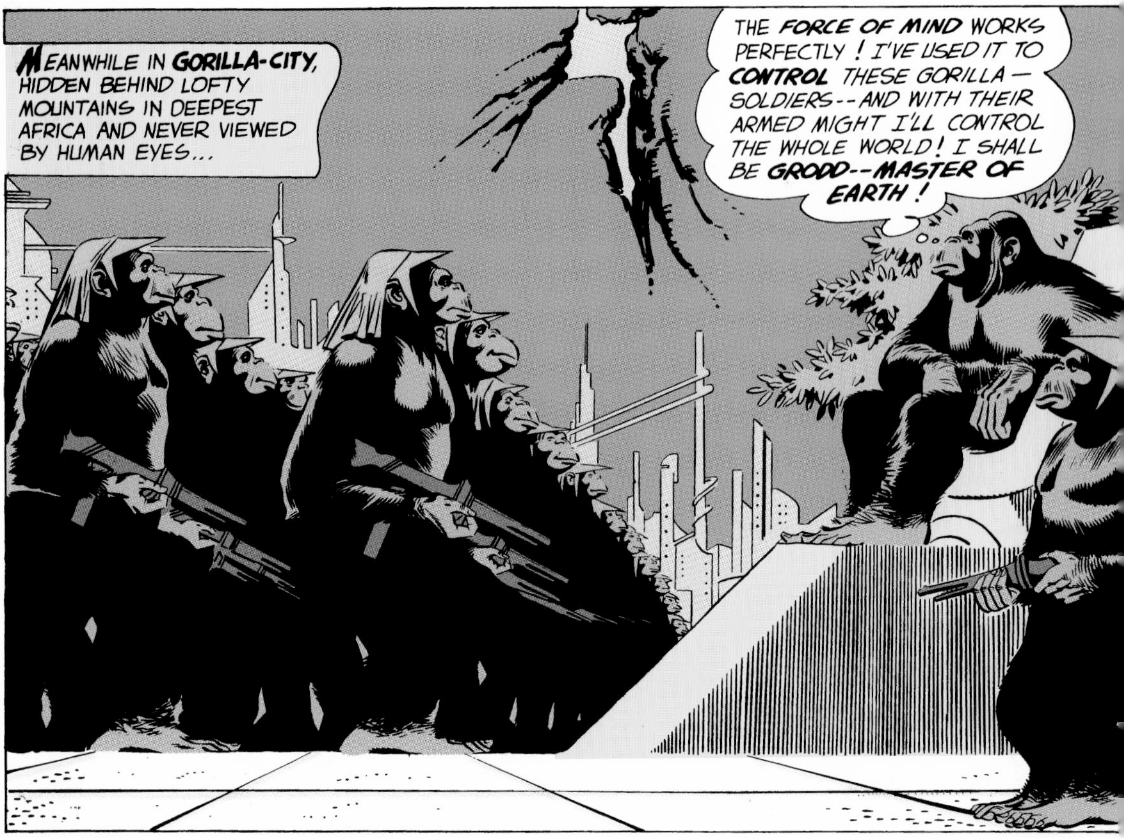
MEANWHILE IN GORILLA-CITY, HIDDEN BEHIND LOFTY MOUNTAINS IN DEEPEST AFRICA AND NEVER VIEWED BY HUMAN EYES...
THE FORCE OF MIND WORKS PERFECTLY! I'VE USED IT TO CONTROL THESE GORILLA-SOLDIERS--AND WITH THEIR ARMED MIGHT I'LL CONTROL THE WHOLE WORLD! I SHALL BE GRODD--MASTER OF EARTH!

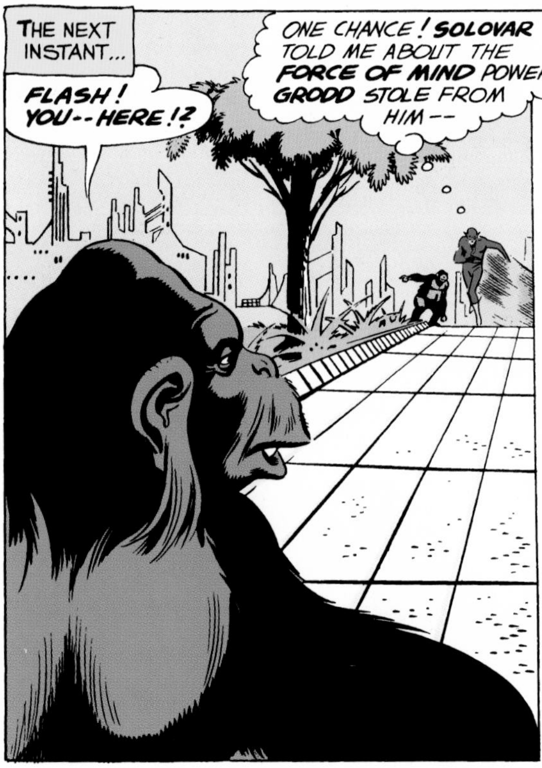
THE NEXT INSTANT...
FLASH! YOU--HERE!?
ONE CHANCE! SOLOVAR TOLD ME ABOUT THE FORCE OF MIND POWER GRODD STOLE FROM HIM--

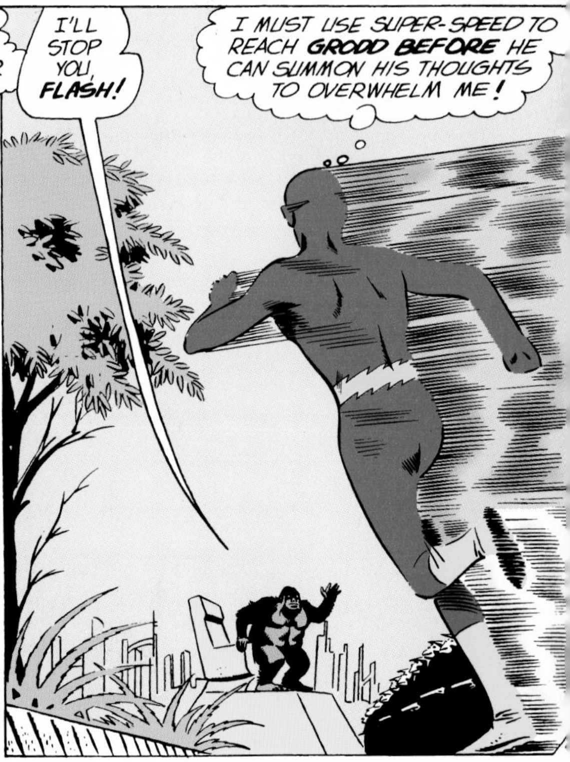
I'LL STOP YOU, FLASH!
I MUST USE SUPER-SPEED TO REACH GRODD BEFORE HE CAN SUMMON HIS THOUGHTS TO OVERWHELM ME!

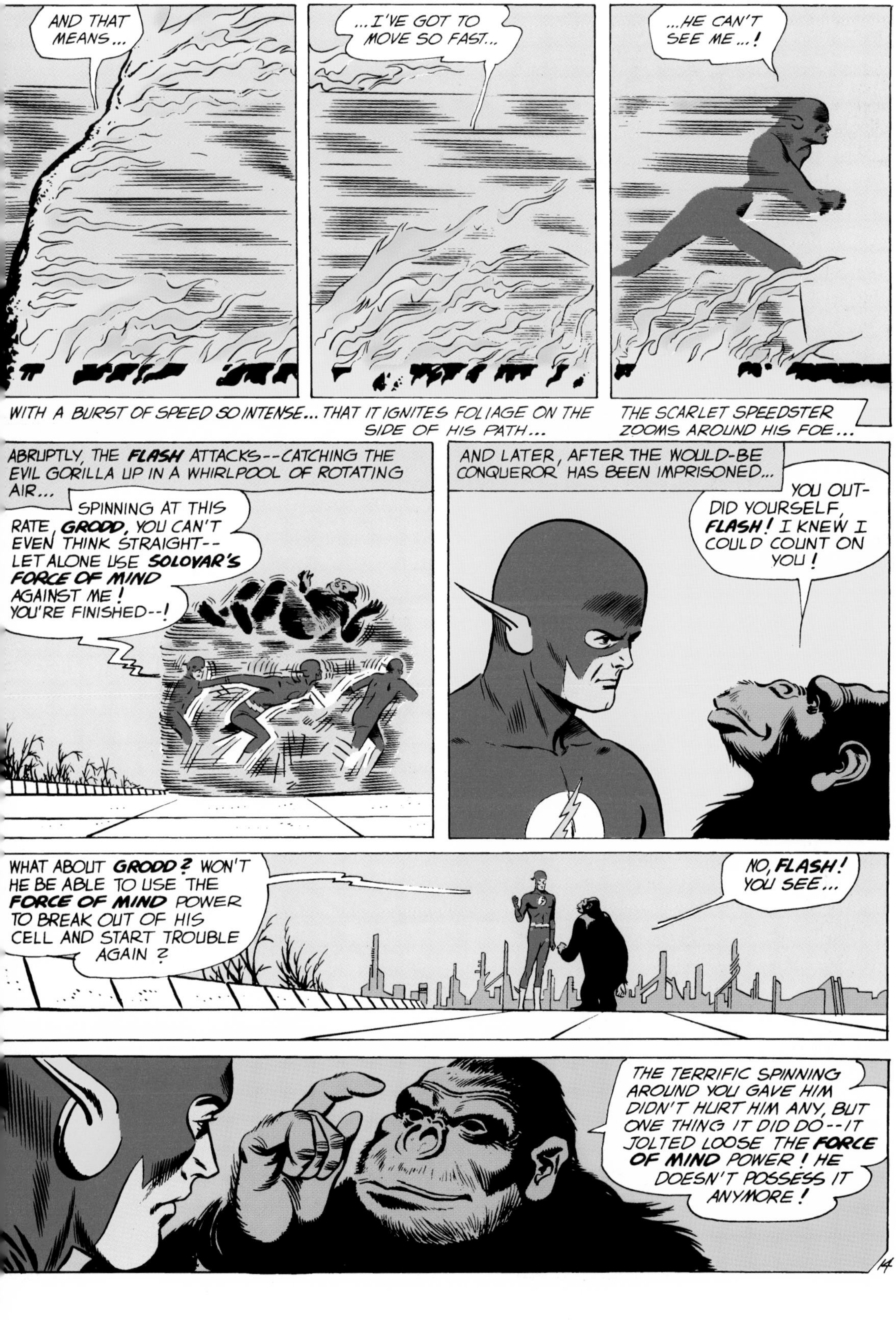
AND THAT MEANS...
...I'VE GOT TO MOVE SO FAST...
...HE CAN'T SEE ME...!
WITH A BURST OF SPEED SO INTENSE... THAT IT IGNITES FOLIAGE ON THE SIDE OF HIS PATH...
THE SCARLET SPEEDSTER ZOOMS AROUND HIS FOE...
ABRUPTLY, THE FLASH ATTACKS--CATCHING THE EVIL GORILLA UP IN A WHIRLPOOL OF ROTATING AIR...
SPINNING AT THIS RATE, GRODD, YOU CAN'T EVEN THINK STRAIGHT-- LET ALONE USE SOLOVAR'S FORCE OF MIND AGAINST ME! YOU'RE FINISHED--!
AND LATER, AFTER THE WOULD-BE CONQUEROR HAS BEEN IMPRISONED...
YOU OUT-DID YOURSELF, FLASH! I KNEW I COULD COUNT ON YOU!
WHAT ABOUT GRODD? WON'T HE BE ABLE TO USE THE FORCE OF MIND POWER TO BREAK OUT OF HIS CELL AND START TROUBLE AGAIN?
NO, FLASH! YOU SEE...
THE TERRIFIC SPINNING AROUND YOU GAVE HIM DIDN'T HURT HIM ANY, BUT ONE THING IT DID DO--IT JOLTED LOOSE THE FORCE OF MIND POWER! HE DOESN'T POSSESS IT ANYMORE!
14

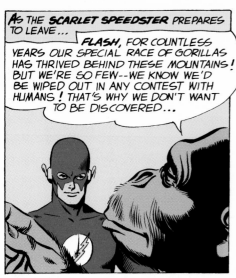

As the **SCARLET SPEEDSTER** PREPARES TO LEAVE...

FLASH, FOR COUNTLESS YEARS OUR SPECIAL RACE OF GORILLAS HAS THRIVED BEHIND THESE MOUNTAINS! BUT WE'RE SO FEW--WE KNOW WE'D BE WIPED OUT IN ANY CONTEST WITH HUMANS! THAT'S WHY WE DON'T WANT TO BE DISCOVERED...

PROMISE ME YOU'LL NEVER REVEAL THE LOCATION OF THIS CITY!

I PROMISE! GOODBYE NOW, **SOLOVAR**-- I MUST RETURN HOME AND SOLVE A FRIEND'S PROBLEM!

BACK IN **CENTRAL CITY**...

FRED, I--ER--CAN'T EXPLAIN WHY, BUT I ASSURE YOU THERE WILL BE NO MORE GORILLA APPEARANCES IN THE STREETS! AND IT **NEVER** WAS YOU!

WHEW! I'M GLAD TO HEAR YOU SAY THAT, **BARRY**...

AS BARRY FINALLY KEEPS HIS DATE WITH IRIS WEST...

TAKING ME TO THE ZOO **!?** I DON'T GET IT!

NOW I'LL NEVER KNOW WHETHER ONE OF THESE GORILLAS IS AN **ORDINARY** GORILLA--OR ONE LIKE **SOLOVAR**-- KEEPING QUIET SO THE **GORILLA-CITY** WILL STAY SECRET!

IN THE NEXT ISSUE OF **THE FLASH**-- ANOTHER SUPER-GORILLA THRILLER!

The End

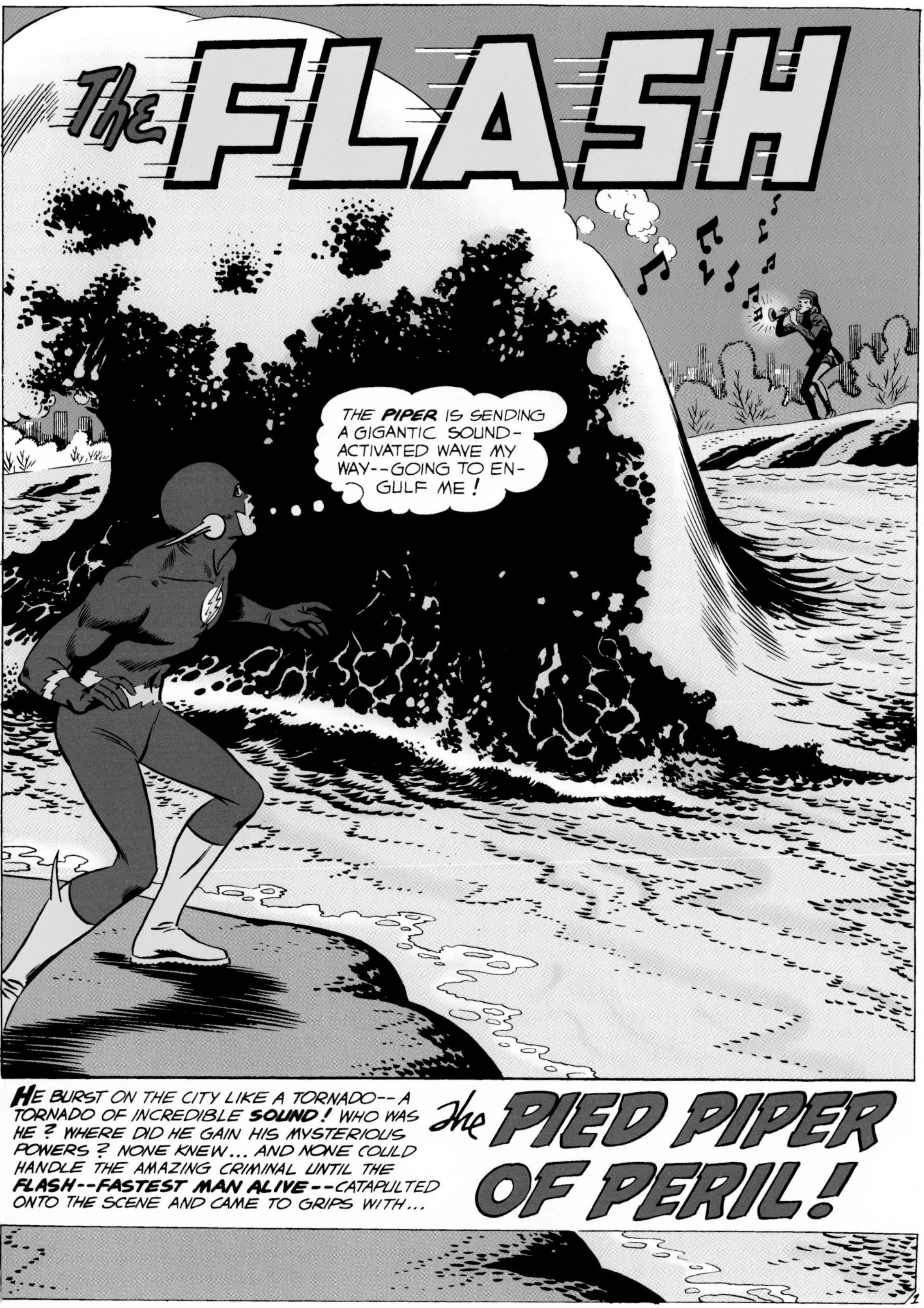

The FLASH
THE PIPER IS SENDING A GIGANTIC SOUND-ACTIVATED WAVE MY WAY--GOING TO ENGULF ME!
HE BURST ON THE CITY LIKE A TORNADO--A TORNADO OF INCREDIBLE SOUND! WHO WAS HE? WHERE DID HE GAIN HIS MYSTERIOUS POWERS? NONE KNEW... AND NONE COULD HANDLE THE AMAZING CRIMINAL UNTIL THE FLASH--FASTEST MAN ALIVE--CATAPULTED ONTO THE SCENE AND CAME TO GRIPS WITH...
The PIED PIPER OF PERIL!
1

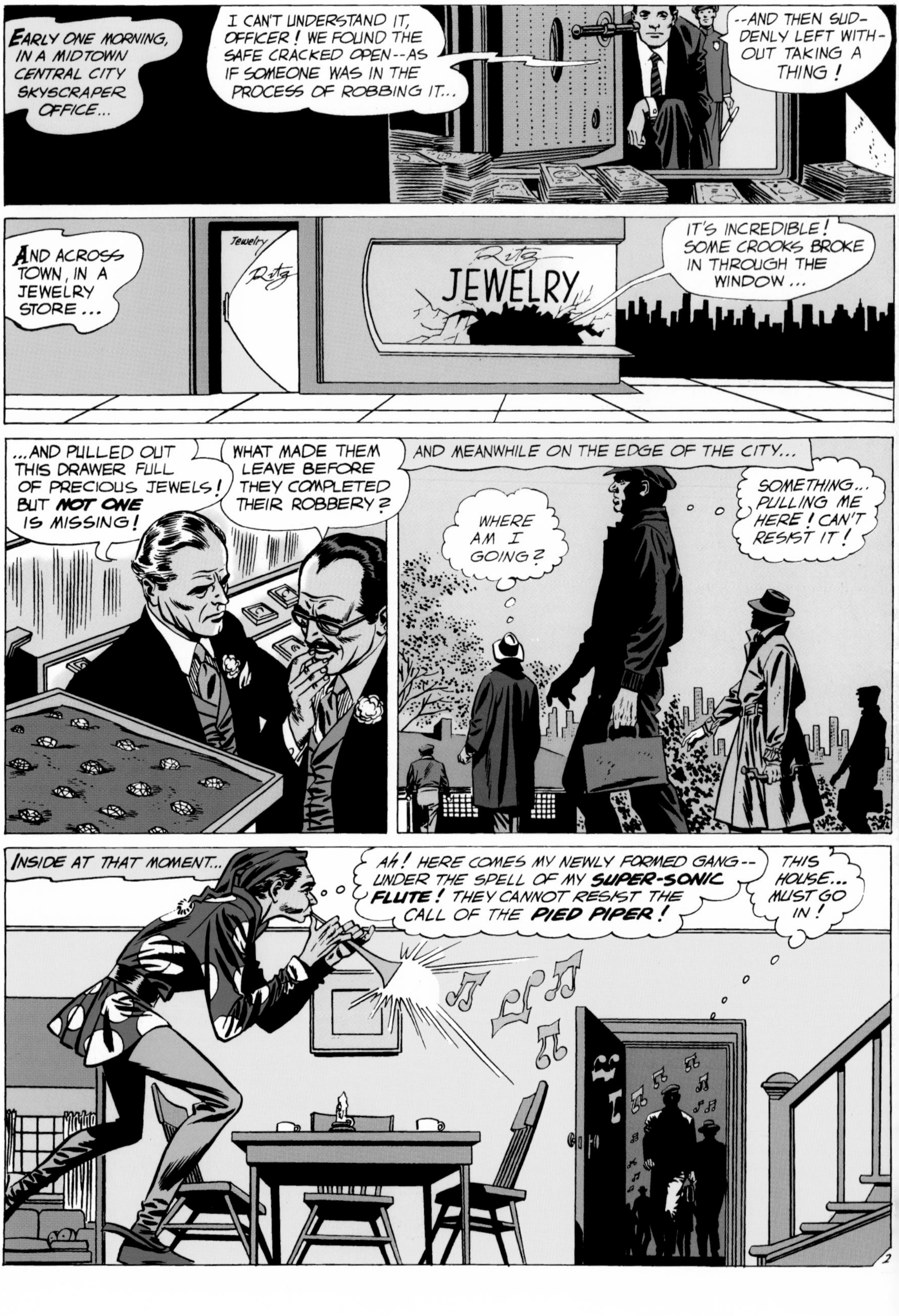
EARLY ONE MORNING, IN A MIDTOWN CENTRAL CITY SKYSCRAPER OFFICE...
I CAN'T UNDERSTAND IT, OFFICER! WE FOUND THE SAFE CRACKED OPEN--AS IF SOMEONE WAS IN THE PROCESS OF ROBBING IT...
--AND THEN SUDDENLY LEFT WITHOUT TAKING A THING!
AND ACROSS TOWN, IN A JEWELRY STORE...
Jewelry
Ritz
JEWELRY
IT'S INCREDIBLE! SOME CROOKS BROKE IN THROUGH THE WINDOW...
...AND PULLED OUT THIS DRAWER FULL OF PRECIOUS JEWELS! BUT **NOT ONE** IS MISSING!
WHAT MADE THEM LEAVE BEFORE THEY COMPLETED THEIR ROBBERY?
AND MEANWHILE ON THE EDGE OF THE CITY...
WHERE AM I GOING?
SOMETHING... PULLING ME HERE! CAN'T RESIST IT!
INSIDE AT THAT MOMENT...
AH! HERE COMES MY NEWLY FORMED GANG--UNDER THE SPELL OF MY **SUPER-SONIC FLUTE**! THEY CANNOT RESIST THE CALL OF THE **PIED PIPER**!
THIS HOUSE... MUST GO IN!
2

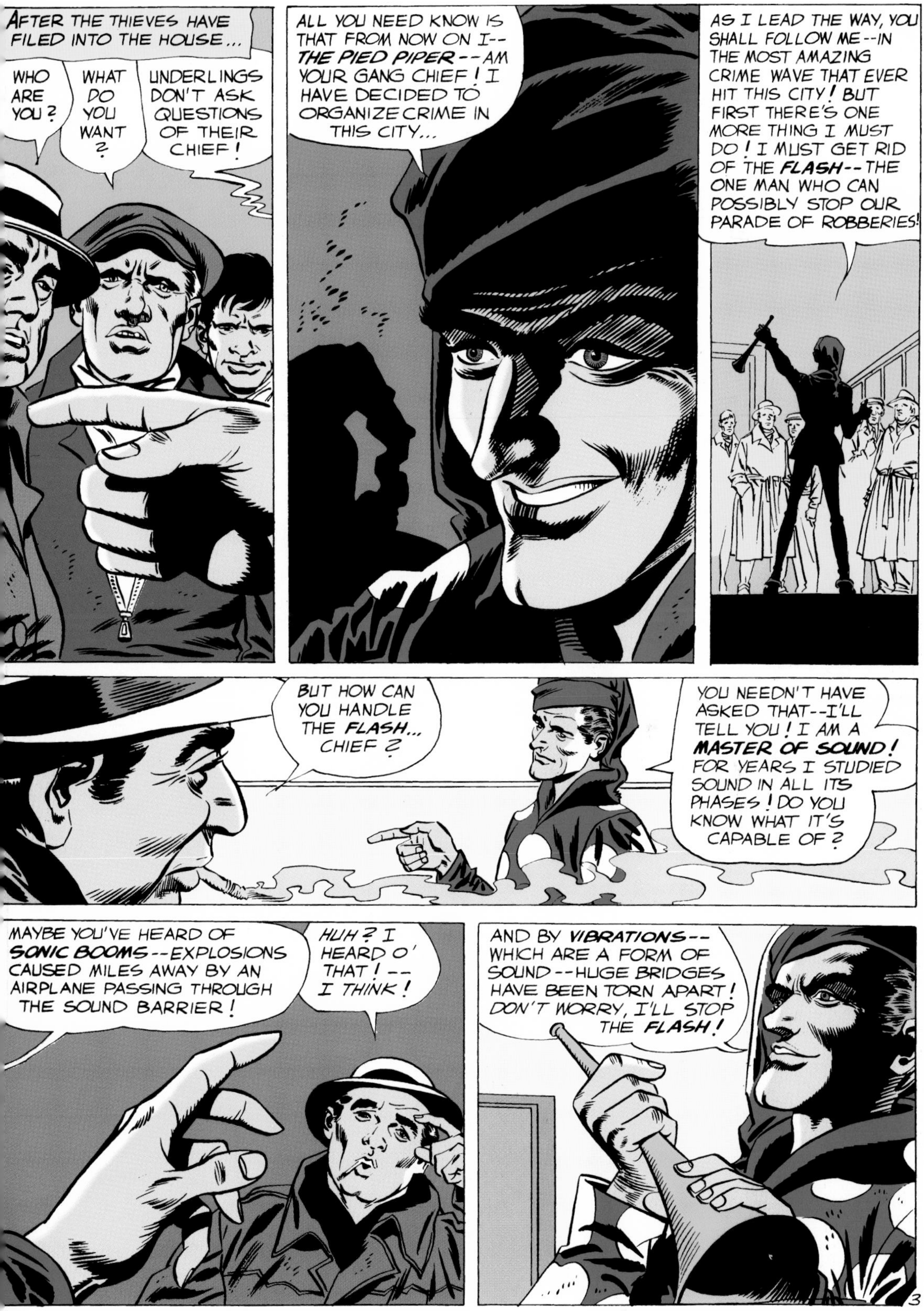
AFTER THE THIEVES HAVE FILED INTO THE HOUSE...
WHO ARE YOU?
WHAT DO YOU WANT?
UNDERLINGS DON'T ASK QUESTIONS OF THEIR CHIEF!
ALL YOU NEED KNOW IS THAT FROM NOW ON I-- THE PIED PIPER--AM YOUR GANG CHIEF! I HAVE DECIDED TO ORGANIZE CRIME IN THIS CITY...
AS I LEAD THE WAY, YOU SHALL FOLLOW ME--IN THE MOST AMAZING CRIME WAVE THAT EVER HIT THIS CITY! BUT FIRST THERE'S ONE MORE THING I MUST DO! I MUST GET RID OF THE FLASH--THE ONE MAN WHO CAN POSSIBLY STOP OUR PARADE OF ROBBERIES!
BUT HOW CAN YOU HANDLE THE FLASH... CHIEF?
YOU NEEDN'T HAVE ASKED THAT--I'LL TELL YOU! I AM A MASTER OF SOUND! FOR YEARS I STUDIED SOUND IN ALL ITS PHASES! DO YOU KNOW WHAT IT'S CAPABLE OF?
MAYBE YOU'VE HEARD OF SONIC BOOMS--EXPLOSIONS CAUSED MILES AWAY BY AN AIRPLANE PASSING THROUGH THE SOUND BARRIER!
HUH? I HEARD O' THAT!--I THINK!
AND BY VIBRATIONS--WHICH ARE A FORM OF SOUND--HUGE BRIDGES HAVE BEEN TORN APART! DON'T WORRY, I'LL STOP THE FLASH!
3

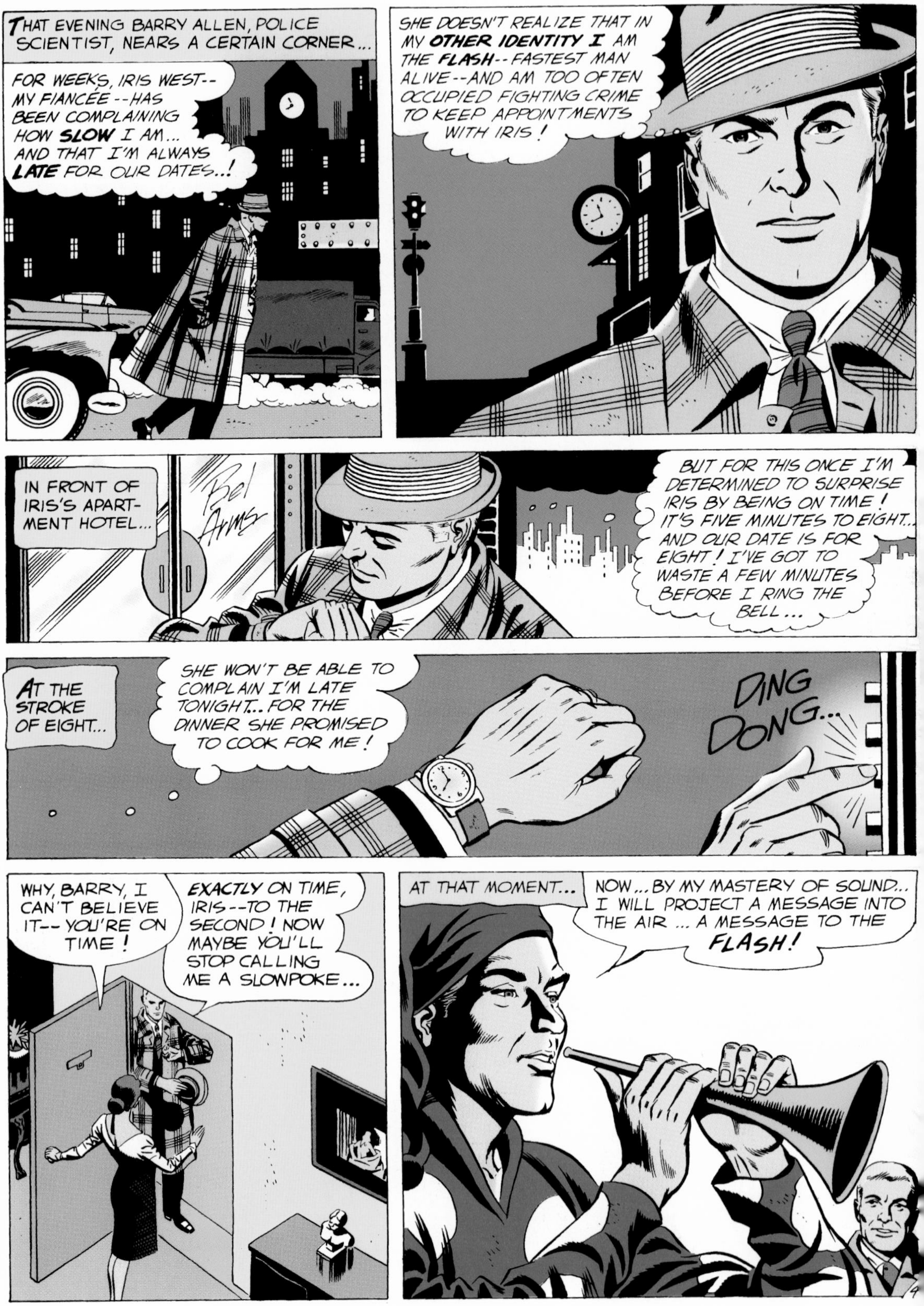
THAT EVENING BARRY ALLEN, POLICE SCIENTIST, NEARS A CERTAIN CORNER...
FOR WEEKS, IRIS WEST--MY FIANCÉE--HAS BEEN COMPLAINING HOW SLOW I AM... AND THAT I'M ALWAYS LATE FOR OUR DATES...!
SHE DOESN'T REALIZE THAT IN MY OTHER IDENTITY I AM THE FLASH--FASTEST MAN ALIVE--AND AM TOO OFTEN OCCUPIED FIGHTING CRIME TO KEEP APPOINTMENTS WITH IRIS!
IN FRONT OF IRIS'S APARTMENT HOTEL...
Bel Arms
BUT FOR THIS ONCE I'M DETERMINED TO SURPRISE IRIS BY BEING ON TIME! IT'S FIVE MINUTES TO EIGHT... AND OUR DATE IS FOR EIGHT! I'VE GOT TO WASTE A FEW MINUTES BEFORE I RING THE BELL...
AT THE STROKE OF EIGHT...
SHE WON'T BE ABLE TO COMPLAIN I'M LATE TONIGHT...FOR THE DINNER SHE PROMISED TO COOK FOR ME!
DING DONG...
WHY, BARRY, I CAN'T BELIEVE IT--YOU'RE ON TIME!
EXACTLY ON TIME, IRIS--TO THE SECOND! NOW MAYBE YOU'LL STOP CALLING ME A SLOWPOKE...
AT THAT MOMENT...
NOW... BY MY MASTERY OF SOUND... I WILL PROJECT A MESSAGE INTO THE AIR ... A MESSAGE TO THE FLASH!
4

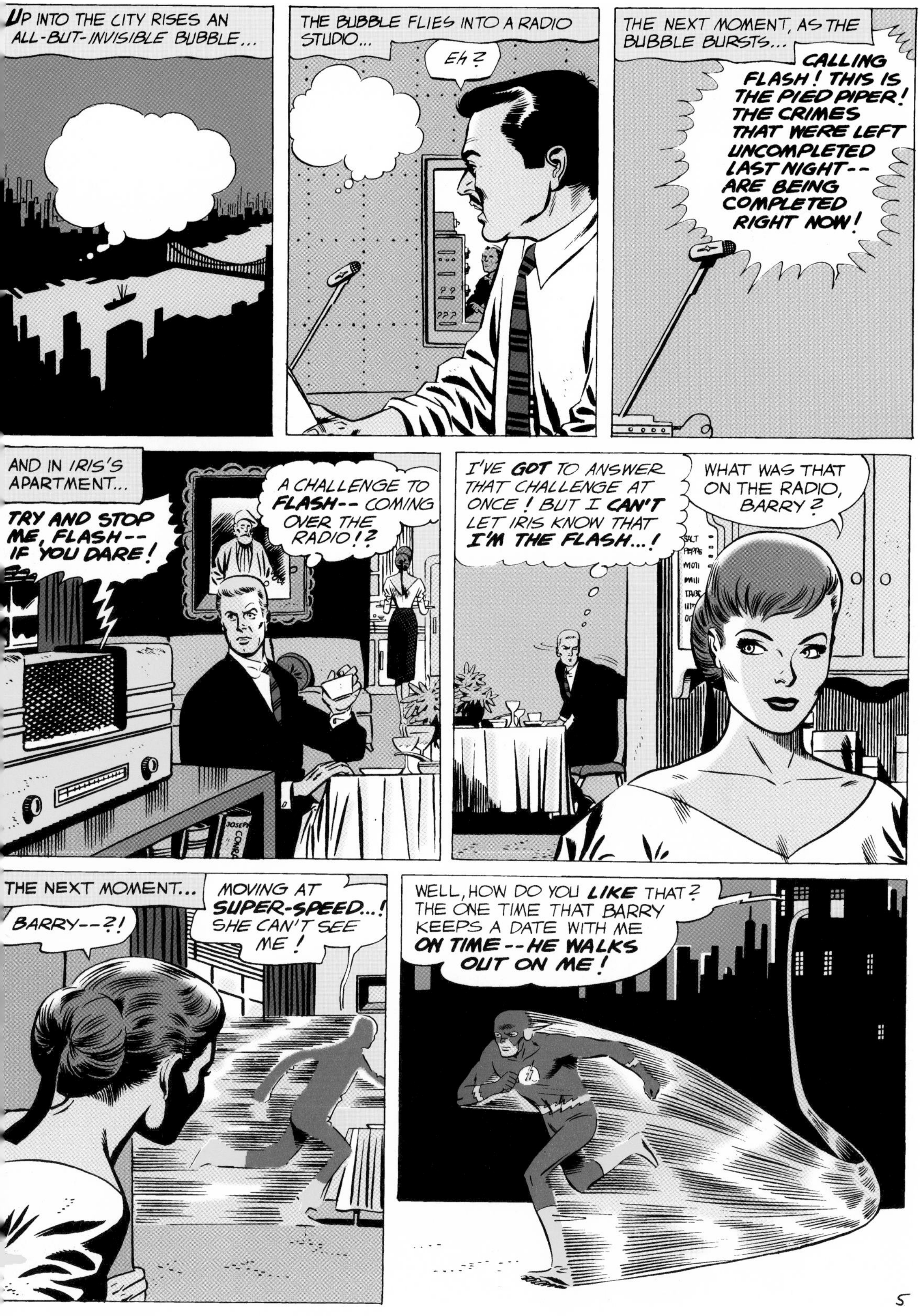
UP INTO THE CITY RISES AN ALL-BUT-INVISIBLE BUBBLE...
THE BUBBLE FLIES INTO A RADIO STUDIO...
Eh?
THE NEXT MOMENT, AS THE BUBBLE BURSTS...
CALLING FLASH! THIS IS THE PIED PIPER! THE CRIMES THAT WERE LEFT UNCOMPLETED LAST NIGHT-- ARE BEING COMPLETED RIGHT NOW!
AND IN IRIS'S APARTMENT...
TRY AND STOP ME, FLASH-- IF YOU DARE!
A CHALLENGE TO FLASH-- COMING OVER THE RADIO!?
I'VE GOT TO ANSWER THAT CHALLENGE AT ONCE! BUT I CAN'T LET IRIS KNOW THAT I'M THE FLASH...!
WHAT WAS THAT ON THE RADIO, BARRY?
THE NEXT MOMENT...
BARRY--?!
MOVING AT SUPER-SPEED...! SHE CAN'T SEE ME!
WELL, HOW DO YOU LIKE THAT? THE ONE TIME THAT BARRY KEEPS A DATE WITH ME ON TIME--HE WALKS OUT ON ME!

As the **WORLD'S FASTEST HUMAN** zooms toward his foe...

ONE OF THOSE **UNCOMPLETED CRIMES** TOOK PLACE IN THIS SKYSCRAPER! I'LL TAKE THE STAIRS--THE ELEVATOR IS TOO SLOW!

SPLIT-INSTANTS LATER...

THAT COSTUMED CHARACTER-- THE SELF-STYLED **PIED PIPER!**

HERE COMES **FLASH**-- RIGHT ON SCHEDULE! WATCH CAREFULLY-- YOU'LL GET A KICK OUT OF THIS!

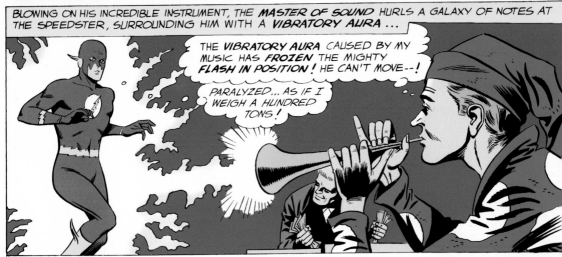

BLOWING ON HIS INCREDIBLE INSTRUMENT, THE **MASTER OF SOUND** HURLS A GALAXY OF NOTES AT THE SPEEDSTER, SURROUNDING HIM WITH A **VIBRATORY AURA**...

THE **VIBRATORY AURA** CAUSED BY MY MUSIC HAS **FROZEN** THE MIGHTY **FLASH IN POSITION!** HE CAN'T MOVE--!

PARALYZED... AS IF I WEIGH A HUNDRED TONS!

THIS WILL CONVINCE **FLASH** NEVER TO INTERFERE IN MY AFFAIRS! HA! IT WILL BE AT LEAST A **HALF HOUR** BEFORE HE CAN BUDGE-- PLENTY OF TIME FOR US--TO MAKE OUR GETAWAY!

BUT SHORT MOMENTS AFTER...

I NEVER SHOULD HAVE UNDERESTIMATED **THE FLASH!** HE'S ALREADY CAUGHT UP TO US!

HE DOESN'T REALIZE MY OWN **VIBRATIONS** COUNTERACTED HIS--WORKED ME LOOSE!

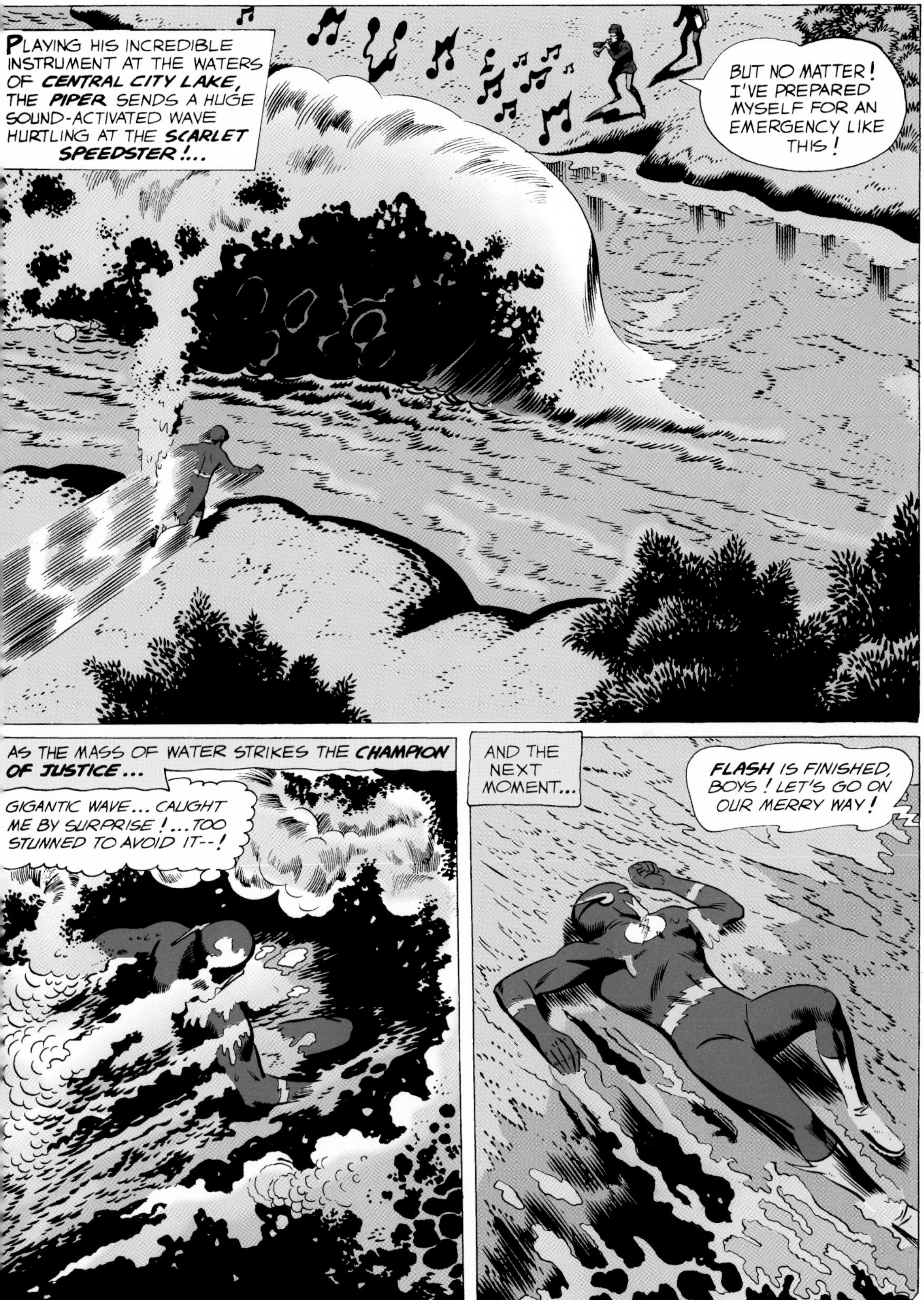
PLAYING HIS INCREDIBLE INSTRUMENT AT THE WATERS OF CENTRAL CITY LAKE, THE PIPER SENDS A HUGE SOUND-ACTIVATED WAVE HURTLING AT THE SCARLET SPEEDSTER!...
BUT NO MATTER! I'VE PREPARED MYSELF FOR AN EMERGENCY LIKE THIS!
AS THE MASS OF WATER STRIKES THE CHAMPION OF JUSTICE...
GIGANTIC WAVE... CAUGHT ME BY SURPRISE!...TOO STUNNED TO AVOID IT--!
AND THE NEXT MOMENT...
FLASH IS FINISHED, BOYS! LET'S GO ON OUR MERRY WAY!

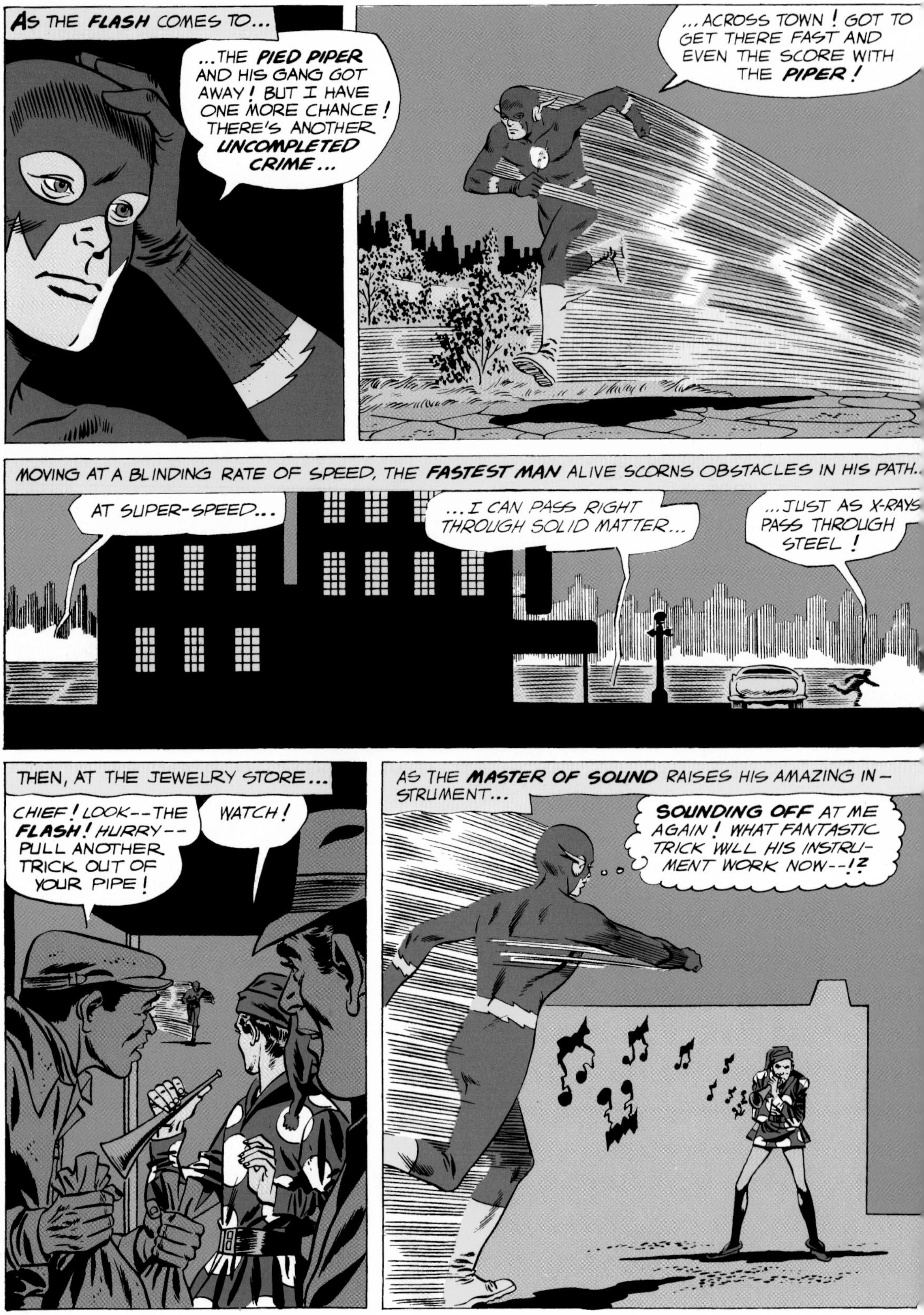
AS THE FLASH COMES TO...
...THE PIED PIPER AND HIS GANG GOT AWAY! BUT I HAVE ONE MORE CHANCE! THERE'S ANOTHER UNCOMPLETED CRIME...
...ACROSS TOWN! GOT TO GET THERE FAST AND EVEN THE SCORE WITH THE PIPER!
MOVING AT A BLINDING RATE OF SPEED, THE FASTEST MAN ALIVE SCORNS OBSTACLES IN HIS PATH...
AT SUPER-SPEED...
...I CAN PASS RIGHT THROUGH SOLID MATTER...
...JUST AS X-RAYS PASS THROUGH STEEL!
THEN, AT THE JEWELRY STORE...
CHIEF! LOOK--THE FLASH! HURRY--PULL ANOTHER TRICK OUT OF YOUR PIPE!
WATCH!
AS THE MASTER OF SOUND RAISES HIS AMAZING IN-STRUMENT...
SOUNDING OFF AT ME AGAIN! WHAT FANTASTIC TRICK WILL HIS INSTRU-MENT WORK NOW--!?

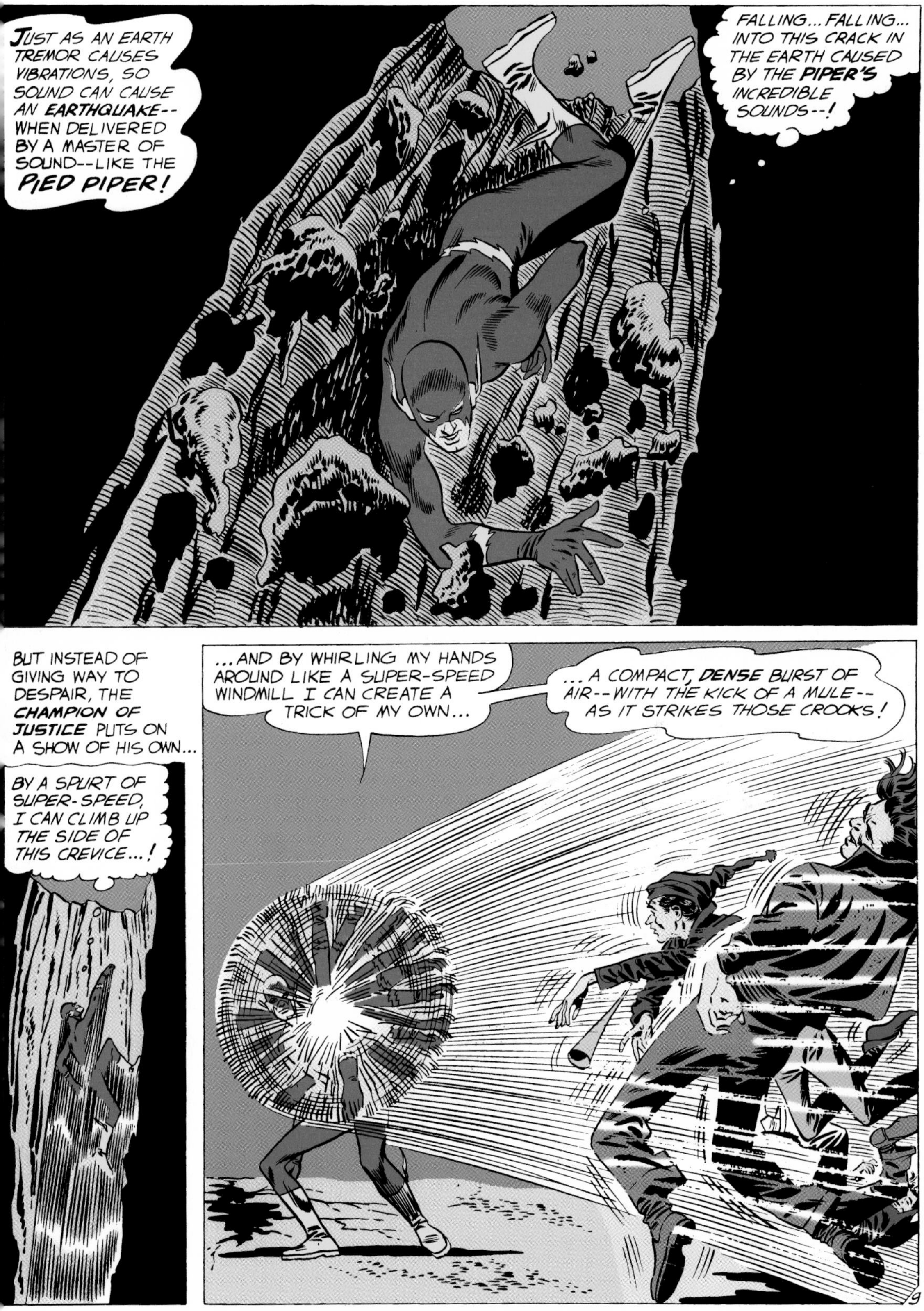
JUST AS AN EARTH TREMOR CAUSES VIBRATIONS, SO SOUND CAN CAUSE AN EARTHQUAKE-- WHEN DELIVERED BY A MASTER OF SOUND--LIKE THE PIED PIPER!
FALLING... FALLING... INTO THIS CRACK IN THE EARTH CAUSED BY THE PIPER'S INCREDIBLE SOUNDS--!
BUT INSTEAD OF GIVING WAY TO DESPAIR, THE CHAMPION OF JUSTICE PUTS ON A SHOW OF HIS OWN...
BY A SPURT OF SUPER-SPEED, I CAN CLIMB UP THE SIDE OF THIS CREVICE...!
...AND BY WHIRLING MY HANDS AROUND LIKE A SUPER-SPEED WINDMILL I CAN CREATE A TRICK OF MY OWN...
...A COMPACT, DENSE BURST OF AIR--WITH THE KICK OF A MULE-- AS IT STRIKES THOSE CROOKS!
9

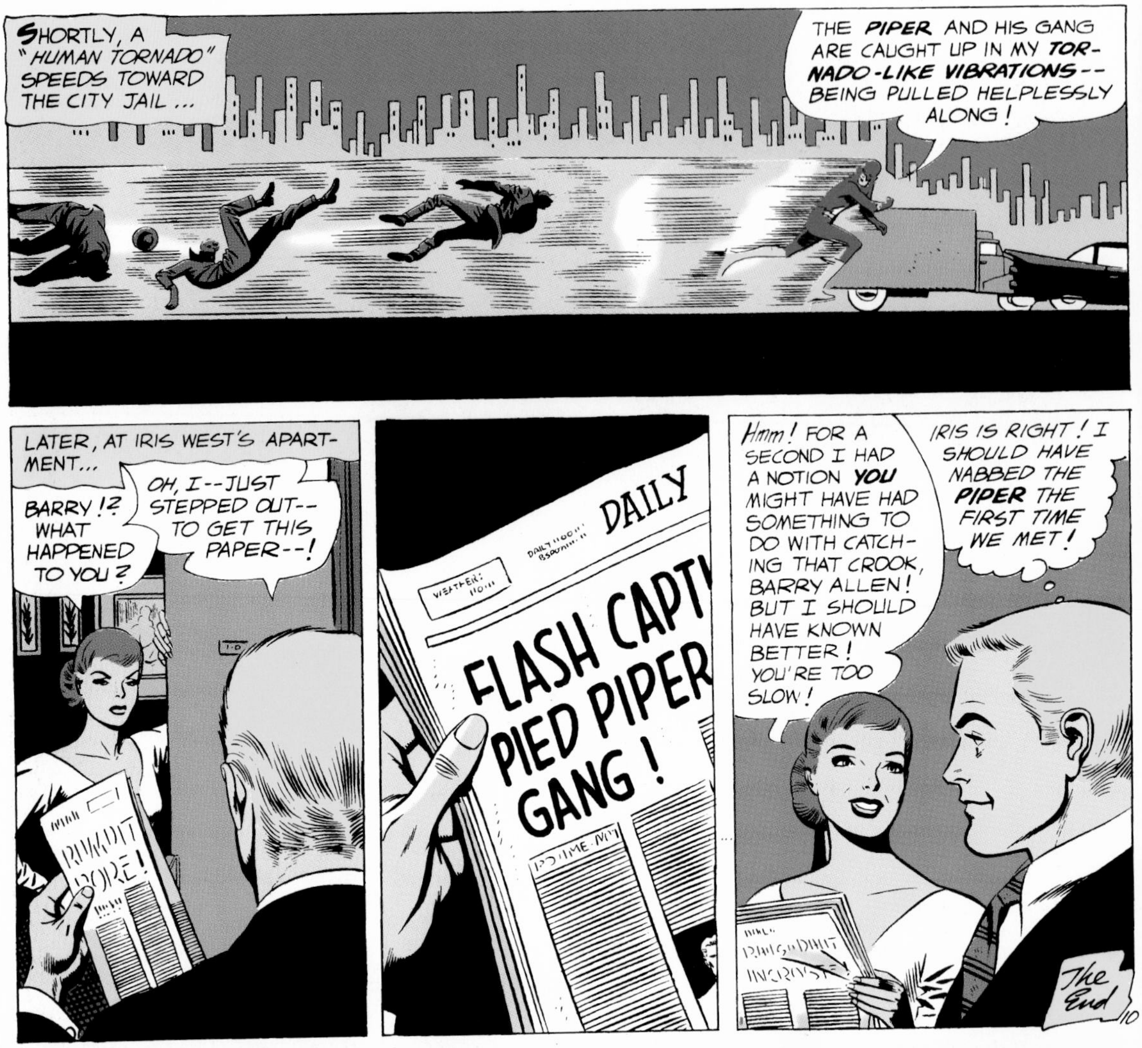
SHORTLY, A "HUMAN TORNADO" SPEEDS TOWARD THE CITY JAIL ...
THE PIPER AND HIS GANG ARE CAUGHT UP IN MY TORNADO-LIKE VIBRATIONS-- BEING PULLED HELPLESSLY ALONG!
LATER, AT IRIS WEST'S APARTMENT...
BARRY!? WHAT HAPPENED TO YOU?
OH, I--JUST STEPPED OUT-- TO GET THIS PAPER--!
DAILY
FLASH CAPT
PIED PIPER
GANG!
Hmm! FOR A SECOND I HAD A NOTION YOU MIGHT HAVE HAD SOMETHING TO DO WITH CATCHING THAT CROOK, BARRY ALLEN! BUT I SHOULD HAVE KNOWN BETTER! YOU'RE TOO SLOW!
IRIS IS RIGHT! I SHOULD HAVE NABBED THE PIPER THE FIRST TIME WE MET!
The End
10

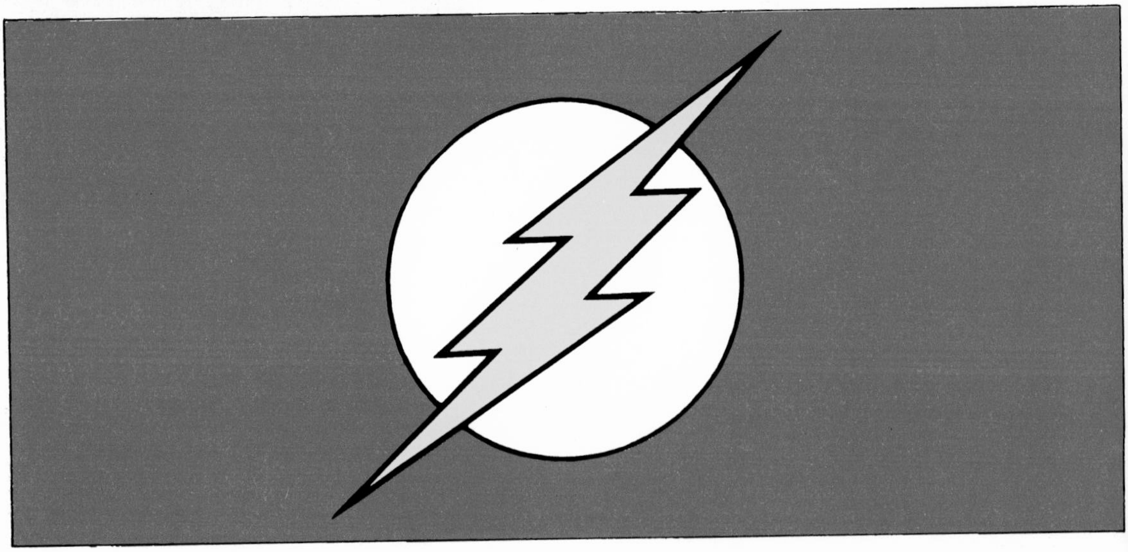

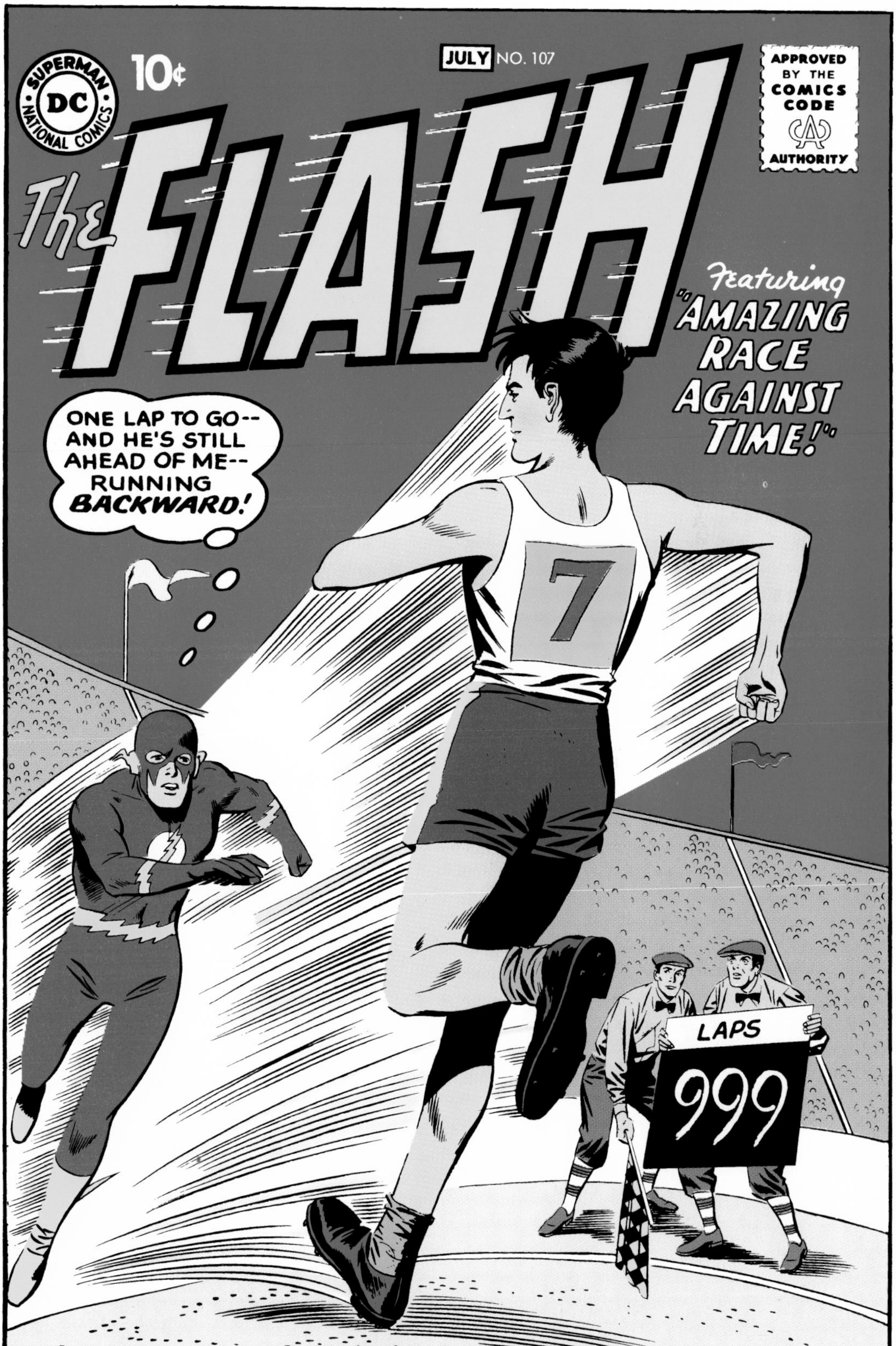
SUPERMAN DC NATIONAL COMICS
10¢
JULY NO. 107
APPROVED BY THE COMICS CODE AUTHORITY
The FLASH
Featuring "AMAZING RACE AGAINST TIME!"
ONE LAP TO GO-- AND HE'S STILL AHEAD OF ME-- RUNNING BACKWARD!
7
LAPS
999

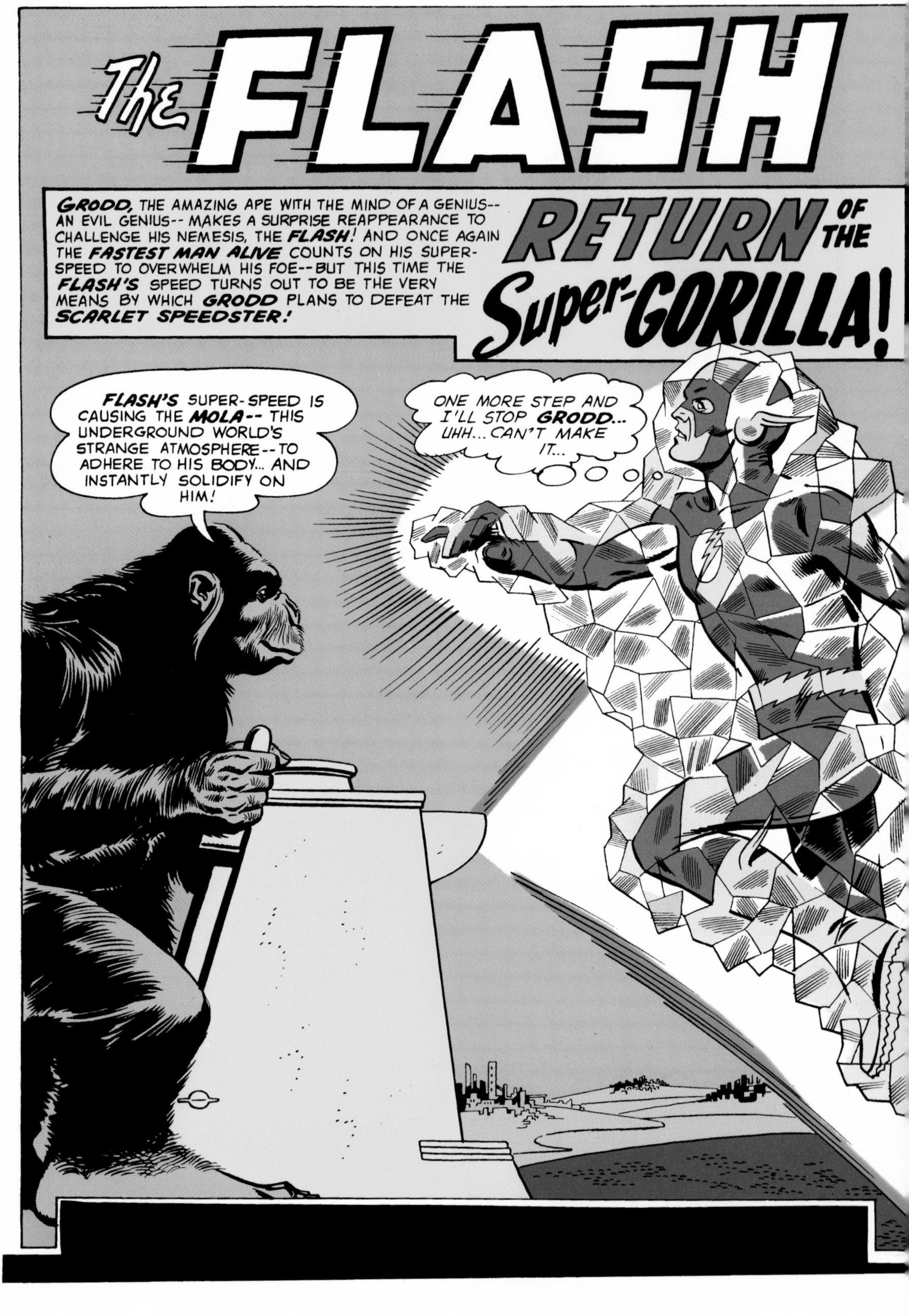
The FLASH
GRODD, THE AMAZING APE WITH THE MIND OF A GENIUS-- AN EVIL GENIUS-- MAKES A SURPRISE REAPPEARANCE TO CHALLENGE HIS NEMESIS, THE FLASH! AND ONCE AGAIN THE FASTEST MAN ALIVE COUNTS ON HIS SUPER-SPEED TO OVERWHELM HIS FOE--BUT THIS TIME THE FLASH'S SPEED TURNS OUT TO BE THE VERY MEANS BY WHICH GRODD PLANS TO DEFEAT THE SCARLET SPEEDSTER!
RETURN OF THE Super-GORILLA!
FLASH'S SUPER-SPEED IS CAUSING THE MOLA-- THIS UNDERGROUND WORLD'S STRANGE ATMOSPHERE--TO ADHERE TO HIS BODY... AND INSTANTLY SOLIDIFY ON HIM!
ONE MORE STEP AND I'LL STOP GRODD... UHH... CAN'T MAKE IT...

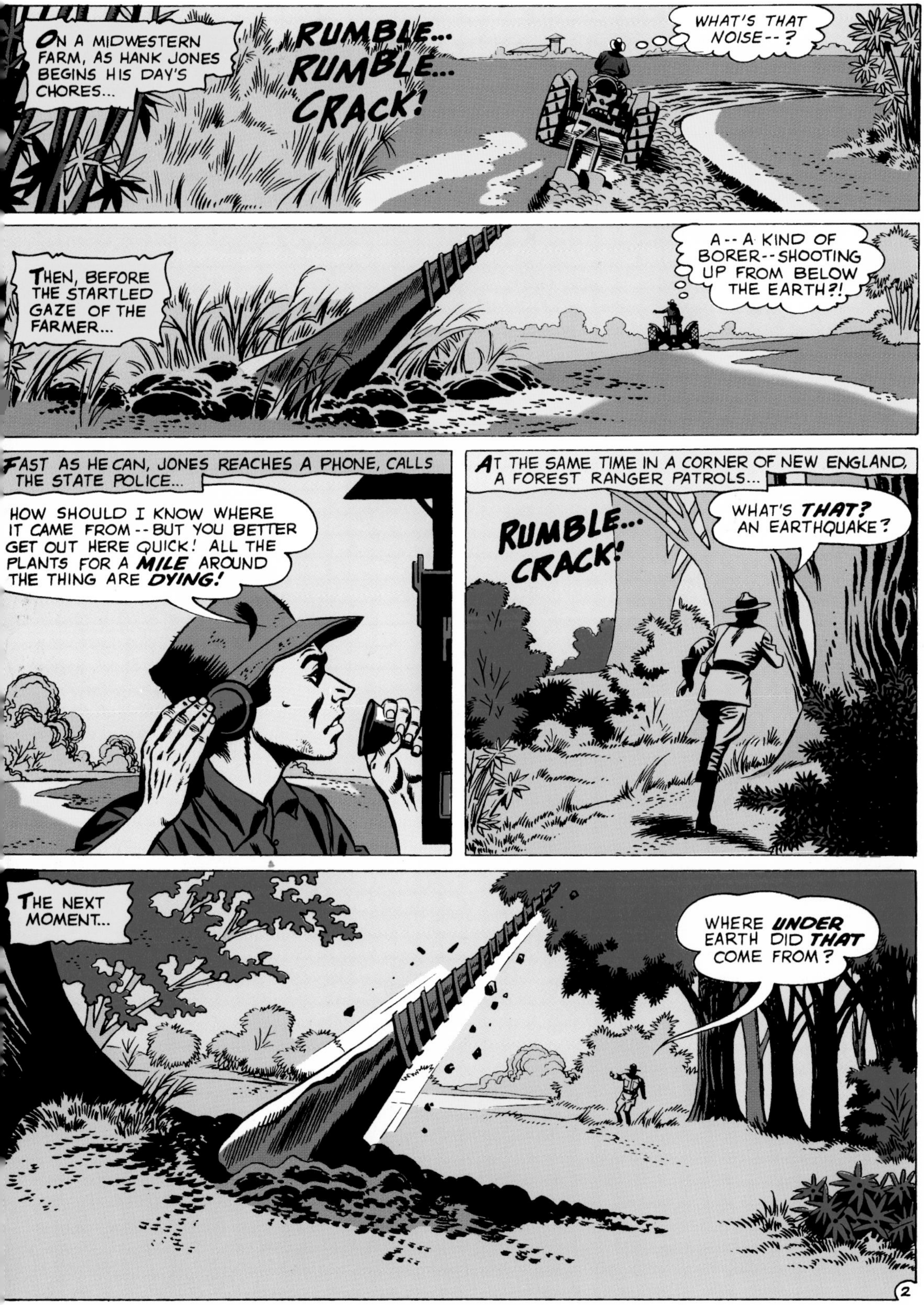
ON A MIDWESTERN FARM, AS HANK JONES BEGINS HIS DAY'S CHORES...
RUMBLE... RUMBLE... CRACK!
WHAT'S THAT NOISE--?
THEN, BEFORE THE STARTLED GAZE OF THE FARMER...
A--A KIND OF BORER--SHOOTING UP FROM BELOW THE EARTH?!
FAST AS HE CAN, JONES REACHES A PHONE, CALLS THE STATE POLICE...
HOW SHOULD I KNOW WHERE IT CAME FROM--BUT YOU BETTER GET OUT HERE QUICK! ALL THE PLANTS FOR A MILE AROUND THE THING ARE DYING!
AT THE SAME TIME IN A CORNER OF NEW ENGLAND, A FOREST RANGER PATROLS...
RUMBLE... CRACK!
WHAT'S THAT? AN EARTHQUAKE?
THE NEXT MOMENT...
WHERE UNDER EARTH DID THAT COME FROM?
2

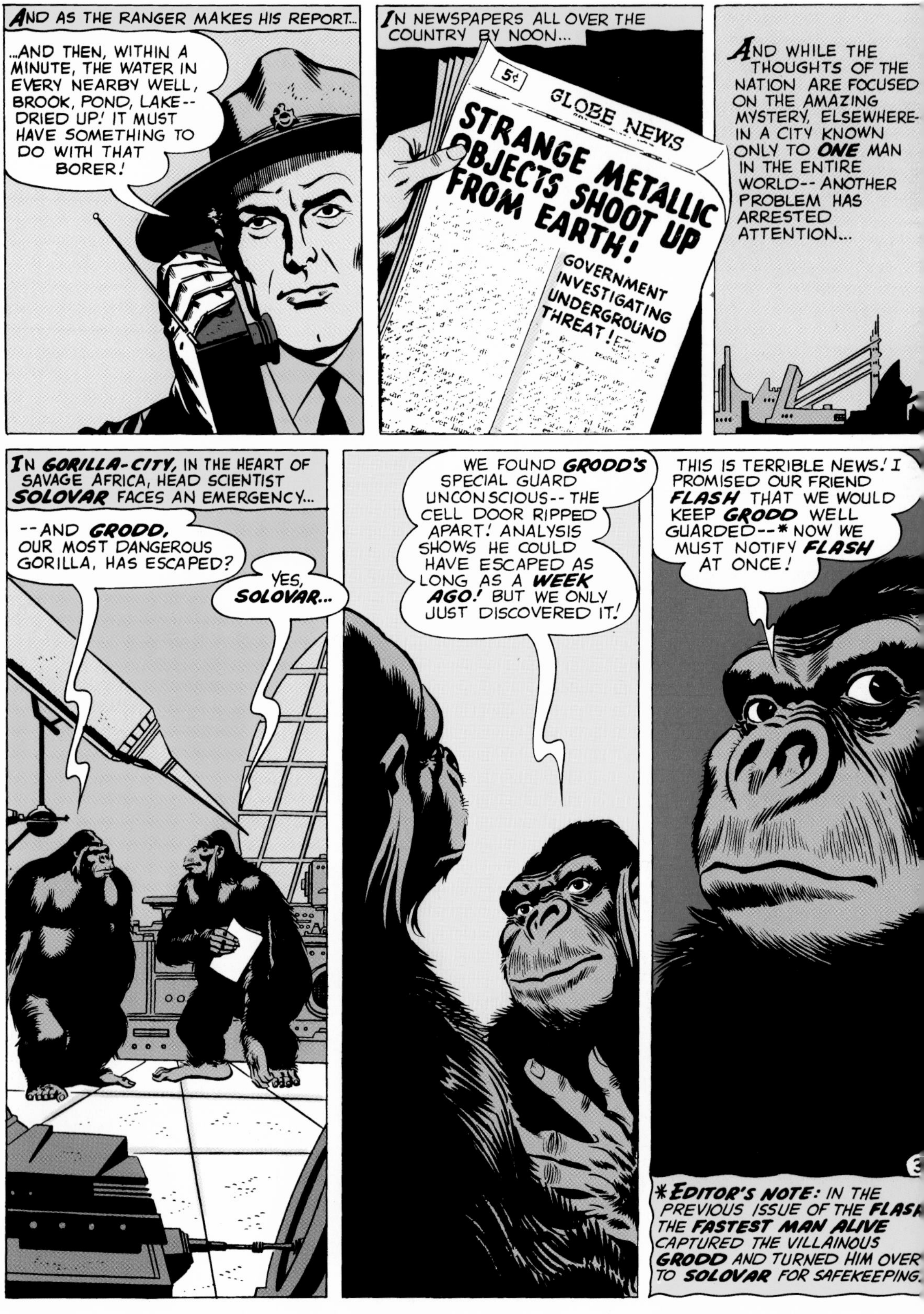
AND AS THE RANGER MAKES HIS REPORT...
...AND THEN, WITHIN A MINUTE, THE WATER IN EVERY NEARBY WELL, BROOK, POND, LAKE--DRIED UP! IT MUST HAVE SOMETHING TO DO WITH THAT BORER!
IN NEWSPAPERS ALL OVER THE COUNTRY BY NOON...
5¢
GLOBE NEWS
STRANGE METALLIC OBJECTS SHOOT UP FROM EARTH!
GOVERNMENT INVESTIGATING UNDERGROUND THREAT!
AND WHILE THE THOUGHTS OF THE NATION ARE FOCUSED ON THE AMAZING MYSTERY, ELSEWHERE-- IN A CITY KNOWN ONLY TO ONE MAN IN THE ENTIRE WORLD-- ANOTHER PROBLEM HAS ARRESTED ATTENTION...
IN GORILLA-CITY, IN THE HEART OF SAVAGE AFRICA, HEAD SCIENTIST SOLOVAR FACES AN EMERGENCY...
--AND GRODD, OUR MOST DANGEROUS GORILLA, HAS ESCAPED?
YES, SOLOVAR...
WE FOUND GRODD'S SPECIAL GUARD UNCONSCIOUS-- THE CELL DOOR RIPPED APART! ANALYSIS SHOWS HE COULD HAVE ESCAPED AS LONG AS A WEEK AGO! BUT WE ONLY JUST DISCOVERED IT!
THIS IS TERRIBLE NEWS! I PROMISED OUR FRIEND FLASH THAT WE WOULD KEEP GRODD WELL GUARDED--* NOW WE MUST NOTIFY FLASH AT ONCE!
*EDITOR'S NOTE: IN THE PREVIOUS ISSUE OF THE FLASH THE FASTEST MAN ALIVE CAPTURED THE VILLAINOUS GRODD AND TURNED HIM OVER TO SOLOVAR FOR SAFEKEEPING.

Swiftly **SOLOVAR** reaches for an instrument on his desk...

INFORMATION? GET ME **FLASH'S** VIBRATION-AURA NUMBER! IT MUST BE ON FILE!

FLASH WAS IN **GORILLA-CITY** NOT LONG AGO--AND THE **VIBRATION RECORDERS** WOULD AUTOMATICALLY HAVE REGISTERED HIS VIBRATION-FREQUENCY!

I'LL CHECK, SIR...

Soon... YOU WERE RIGHT, SCIENTIST **SOLOVAR!** OUR RECORDERS DID REGISTER **FLASH'S** VIBRATION-AURA! THE NUMBER IS **GAMMA FREQUENCY 54-8321!**

CONTACT **FLASH** AT ONCE! I'LL HOLD ON--

YES, SIR!

FROM THE HIDDEN GORILLA-CITY AN ENERGY-BURST FLARES UPWARD...

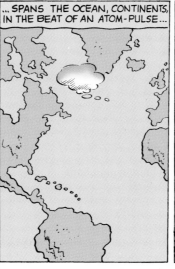

...SPANS THE OCEAN, CONTINENTS, IN THE BEAT OF AN ATOM-PULSE...

...INTO THE POLICE LABORATORY IN CENTRAL CITY WHERE **CHEMIST BARRY ALLEN** WORKS...

HUH? SOME-ONE CALLING ME?

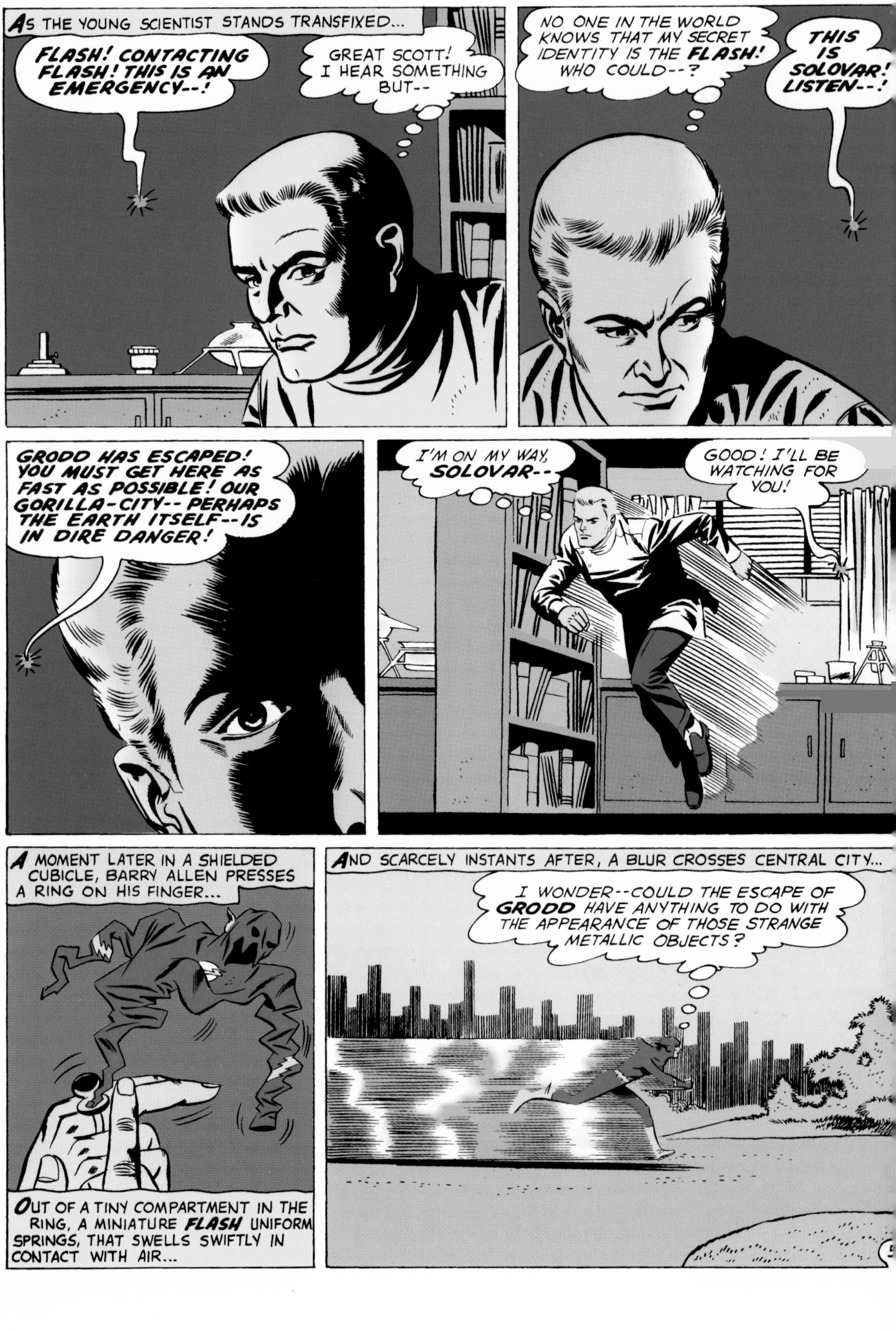
AS THE YOUNG SCIENTIST STANDS TRANSFIXED...
FLASH! CONTACTING FLASH! THIS IS AN EMERGENCY--!
GREAT SCOTT! I HEAR SOMETHING BUT--
NO ONE IN THE WORLD KNOWS THAT MY SECRET IDENTITY IS THE FLASH! WHO COULD--?
THIS IS SOLOVAR! LISTEN--!
GRODD HAS ESCAPED! YOU MUST GET HERE AS FAST AS POSSIBLE! OUR GORILLA-CITY-- PERHAPS THE EARTH ITSELF--IS IN DIRE DANGER!
I'M ON MY WAY, SOLOVAR--
GOOD! I'LL BE WATCHING FOR YOU!
A MOMENT LATER IN A SHIELDED CUBICLE, BARRY ALLEN PRESSES A RING ON HIS FINGER...
OUT OF A TINY COMPARTMENT IN THE RING, A MINIATURE FLASH UNIFORM SPRINGS, THAT SWELLS SWIFTLY IN CONTACT WITH AIR...
AND SCARCELY INSTANTS AFTER, A BLUR CROSSES CENTRAL CITY...
I WONDER--COULD THE ESCAPE OF GRODD HAVE ANYTHING TO DO WITH THE APPEARANCE OF THOSE STRANGE METALLIC OBJECTS?

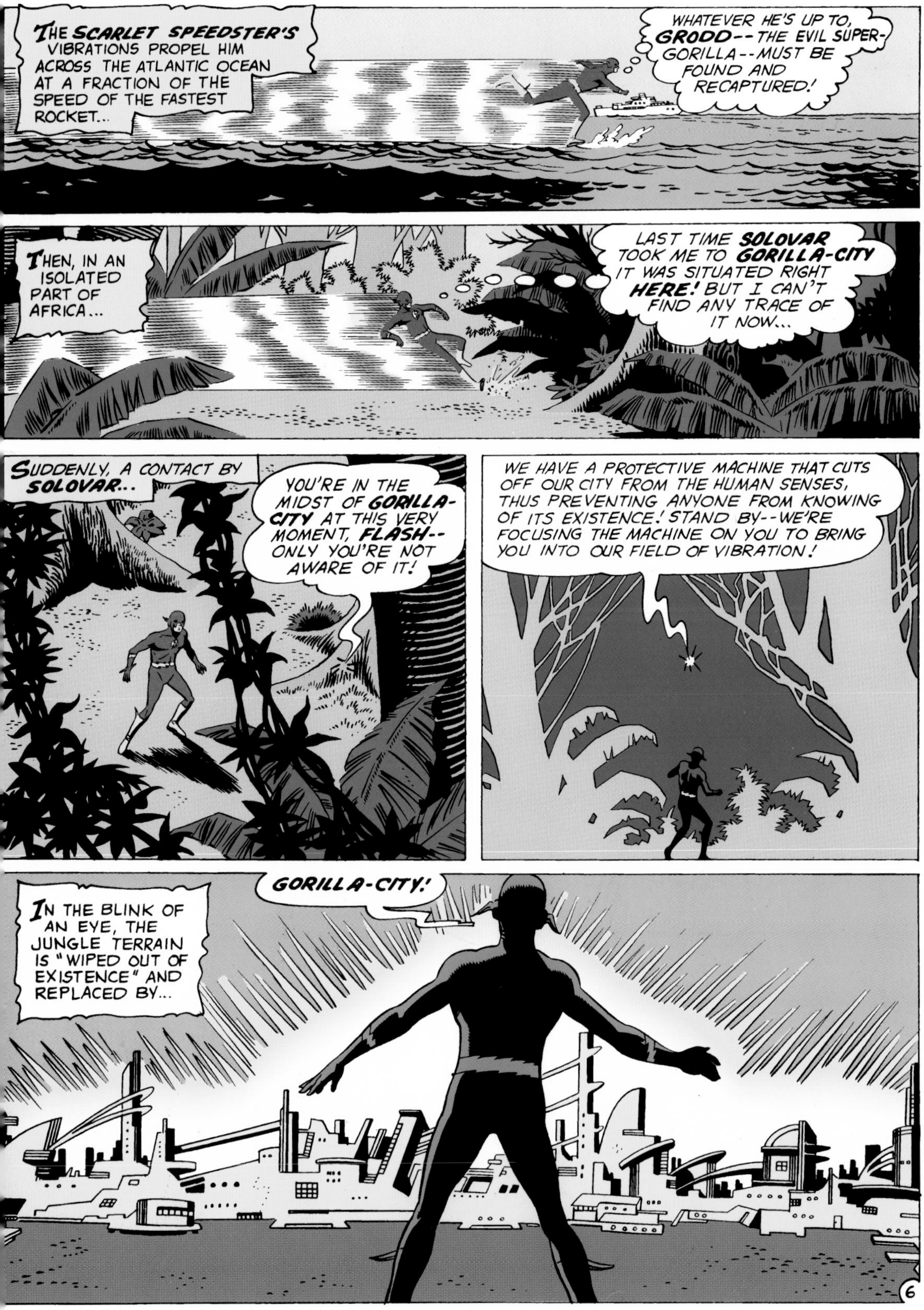
THE SCARLET SPEEDSTER'S VIBRATIONS PROPEL HIM ACROSS THE ATLANTIC OCEAN AT A FRACTION OF THE SPEED OF THE FASTEST ROCKET...
WHATEVER HE'S UP TO, GRODD--THE EVIL SUPER-GORILLA--MUST BE FOUND AND RECAPTURED!
THEN, IN AN ISOLATED PART OF AFRICA...
LAST TIME SOLOVAR TOOK ME TO GORILLA-CITY IT WAS SITUATED RIGHT HERE! BUT I CAN'T FIND ANY TRACE OF IT NOW...
SUDDENLY, A CONTACT BY SOLOVAR...
YOU'RE IN THE MIDST OF GORILLA-CITY AT THIS VERY MOMENT, FLASH--ONLY YOU'RE NOT AWARE OF IT!
WE HAVE A PROTECTIVE MACHINE THAT CUTS OFF OUR CITY FROM THE HUMAN SENSES, THUS PREVENTING ANYONE FROM KNOWING OF ITS EXISTENCE! STAND BY--WE'RE FOCUSING THE MACHINE ON YOU TO BRING YOU INTO OUR FIELD OF VIBRATION!
IN THE BLINK OF AN EYE, THE JUNGLE TERRAIN IS "WIPED OUT OF EXISTENCE" AND REPLACED BY...
GORILLA-CITY!
6

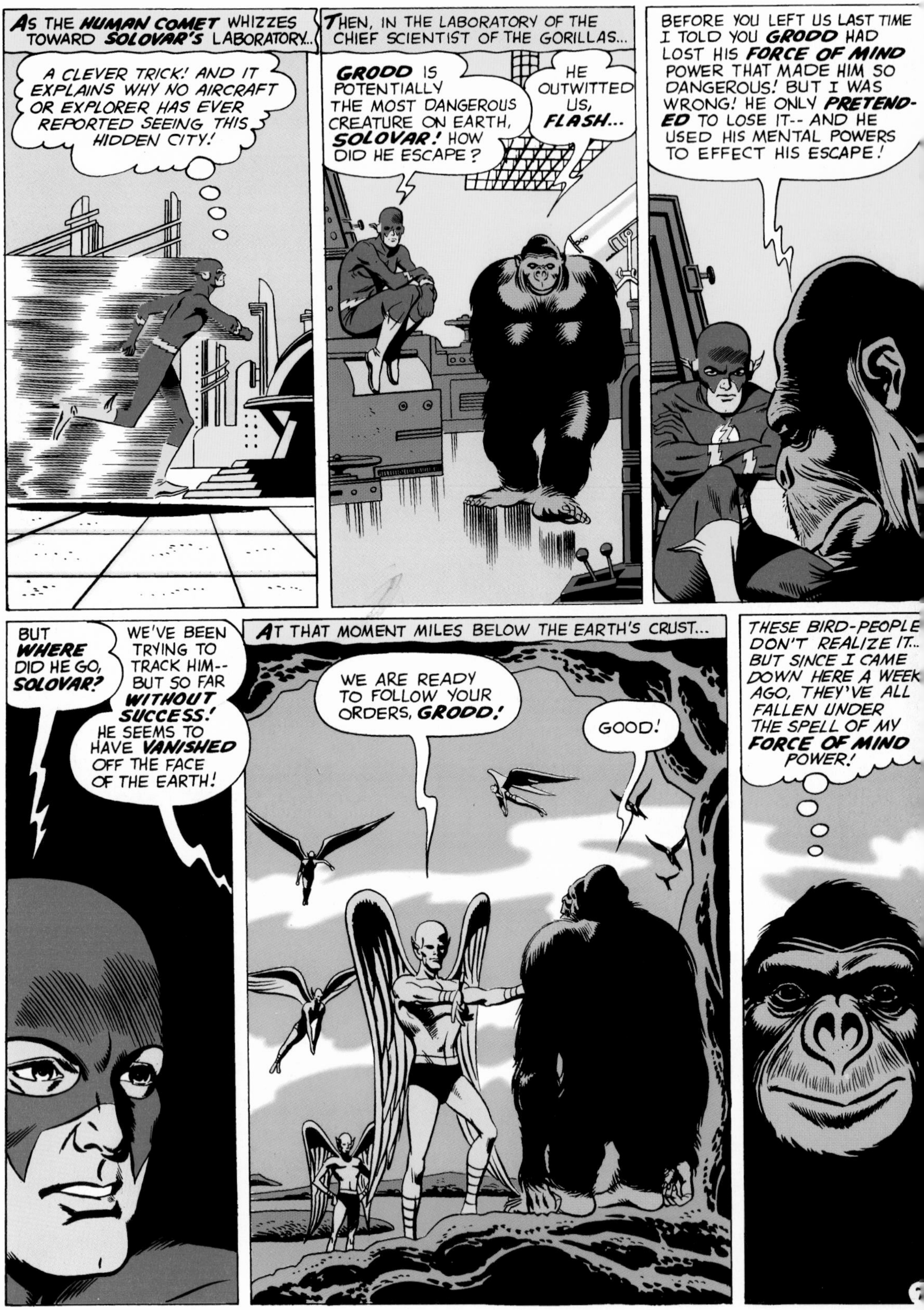
AS THE HUMAN COMET WHIZZES TOWARD SOLOVAR'S LABORATORY...
A CLEVER TRICK! AND IT EXPLAINS WHY NO AIRCRAFT OR EXPLORER HAS EVER REPORTED SEEING THIS HIDDEN CITY!
THEN, IN THE LABORATORY OF THE CHIEF SCIENTIST OF THE GORILLAS...
GRODD IS POTENTIALLY THE MOST DANGEROUS CREATURE ON EARTH, SOLOVAR! HOW DID HE ESCAPE?
HE OUTWITTED US, FLASH...
BEFORE YOU LEFT US LAST TIME I TOLD YOU GRODD HAD LOST HIS FORCE OF MIND POWER THAT MADE HIM SO DANGEROUS! BUT I WAS WRONG! HE ONLY PRETENDED TO LOSE IT-- AND HE USED HIS MENTAL POWERS TO EFFECT HIS ESCAPE!
BUT WHERE DID HE GO, SOLOVAR?
WE'VE BEEN TRYING TO TRACK HIM-- BUT SO FAR WITHOUT SUCCESS! HE SEEMS TO HAVE VANISHED OFF THE FACE OF THE EARTH!
AT THAT MOMENT MILES BELOW THE EARTH'S CRUST...
WE ARE READY TO FOLLOW YOUR ORDERS, GRODD!
GOOD!
THESE BIRD-PEOPLE DON'T REALIZE IT... BUT SINCE I CAME DOWN HERE A WEEK AGO, THEY'VE ALL FALLEN UNDER THE SPELL OF MY FORCE OF MIND POWER!

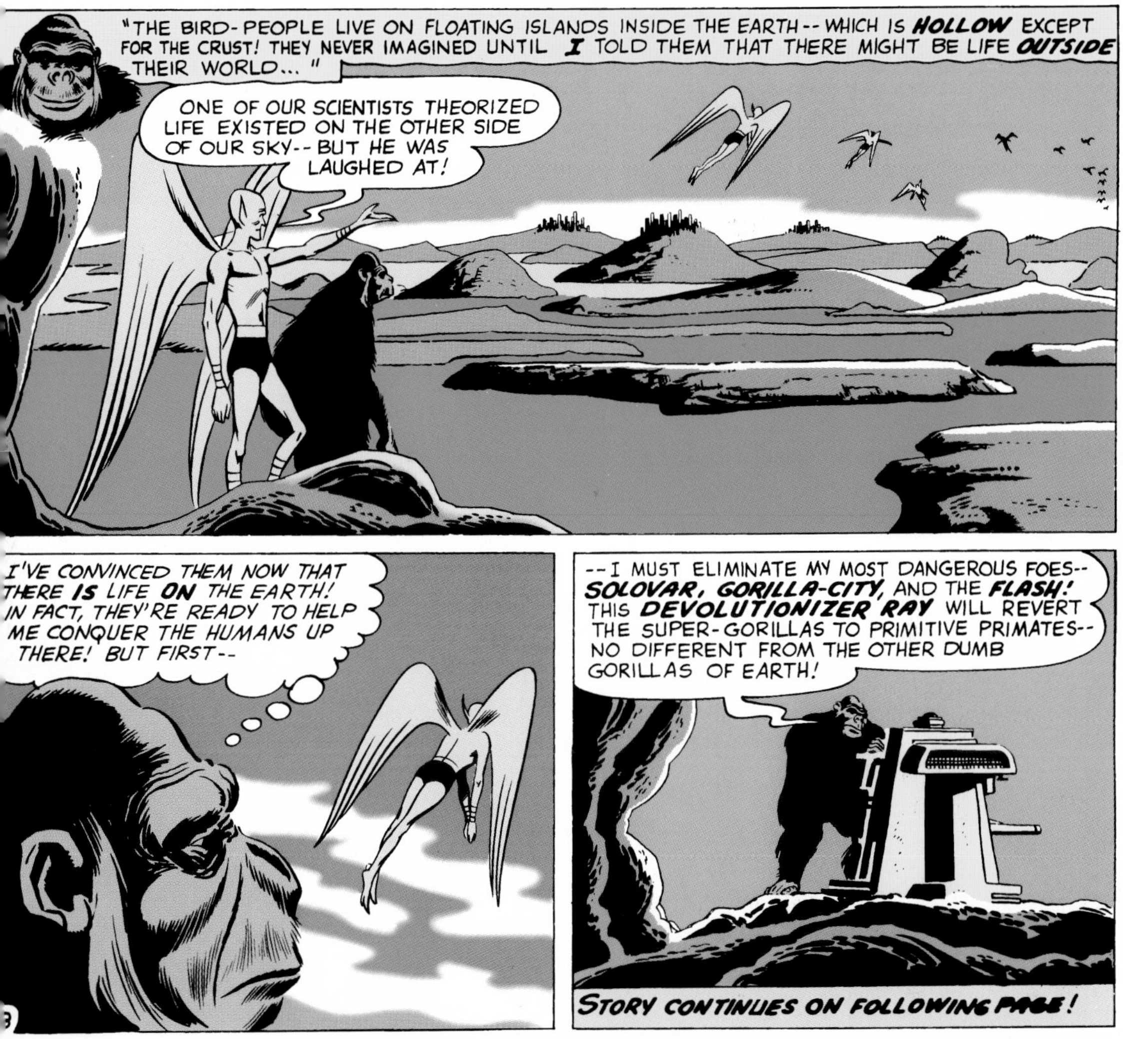
"THE BIRD-PEOPLE LIVE ON FLOATING ISLANDS INSIDE THE EARTH--WHICH IS HOLLOW EXCEPT FOR THE CRUST! THEY NEVER IMAGINED UNTIL I TOLD THEM THAT THERE MIGHT BE LIFE OUTSIDE THEIR WORLD..."
ONE OF OUR SCIENTISTS THEORIZED LIFE EXISTED ON THE OTHER SIDE OF OUR SKY--BUT HE WAS LAUGHED AT!
I'VE CONVINCED THEM NOW THAT THERE IS LIFE ON THE EARTH! IN FACT, THEY'RE READY TO HELP ME CONQUER THE HUMANS UP THERE! BUT FIRST--
--I MUST ELIMINATE MY MOST DANGEROUS FOES--SOLOVAR, GORILLA-CITY, AND THE FLASH! THIS DEVOLUTIONIZER RAY WILL REVERT THE SUPER-GORILLAS TO PRIMITIVE PRIMATES--NO DIFFERENT FROM THE OTHER DUMB GORILLAS OF EARTH!
STORY CONTINUES ON FOLLOWING PAGE!

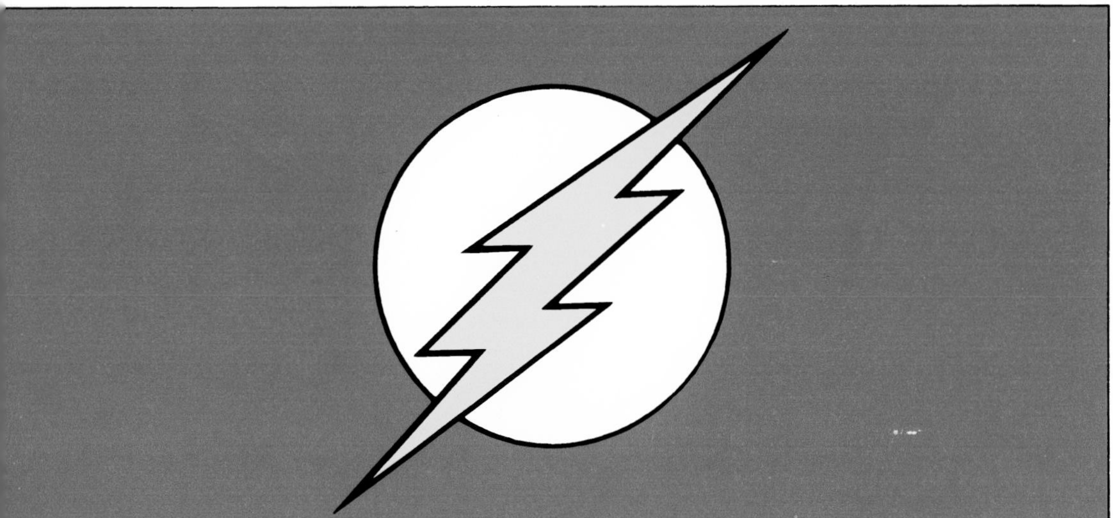

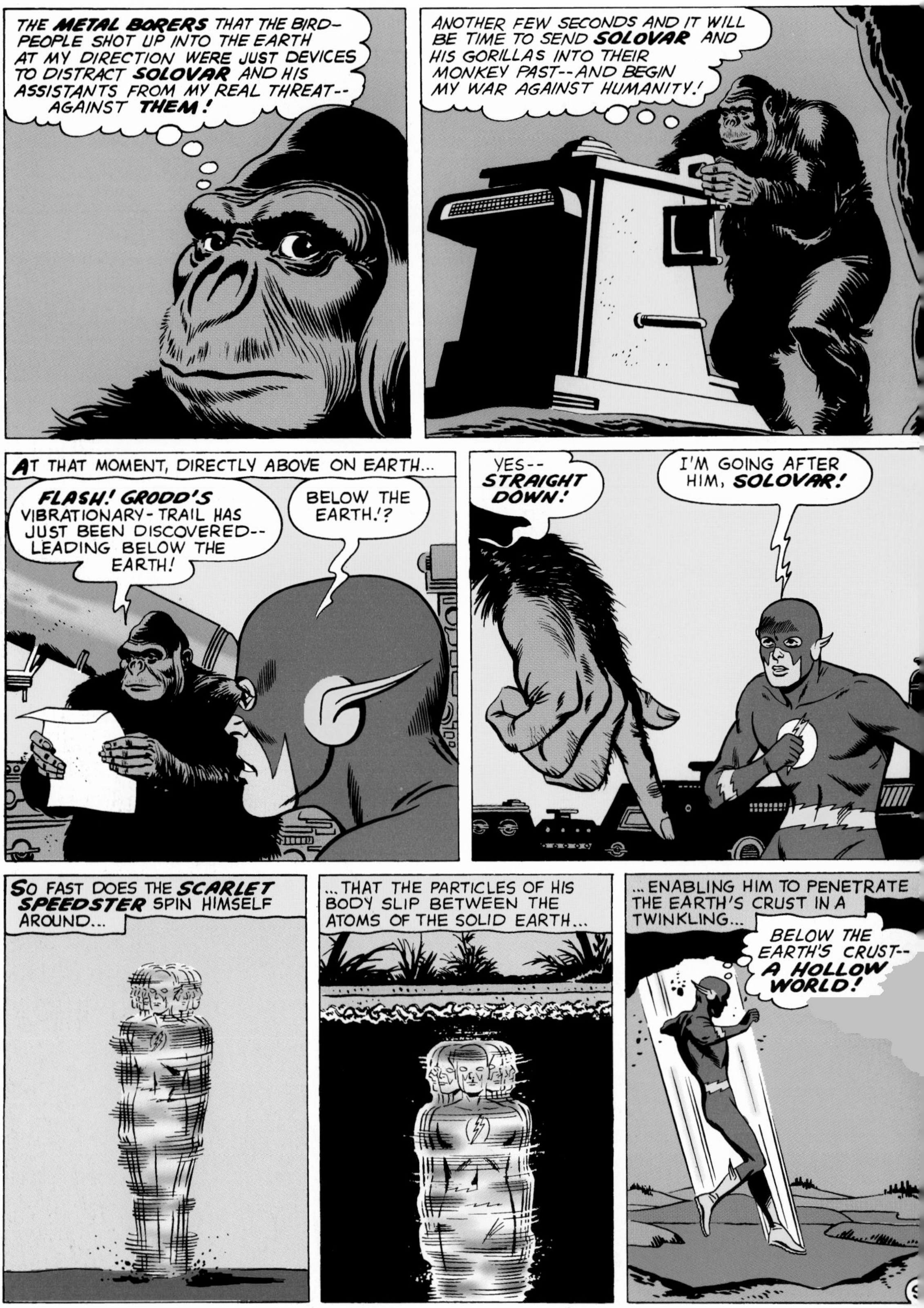
THE METAL BORERS THAT THE BIRD-PEOPLE SHOT UP INTO THE EARTH AT MY DIRECTION WERE JUST DEVICES TO DISTRACT SOLOVAR AND HIS ASSISTANTS FROM MY REAL THREAT--AGAINST THEM!
ANOTHER FEW SECONDS AND IT WILL BE TIME TO SEND SOLOVAR AND HIS GORILLAS INTO THEIR MONKEY PAST--AND BEGIN MY WAR AGAINST HUMANITY!
AT THAT MOMENT, DIRECTLY ABOVE ON EARTH...
FLASH! GRODD'S VIBRATIONARY-TRAIL HAS JUST BEEN DISCOVERED--LEADING BELOW THE EARTH!
BELOW THE EARTH!?
YES--STRAIGHT DOWN!
I'M GOING AFTER HIM, SOLOVAR!
SO FAST DOES THE SCARLET SPEEDSTER SPIN HIMSELF AROUND...
...THAT THE PARTICLES OF HIS BODY SLIP BETWEEN THE ATOMS OF THE SOLID EARTH...
...ENABLING HIM TO PENETRATE THE EARTH'S CRUST IN A TWINKLING...
BELOW THE EARTH'S CRUST--A HOLLOW WORLD!

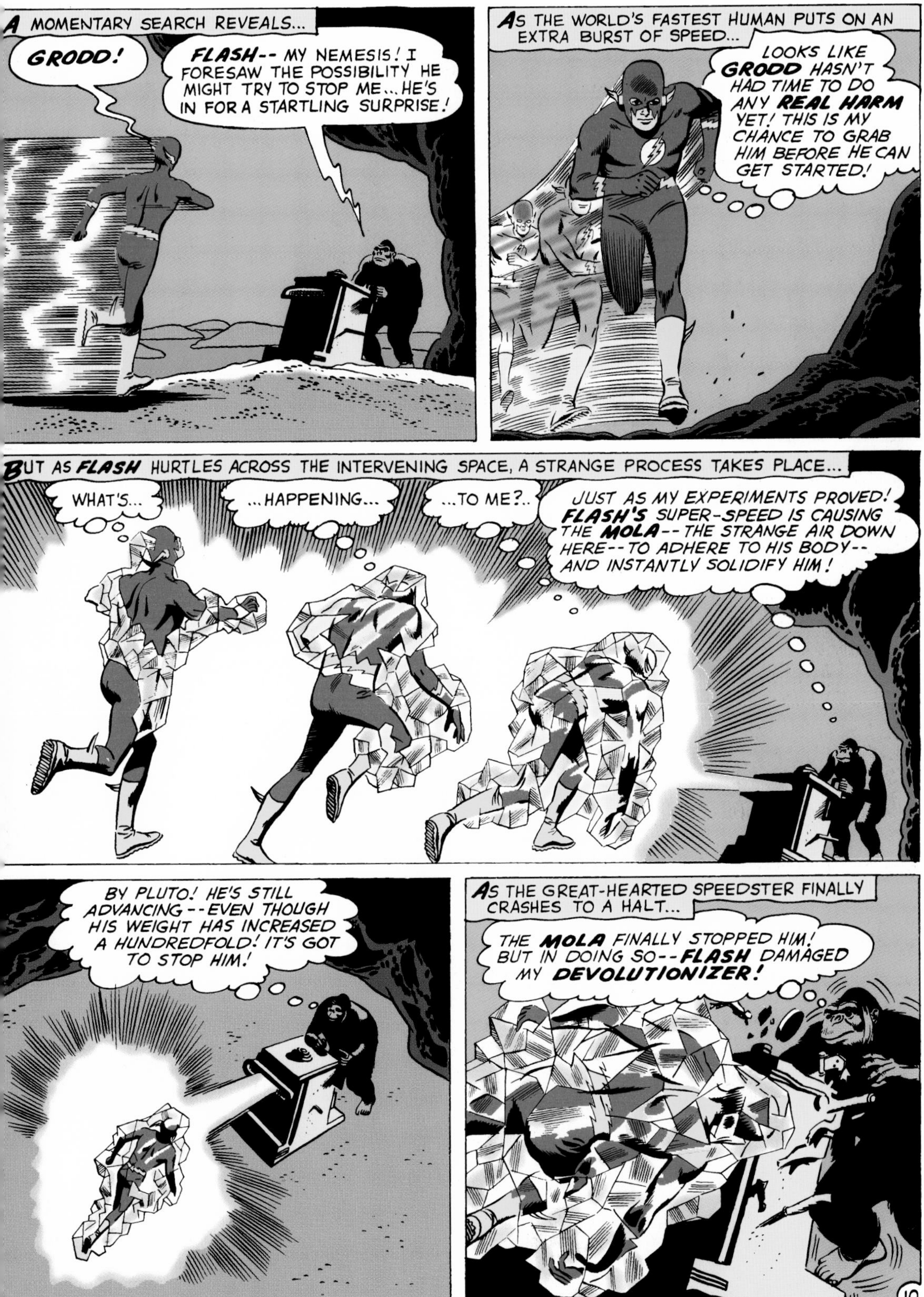
A MOMENTARY SEARCH REVEALS...
GRODD!
FLASH-- MY NEMESIS! I FORESAW THE POSSIBILITY HE MIGHT TRY TO STOP ME... HE'S IN FOR A STARTLING SURPRISE!
AS THE WORLD'S FASTEST HUMAN PUTS ON AN EXTRA BURST OF SPEED...
LOOKS LIKE GRODD HASN'T HAD TIME TO DO ANY REAL HARM YET! THIS IS MY CHANCE TO GRAB HIM BEFORE HE CAN GET STARTED!
BUT AS FLASH HURTLES ACROSS THE INTERVENING SPACE, A STRANGE PROCESS TAKES PLACE...
WHAT'S...
...HAPPENING...
...TO ME?..
JUST AS MY EXPERIMENTS PROVED! FLASH'S SUPER-SPEED IS CAUSING THE MOLA-- THE STRANGE AIR DOWN HERE-- TO ADHERE TO HIS BODY-- AND INSTANTLY SOLIDIFY HIM!
BY PLUTO! HE'S STILL ADVANCING-- EVEN THOUGH HIS WEIGHT HAS INCREASED A HUNDREDFOLD! IT'S GOT TO STOP HIM!
AS THE GREAT-HEARTED SPEEDSTER FINALLY CRASHES TO A HALT...
THE MOLA FINALLY STOPPED HIM! BUT IN DOING SO-- FLASH DAMAGED MY DEVOLUTIONIZER!
10

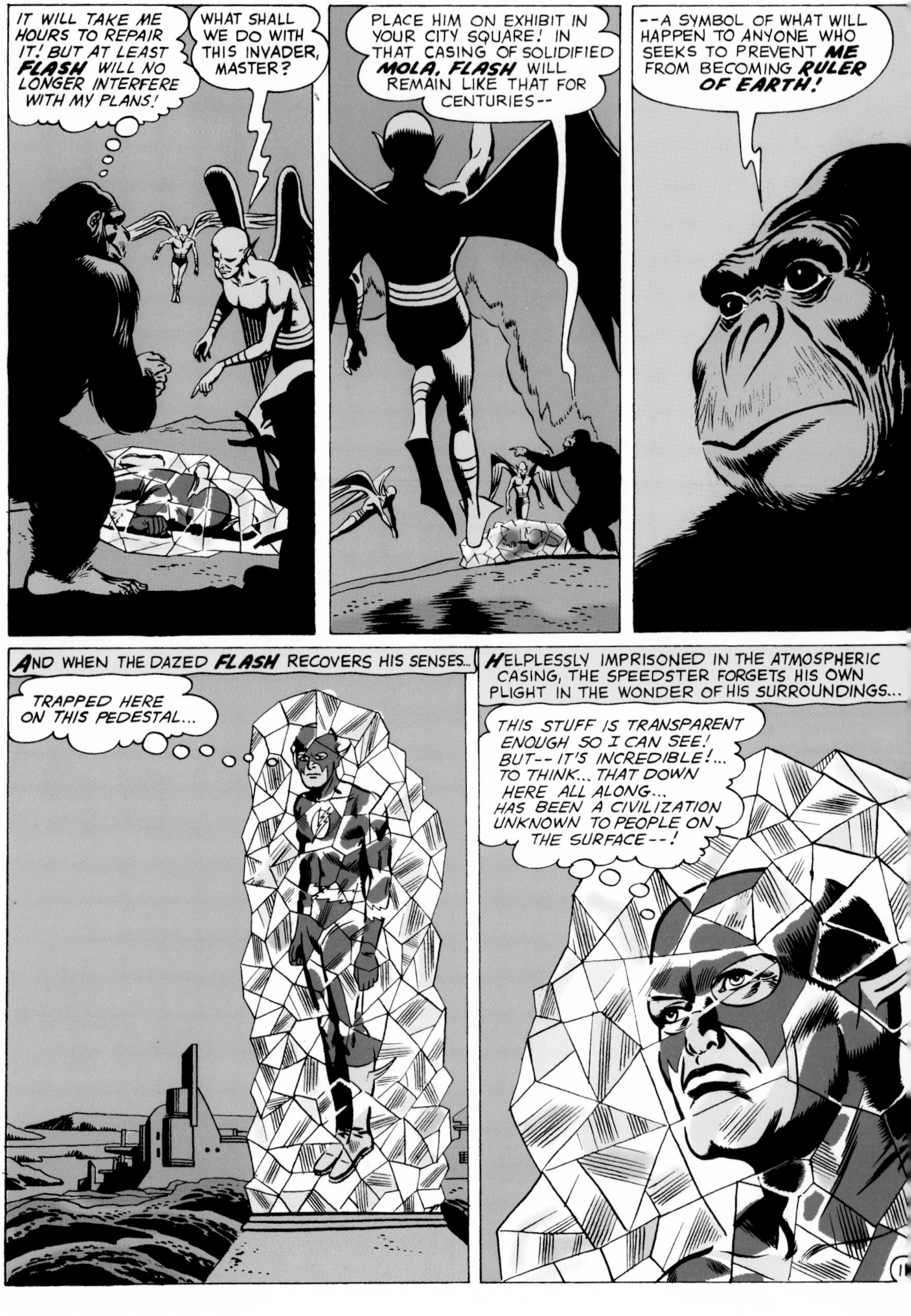
IT WILL TAKE ME HOURS TO REPAIR IT! BUT AT LEAST FLASH WILL NO LONGER INTERFERE WITH MY PLANS!
WHAT SHALL WE DO WITH THIS INVADER, MASTER?
PLACE HIM ON EXHIBIT IN YOUR CITY SQUARE! IN THAT CASING OF SOLIDIFIED MOLA, FLASH WILL REMAIN LIKE THAT FOR CENTURIES--
--A SYMBOL OF WHAT WILL HAPPEN TO ANYONE WHO SEEKS TO PREVENT ME FROM BECOMING RULER OF EARTH!
AND WHEN THE DAZED FLASH RECOVERS HIS SENSES...
TRAPPED HERE ON THIS PEDESTAL...
HELPLESSLY IMPRISONED IN THE ATMOSPHERIC CASING, THE SPEEDSTER FORGETS HIS OWN PLIGHT IN THE WONDER OF HIS SURROUNDINGS...
THIS STUFF IS TRANSPARENT ENOUGH SO I CAN SEE! BUT-- IT'S INCREDIBLE!... TO THINK... THAT DOWN HERE ALL ALONG... HAS BEEN A CIVILIZATION UNKNOWN TO PEOPLE ON THE SURFACE--!

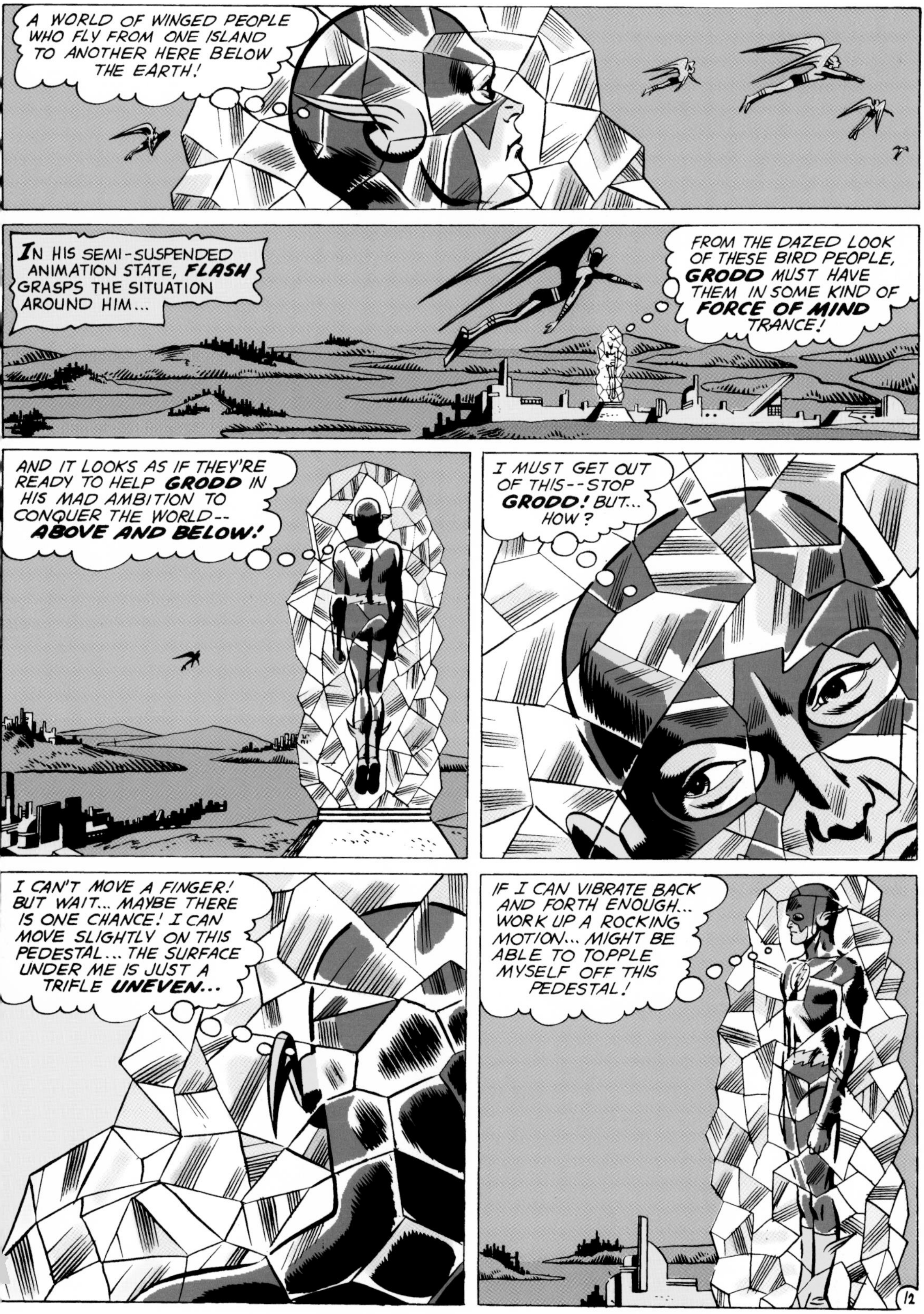
A WORLD OF WINGED PEOPLE WHO FLY FROM ONE ISLAND TO ANOTHER HERE BELOW THE EARTH!
IN HIS SEMI-SUSPENDED ANIMATION STATE, FLASH GRASPS THE SITUATION AROUND HIM...
FROM THE DAZED LOOK OF THESE BIRD PEOPLE, GRODD MUST HAVE THEM IN SOME KIND OF FORCE OF MIND TRANCE!
AND IT LOOKS AS IF THEY'RE READY TO HELP GRODD IN HIS MAD AMBITION TO CONQUER THE WORLD-- ABOVE AND BELOW!
I MUST GET OUT OF THIS--STOP GRODD! BUT... HOW?
I CAN'T MOVE A FINGER! BUT WAIT... MAYBE THERE IS ONE CHANCE! I CAN MOVE SLIGHTLY ON THIS PEDESTAL... THE SURFACE UNDER ME IS JUST A TRIFLE UNEVEN...
IF I CAN VIBRATE BACK AND FORTH ENOUGH... WORK UP A ROCKING MOTION... MIGHT BE ABLE TO TOPPLE MYSELF OFF THIS PEDESTAL!
12

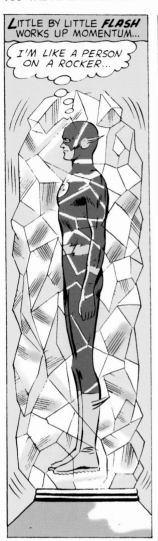

LITTLE BY LITTLE *FLASH* WORKS UP MOMENTUM...

I'M LIKE A PERSON ON A ROCKER...

...TRYING TO MAKE THE ROCKER *TOPPLE OVER*...

BY ROCKING *HARD ENOUGH!* ONCE MORE--!

*T*HEN... I'M ON THE EDGE... *I'M GOING OVER!*

*A*S THE "HUMAN STATUE" HITS THE GROUND...

JUST AS I HOPED, THE CRYSTAL-LIKE MASS AROUND ME IS SHATTERING ON THE GROUND--

--BUT IT'S LEFT ME UNHURT! NOW TO GET AFTER *GRODD* AGAIN--

AT THAT MOMENT... AT LAST-- I'VE GOT MY *DEVOLUTIONIZER* IN WORKING ORDER AGAIN! TOO BAD I CAN'T BE UP THERE TO WATCH *SOLOVAR* TURN INTO A BABBLING GORILLA *AS I PRESS THIS LEVER--*

BEFORE THE *SUPER-GORILLA* CAN MAKE A MOVE...

FLASH-- AGAIN?

GOT TO CONTROL MY SPEED--KEEP IT JUST *UNDER* THE CRITICAL POINT WHERE IT WILL SOLIDIFY THIS ATMOSPHERE AROUND ME!

AS THE HUMAN COMET THROWS A WHORL OF AIR MOVING AT TORNADO SPEED AROUND HIS FOE...

AHH!

THAT SHOULD HOLD HIM!

BUT THE NEXT MOMENT, AMAZINGLY...

HIS STRENGTH IS...FANTASTIC! HE BURST OUT OF THE WHIRLWIND I CAUSED AROUND HIM! NO ONE'S EVER DONE THAT BEFORE!

YOU WON'T STOP *ME*, FLASH!

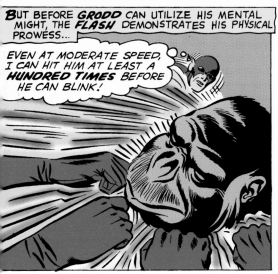

BUT BEFORE *GRODD* CAN UTILIZE HIS MENTAL MIGHT, THE *FLASH* DEMONSTRATES HIS PHYSICAL PROWESS...

EVEN AT MODERATE SPEED, I CAN HIT HIM AT LEAST A *HUNDRED TIMES* BEFORE HE CAN BLINK!

AND WHEN THE FLURRY OF ACTION IS OVER...

MAYBE *THAT* KNOCKED THE *FORCE OF MIND* POWER FROM HIM! I HOPE IT DID! AT LEAST... HE HAD NO CHANCE TO USE IT AGAINST ME--!

14

LATER...

YES...**GRODD** HAD US IN SOME KIND OF **SPELL!** BUT WHEN YOU KNOCKED HIM OUT, HIS HOLD ON US WAS BROKEN! WE'RE FREE NOW!

AS THE **FASTEST HUMAN** AND HIS CAPTIVE ZOOM BACK TOWARD THE SURFACE...

THE BIRD-PEOPLE ARE PEACEFUL! SOMEDAY WHEN THEY ARE READY THEY WILL PAY A VISIT TO THE SURFACE! UNTIL THEN, PERHAPS IT WOULD BE BEST FOR ME NOT TO SAY ANYTHING ABOUT THEIR SUBTERRANEAN EXISTENCE!

IN **GORILLA-CITY** SOON AFTER...

WE'LL BE MORE CAREFUL ABOUT WATCHING **GRODD** THIS TIME, **FLASH!** THANKS FOR CAPTURING HIM AGAIN!

GOODBYE, **SOLOVAR!** TIME FOR ME TO RETURN HOME...

15

AS BARRY "**FLASH**" ALLEN READS THE PAPERS LATER...

I SEE THAT THE "STRANGE METAL OBJECTS" VANISHED AS MYSTERIOUSLY AS THEY APPEARED! I HOPE THAT'S THE LAST I EVER HEAR OF THE EVIL-MINDED **GRODD!**

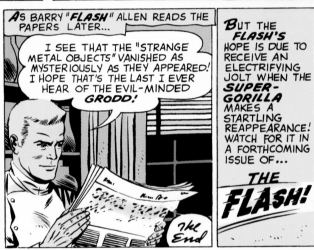

THE End

BUT THE **FLASH'S** HOPE IS DUE TO RECEIVE AN ELECTRIFYING JOLT WHEN THE **SUPER-GORILLA** MAKES A STARTLING REAPPEARANCE! WATCH FOR IT IN A FORTHCOMING ISSUE OF...

THE FLASH!

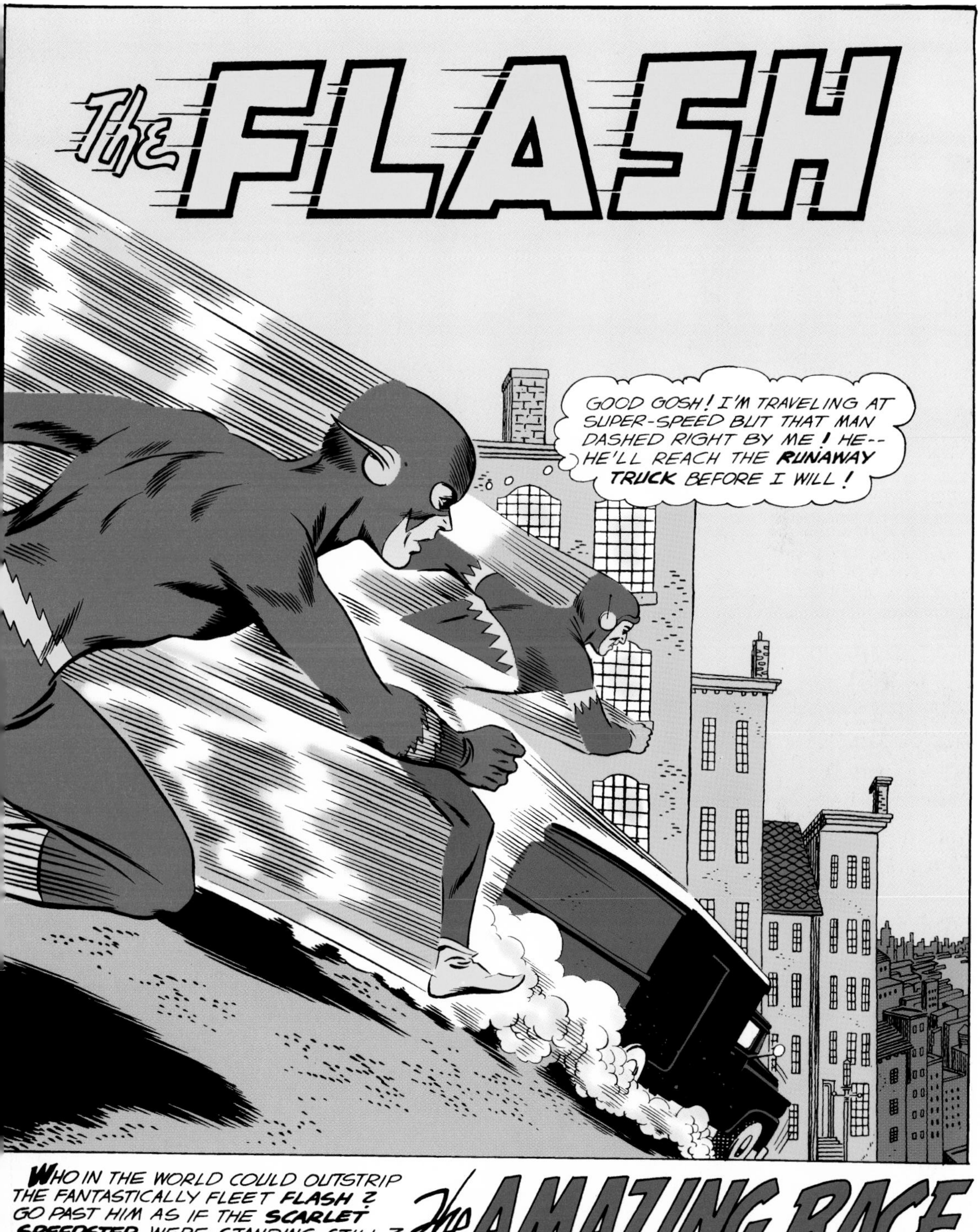
The FLASH
GOOD GOSH! I'M TRAVELING AT SUPER-SPEED BUT THAT MAN DASHED RIGHT BY ME! HE--HE'LL REACH THE RUNAWAY TRUCK BEFORE I WILL!
WHO IN THE WORLD COULD OUTSTRIP THE FANTASTICALLY FLEET FLASH? GO PAST HIM AS IF THE SCARLET SPEEDSTER WERE STANDING STILL? FOR THE STARTLING AND ELECTRIFYING TRUTH BEHIND THIS ASTONISHING EVENT--READ...
The AMAZING RACE AGAINST TIME!

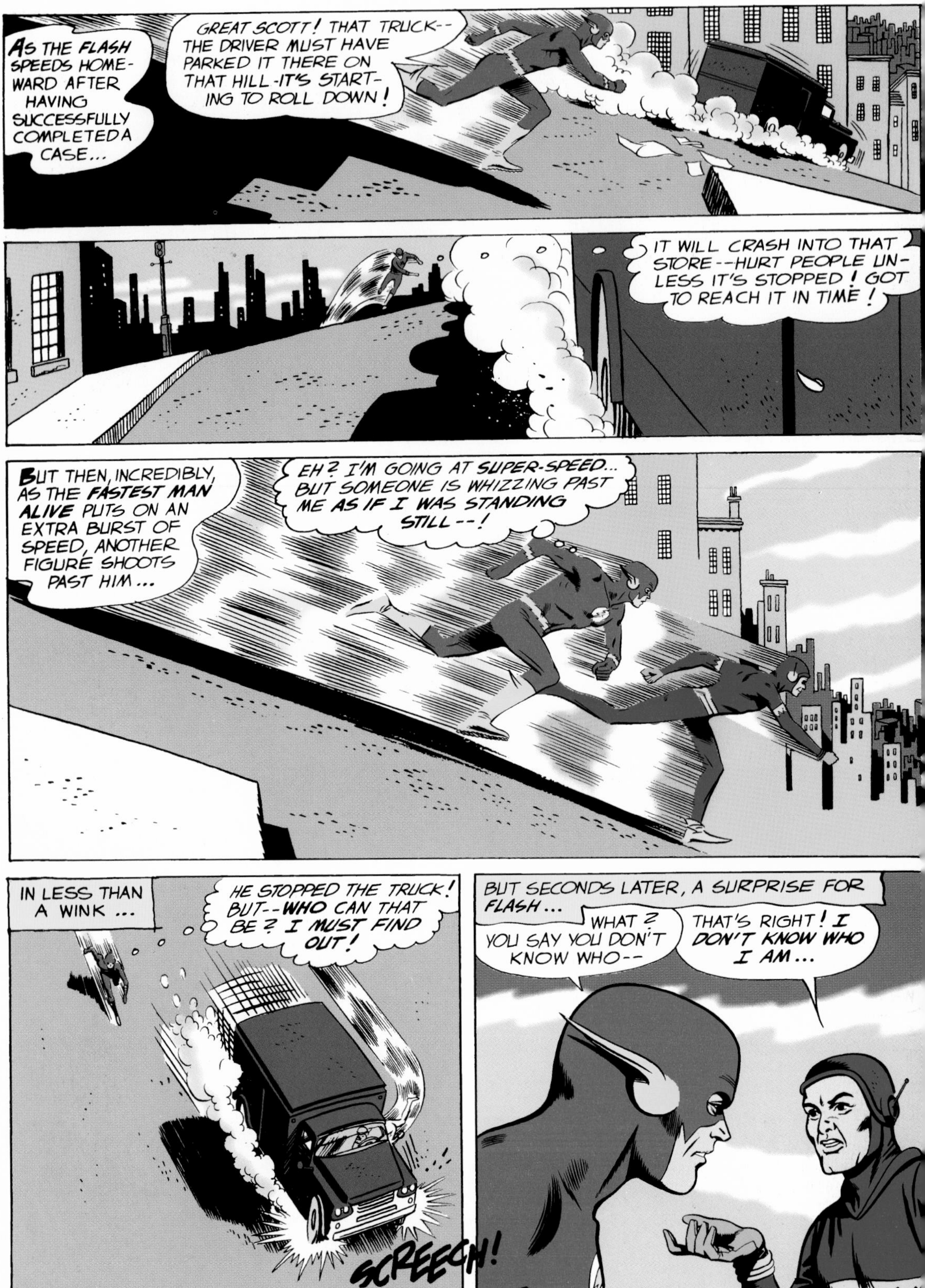
AS THE FLASH SPEEDS HOMEWARD AFTER HAVING SUCCESSFULLY COMPLETED A CASE...
GREAT SCOTT! THAT TRUCK-- THE DRIVER MUST HAVE PARKED IT THERE ON THAT HILL-IT'S STARTING TO ROLL DOWN!
IT WILL CRASH INTO THAT STORE--HURT PEOPLE UNLESS IT'S STOPPED! GOT TO REACH IT IN TIME!
BUT THEN, INCREDIBLY, AS THE FASTEST MAN ALIVE PUTS ON AN EXTRA BURST OF SPEED, ANOTHER FIGURE SHOOTS PAST HIM...
EH? I'M GOING AT SUPER-SPEED... BUT SOMEONE IS WHIZZING PAST ME AS IF I WAS STANDING STILL--!
IN LESS THAN A WINK...
HE STOPPED THE TRUCK! BUT--WHO CAN THAT BE? I MUST FIND OUT!
SCREECH!
BUT SECONDS LATER, A SURPRISE FOR FLASH...
WHAT? YOU SAY YOU DON'T KNOW WHO--
THAT'S RIGHT! I DON'T KNOW WHO I AM...

*LATER, IN AN APARTMENT THAT **FLASH** KEEPS TO PROTECT HIS DUAL IDENTITY OF BARRY ALLEN, POLICE SCIENTIST...*

I HAD TO BRING HIM HERE! I HAD TO FIND OUT ALL I COULD ABOUT A MAN WHO COULD **OUTSTRIP ME** IN SPEED!

AND YOU SAY THAT ALL YOU REMEMBER IS THAT EARLY THIS AFTERNOON YOU FOUND YOURSELF WANDERING ON THE OUTSKIRTS OF THE CITY?

THAT'S RIGHT, **FLASH**...

WHY, I DIDN'T EVEN KNOW **YOUR** NAME--UNTIL YOU TOLD IT TO ME A FEW MINUTES AGO!

IT'S A CLEAR CASE OF AMNESIA...

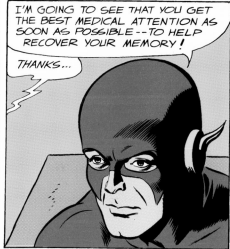

I'M GOING TO SEE THAT YOU GET THE BEST MEDICAL ATTENTION AS SOON AS POSSIBLE--TO HELP RECOVER YOUR MEMORY!

THANKS...

*BUT UNKNOWN TO THE **SCARLET SPEEDSTER** AT THIS MOMENT...*

...AND EYE-WITNESSES SAY THE **STRANGER** SPRINTED RIGHT PAST THE **FLASH**! DO YOU REALIZE WHAT THAT MEANS, CHIEF?

ER--NOT QUITE, IRIS!

*AS IRIS WEST, OF **PICTURE NEWS**, DETAILS AN ANGLE TO HER EDITOR...*

THIS THING COULD BE BUILT UP AS A **TERRIFIC PUBLICITY STUNT**! EVERYONE BELIEVES **FLASH** IS THE **WORLD'S FASTEST HUMAN**--!

3

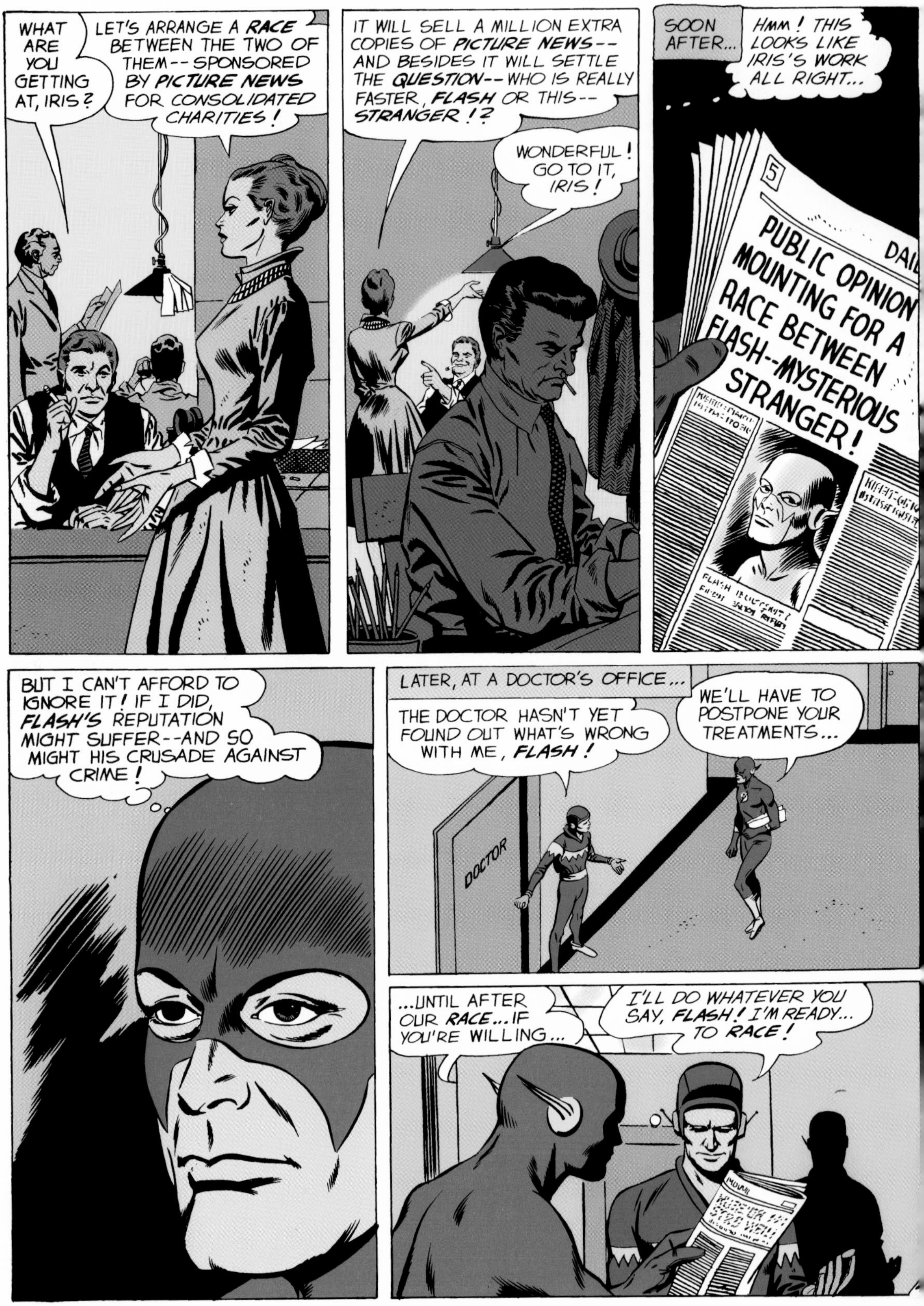
WHAT ARE YOU GETTING AT, IRIS?
LET'S ARRANGE A RACE BETWEEN THE TWO OF THEM--SPONSORED BY PICTURE NEWS FOR CONSOLIDATED CHARITIES!
IT WILL SELL A MILLION EXTRA COPIES OF PICTURE NEWS--AND BESIDES IT WILL SETTLE THE QUESTION--WHO IS REALLY FASTER, FLASH OR THIS--STRANGER!?
WONDERFUL! GO TO IT, IRIS!
SOON AFTER...
HMM! THIS LOOKS LIKE IRIS'S WORK ALL RIGHT...
5
DAI
PUBLIC OPINION MOUNTING FOR A RACE BETWEEN FLASH--MYSTERIOUS STRANGER!
BUT I CAN'T AFFORD TO IGNORE IT! IF I DID, FLASH'S REPUTATION MIGHT SUFFER--AND SO MIGHT HIS CRUSADE AGAINST CRIME!
LATER, AT A DOCTOR'S OFFICE...
THE DOCTOR HASN'T YET FOUND OUT WHAT'S WRONG WITH ME, FLASH!
WE'LL HAVE TO POSTPONE YOUR TREATMENTS...
DOCTOR
...UNTIL AFTER OUR RACE... IF YOU'RE WILLING...
I'LL DO WHATEVER YOU SAY, FLASH! I'M READY... TO RACE!

AS THE DAY OF THE GREAT EVENT DAWNS...

I DON'T GET IT, IRIS-- WHY IS THE **STRANGER** FACING THE STARTING LINE **BACKWARDS**?

I CAN EXPLAIN THAT, CHIEF--

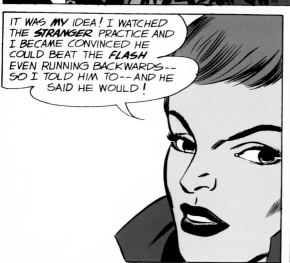

IT WAS **MY** IDEA! I WATCHED THE **STRANGER** PRACTICE AND I BECAME CONVINCED HE COULD BEAT THE **FLASH** EVEN RUNNING BACKWARDS-- SO I TOLD HIM TO-- AND HE SAID HE WOULD!

IT'LL MAKE AN EVEN **BETTER** STORY THIS WAY-- IF FLASH GETS BEATEN!

BANG!

THE STARTING GUN--THEY'RE OFF!

IN LESS TIME THAN IT TAKES TO DRAW A COUPLE OF BREATHS, THE TWO SPEEDSTERS HAVE ROUNDED THE FIELD AN INCREDIBLE **999** TIMES IN THE **1,000**-LAP RACE...

TOOK ME A SPLIT-SECOND TO BUILD UP SPEED--BUT HE **INSTANTLY** STARTED OFF AT HIGH SPEED-- AND IS MAINTAINING HIS SLIGHT LEAD!

GASP! HARD TO SEE... THEY MOVE SO FAST!

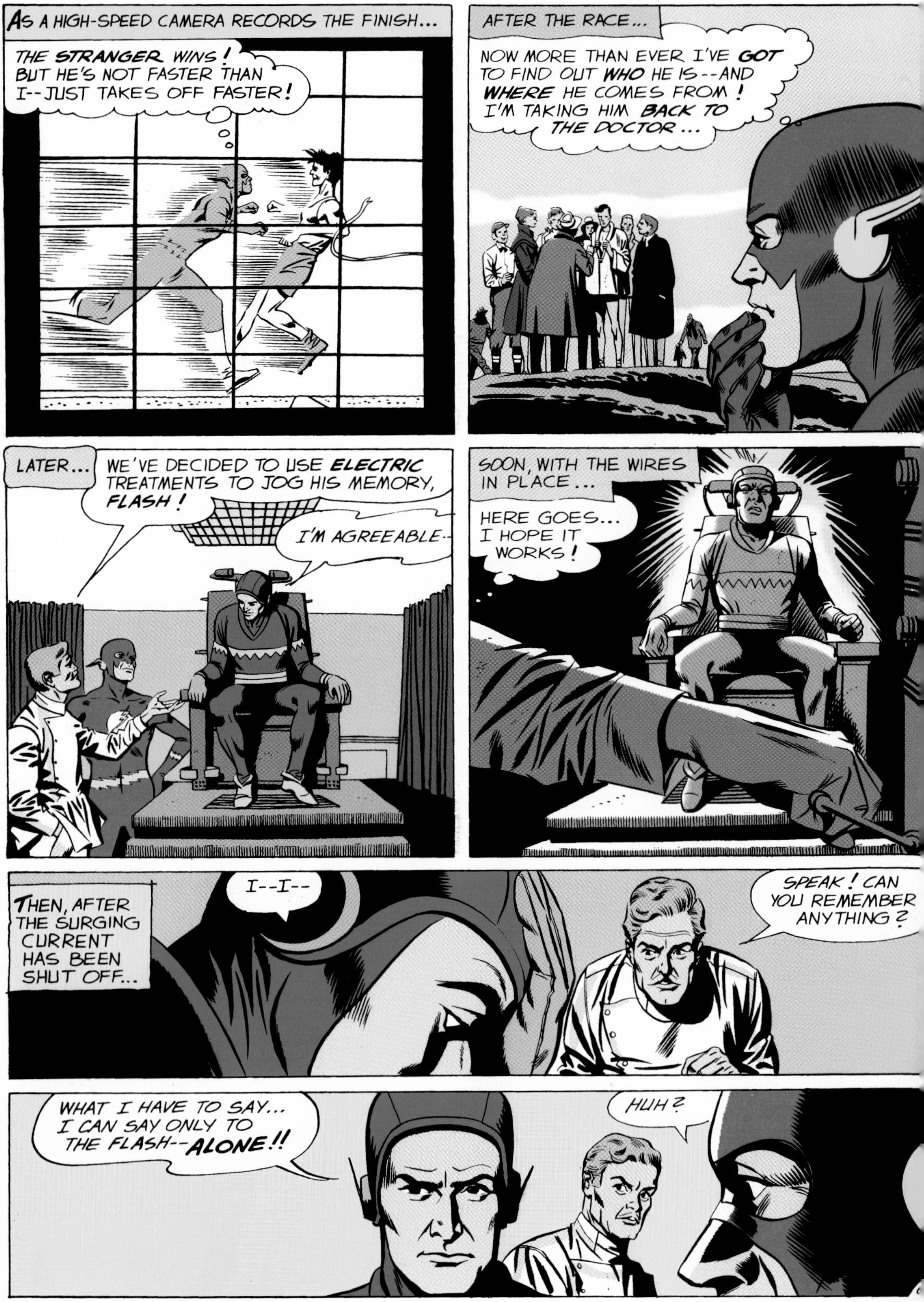
AS A HIGH-SPEED CAMERA RECORDS THE FINISH...
THE STRANGER WINS! BUT HE'S NOT FASTER THAN I--JUST TAKES OFF FASTER!
AFTER THE RACE...
NOW MORE THAN EVER I'VE GOT TO FIND OUT WHO HE IS--AND WHERE HE COMES FROM! I'M TAKING HIM BACK TO THE DOCTOR...
LATER...
WE'VE DECIDED TO USE ELECTRIC TREATMENTS TO JOG HIS MEMORY, FLASH!
I'M AGREEABLE--
SOON, WITH THE WIRES IN PLACE...
HERE GOES... I HOPE IT WORKS!
THEN, AFTER THE SURGING CURRENT HAS BEEN SHUT OFF...
I--I--
SPEAK! CAN YOU REMEMBER ANYTHING?
WHAT I HAVE TO SAY... I CAN SAY ONLY TO THE FLASH--ALONE!!
HUH?

OUTSIDE THE DOCTOR'S OFFICE, MOMENTS LATER...

FLASH, LISTEN-- I KNOW WHO I AM NOW! BUT I ALSO KNOW THAT **SOME-THING** HAS HAPPENED TO ME!

WHAT DO YOU MEAN?

WHEN THAT ELECTRICITY SURGED THROUGH ME IT NOT ONLY **BROUGHT BACK MY MEMORY**-- IT ALSO DESTROYED MY SPEED! I SENSED IT THE MOMENT IT HAPPENED--! TO PROVE IT--

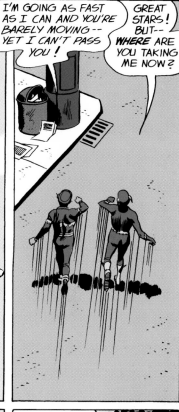

I'M GOING AS FAST AS I CAN AND YOU'RE BARELY MOVING-- YET I CAN'T PASS YOU!

GREAT STARS! BUT-- **WHERE** ARE YOU TAKING ME NOW?

I'LL SHOW YOU... ONE OF THE THINGS I REMEMBERED WAS **HOW** I CAME HERE TO YOUR PLANET! YOU SEE-- I'M NOT OF YOUR WORLD, FLASH!

I CAME HERE BY SPACESHIP-- BUT MY SHIP CRASHED! THE CRASH ROBBED ME OF MY MEMORY...

BUT NOW I KNOW THAT YOU MUST HELP ME... BY PERFORMING A TASK OF THE **UTMOST** URGENCY--!

WHAT TASK--?

7

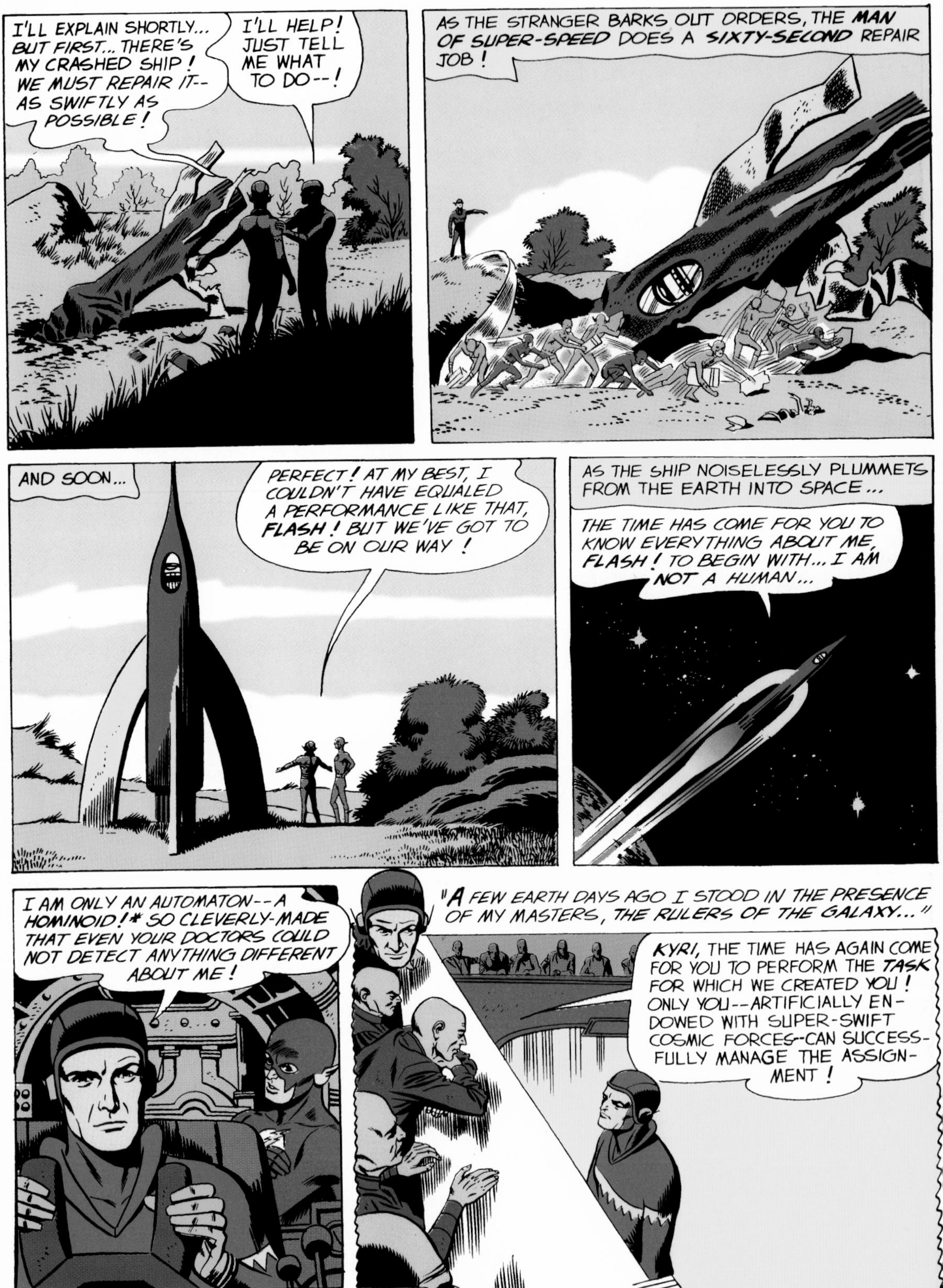
I'LL EXPLAIN SHORTLY... BUT FIRST... THERE'S MY CRASHED SHIP! WE MUST REPAIR IT-- AS SWIFTLY AS POSSIBLE!
I'LL HELP! JUST TELL ME WHAT TO DO--!
AS THE STRANGER BARKS OUT ORDERS, THE MAN OF SUPER-SPEED DOES A SIXTY-SECOND REPAIR JOB!
AND SOON...
PERFECT! AT MY BEST, I COULDN'T HAVE EQUALED A PERFORMANCE LIKE THAT, FLASH! BUT WE'VE GOT TO BE ON OUR WAY!
AS THE SHIP NOISELESSLY PLUMMETS FROM THE EARTH INTO SPACE...
THE TIME HAS COME FOR YOU TO KNOW EVERYTHING ABOUT ME, FLASH! TO BEGIN WITH... I AM NOT A HUMAN...
I AM ONLY AN AUTOMATON--A HOMINOID!* SO CLEVERLY-MADE THAT EVEN YOUR DOCTORS COULD NOT DETECT ANYTHING DIFFERENT ABOUT ME!
"A FEW EARTH DAYS AGO I STOOD IN THE PRESENCE OF MY MASTERS, THE RULERS OF THE GALAXY..."
KYRI, THE TIME HAS AGAIN COME FOR YOU TO PERFORM THE TASK FOR WHICH WE CREATED YOU! ONLY YOU--ARTIFICIALLY ENDOWED WITH SUPER-SWIFT COSMIC FORCES--CAN SUCCESSFULLY MANAGE THE ASSIGNMENT!
8

Editor's Note: A HOMINOID IS A HUMAN-LIKE ROBOT!

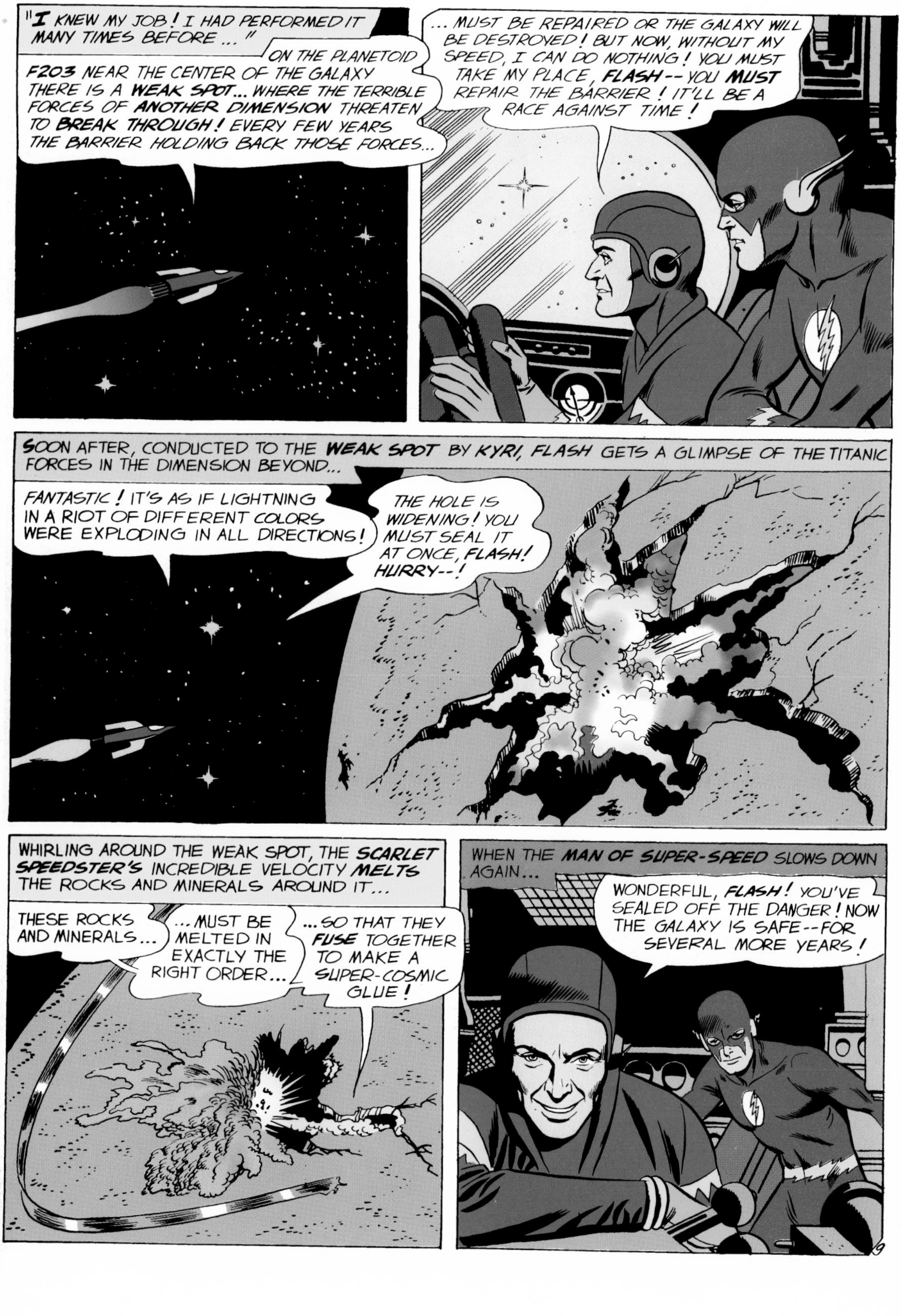
"I KNEW MY JOB! I HAD PERFORMED IT MANY TIMES BEFORE ..."
ON THE PLANETOID F203 NEAR THE CENTER OF THE GALAXY THERE IS A WEAK SPOT... WHERE THE TERRIBLE FORCES OF ANOTHER DIMENSION THREATEN TO BREAK THROUGH! EVERY FEW YEARS THE BARRIER HOLDING BACK THOSE FORCES...
... MUST BE REPAIRED OR THE GALAXY WILL BE DESTROYED! BUT NOW, WITHOUT MY SPEED, I CAN DO NOTHING! YOU MUST TAKE MY PLACE, FLASH -- YOU MUST REPAIR THE BARRIER! IT'LL BE A RACE AGAINST TIME!
SOON AFTER, CONDUCTED TO THE WEAK SPOT BY KYRI, FLASH GETS A GLIMPSE OF THE TITANIC FORCES IN THE DIMENSION BEYOND...
FANTASTIC! IT'S AS IF LIGHTNING IN A RIOT OF DIFFERENT COLORS WERE EXPLODING IN ALL DIRECTIONS!
THE HOLE IS WIDENING! YOU MUST SEAL IT AT ONCE, FLASH! HURRY--!
WHIRLING AROUND THE WEAK SPOT, THE SCARLET SPEEDSTER'S INCREDIBLE VELOCITY MELTS THE ROCKS AND MINERALS AROUND IT...
THESE ROCKS AND MINERALS...
...MUST BE MELTED IN EXACTLY THE RIGHT ORDER...
...SO THAT THEY FUSE TOGETHER TO MAKE A SUPER-COSMIC GLUE!
WHEN THE MAN OF SUPER-SPEED SLOWS DOWN AGAIN...
WONDERFUL, FLASH! YOU'VE SEALED OFF THE DANGER! NOW THE GALAXY IS SAFE--FOR SEVERAL MORE YEARS!
9

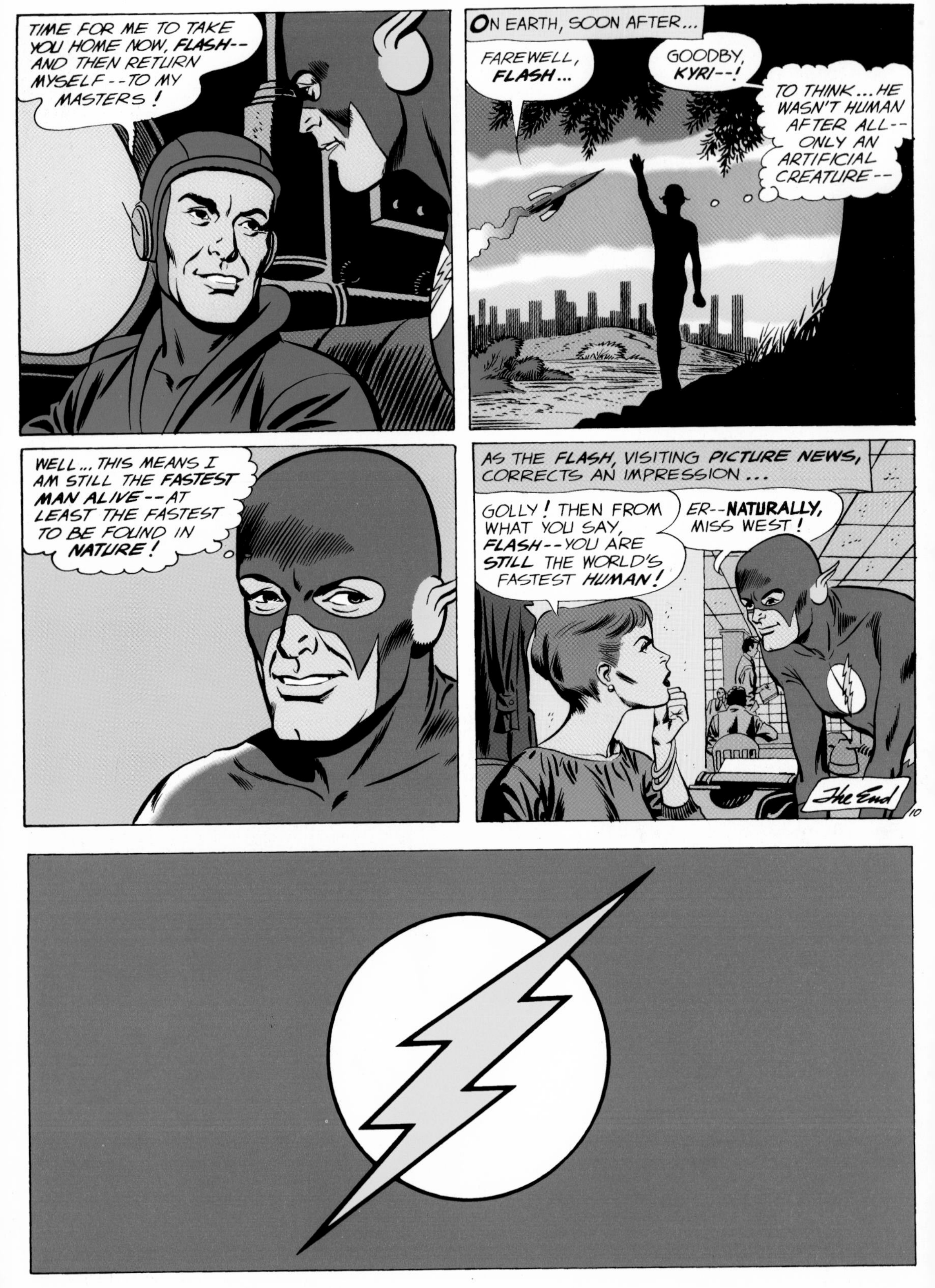
TIME FOR ME TO TAKE YOU HOME NOW, FLASH-- AND THEN RETURN MYSELF--TO MY MASTERS!
ON EARTH, SOON AFTER...
FAREWELL, FLASH...
GOODBY, KYRI--!
TO THINK...HE WASN'T HUMAN AFTER ALL-- ONLY AN ARTIFICIAL CREATURE--
WELL... THIS MEANS I AM STILL THE FASTEST MAN ALIVE--AT LEAST THE FASTEST TO BE FOUND IN NATURE!
AS THE FLASH, VISITING PICTURE NEWS, CORRECTS AN IMPRESSION...
GOLLY! THEN FROM WHAT YOU SAY, FLASH--YOU ARE STILL THE WORLD'S FASTEST HUMAN!
ER--NATURALLY, MISS WEST!
The End
10

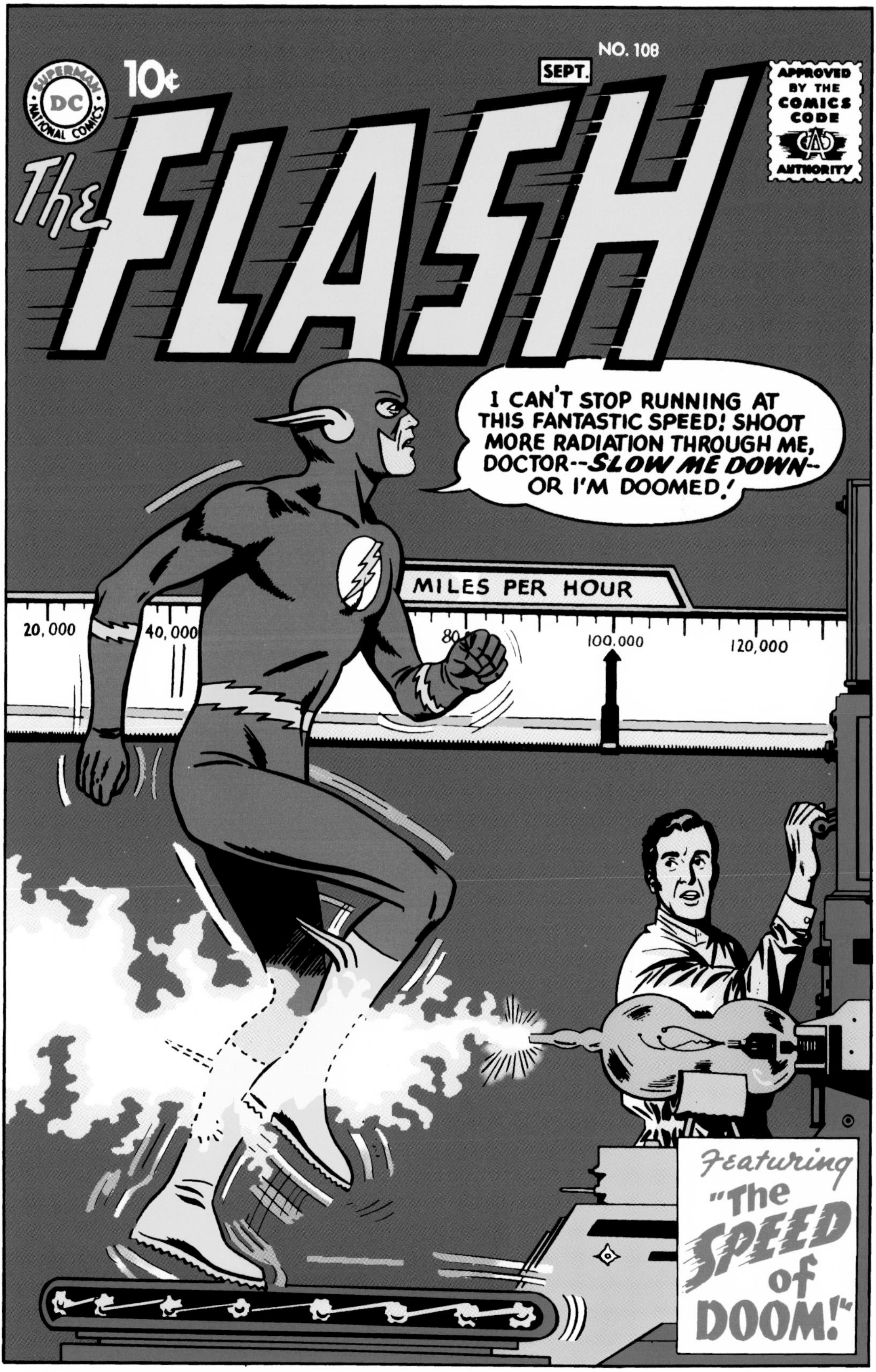

NO. 108
SEPT.
10¢
SUPERMAN DC NATIONAL COMICS
APPROVED BY THE COMICS CODE AUTHORITY
The FLASH
I CAN'T STOP RUNNING AT THIS FANTASTIC SPEED! SHOOT MORE RADIATION THROUGH ME, DOCTOR--SLOW ME DOWN--OR I'M DOOMED!
MILES PER HOUR
20,000
40,000
100,000
120,000
Featuring "The SPEED of DOOM!"

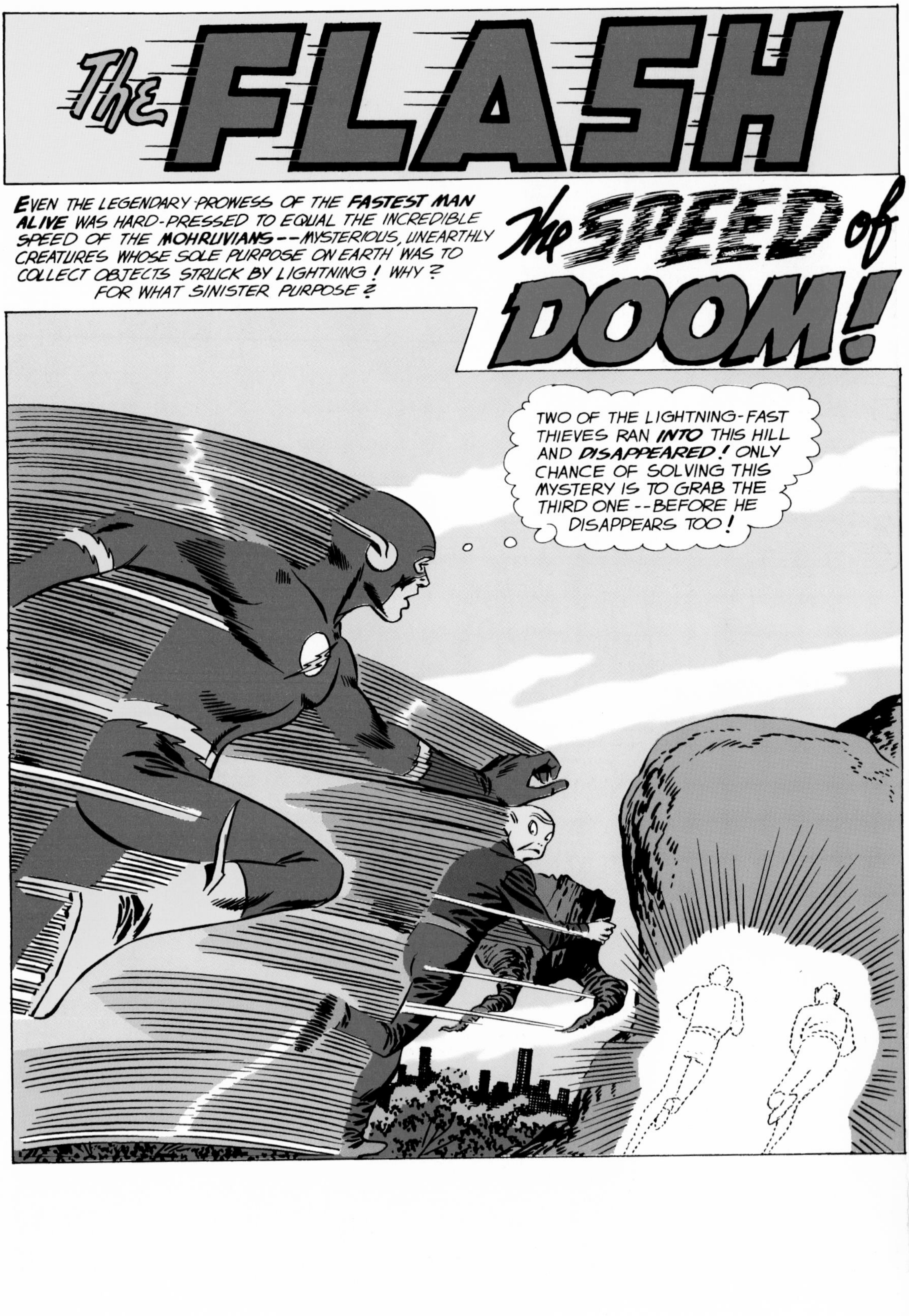
The FLASH
EVEN THE LEGENDARY PROWESS OF THE FASTEST MAN ALIVE WAS HARD-PRESSED TO EQUAL THE INCREDIBLE SPEED OF THE MOHRUVIANS--MYSTERIOUS, UNEARTHLY CREATURES WHOSE SOLE PURPOSE ON EARTH WAS TO COLLECT OBJECTS STRUCK BY LIGHTNING! WHY? FOR WHAT SINISTER PURPOSE?
The SPEED of DOOM!
TWO OF THE LIGHTNING-FAST THIEVES RAN INTO THIS HILL AND DISAPPEARED! ONLY CHANCE OF SOLVING THIS MYSTERY IS TO GRAB THE THIRD ONE--BEFORE HE DISAPPEARS TOO!

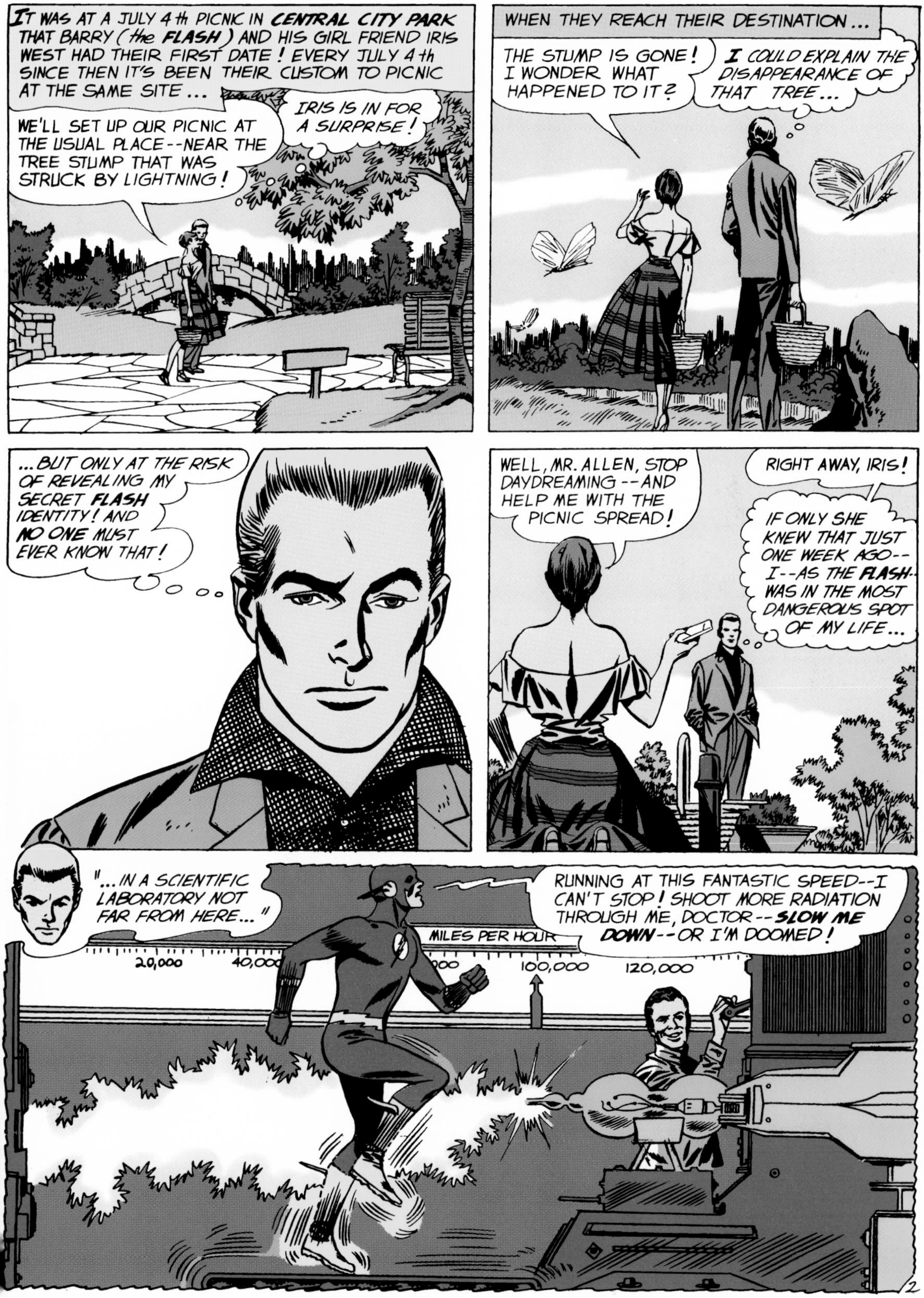
IT WAS AT A JULY 4th PICNIC IN CENTRAL CITY PARK THAT BARRY (the FLASH) AND HIS GIRL FRIEND IRIS WEST HAD THEIR FIRST DATE! EVERY JULY 4th SINCE THEN IT'S BEEN THEIR CUSTOM TO PICNIC AT THE SAME SITE...
WE'LL SET UP OUR PICNIC AT THE USUAL PLACE--NEAR THE TREE STUMP THAT WAS STRUCK BY LIGHTNING!
IRIS IS IN FOR A SURPRISE!
WHEN THEY REACH THEIR DESTINATION...
THE STUMP IS GONE! I WONDER WHAT HAPPENED TO IT?
I COULD EXPLAIN THE DISAPPEARANCE OF THAT TREE...
...BUT ONLY AT THE RISK OF REVEALING MY SECRET FLASH IDENTITY! AND NO ONE MUST EVER KNOW THAT!
WELL, MR. ALLEN, STOP DAYDREAMING--AND HELP ME WITH THE PICNIC SPREAD!
RIGHT AWAY, IRIS!
IF ONLY SHE KNEW THAT JUST ONE WEEK AGO--I--AS THE FLASH--WAS IN THE MOST DANGEROUS SPOT OF MY LIFE...
"...IN A SCIENTIFIC LABORATORY NOT FAR FROM HERE..."
RUNNING AT THIS FANTASTIC SPEED--I CAN'T STOP! SHOOT MORE RADIATION THROUGH ME, DOCTOR--SLOW ME DOWN--OR I'M DOOMED!
MILES PER HOUR
20,000
40,000
100,000
120,000
2

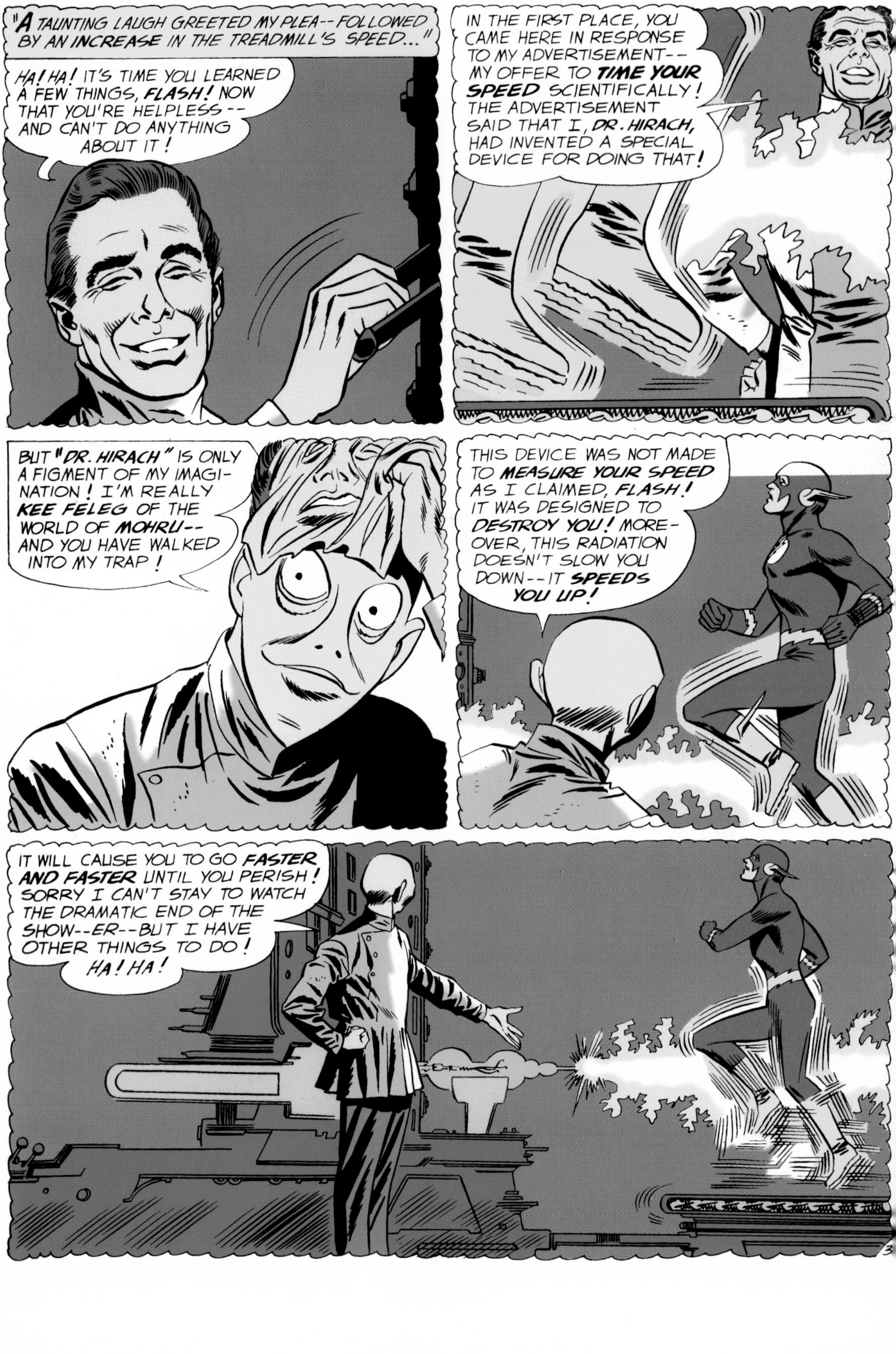
"A TAUNTING LAUGH GREETED MY PLEA--FOLLOWED BY AN INCREASE IN THE TREADMILL'S SPEED..."
HA! HA! IT'S TIME YOU LEARNED A FEW THINGS, FLASH! NOW THAT YOU'RE HELPLESS -- AND CAN'T DO ANYTHING ABOUT IT!
IN THE FIRST PLACE, YOU CAME HERE IN RESPONSE TO MY ADVERTISEMENT-- MY OFFER TO TIME YOUR SPEED SCIENTIFICALLY! THE ADVERTISEMENT SAID THAT I, DR. HIRACH, HAD INVENTED A SPECIAL DEVICE FOR DOING THAT!
BUT "DR. HIRACH" IS ONLY A FIGMENT OF MY IMAGINATION! I'M REALLY KEE FELEG OF THE WORLD OF MOHRU-- AND YOU HAVE WALKED INTO MY TRAP!
THIS DEVICE WAS NOT MADE TO MEASURE YOUR SPEED AS I CLAIMED, FLASH! IT WAS DESIGNED TO DESTROY YOU! MOREOVER, THIS RADIATION DOESN'T SLOW YOU DOWN--IT SPEEDS YOU UP!
IT WILL CAUSE YOU TO GO FASTER AND FASTER UNTIL YOU PERISH! SORRY I CAN'T STAY TO WATCH THE DRAMATIC END OF THE SHOW--ER--BUT I HAVE OTHER THINGS TO DO! HA! HA!
3

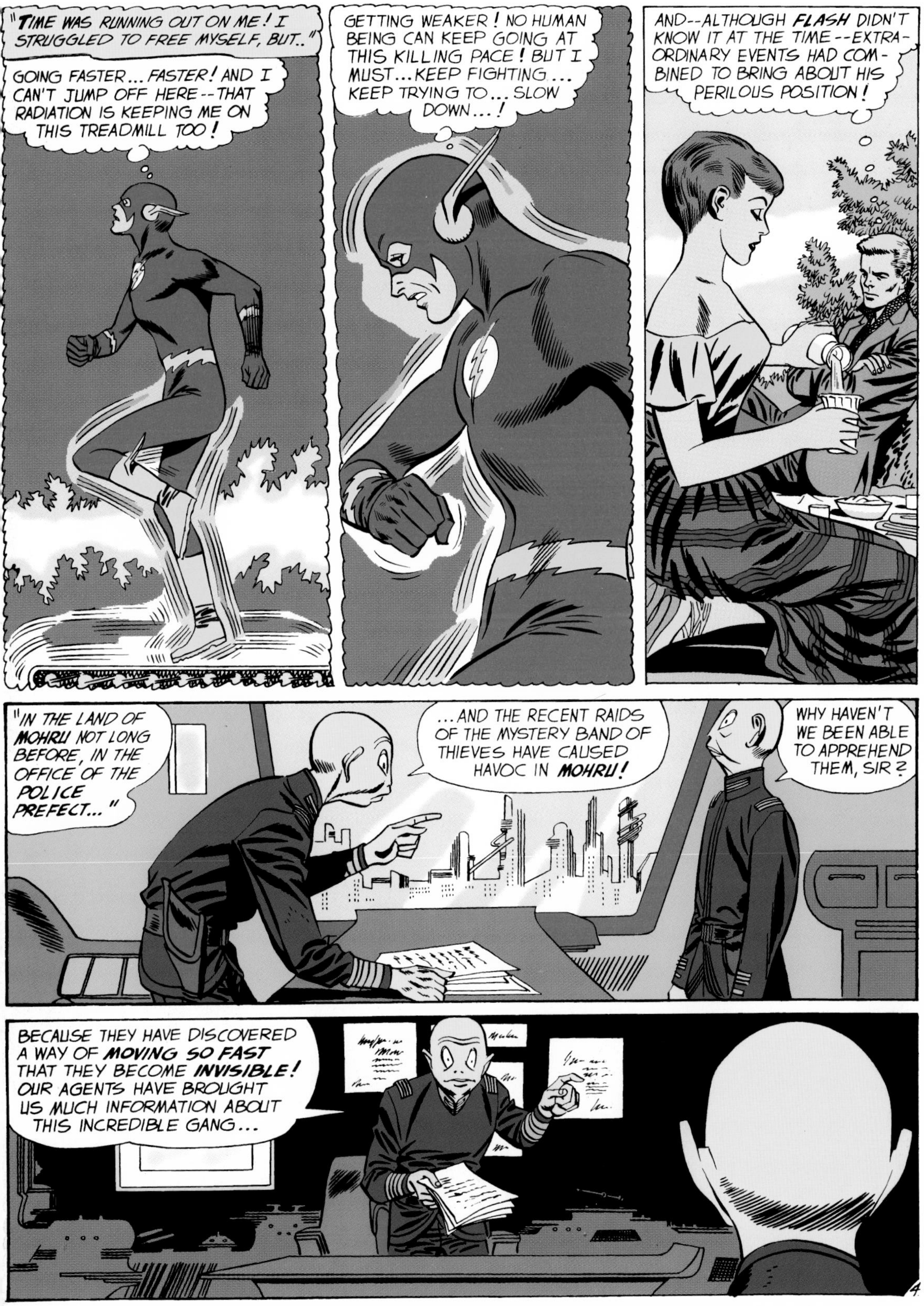
"TIME WAS RUNNING OUT ON ME! I STRUGGLED TO FREE MYSELF, BUT.."
GOING FASTER... FASTER! AND I CAN'T JUMP OFF HERE--THAT RADIATION IS KEEPING ME ON THIS TREADMILL TOO!
GETTING WEAKER! NO HUMAN BEING CAN KEEP GOING AT THIS KILLING PACE! BUT I MUST...KEEP FIGHTING... KEEP TRYING TO... SLOW DOWN...!
AND--ALTHOUGH FLASH DIDN'T KNOW IT AT THE TIME--EXTRA-ORDINARY EVENTS HAD COM-BINED TO BRING ABOUT HIS PERILOUS POSITION!
"IN THE LAND OF MOHRU NOT LONG BEFORE, IN THE OFFICE OF THE POLICE PREFECT..."
...AND THE RECENT RAIDS OF THE MYSTERY BAND OF THIEVES HAVE CAUSED HAVOC IN MOHRU!
WHY HAVEN'T WE BEEN ABLE TO APPREHEND THEM, SIR?
BECAUSE THEY HAVE DISCOVERED A WAY OF MOVING SO FAST THAT THEY BECOME INVISIBLE! OUR AGENTS HAVE BROUGHT US MUCH INFORMATION ABOUT THIS INCREDIBLE GANG...
4

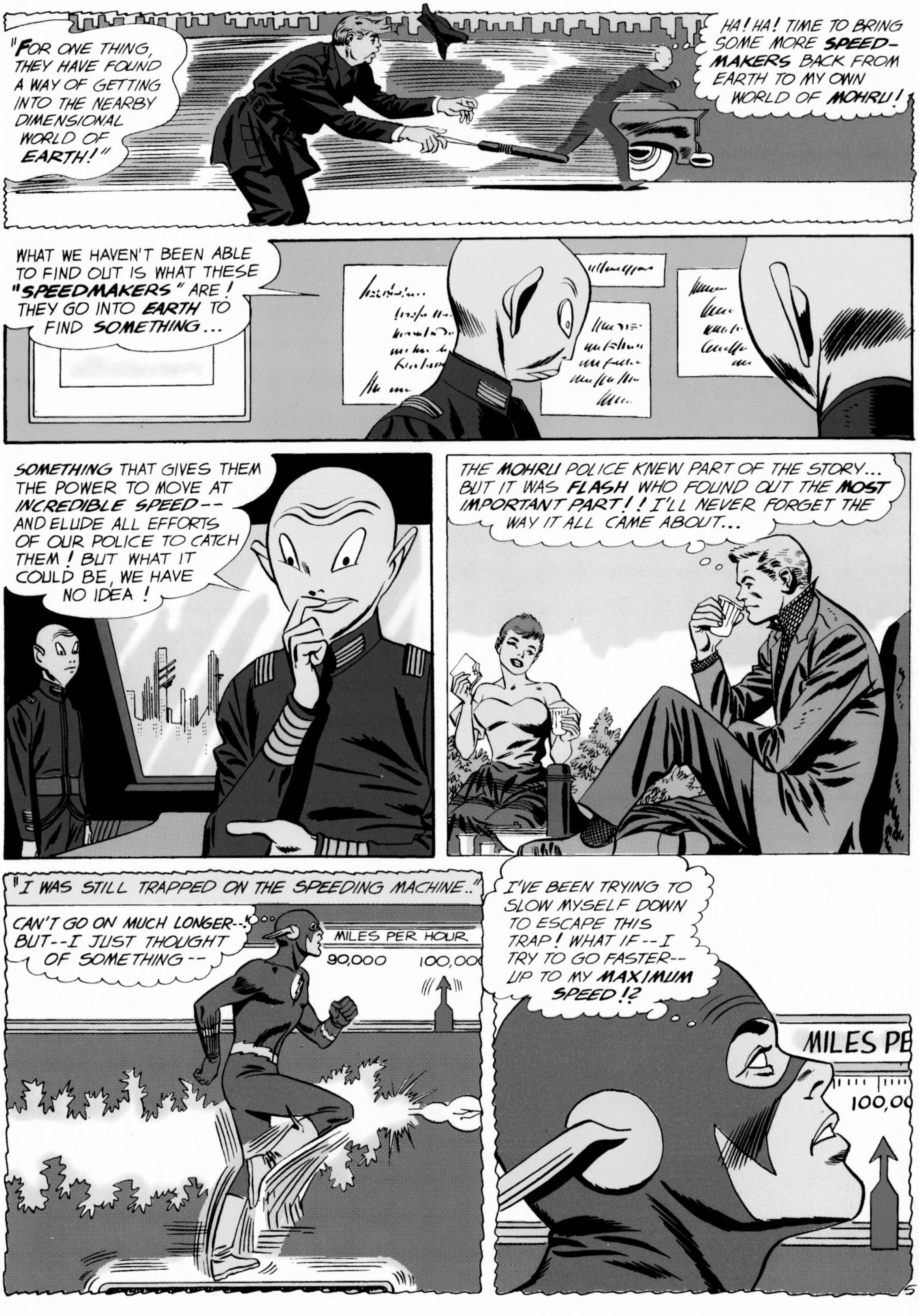
"FOR ONE THING, THEY HAVE FOUND A WAY OF GETTING INTO THE NEARBY DIMENSIONAL WORLD OF EARTH!"
HA! HA! TIME TO BRING SOME MORE SPEED-MAKERS BACK FROM EARTH TO MY OWN WORLD OF MOHRU!
WHAT WE HAVEN'T BEEN ABLE TO FIND OUT IS WHAT THESE "SPEEDMAKERS" ARE! THEY GO INTO EARTH TO FIND SOMETHING...
SOMETHING THAT GIVES THEM THE POWER TO MOVE AT INCREDIBLE SPEED-- AND ELUDE ALL EFFORTS OF OUR POLICE TO CATCH THEM! BUT WHAT IT COULD BE, WE HAVE NO IDEA!
THE MOHRU POLICE KNEW PART OF THE STORY... BUT IT WAS FLASH WHO FOUND OUT THE MOST IMPORTANT PART!! I'LL NEVER FORGET THE WAY IT ALL CAME ABOUT...
"I WAS STILL TRAPPED ON THE SPEEDING MACHINE.."
CAN'T GO ON MUCH LONGER--! BUT--I JUST THOUGHT OF SOMETHING--
MILES PER HOUR
90,000
100,00
I'VE BEEN TRYING TO SLOW MYSELF DOWN TO ESCAPE THIS TRAP! WHAT IF--I TRY TO GO FASTER-- UP TO MY MAXIMUM SPEED!?
MILES PE
100,00
5

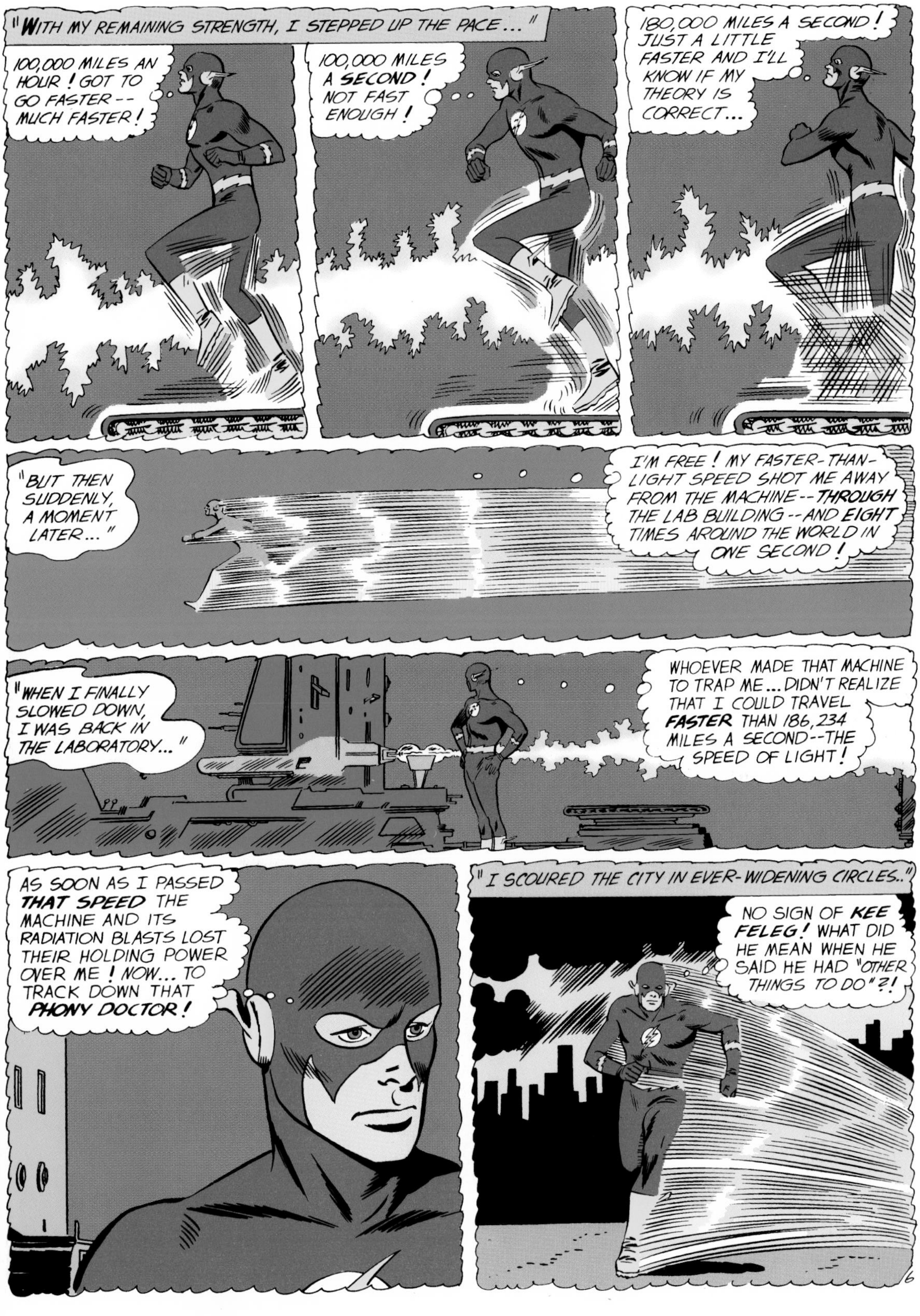
"WITH MY REMAINING STRENGTH, I STEPPED UP THE PACE..."
100,000 MILES AN HOUR! GOT TO GO FASTER-- MUCH FASTER!
100,000 MILES A SECOND! NOT FAST ENOUGH!
180,000 MILES A SECOND! JUST A LITTLE FASTER AND I'LL KNOW IF MY THEORY IS CORRECT...
"BUT THEN SUDDENLY, A MOMENT LATER..."
I'M FREE! MY FASTER-THAN-LIGHT SPEED SHOT ME AWAY FROM THE MACHINE--THROUGH THE LAB BUILDING--AND EIGHT TIMES AROUND THE WORLD IN ONE SECOND!
"WHEN I FINALLY SLOWED DOWN, I WAS BACK IN THE LABORATORY..."
WHOEVER MADE THAT MACHINE TO TRAP ME... DIDN'T REALIZE THAT I COULD TRAVEL FASTER THAN 186,234 MILES A SECOND--THE SPEED OF LIGHT!
AS SOON AS I PASSED THAT SPEED THE MACHINE AND ITS RADIATION BLASTS LOST THEIR HOLDING POWER OVER ME! NOW... TO TRACK DOWN THAT PHONY DOCTOR!
"I SCOURED THE CITY IN EVER-WIDENING CIRCLES.."
NO SIGN OF KEE FELEG! WHAT DID HE MEAN WHEN HE SAID HE HAD "OTHER THINGS TO DO"?!
6

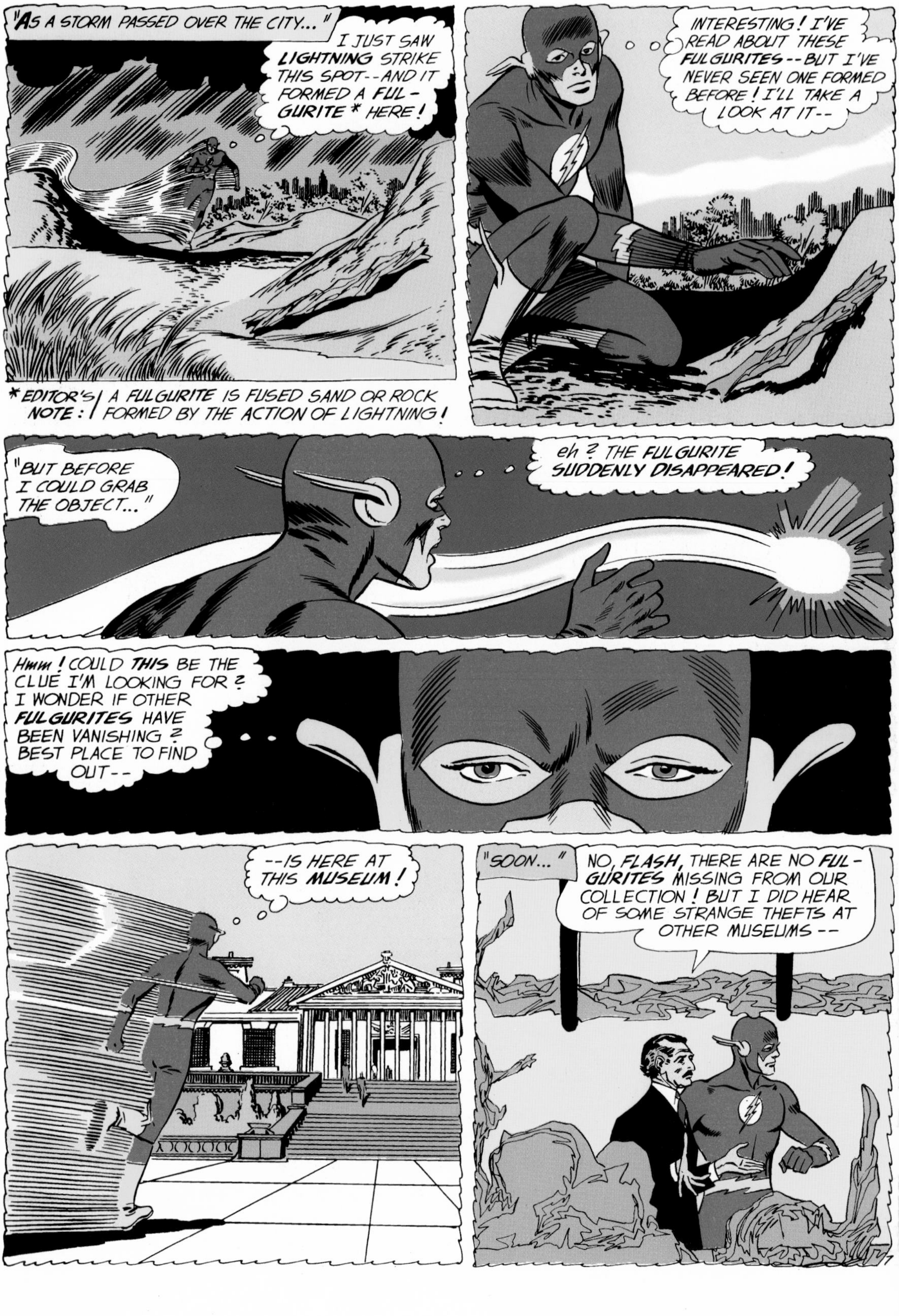
"AS A STORM PASSED OVER THE CITY..."
I JUST SAW LIGHTNING STRIKE THIS SPOT--AND IT FORMED A FUL-GURITE * HERE!
* EDITOR'S NOTE: A FULGURITE IS FUSED SAND OR ROCK FORMED BY THE ACTION OF LIGHTNING!
INTERESTING! I'VE READ ABOUT THESE FULGURITES--BUT I'VE NEVER SEEN ONE FORMED BEFORE! I'LL TAKE A LOOK AT IT--
"BUT BEFORE I COULD GRAB THE OBJECT..."
eh? THE FULGURITE SUDDENLY DISAPPEARED!
Hmm! COULD THIS BE THE CLUE I'M LOOKING FOR? I WONDER IF OTHER FULGURITES HAVE BEEN VANISHING? BEST PLACE TO FIND OUT--
--IS HERE AT THIS MUSEUM!
"SOON..."
NO, FLASH, THERE ARE NO FUL-GURITES MISSING FROM OUR COLLECTION! BUT I DID HEAR OF SOME STRANGE THEFTS AT OTHER MUSEUMS--
7

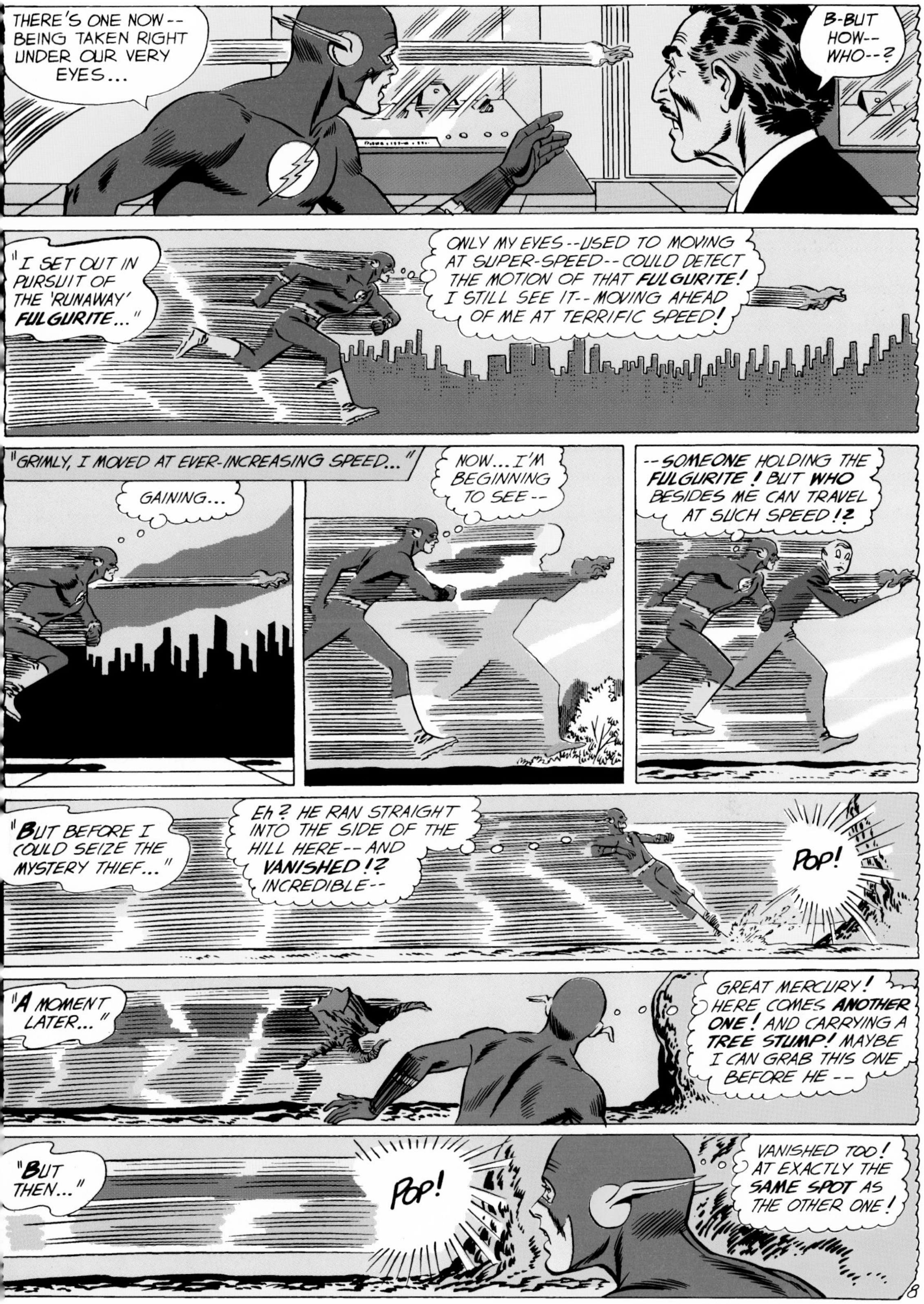
THERE'S ONE NOW -- BEING TAKEN RIGHT UNDER OUR VERY EYES...
B-BUT HOW-- WHO--?
"I SET OUT IN PURSUIT OF THE 'RUNAWAY' FULGURITE..."
ONLY MY EYES--USED TO MOVING AT SUPER-SPEED--COULD DETECT THE MOTION OF THAT FULGURITE! I STILL SEE IT--MOVING AHEAD OF ME AT TERRIFIC SPEED!
"GRIMLY, I MOVED AT EVER-INCREASING SPEED..."
GAINING...
NOW... I'M BEGINNING TO SEE--
--SOMEONE HOLDING THE FULGURITE! BUT WHO BESIDES ME CAN TRAVEL AT SUCH SPEED!?
"BUT BEFORE I COULD SEIZE THE MYSTERY THIEF..."
Eh? HE RAN STRAIGHT INTO THE SIDE OF THE HILL HERE--AND VANISHED!? INCREDIBLE--
POP!
"A MOMENT LATER..."
GREAT MERCURY! HERE COMES ANOTHER ONE! AND CARRYING A TREE STUMP! MAYBE I CAN GRAB THIS ONE BEFORE HE--
"BUT THEN..."
POP!
VANISHED TOO! AT EXACTLY THE SAME SPOT AS THE OTHER ONE!
8

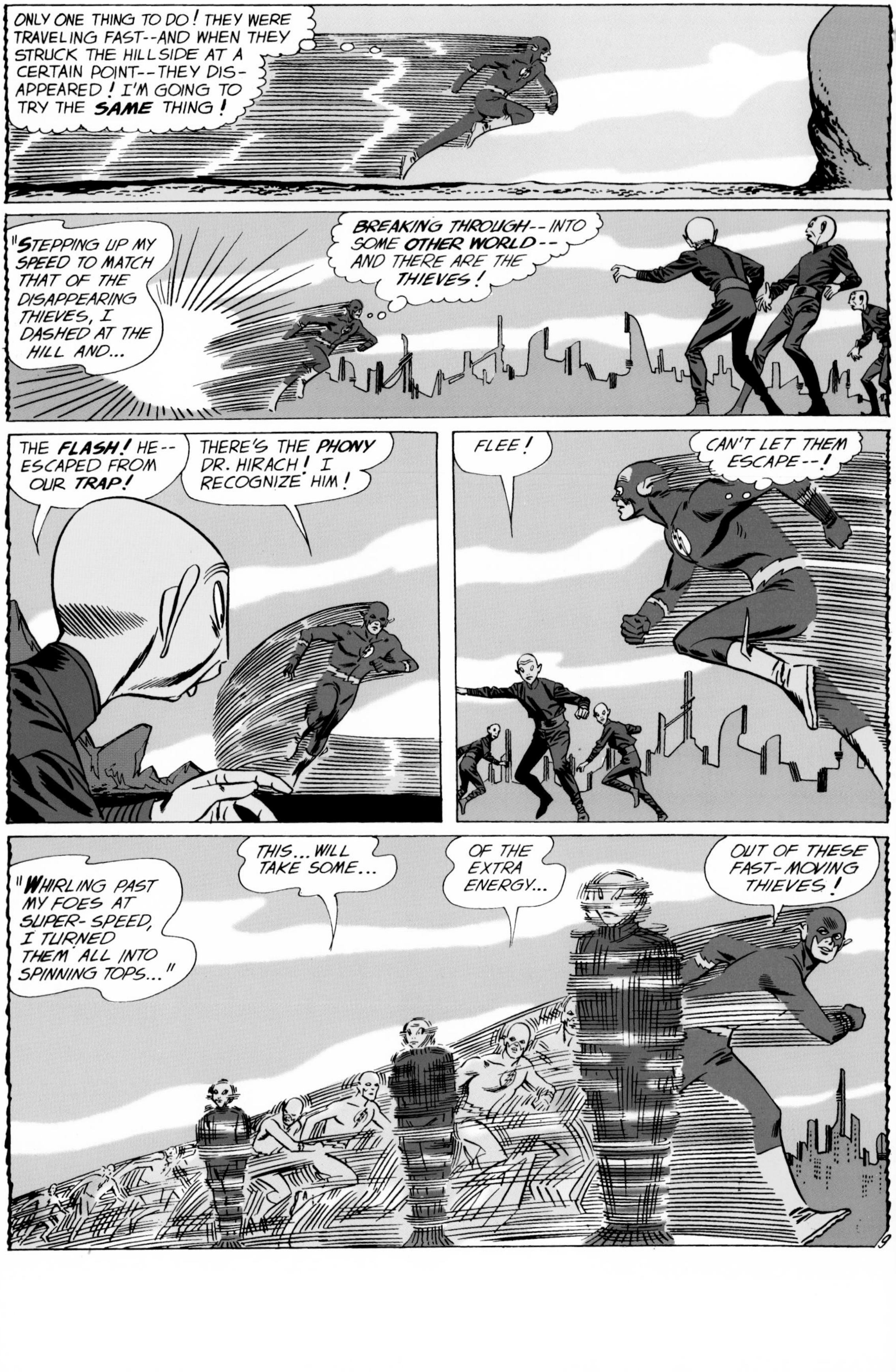
ONLY ONE THING TO DO! THEY WERE TRAVELING FAST--AND WHEN THEY STRUCK THE HILLSIDE AT A CERTAIN POINT--THEY DISAPPEARED! I'M GOING TO TRY THE SAME THING!
"STEPPING UP MY SPEED TO MATCH THAT OF THE DISAPPEARING THIEVES, I DASHED AT THE HILL AND...
BREAKING THROUGH--INTO SOME OTHER WORLD--AND THERE ARE THE THIEVES!
THE FLASH! HE--ESCAPED FROM OUR TRAP!
THERE'S THE PHONY DR. HIRACH! I RECOGNIZE HIM!
FLEE!
CAN'T LET THEM ESCAPE--!
"WHIRLING PAST MY FOES AT SUPER-SPEED, I TURNED THEM ALL INTO SPINNING TOPS..."
THIS...WILL TAKE SOME...
OF THE EXTRA ENERGY...
OUT OF THESE FAST-MOVING THIEVES!
9

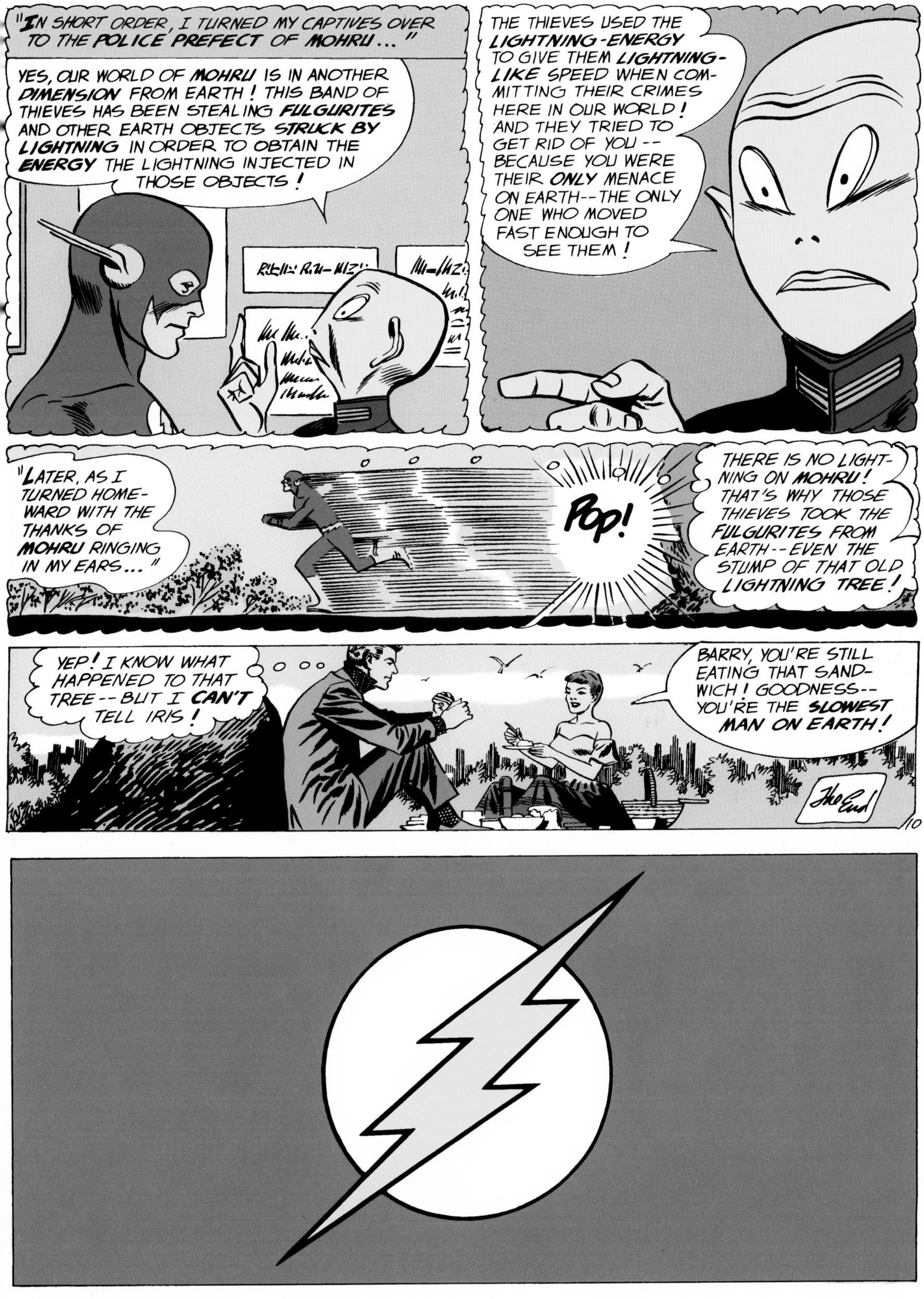
"IN SHORT ORDER, I TURNED MY CAPTIVES OVER TO THE POLICE PREFECT OF MOHRU..."
YES, OUR WORLD OF MOHRU IS IN ANOTHER DIMENSION FROM EARTH! THIS BAND OF THIEVES HAS BEEN STEALING FULGURITES AND OTHER EARTH OBJECTS STRUCK BY LIGHTNING IN ORDER TO OBTAIN THE ENERGY THE LIGHTNING INJECTED IN THOSE OBJECTS!
THE THIEVES USED THE LIGHTNING-ENERGY TO GIVE THEM LIGHTNING-LIKE SPEED WHEN COMMITTING THEIR CRIMES HERE IN OUR WORLD! AND THEY TRIED TO GET RID OF YOU -- BECAUSE YOU WERE THEIR ONLY MENACE ON EARTH--THE ONLY ONE WHO MOVED FAST ENOUGH TO SEE THEM!
"LATER, AS I TURNED HOMEWARD WITH THE THANKS OF MOHRU RINGING IN MY EARS..."
POP!
THERE IS NO LIGHTNING ON MOHRU! THAT'S WHY THOSE THIEVES TOOK THE FULGURITES FROM EARTH--EVEN THE STUMP OF THAT OLD LIGHTNING TREE!
YEP! I KNOW WHAT HAPPENED TO THAT TREE--BUT I CAN'T TELL IRIS!
BARRY, YOU'RE STILL EATING THAT SANDWICH! GOODNESS--YOU'RE THE SLOWEST MAN ON EARTH!
The End
10

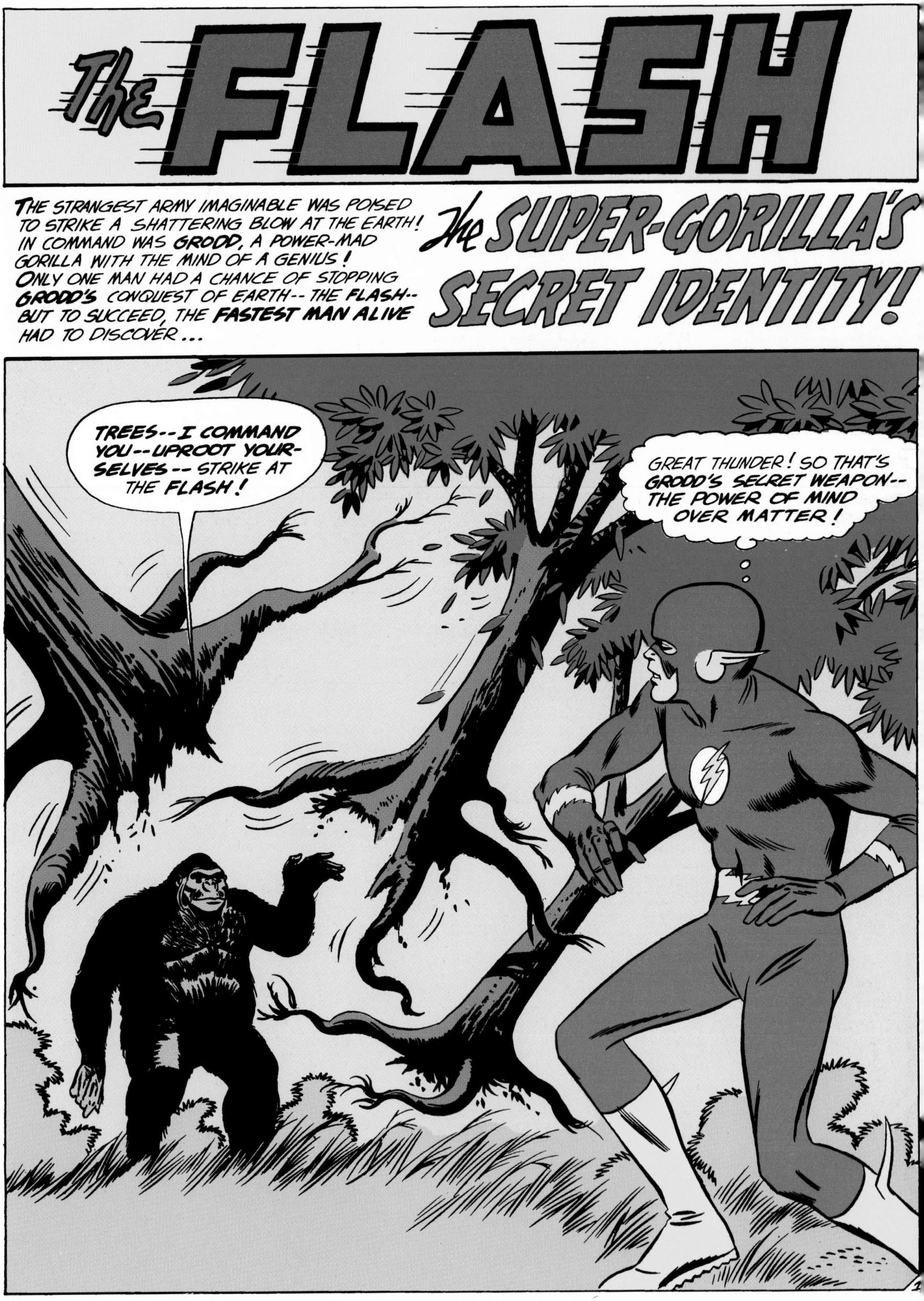
The FLASH
THE STRANGEST ARMY IMAGINABLE WAS POISED TO STRIKE A SHATTERING BLOW AT THE EARTH! IN COMMAND WAS GRODD, A POWER-MAD GORILLA WITH THE MIND OF A GENIUS! ONLY ONE MAN HAD A CHANCE OF STOPPING GRODD'S CONQUEST OF EARTH-- THE FLASH-- BUT TO SUCCEED, THE FASTEST MAN ALIVE HAD TO DISCOVER...
The SUPER-GORILLA'S SECRET IDENTITY!
TREES--I COMMAND YOU--UPROOT YOURSELVES-- STRIKE AT THE FLASH!
GREAT THUNDER! SO THAT'S GRODD'S SECRET WEAPON-- THE POWER OF MIND OVER MATTER!

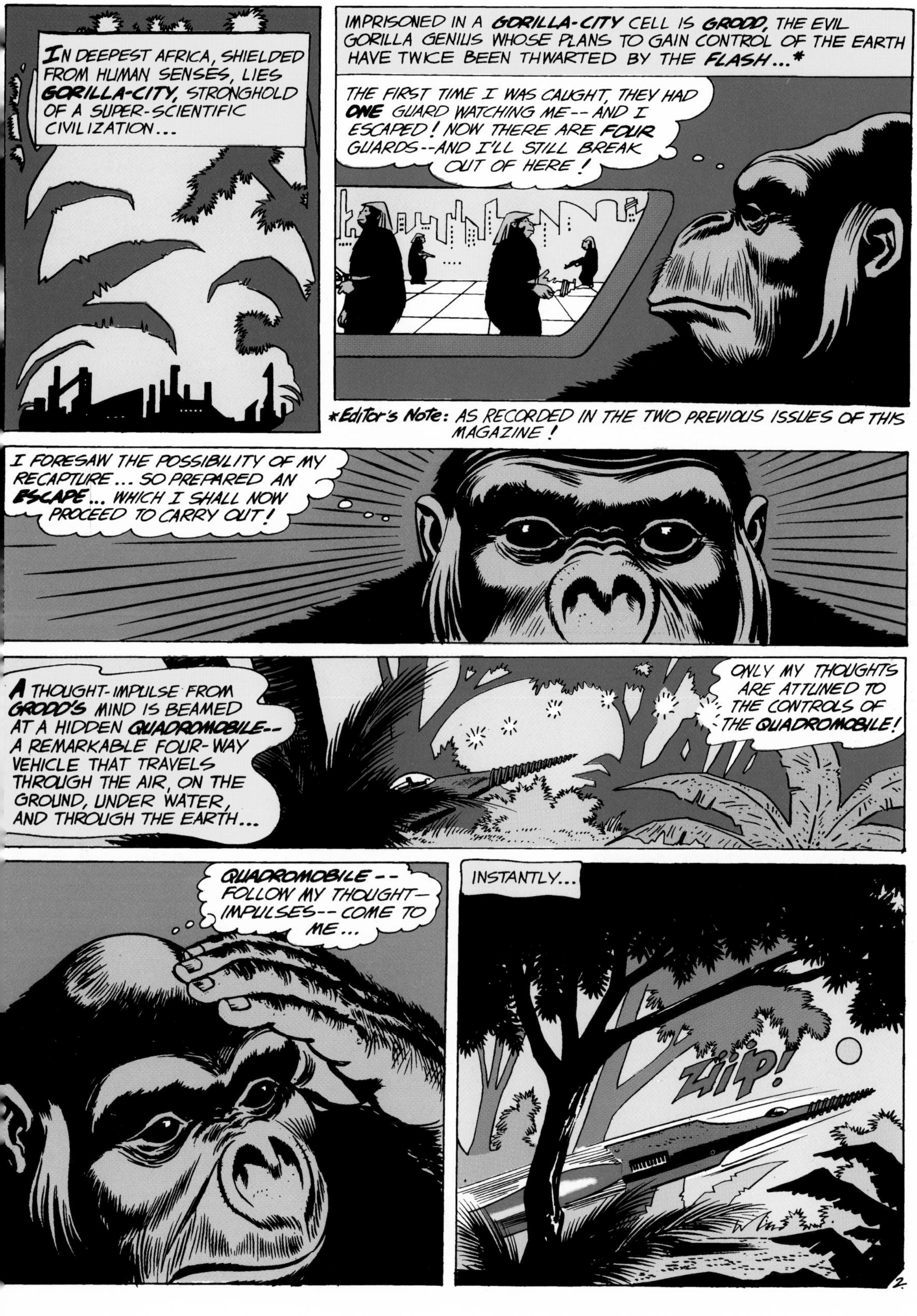
IN DEEPEST AFRICA, SHIELDED FROM HUMAN SENSES, LIES GORILLA-CITY, STRONGHOLD OF A SUPER-SCIENTIFIC CIVILIZATION...
IMPRISONED IN A GORILLA-CITY CELL IS GRODD, THE EVIL GORILLA GENIUS WHOSE PLANS TO GAIN CONTROL OF THE EARTH HAVE TWICE BEEN THWARTED BY THE FLASH...*
THE FIRST TIME I WAS CAUGHT, THEY HAD ONE GUARD WATCHING ME-- AND I ESCAPED! NOW THERE ARE FOUR GUARDS--AND I'LL STILL BREAK OUT OF HERE!
*Editor's Note: AS RECORDED IN THE TWO PREVIOUS ISSUES OF THIS MAGAZINE!
I FORESAW THE POSSIBILITY OF MY RECAPTURE... SO PREPARED AN ESCAPE... WHICH I SHALL NOW PROCEED TO CARRY OUT!
A THOUGHT-IMPULSE FROM GRODD'S MIND IS BEAMED AT A HIDDEN QUADROMOBILE-- A REMARKABLE FOUR-WAY VEHICLE THAT TRAVELS THROUGH THE AIR, ON THE GROUND, UNDER WATER, AND THROUGH THE EARTH...
ONLY MY THOUGHTS ARE ATTUNED TO THE CONTROLS OF THE QUADROMOBILE!
QUADROMOBILE -- FOLLOW MY THOUGHT-IMPULSES-- COME TO ME...
INSTANTLY...
ZIP!
2

THE FOLLOWING MOMENT...

FULL SPEED-- RIGHT THROUGH THE CELL WALL-- NOW *STOP!*

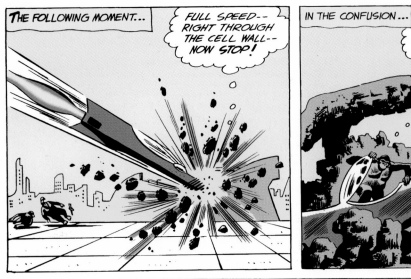

IN THE CONFUSION...

THIS WILL TEACH CHIEF *SOLOVAR* AND HIS *GORILLA-MINIONS* THAT NO PRISON OF THEIRS CAN HOLD ME!

LIKE A FAST-AS-LIGHT MISSILE, THE *QUADRO-MOBILE* SHOOTS SKYWARD...

HA HA...

OVER MID-OCEAN GRODD'S INCREDIBLE CRAFT DARTS DOWN-WARD...

NOW TO CARRY OUT THE NEXT PHASE OF MY *PREPARED PLAN...*

...ACTIVATE MY *EVOLUTION-ACCELERATOR!* THIS INVENTION OF MY *SUPER-BRAIN* WILL ADVANCE ME FAR ALONG THE EVOLUTIONARY TRACK--

--THE NEXT STEP AFTER MODERN MAN!

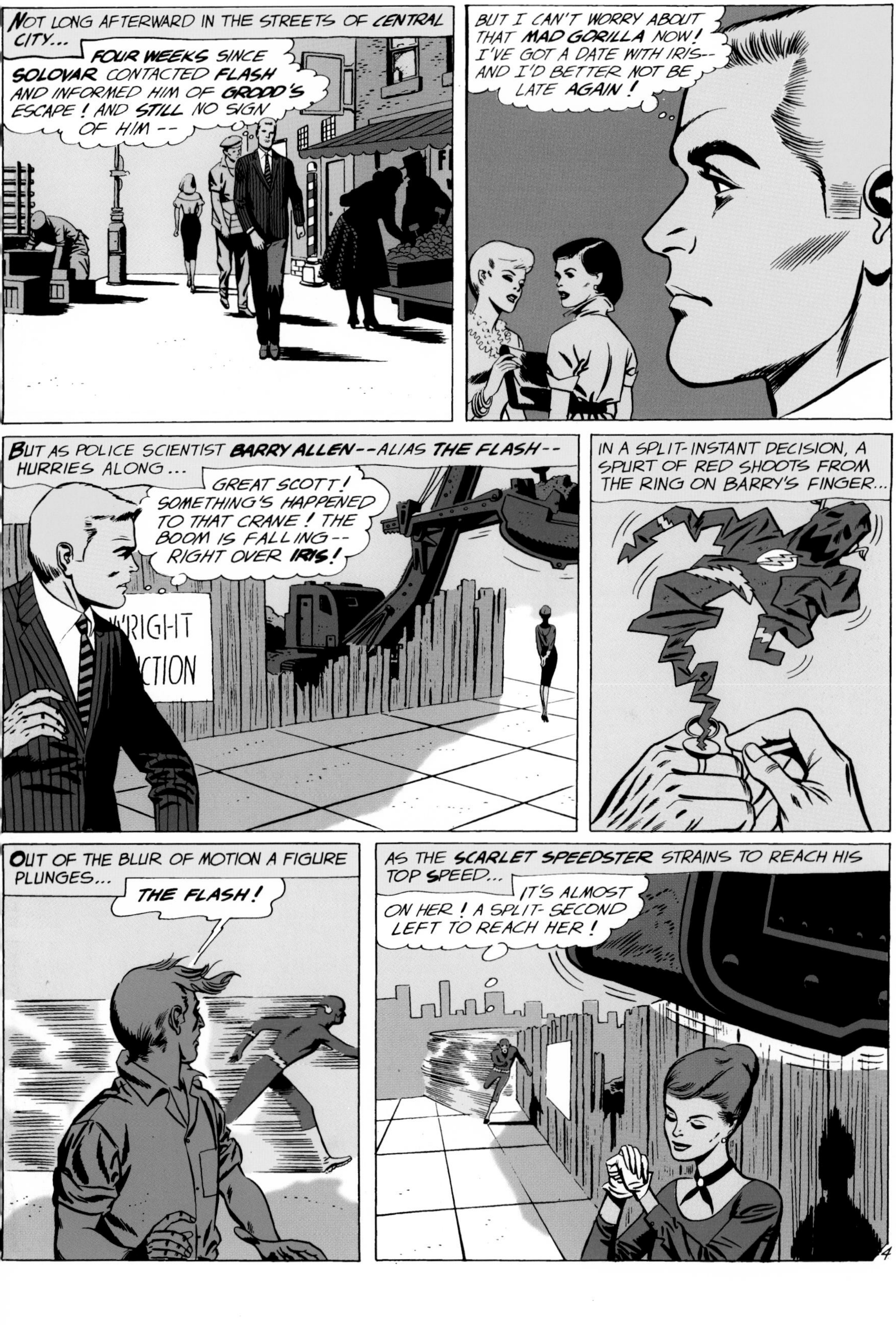
NOT LONG AFTERWARD IN THE STREETS OF CENTRAL CITY...
FOUR WEEKS SINCE SOLOVAR CONTACTED FLASH AND INFORMED HIM OF GRODD'S ESCAPE! AND STILL NO SIGN OF HIM --
BUT I CAN'T WORRY ABOUT THAT MAD GORILLA NOW! I'VE GOT A DATE WITH IRIS-- AND I'D BETTER NOT BE LATE AGAIN!
BUT AS POLICE SCIENTIST BARRY ALLEN--ALIAS THE FLASH-- HURRIES ALONG...
GREAT SCOTT! SOMETHING'S HAPPENED TO THAT CRANE! THE BOOM IS FALLING-- RIGHT OVER IRIS!
WRIGHT
CTION
IN A SPLIT-INSTANT DECISION, A SPURT OF RED SHOOTS FROM THE RING ON BARRY'S FINGER...
OUT OF THE BLUR OF MOTION A FIGURE PLUNGES...
THE FLASH!
AS THE SCARLET SPEEDSTER STRAINS TO REACH HIS TOP SPEED...
IT'S ALMOST ON HER! A SPLIT-SECOND LEFT TO REACH HER!
4

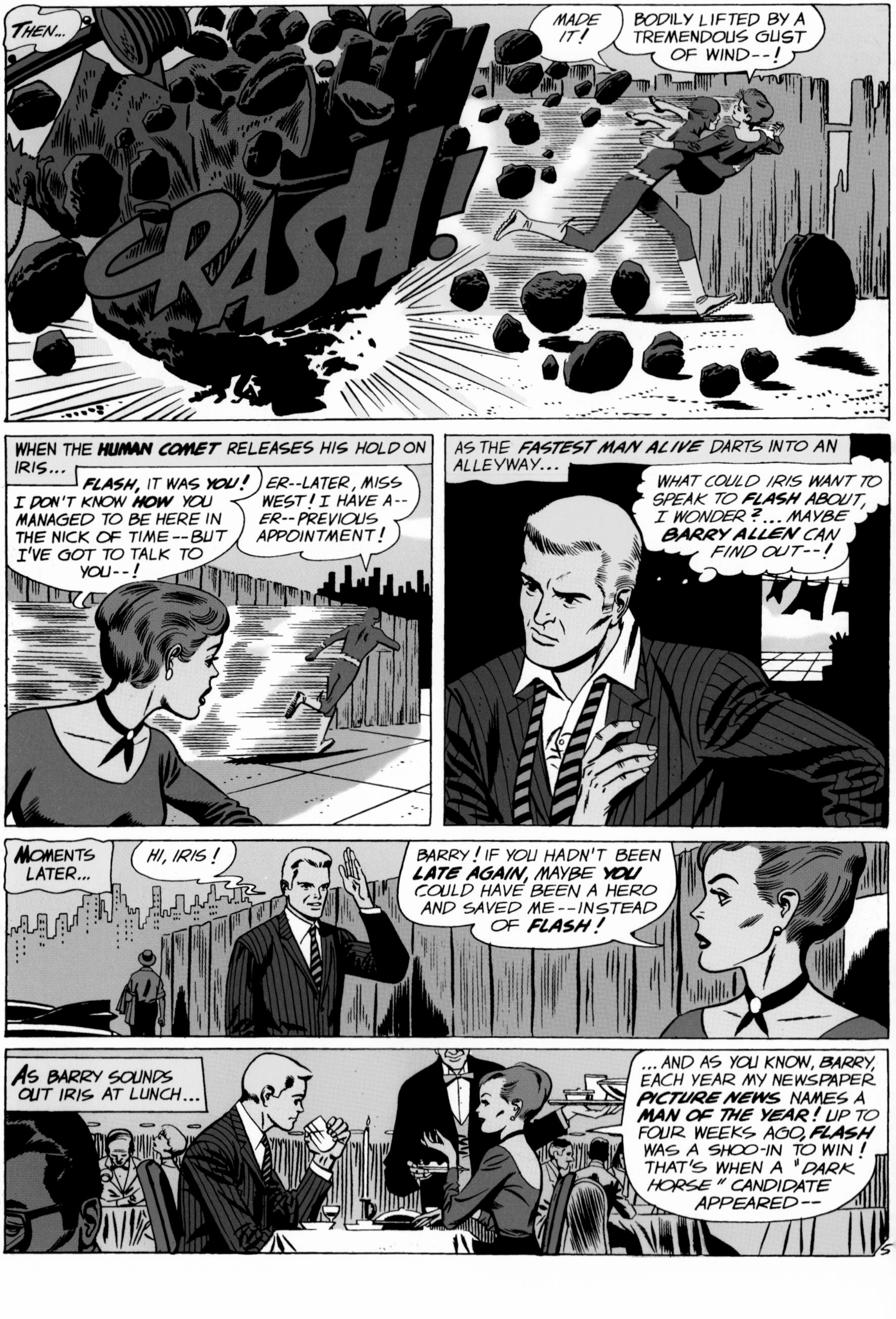
THEN...
CRASH!
MADE IT!
BODILY LIFTED BY A TREMENDOUS GUST OF WIND--!
WHEN THE HUMAN COMET RELEASES HIS HOLD ON IRIS...
FLASH, IT WAS YOU! I DON'T KNOW HOW YOU MANAGED TO BE HERE IN THE NICK OF TIME--BUT I'VE GOT TO TALK TO YOU--!
ER--LATER, MISS WEST! I HAVE A--ER--PREVIOUS APPOINTMENT!
AS THE FASTEST MAN ALIVE DARTS INTO AN ALLEYWAY...
WHAT COULD IRIS WANT TO SPEAK TO FLASH ABOUT, I WONDER?... MAYBE BARRY ALLEN CAN FIND OUT--!
MOMENTS LATER...
HI, IRIS!
BARRY! IF YOU HADN'T BEEN LATE AGAIN, MAYBE YOU COULD HAVE BEEN A HERO AND SAVED ME--INSTEAD OF FLASH!
AS BARRY SOUNDS OUT IRIS AT LUNCH...
...AND AS YOU KNOW, BARRY, EACH YEAR MY NEWSPAPER PICTURE NEWS NAMES A MAN OF THE YEAR! UP TO FOUR WEEKS AGO, FLASH WAS A SHOO-IN TO WIN! THAT'S WHEN A "DARK HORSE" CANDIDATE APPEARED--
5

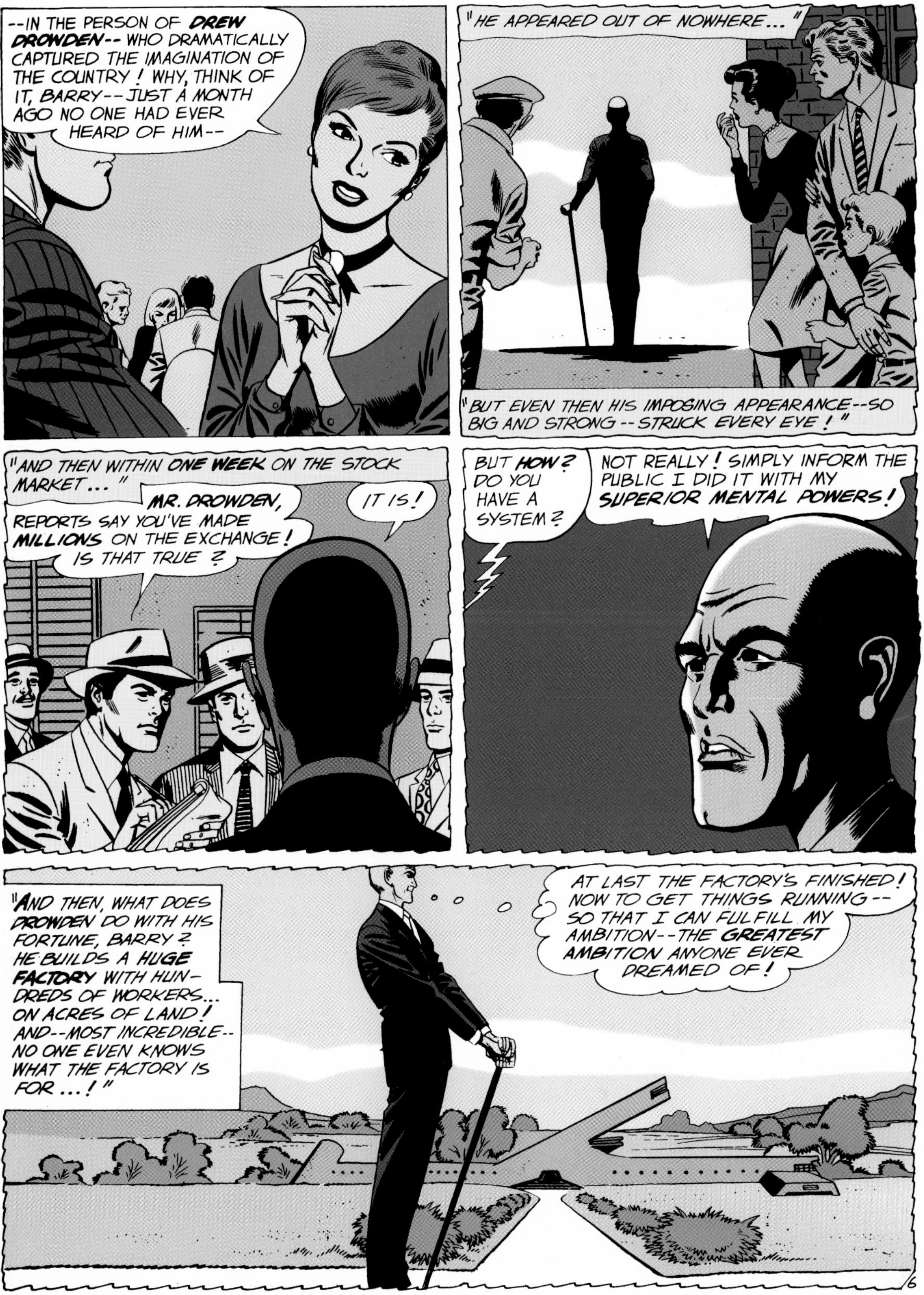
--IN THE PERSON OF DREW DROWDEN-- WHO DRAMATICALLY CAPTURED THE IMAGINATION OF THE COUNTRY! WHY, THINK OF IT, BARRY--JUST A MONTH AGO NO ONE HAD EVER HEARD OF HIM--
"HE APPEARED OUT OF NOWHERE..."
"BUT EVEN THEN HIS IMPOSING APPEARANCE--SO BIG AND STRONG--STRUCK EVERY EYE!"
"AND THEN WITHIN ONE WEEK ON THE STOCK MARKET..."
MR. DROWDEN, REPORTS SAY YOU'VE MADE MILLIONS ON THE EXCHANGE! IS THAT TRUE?
IT IS!
BUT HOW? DO YOU HAVE A SYSTEM?
NOT REALLY! SIMPLY INFORM THE PUBLIC I DID IT WITH MY SUPERIOR MENTAL POWERS!
"AND THEN, WHAT DOES DROWDEN DO WITH HIS FORTUNE, BARRY? HE BUILDS A HUGE FACTORY WITH HUNDREDS OF WORKERS... ON ACRES OF LAND! AND--MOST INCREDIBLE--NO ONE EVEN KNOWS WHAT THE FACTORY IS FOR...!"
AT LAST THE FACTORY'S FINISHED! NOW TO GET THINGS RUNNING--SO THAT I CAN FULFILL MY AMBITION--THE GREATEST AMBITION ANYONE EVER DREAMED OF!
6

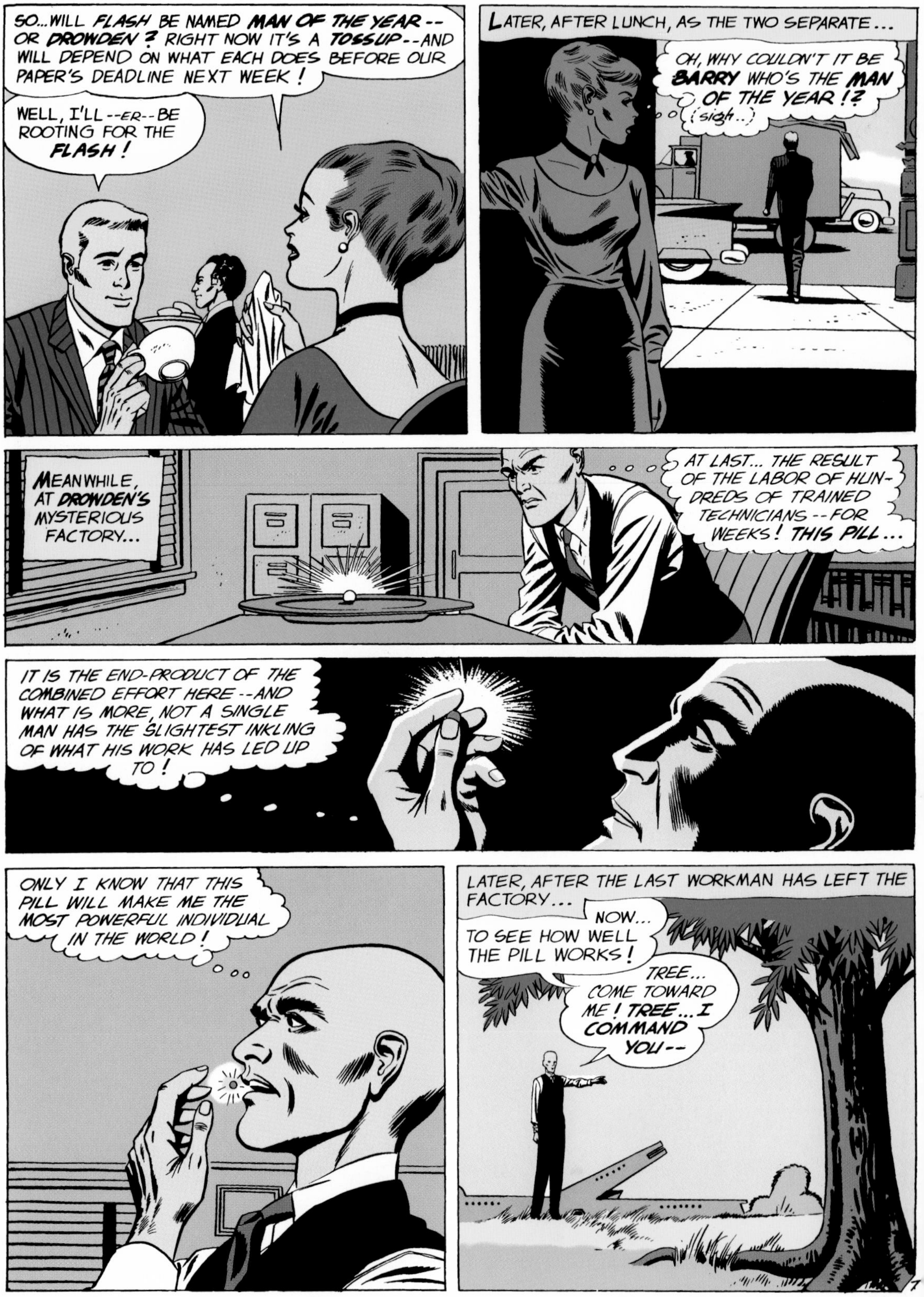
SO...WILL FLASH BE NAMED MAN OF THE YEAR -- OR DROWDEN? RIGHT NOW IT'S A TOSSUP--AND WILL DEPEND ON WHAT EACH DOES BEFORE OUR PAPER'S DEADLINE NEXT WEEK!
WELL, I'LL --ER-- BE ROOTING FOR THE FLASH!
LATER, AFTER LUNCH, AS THE TWO SEPARATE...
OH, WHY COULDN'T IT BE BARRY WHO'S THE MAN OF THE YEAR!?
(sigh..)
MEANWHILE, AT DROWDEN'S MYSTERIOUS FACTORY...
AT LAST... THE RESULT OF THE LABOR OF HUNDREDS OF TRAINED TECHNICIANS --FOR WEEKS! THIS PILL...
IT IS THE END-PRODUCT OF THE COMBINED EFFORT HERE --AND WHAT IS MORE, NOT A SINGLE MAN HAS THE SLIGHTEST INKLING OF WHAT HIS WORK HAS LED UP TO!
ONLY I KNOW THAT THIS PILL WILL MAKE ME THE MOST POWERFUL INDIVIDUAL IN THE WORLD!
LATER, AFTER THE LAST WORKMAN HAS LEFT THE FACTORY...
NOW... TO SEE HOW WELL THE PILL WORKS!
TREE... COME TOWARD ME! TREE...I COMMAND YOU--
7

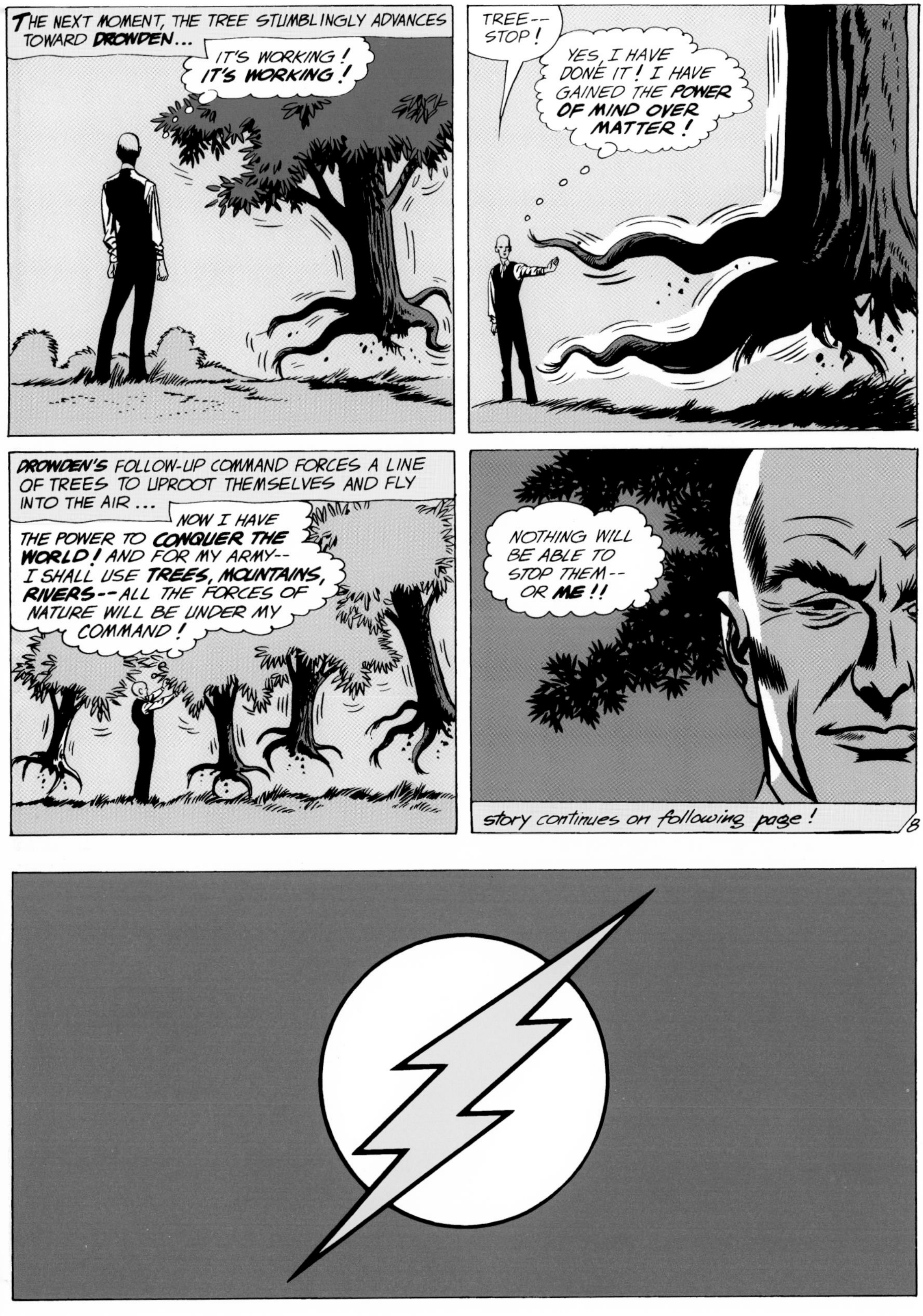
THE NEXT MOMENT, THE TREE STUMBLINGLY ADVANCES TOWARD DROWDEN...
IT'S WORKING! IT'S WORKING!
TREE-- STOP!
YES, I HAVE DONE IT! I HAVE GAINED THE POWER OF MIND OVER MATTER!
DROWDEN'S FOLLOW-UP COMMAND FORCES A LINE OF TREES TO UPROOT THEMSELVES AND FLY INTO THE AIR...
NOW I HAVE THE POWER TO CONQUER THE WORLD! AND FOR MY ARMY-- I SHALL USE TREES, MOUNTAINS, RIVERS-- ALL THE FORCES OF NATURE WILL BE UNDER MY COMMAND!
NOTHING WILL BE ABLE TO STOP THEM-- OR ME!!
story continues on following page!
8

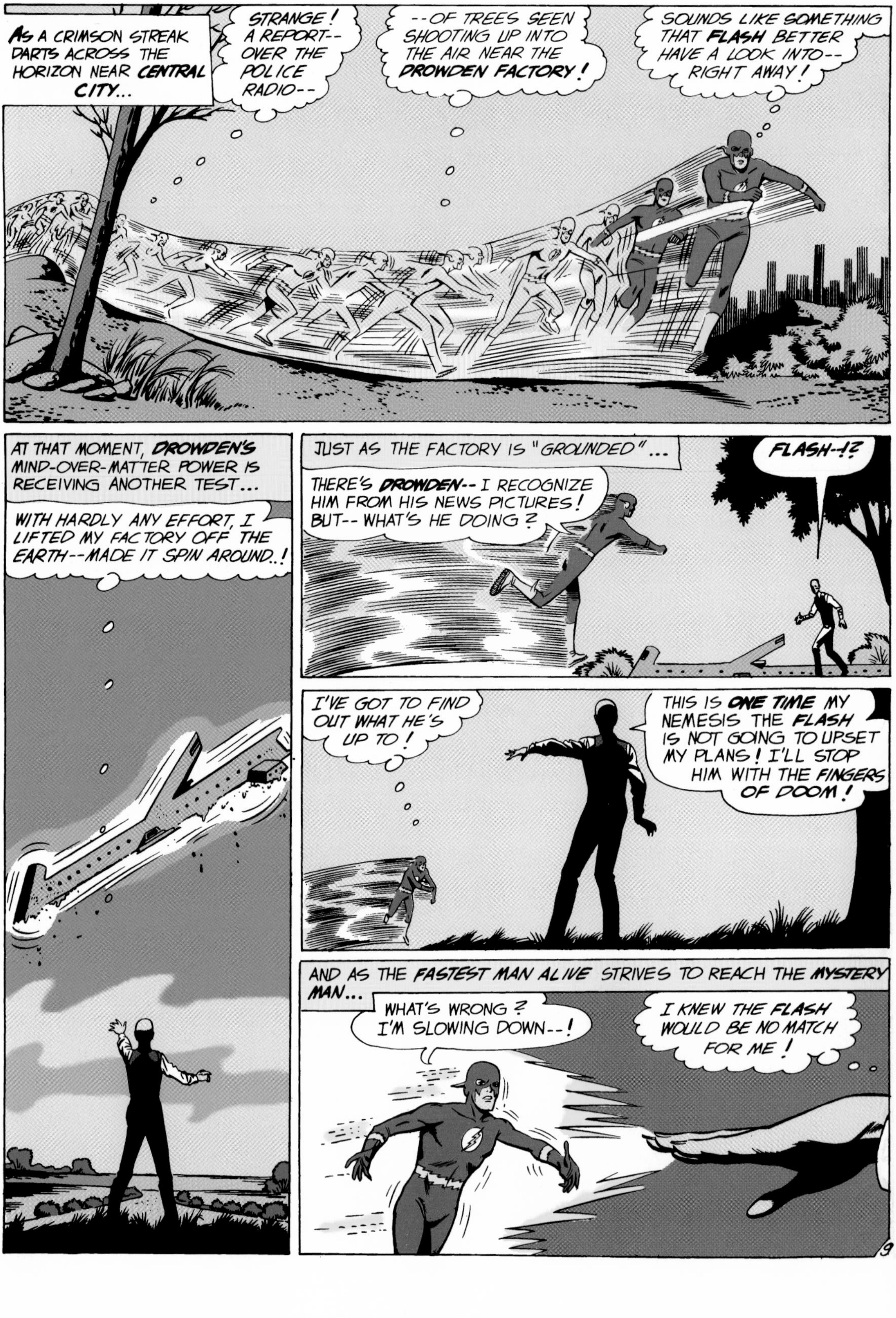
AS A CRIMSON STREAK DARTS ACROSS THE HORIZON NEAR CENTRAL CITY...
STRANGE! A REPORT-- OVER THE POLICE RADIO--
--OF TREES SEEN SHOOTING UP INTO THE AIR NEAR THE DROWDEN FACTORY!
SOUNDS LIKE SOMETHING THAT FLASH BETTER HAVE A LOOK INTO-- RIGHT AWAY!
AT THAT MOMENT, DROWDEN'S MIND-OVER-MATTER POWER IS RECEIVING ANOTHER TEST...
WITH HARDLY ANY EFFORT, I LIFTED MY FACTORY OFF THE EARTH--MADE IT SPIN AROUND..!
JUST AS THE FACTORY IS "GROUNDED"...
THERE'S DROWDEN-- I RECOGNIZE HIM FROM HIS NEWS PICTURES! BUT-- WHAT'S HE DOING?
FLASH-!?
I'VE GOT TO FIND OUT WHAT HE'S UP TO!
THIS IS ONE TIME MY NEMESIS THE FLASH IS NOT GOING TO UPSET MY PLANS! I'LL STOP HIM WITH THE FINGERS OF DOOM!
AND AS THE FASTEST MAN ALIVE STRIVES TO REACH THE MYSTERY MAN...
WHAT'S WRONG? I'M SLOWING DOWN--!
I KNEW THE FLASH WOULD BE NO MATCH FOR ME!
9

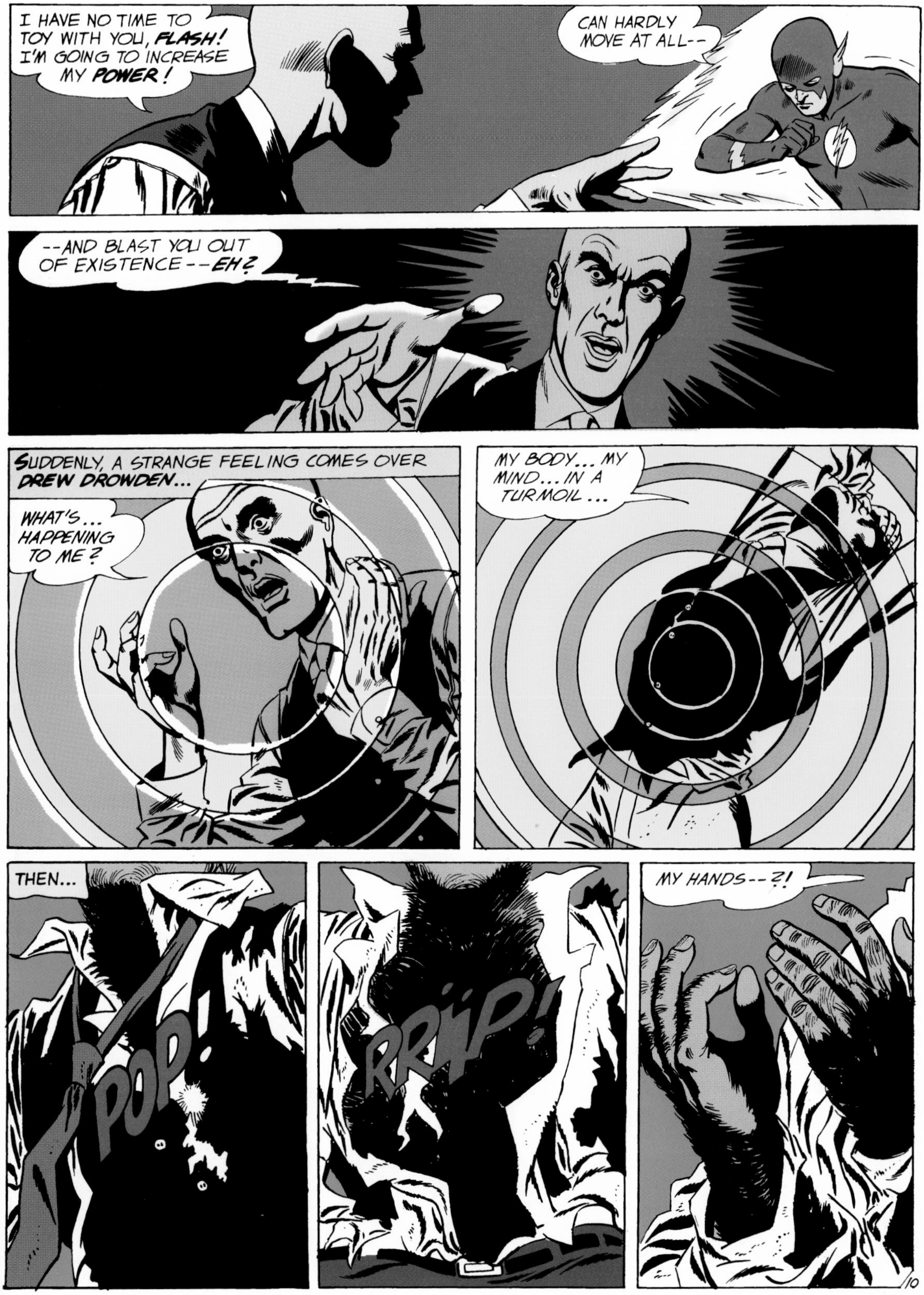
I HAVE NO TIME TO TOY WITH YOU, FLASH! I'M GOING TO INCREASE MY POWER!
CAN HARDLY MOVE AT ALL--
--AND BLAST YOU OUT OF EXISTENCE--EH?
SUDDENLY, A STRANGE FEELING COMES OVER DREW DROWDEN...
WHAT'S... HAPPENING TO ME?
MY BODY... MY MIND... IN A TURMOIL...
THEN...
POP!
RRIIP!
MY HANDS--?!
10

AND AS *FLASH* STARES AGHAST...

INCREDIBLE--!! *DREW DROWDEN*--CHANGING INTO--

GRODD-- THE *EVIL SUPER-GORILLA!* NO WONDER WE COULDN'T FIND ANY TRACE OF HIM!

YOU'LL NEVER REVEAL MY SECRET, *FLASH!*

*B*UT THIS TIME, WHEN *GRODD* POINTS HIS FINGER AT HIS FOE...

I CAN MOVE AGAIN!

MY *POWER*-- IT'S GONE!

IT'S ONLY AS A *HUMAN* THAT I HAVE THE MIND-OVER-MATTER POWER-- BECAUSE AS A *HUMAN* MY BRAIN IS ON A HIGHER EVOLUTIONARY LEVEL! MY GORILLA BRAIN CAN'T USE THE POWER!

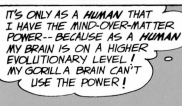

GOT TO REACH MY *EVOLUTION-ACCELERATOR!* TURN IT ON-- MAKE ME *HUMAN AGAIN!*

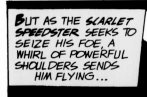

*B*UT AS THE *SCARLET SPEEDSTER* SEEKS TO SEIZE HIS FOE, A WHIRL OF POWERFUL SHOULDERS SENDS HIM FLYING...

I'VE STILL GOT MY *SUPER-GORILLA* STRENGTH, *FLASH!* YOU'LL NEVER CAPTURE ME!

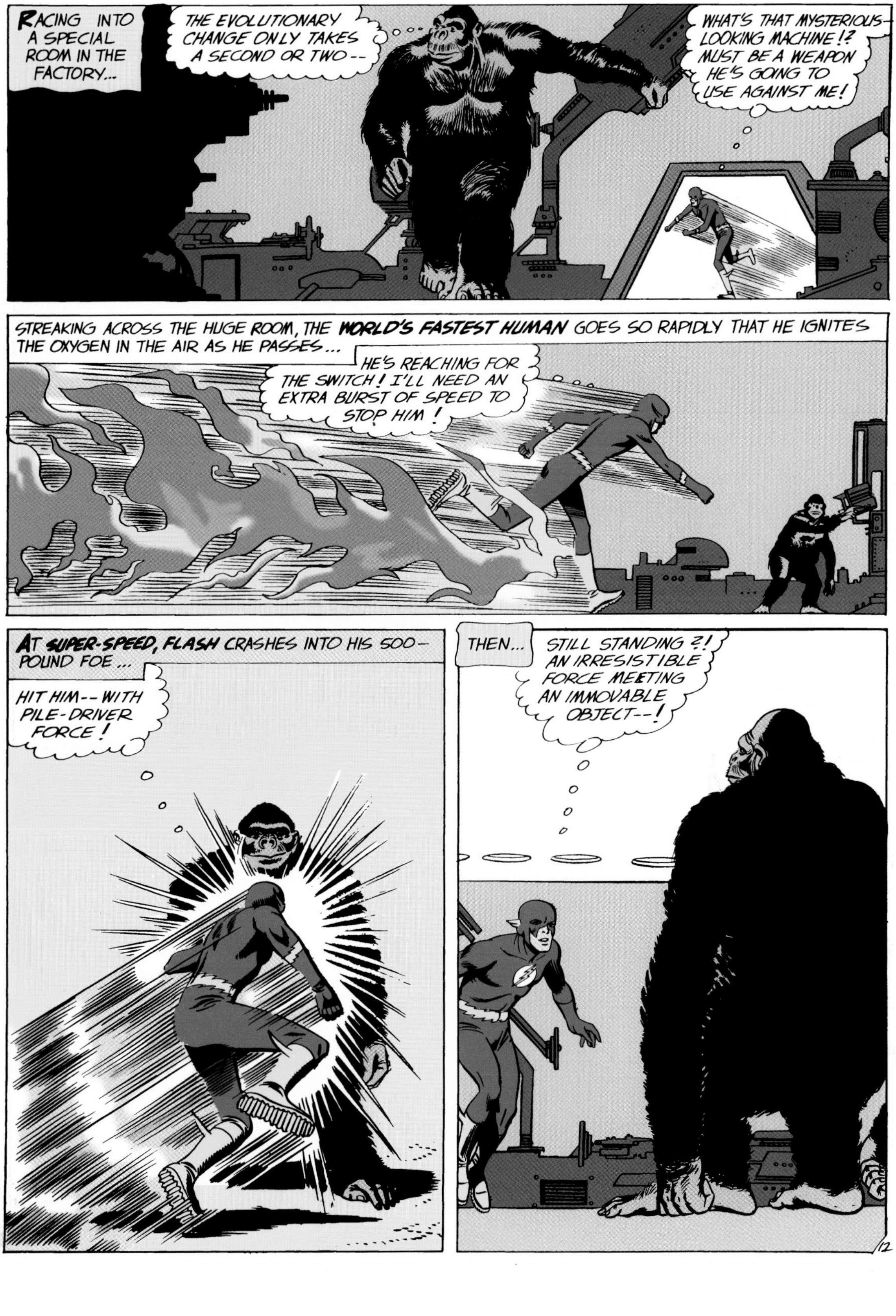
RACING INTO A SPECIAL ROOM IN THE FACTORY...
THE EVOLUTIONARY CHANGE ONLY TAKES A SECOND OR TWO--
WHAT'S THAT MYSTERIOUS-LOOKING MACHINE!? MUST BE A WEAPON HE'S GOING TO USE AGAINST ME!
STREAKING ACROSS THE HUGE ROOM, THE WORLD'S FASTEST HUMAN GOES SO RAPIDLY THAT HE IGNITES THE OXYGEN IN THE AIR AS HE PASSES...
HE'S REACHING FOR THE SWITCH! I'LL NEED AN EXTRA BURST OF SPEED TO STOP HIM!
AT SUPER-SPEED, FLASH CRASHES INTO HIS 500-POUND FOE...
HIT HIM--WITH PILE-DRIVER FORCE!
THEN...
STILL STANDING?! AN IRRESISTIBLE FORCE MEETING AN IMMOVABLE OBJECT--!
12

I'VE CHANGED MY MIND, *FLASH!* I'LL ENJOY MY TRIUMPH MORE BY ELIMINATING YOU IN MY *GORILLA-FORM!*

AFTER THAT, AS *DREW DROWDEN--* WITH ABSOLUTE CONTROL OF MIND OVER MATTER--I SHALL RULE THE WORLD!

THEN THE FATE OF THE WORLD RESTS IN MY HANDS-- *HANDS!* THAT'S IT! I KNOW HOW TO STOP HIM!

AS THE *FASTEST MAN ALIVE* FOLLOWS THROUGH WITH HIS IDEA...

IF *YOU* WON'T USE YOUR MACHINE, *GRODD--* I WILL!

BACK AND FORTH OVER THE MACHINE RUB THE *FLASH'S* HANDS--SO FAST THAT THE FRICTION-HEAT CAUSES THE METAL TO MELT...

MY EVOLUTION-ACCELERATOR-- WHAT'S HE DOING TO IT?

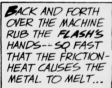

THE NEXT MOMENT, AS THE EVIL ANTHROPOID TRIES TO INTERCEPT THE *SCARLET SPEEDSTER* ...

THERE! THAT'LL HOLD YOU!

UH--! HANDCUFFED!

KLIK!

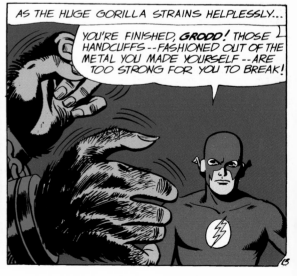

AS THE HUGE GORILLA STRAINS HELPLESSLY...

YOU'RE FINISHED, *GRODD!* THOSE HANDCUFFS--FASHIONED OUT OF THE METAL YOU MADE YOURSELF --ARE TOO STRONG FOR YOU TO BREAK!

13

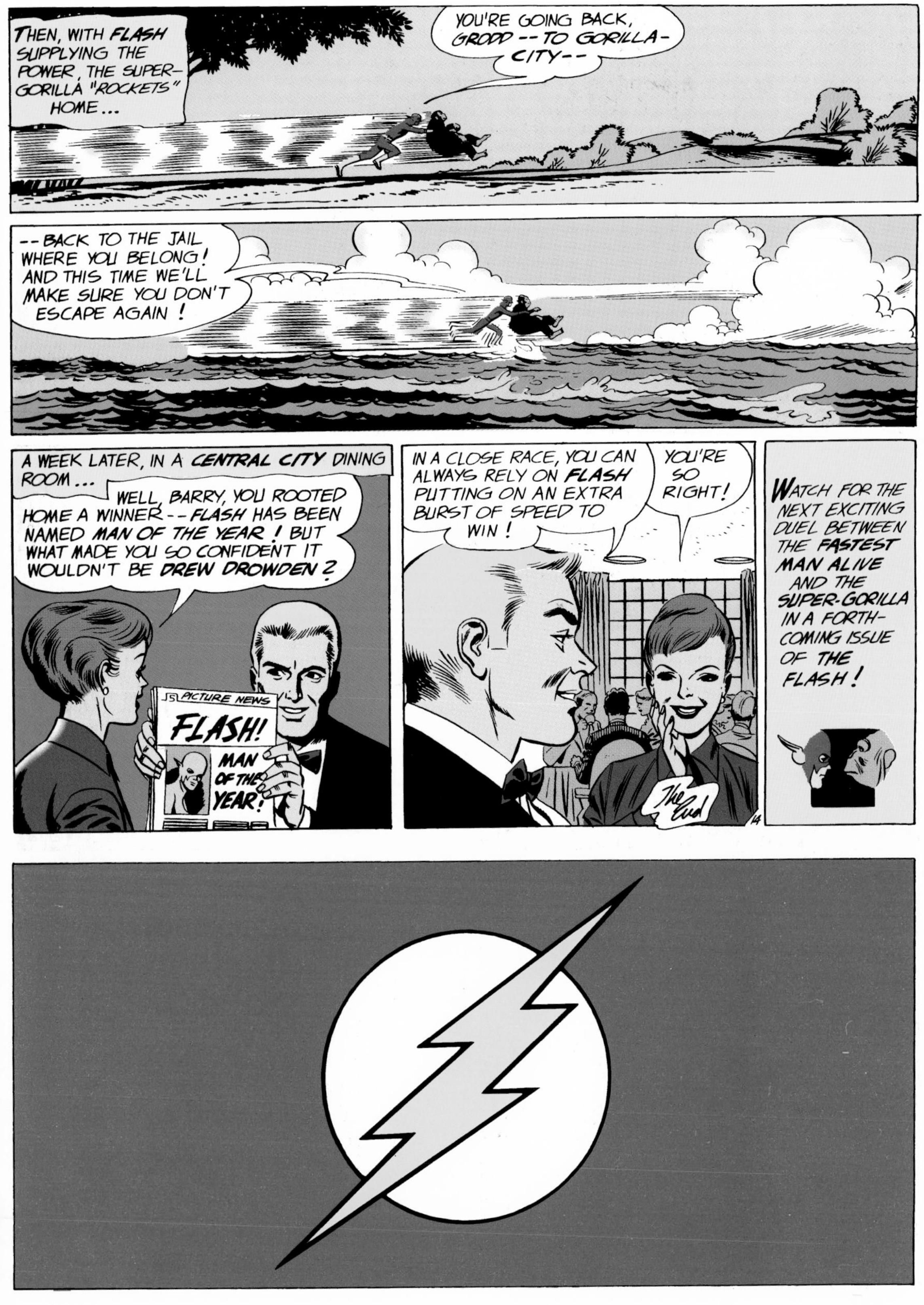
THEN, WITH FLASH SUPPLYING THE POWER, THE SUPER-GORILLA "ROCKETS" HOME...
YOU'RE GOING BACK, GRODD -- TO GORILLA-CITY--
-- BACK TO THE JAIL WHERE YOU BELONG! AND THIS TIME WE'LL MAKE SURE YOU DON'T ESCAPE AGAIN!
A WEEK LATER, IN A CENTRAL CITY DINING ROOM...
WELL, BARRY, YOU ROOTED HOME A WINNER -- FLASH HAS BEEN NAMED MAN OF THE YEAR! BUT WHAT MADE YOU SO CONFIDENT IT WOULDN'T BE DREW DROWDEN?
PICTURE NEWS
FLASH!
MAN OF THE YEAR!
IN A CLOSE RACE, YOU CAN ALWAYS RELY ON FLASH PUTTING ON AN EXTRA BURST OF SPEED TO WIN!
YOU'RE SO RIGHT!
The End
14
WATCH FOR THE NEXT EXCITING DUEL BETWEEN THE FASTEST MAN ALIVE AND THE SUPER-GORILLA IN A FORTH-COMING ISSUE OF THE FLASH!

JOHN BROOME

John Broome scripted the majority of the Silver Age Flash stories, beginning with the second tale in SHOWCASE #4, the character's first appearance, and continuing on the title until 1970. Prior to Flash, Broome had accumulated a lively résumé of comic-book credits, including Captain Marvel and the rest of the Marvel Family, the Golden Age Green Lantern, the Justice Society of America, Captain Comet, the Silver Age revival of Green Lantern, the Atomic Knights, Batman, Star Hawkins, Rex the Wonder Dog, Detective Chimp, and a variety of science-fiction tales. Broome retired from comics in the 1970s to travel the world, and eventually settled in Japan. He passed away on March 14, 1999.

FRANK GIACOIA

Frank Giacoia entered comics in the mid-1940s along with his friend Carmine Infantino. During his long career, Giacoia frequently worked with his friend Infantino, including runs on the Golden Age Flash and Black Canary, The Phantom Stranger, and other features, including, of course, the Silver Age Flash. Giacoia's work as both a penciller and inker has also appeared in syndicated newspaper strips, a variety of super-hero and genre stories for DC and other publishers, as well as long runs on *Spider-Man* and other titles for Marvel Comics. Giacoia's clean and distinctive inking style continued to grace the comic-book field until his death in the 1980s.

JOE GIELLA

Inker Joe Giella began his career in the 1940s as an inker for Hillman Publications and Timely Comics, the company that was later to become Marvel. Joe first worked for DC Comics in 1951 where, in the 1960s, his style of embellishment became associated with some of the company's greatest heroes, including Batman (over the work of penciller Sheldon Moldoff), The Flash (with artist Carmine Infantino), and The Atom (with penciller Gil Kane). Giella, who also pencilled and inked a run of the *Batman* syndicated newspaper strip during the 1960s, retired from comics in the early 1980s.

CARMINE INFANTINO

The man most closely associated with the Silver Age Flash, Carmine Infantino began working in comics in the mid-1940s as the artist on such features as Green Lantern, Black Canary, Ghost Patrol... and the original Golden Age Flash. Infantino's unique style continued to grace a variety of super-hero, supernatural, and Western features throughout the 1950s, until he was tapped to pencil the 1956 revival of The Flash. He went on to pencil Flash for an impressive number of issues, while also providing the art for other strips, including Batman, The Elongated Man, and Adam Strange. Infantino became DC's editorial director in 1967 and, later, publisher before returning to freelancing in 1976 since which time he has pencilled and inked numerous features, including the *Batman* newspaper strip, The Green Lantern Corps, and Danger Trail.

ROBERT KANIGHER

Robert Kanigher has long been recognized as one of the most prolific and innovative writers and editors in the comic-book field. Since the 1940s, Kanigher has written and/or created more characters than nearly anyone else. These include Blue Beetle, Steel Sterling, Black Canary, Captain Marvel, Flash, Sgt. Rock, The Haunted Tank, Wonder Woman, Lois Lane, and too many war, horror, and romance scripts to count. After scripting Flash's origin story in SHOWCASE #4, Kanigher contributed several more tales to subsequent SHOWCASE appearances, finally returning to the character for an extended run as regular writer on THE FLASH in 1970.

JOE KUBERT

Beginning his career in comics while still in high school, Joe Kubert is acknowledged as one of the leading talents in the comic-book field. He has functioned as a comics artist, writer, editor, publisher, and teacher. During the 1940s, Kubert lent his artistic abilities to numerous DC features, including Hawkman, before moving on to work for other publishers, including his own St. John's Publishing, under whose banner he pioneered the popular 3-D comics genre. Since his involvement in the relaunching of The Flash, Kubert has illustrated a variety of characters for DC, including Hawkman, Sgt. Rock, and Viking Prince, as well as strips for Marvel and his series of Abraham Stone and Tor graphic novels. In 1976, he launched the Joe Kubert School of Visual Arts, which has turned out many of the finest young talents in comics today.

JULIUS SCHWARTZ

Comic books were Julius Schwartz's second career, following almost a decade in the 1930s as a successful science-fiction literary agent for such clients as Edmond Hamilton, H.P. Lovecraft, and Ray Bradbury. Schwartz joined DC as an editor in 1944 and remained on staff until the mid-1980s, during which time he had a creative hand in most of DC's characters. It was Schwartz's experience editing the Golden Age Flash that landed him the editorial assignment of reviving the character in 1956. His success with Flash led to other revivals, including Green Lantern, The Atom, and Hawkman. He has also edited JUSTICE LEAGUE OF AMERICA, MYSTERY IN SPACE, BATMAN, SUPERMAN, and just about everything in between. Since retiring from active editing, Schwartz has served as DC's unofficial goodwill ambassador, traveling to as xmany as two dozen comic-book and science-fiction conventions a year.